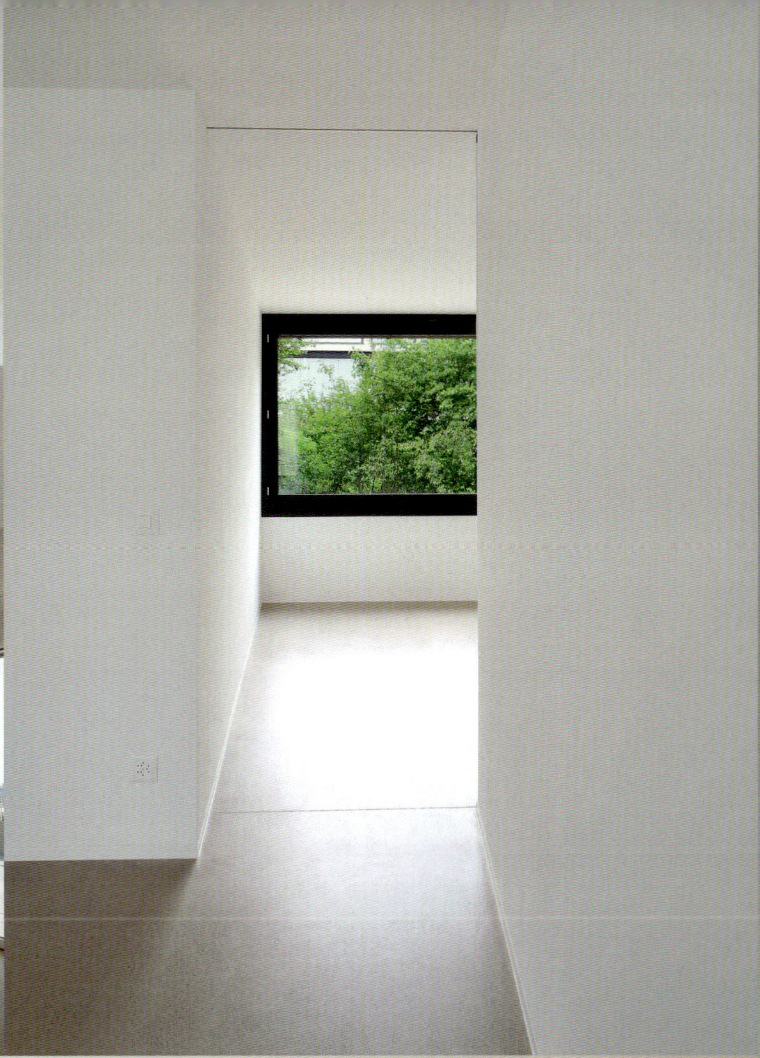
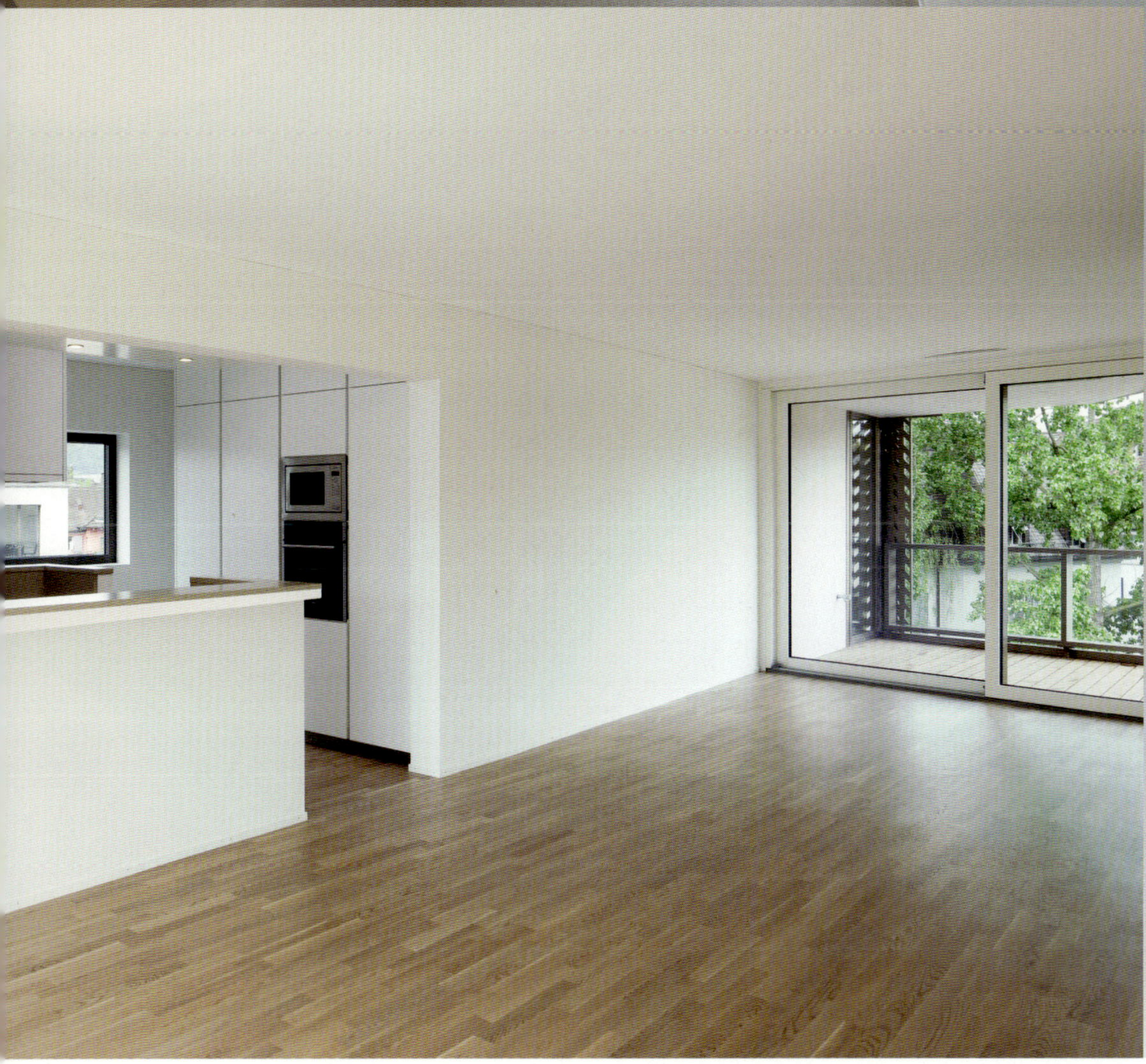

5

6

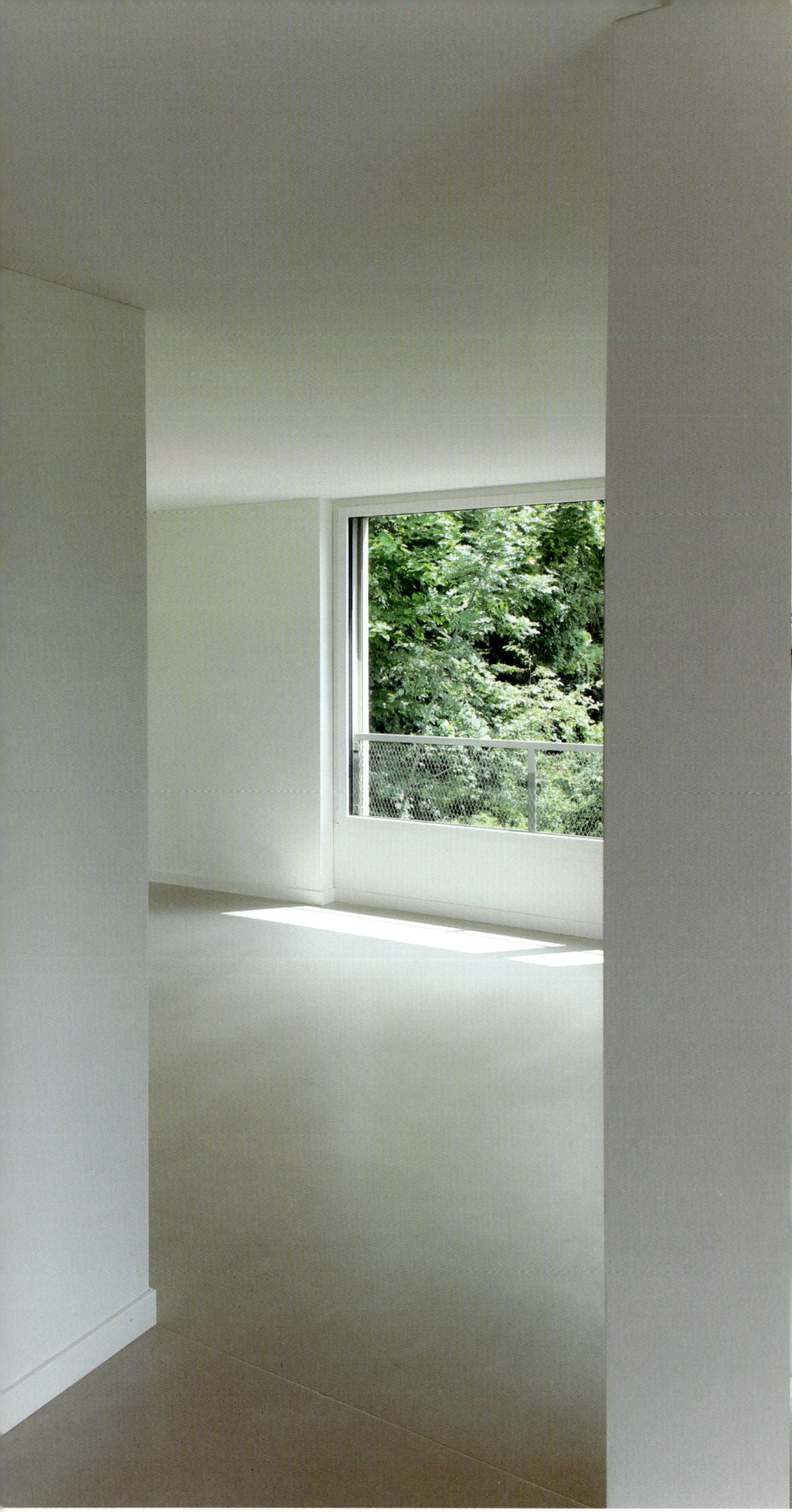

7
8
9

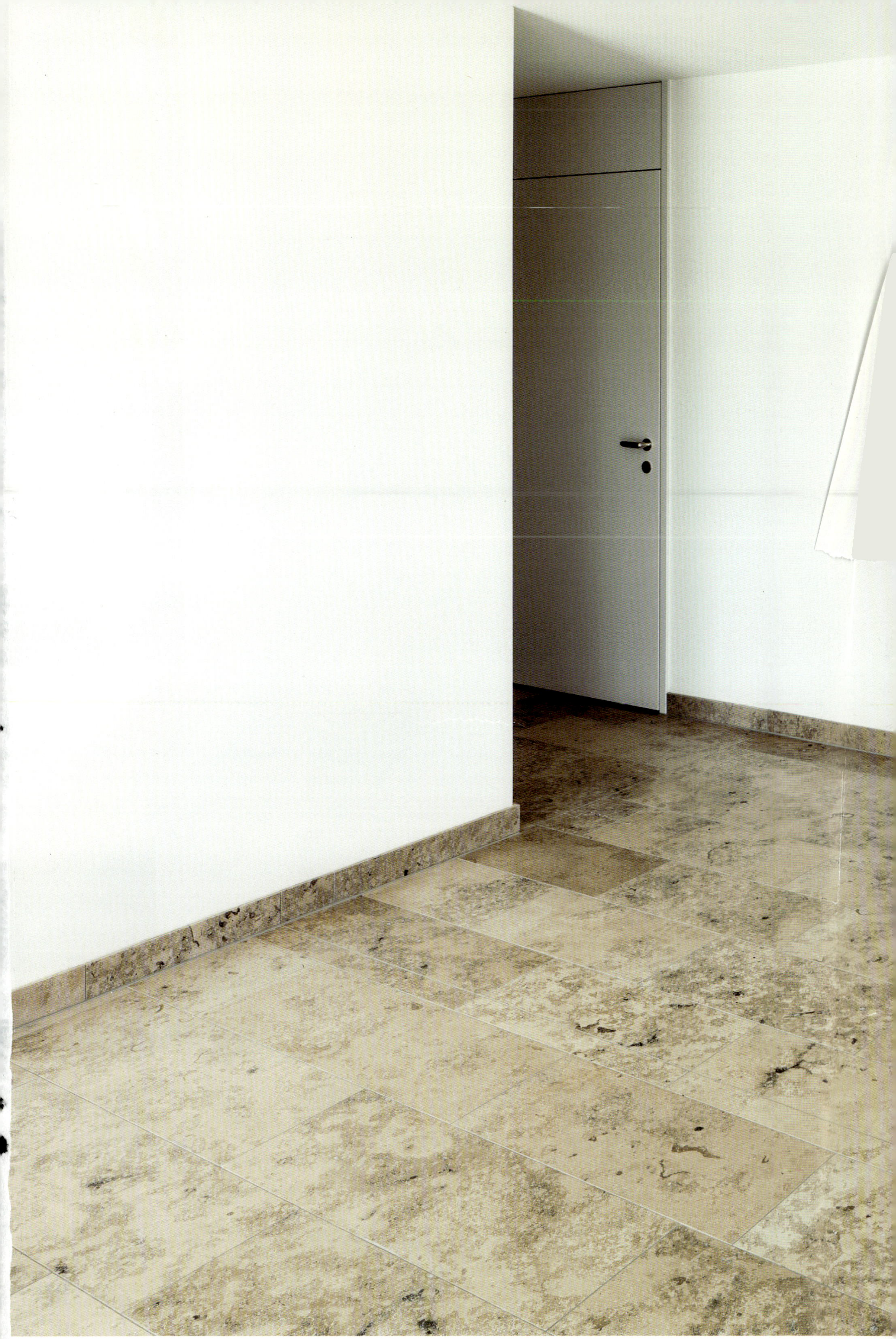

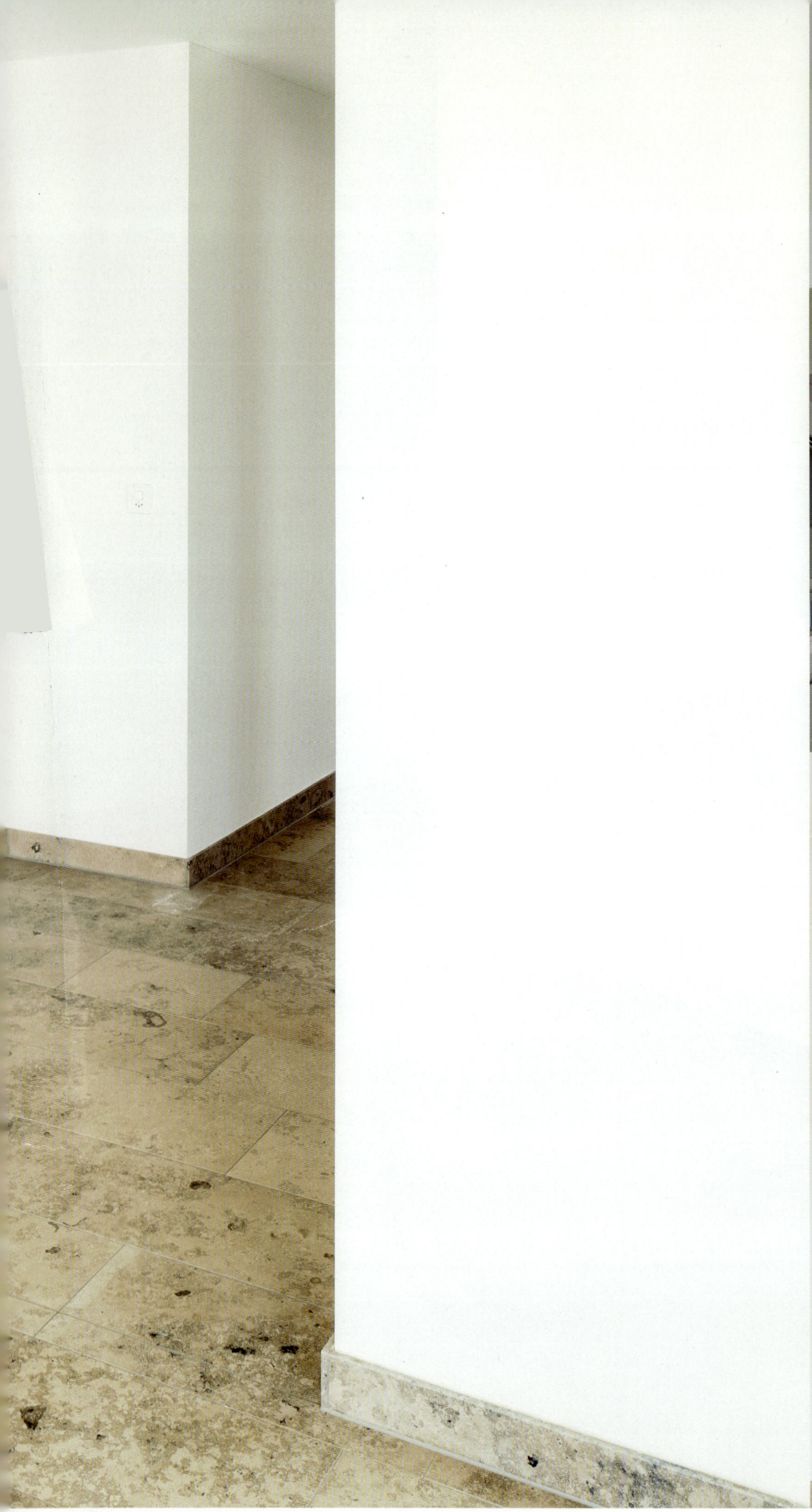

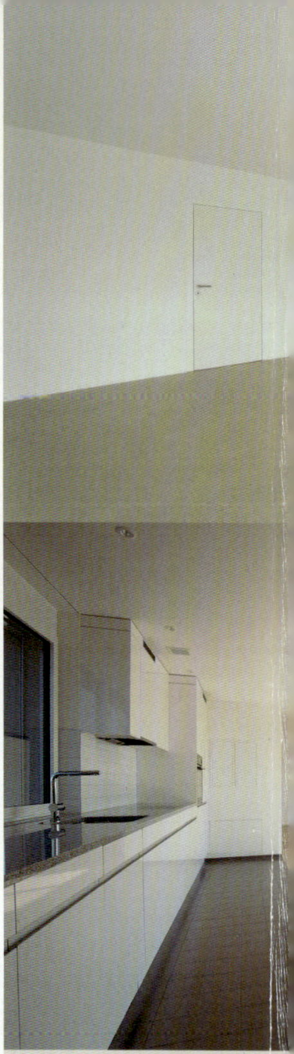

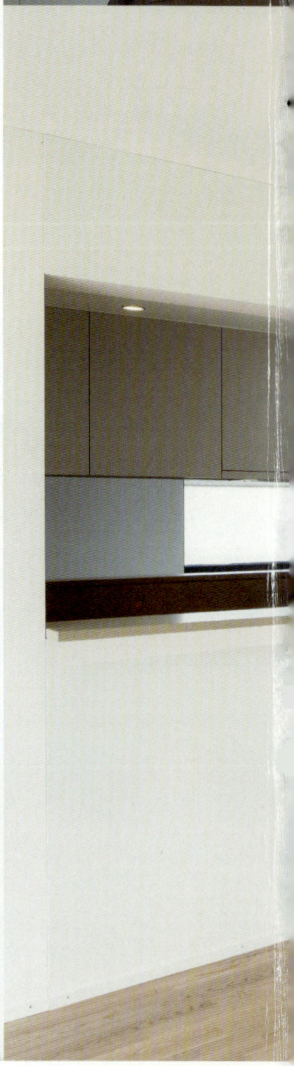

2
3

4

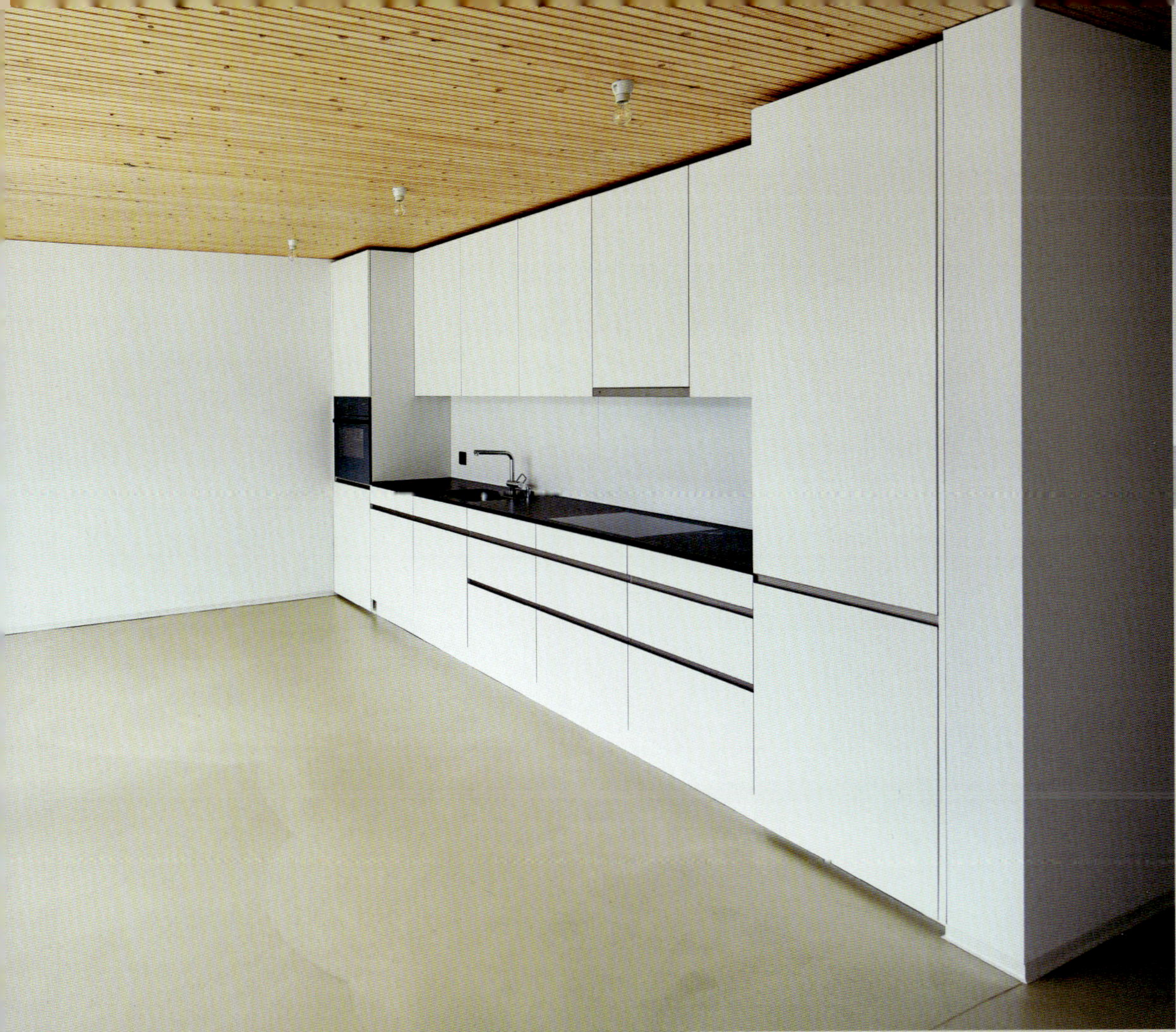

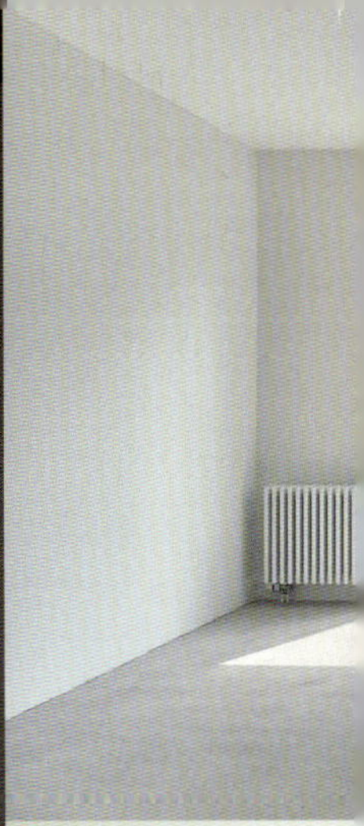

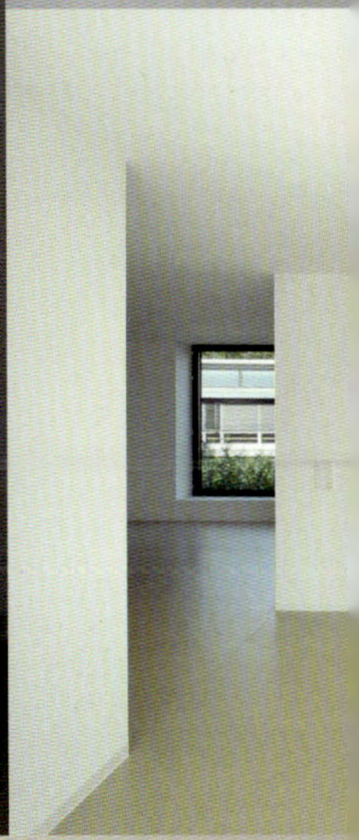

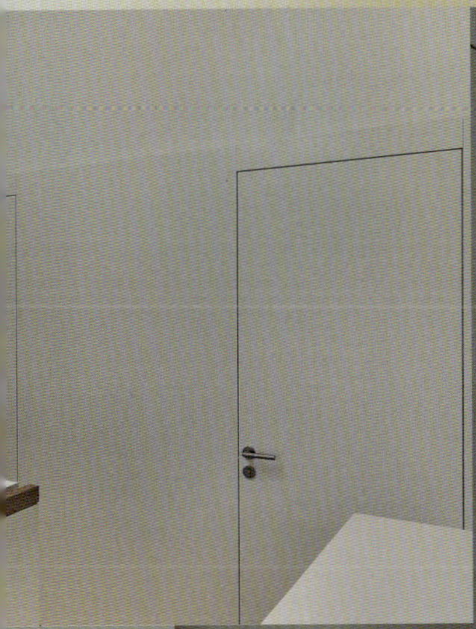

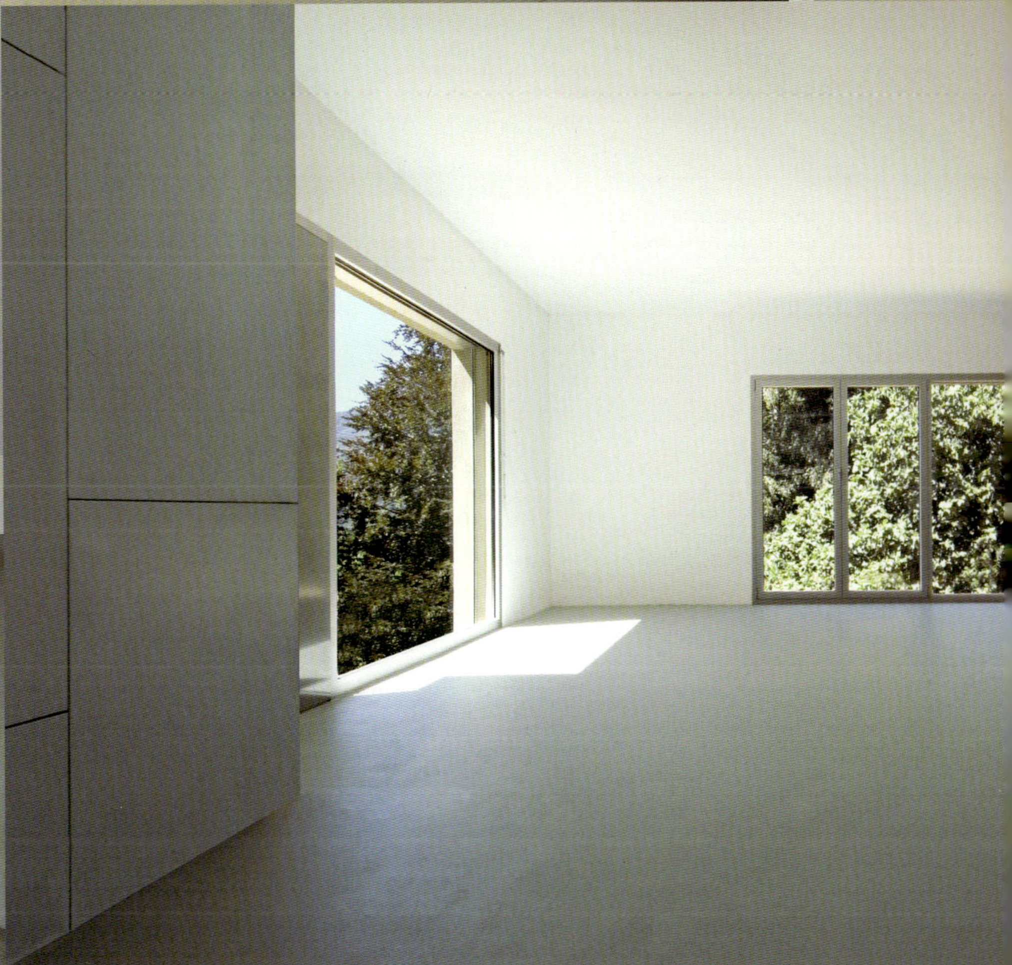

11
12

10

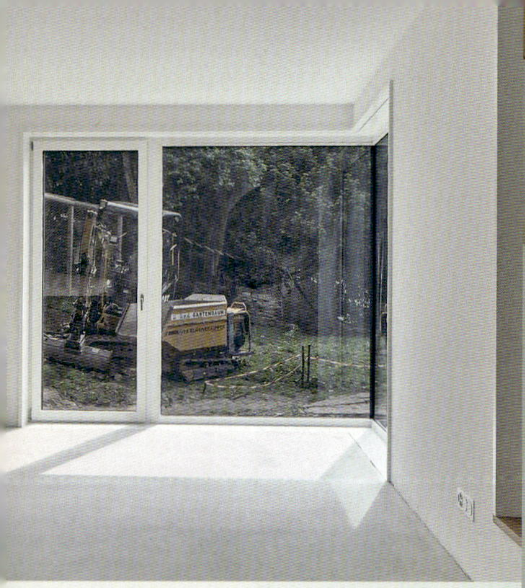

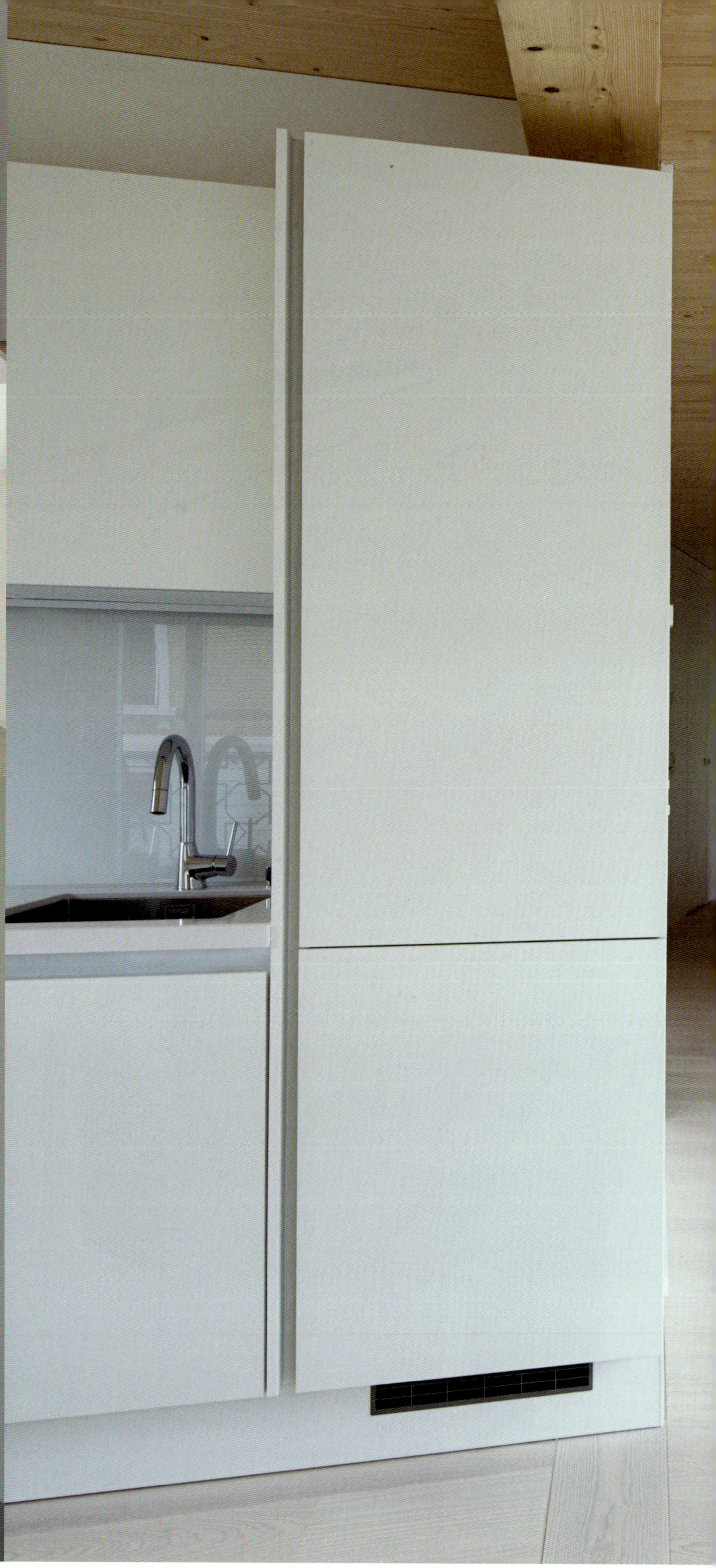

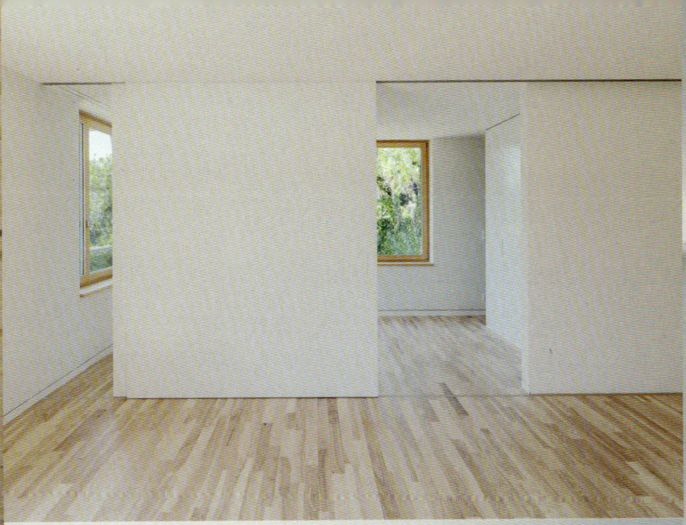
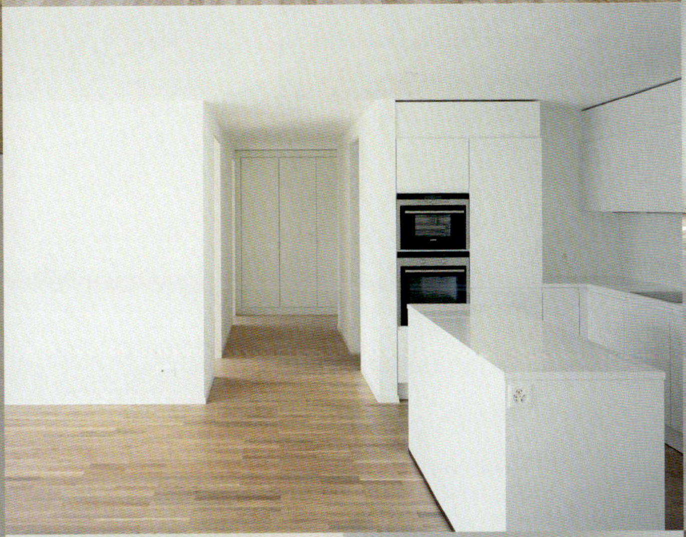
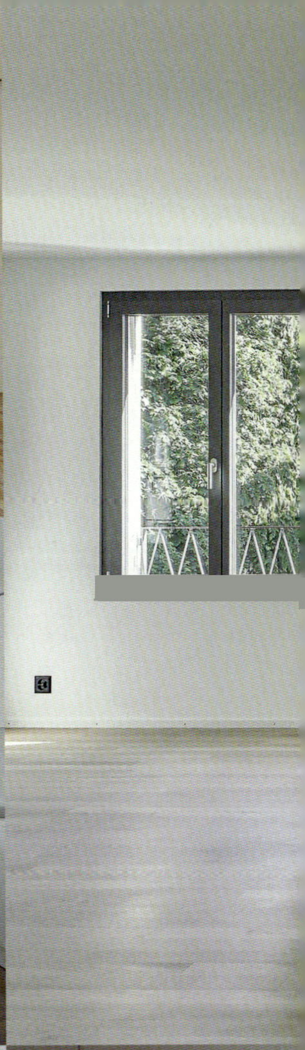
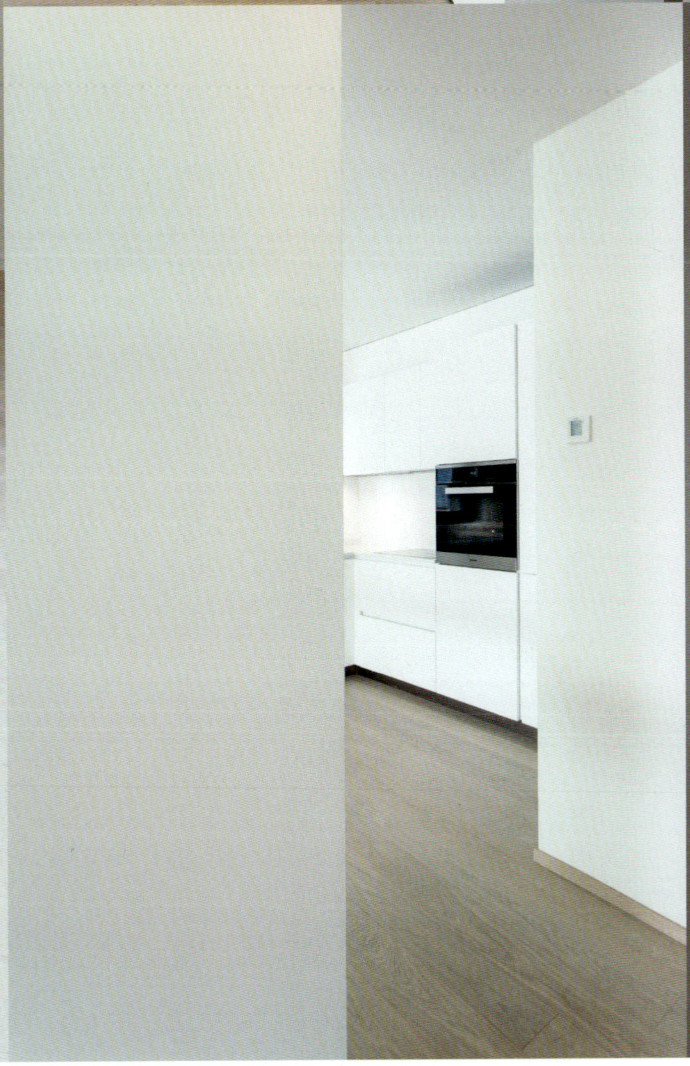

14
15

16

17

18

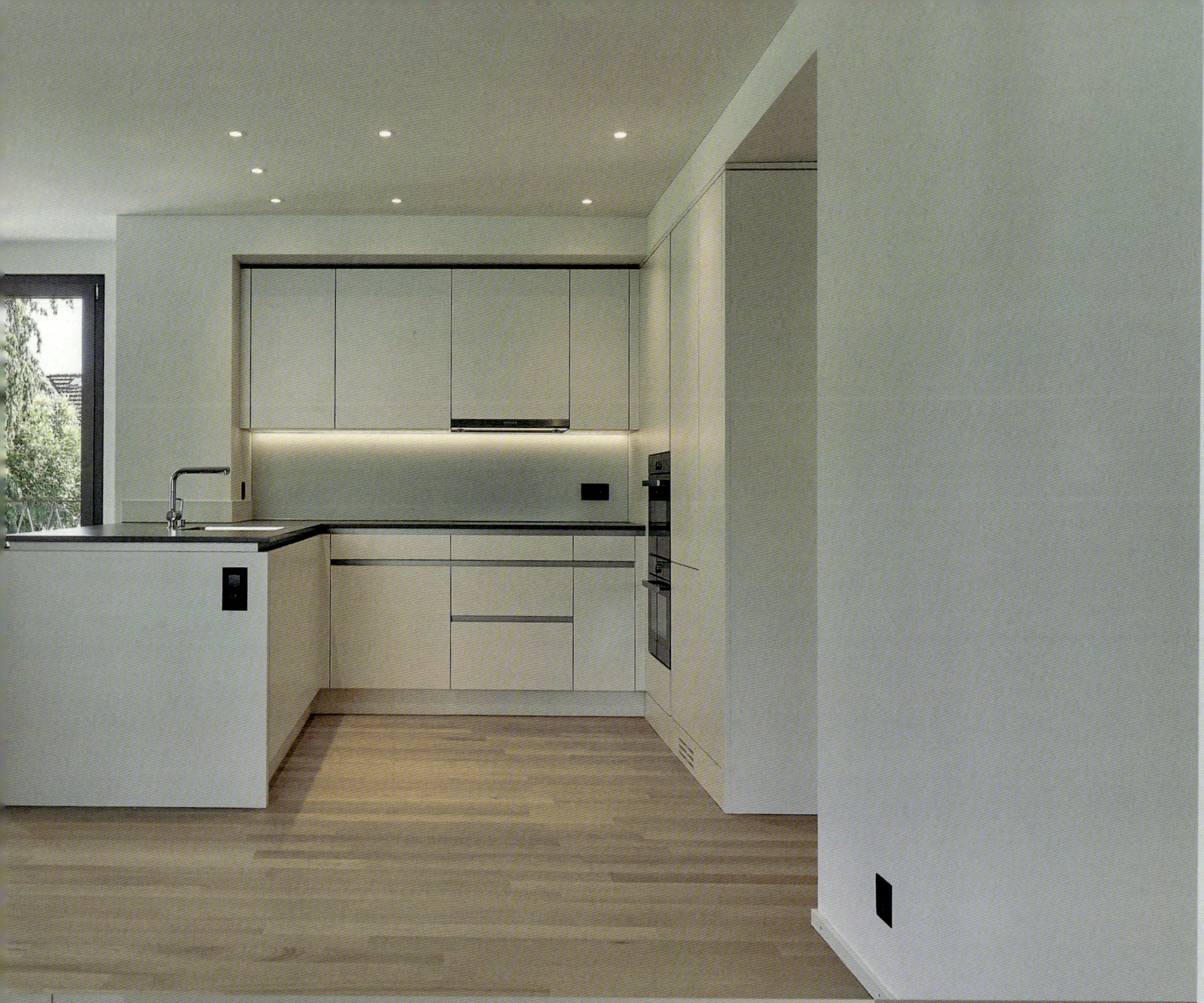

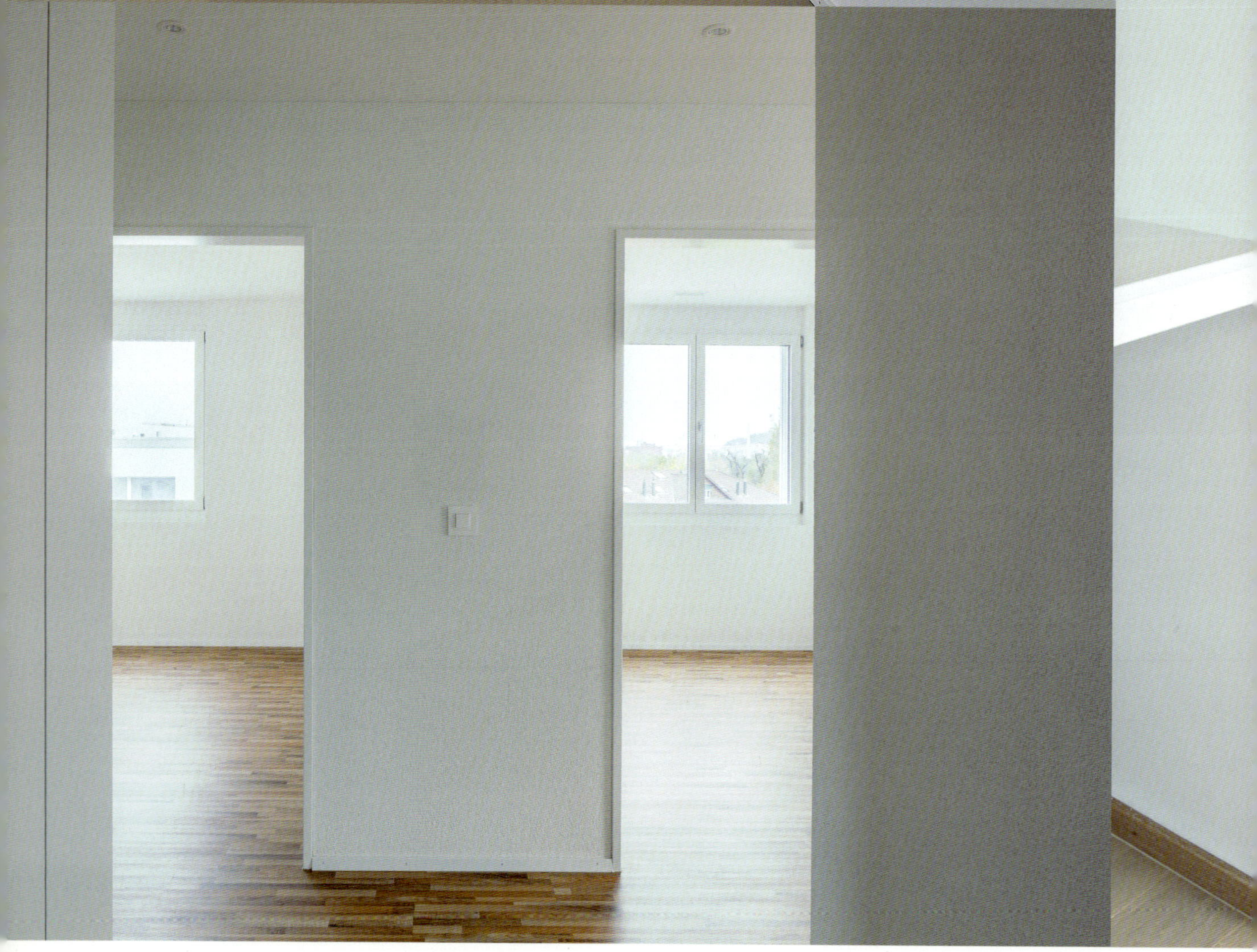

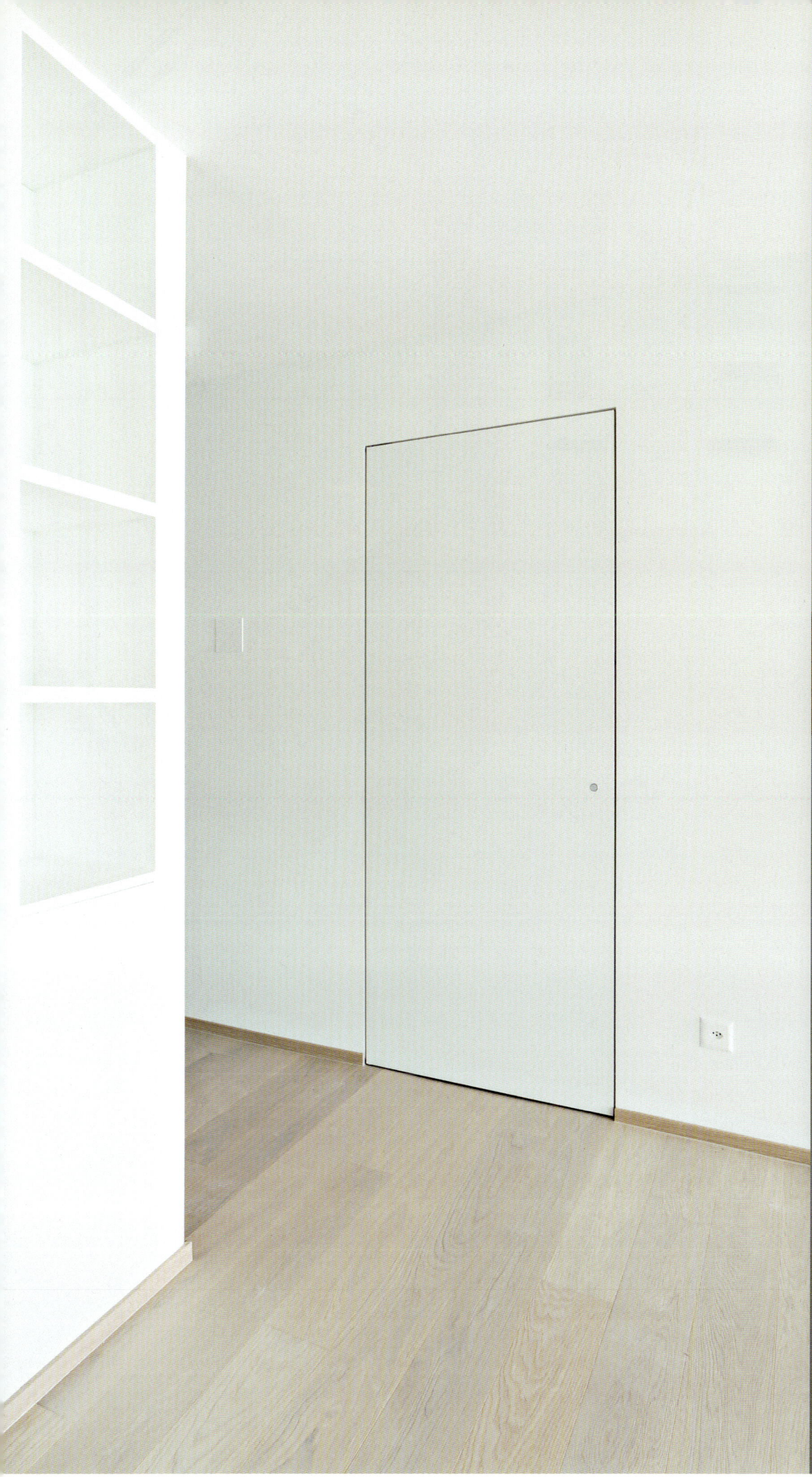
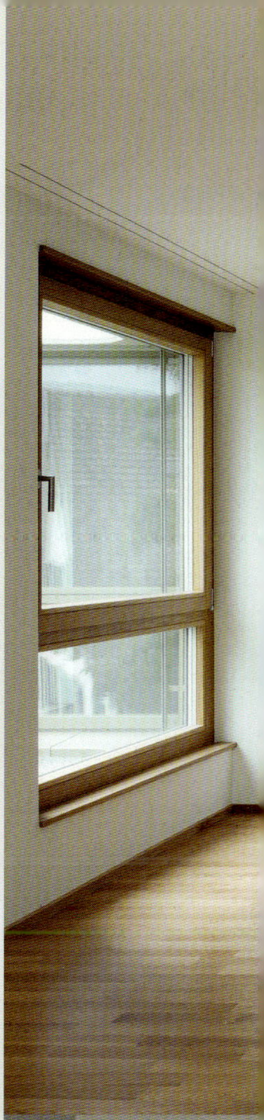

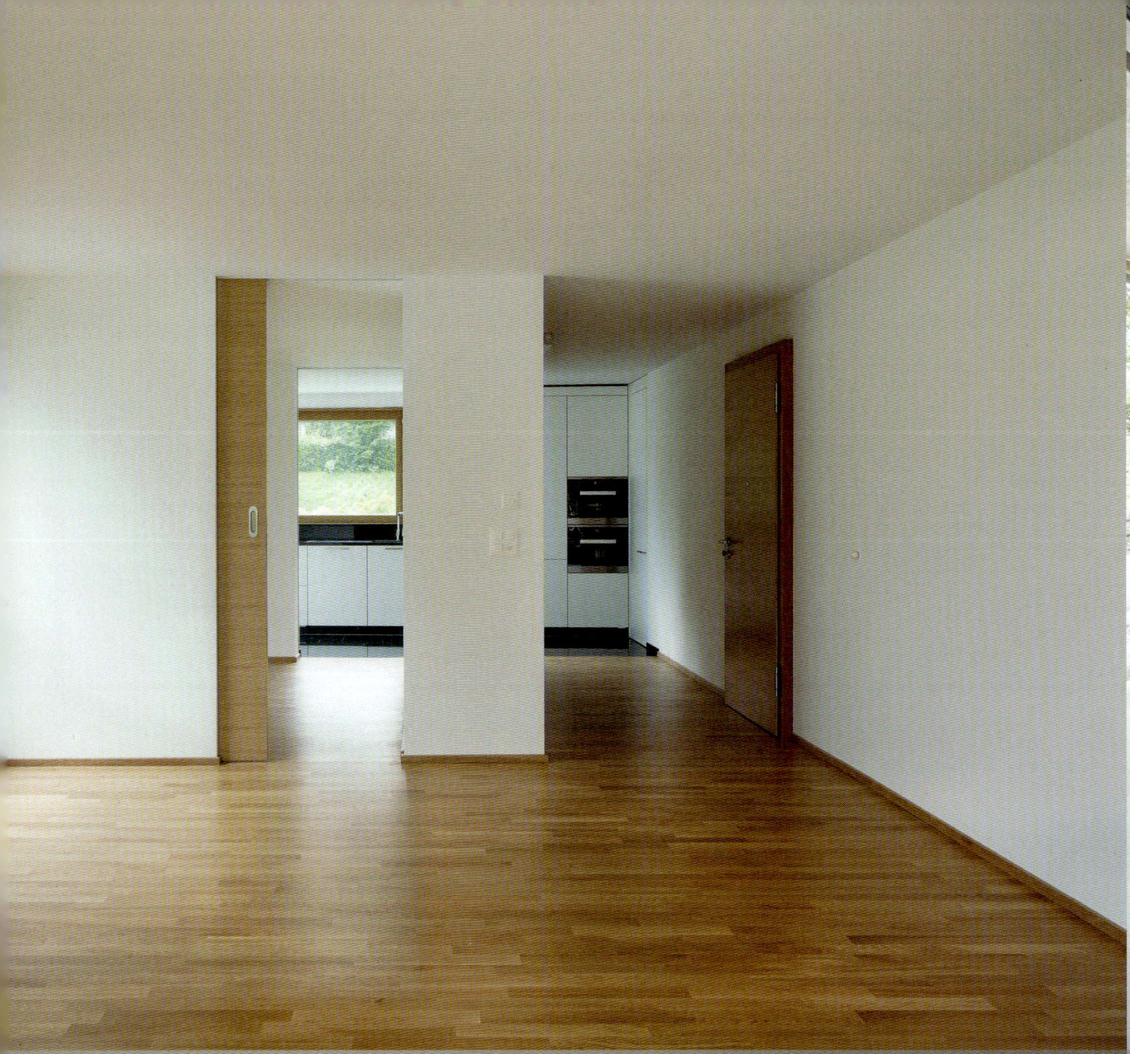
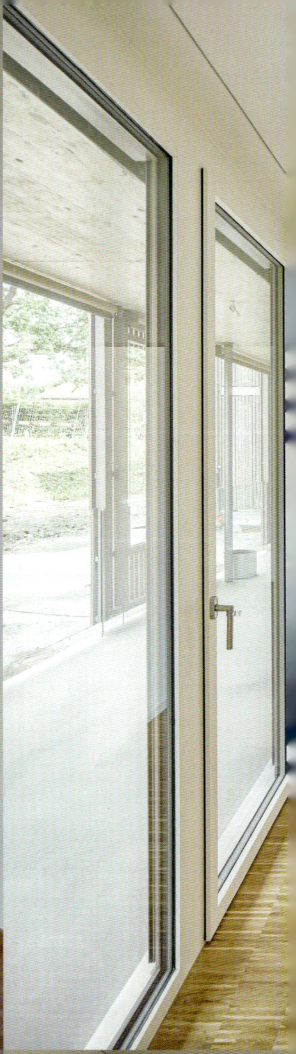
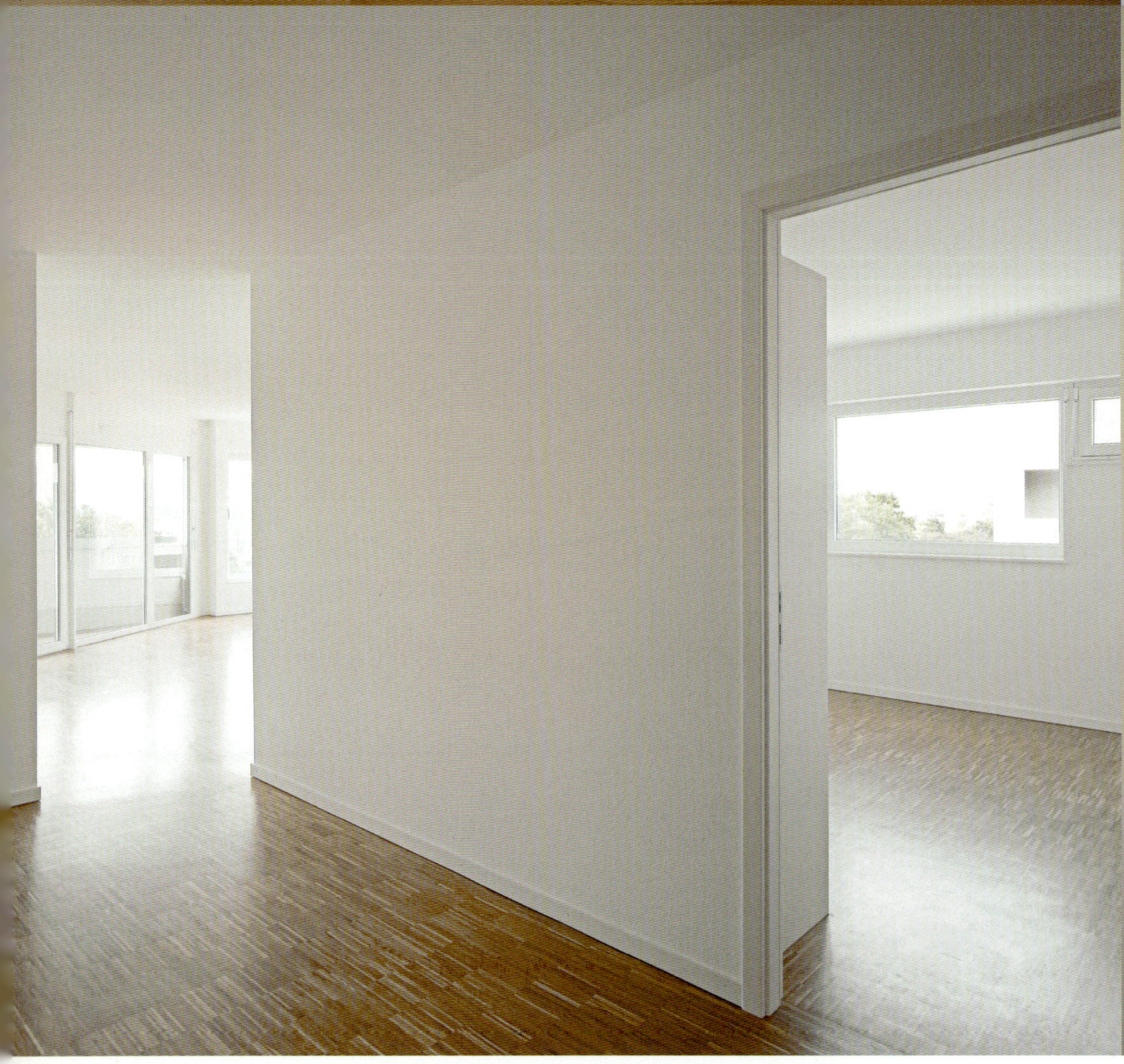

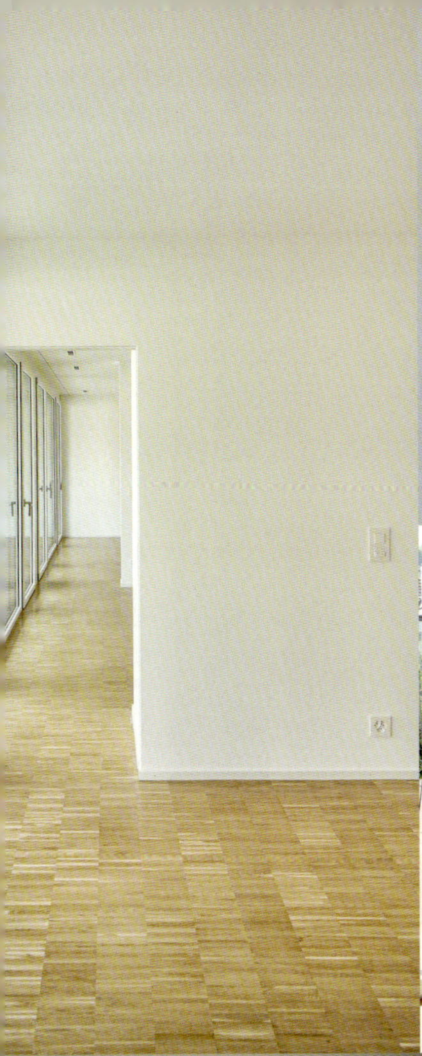
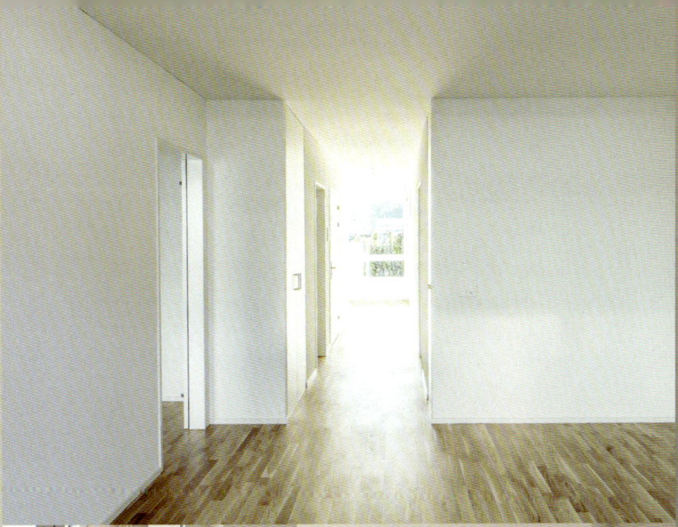
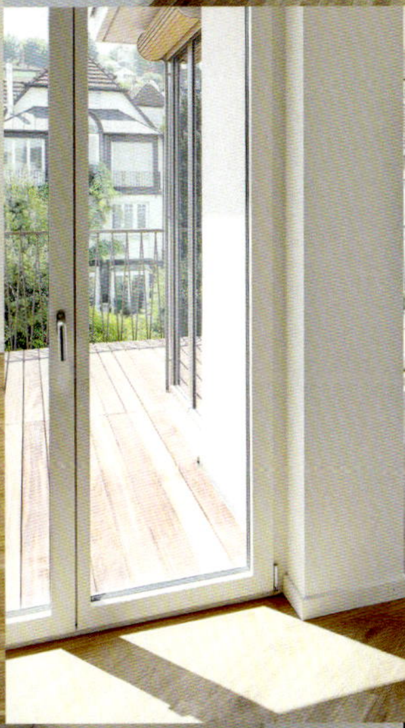
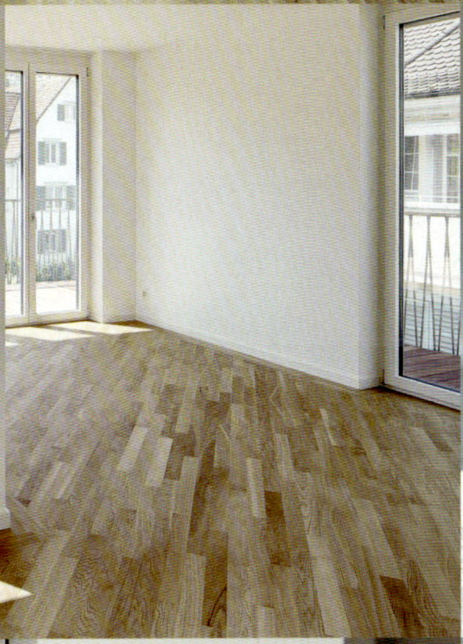
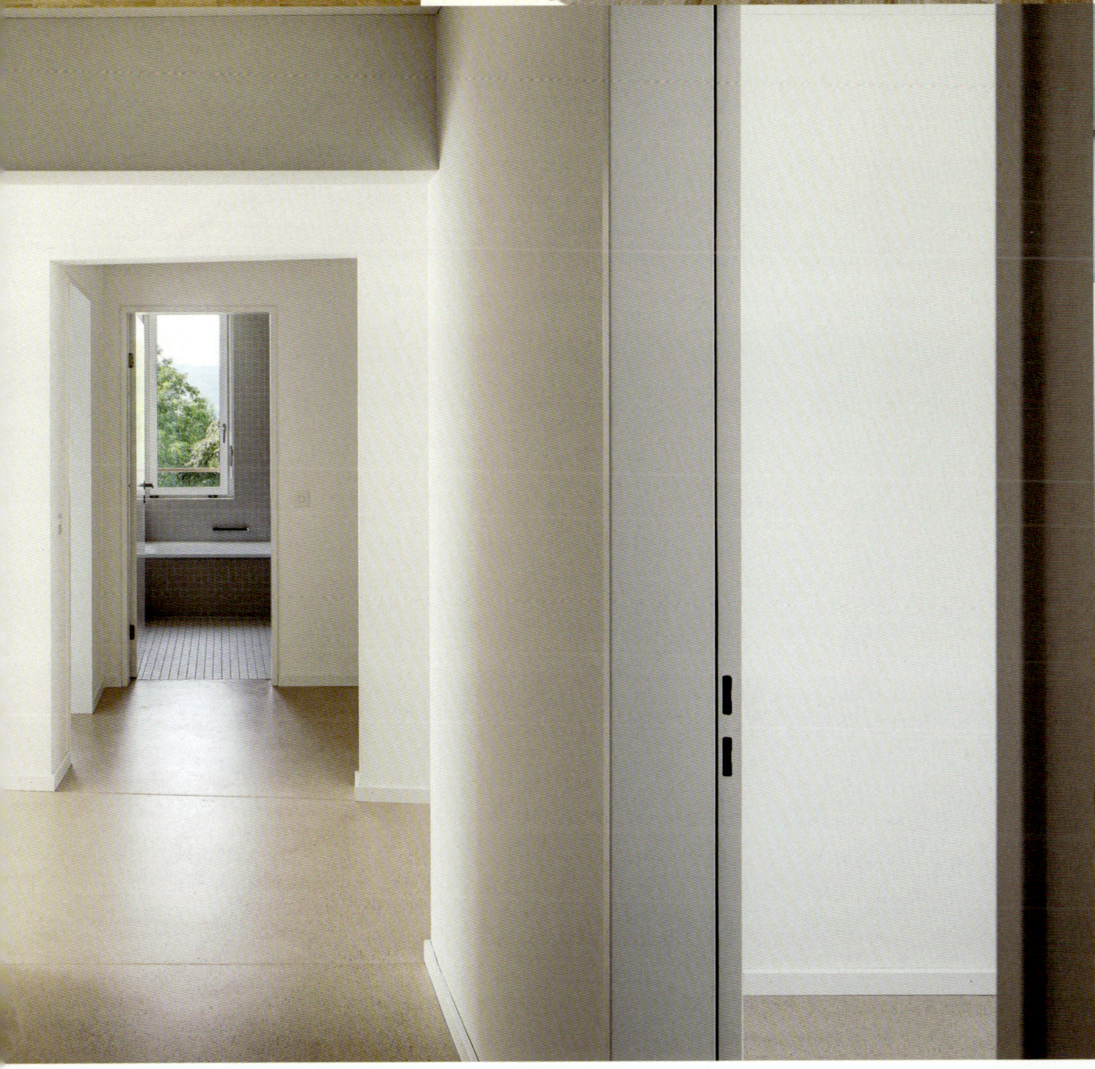
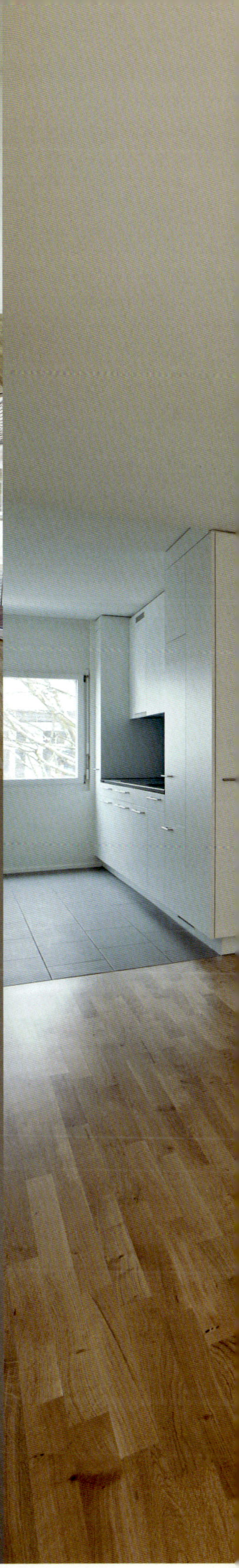

24
25

26

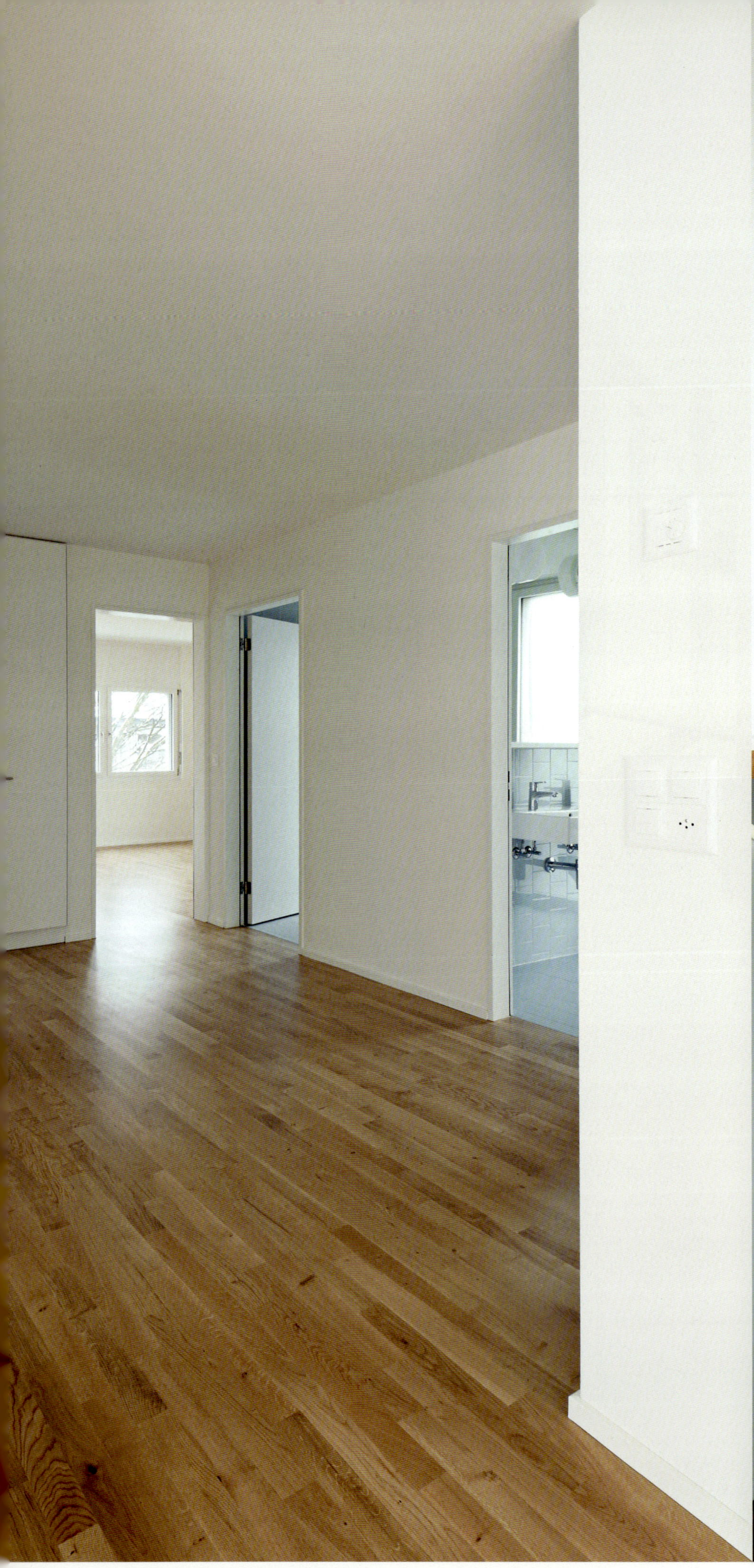
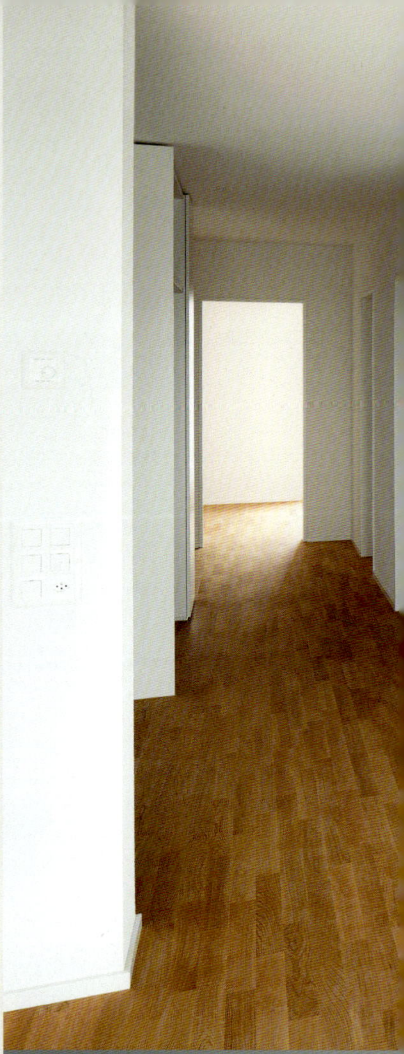
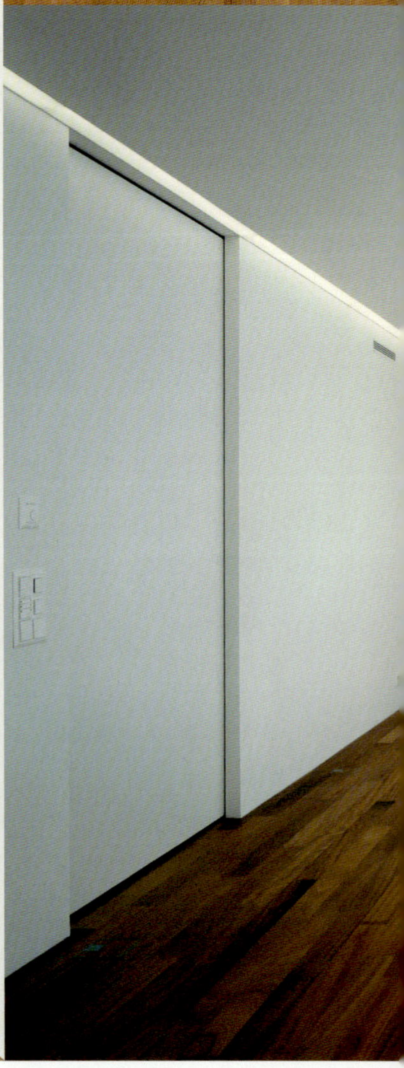

27

28

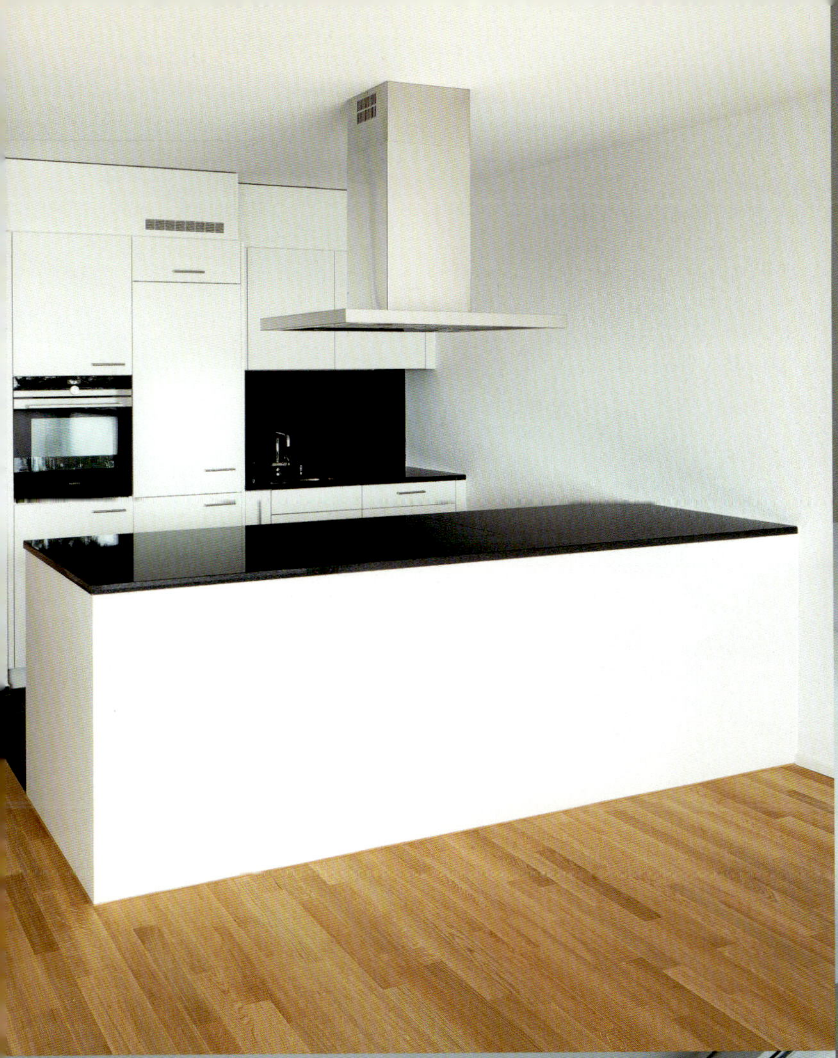
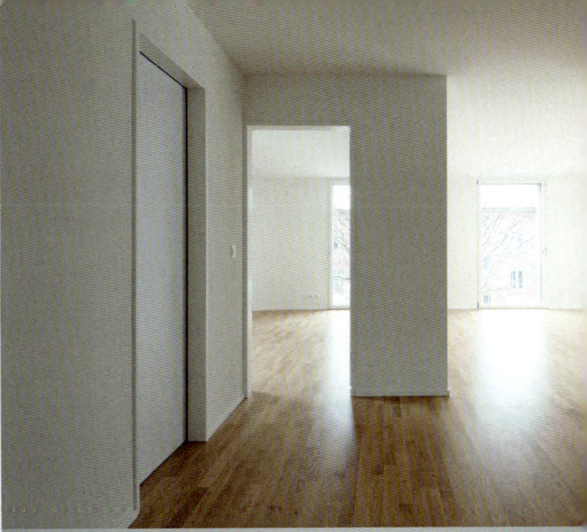
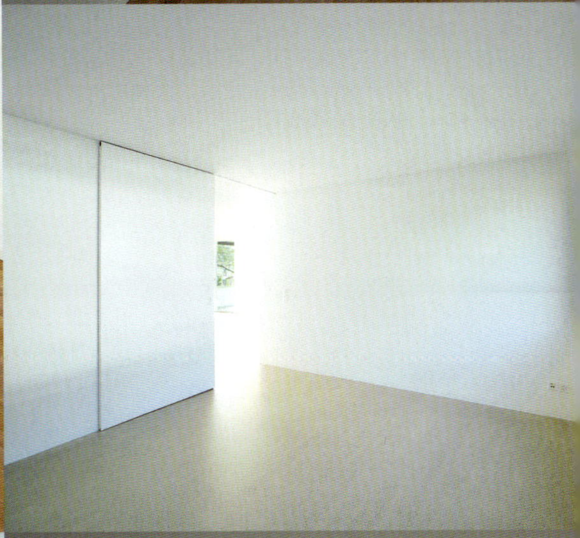
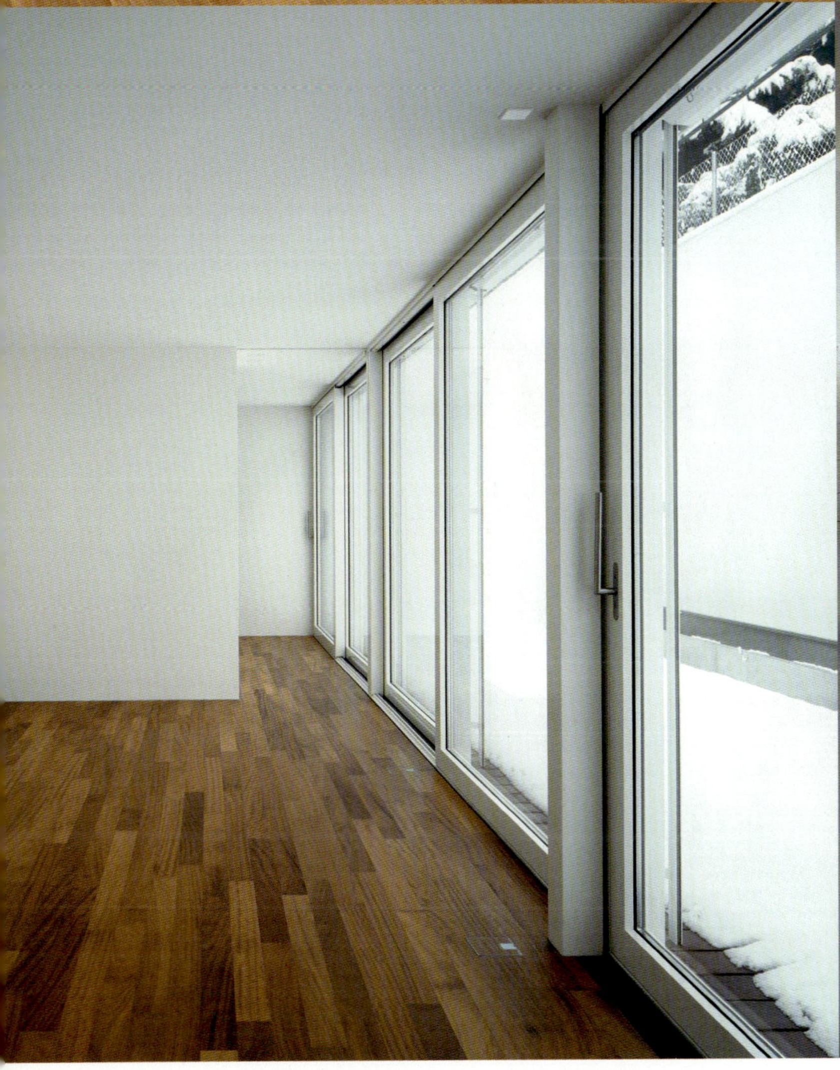
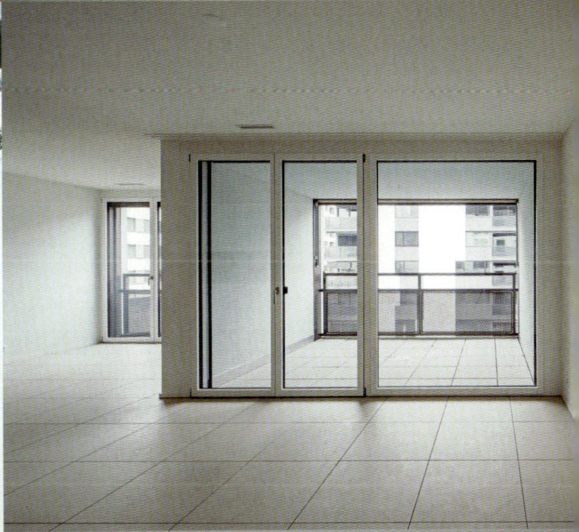
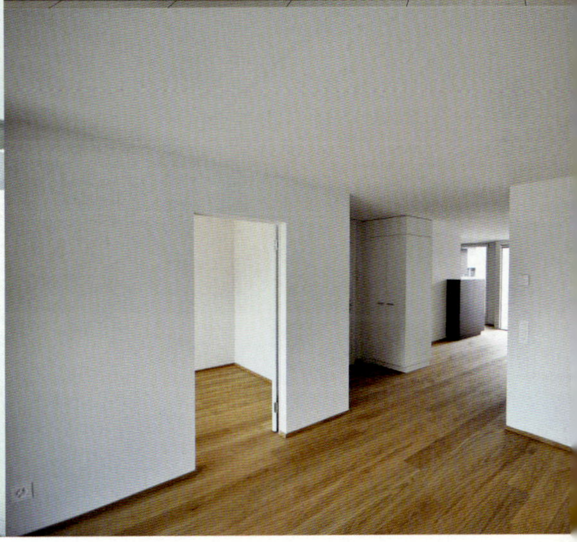

29
30
31
32

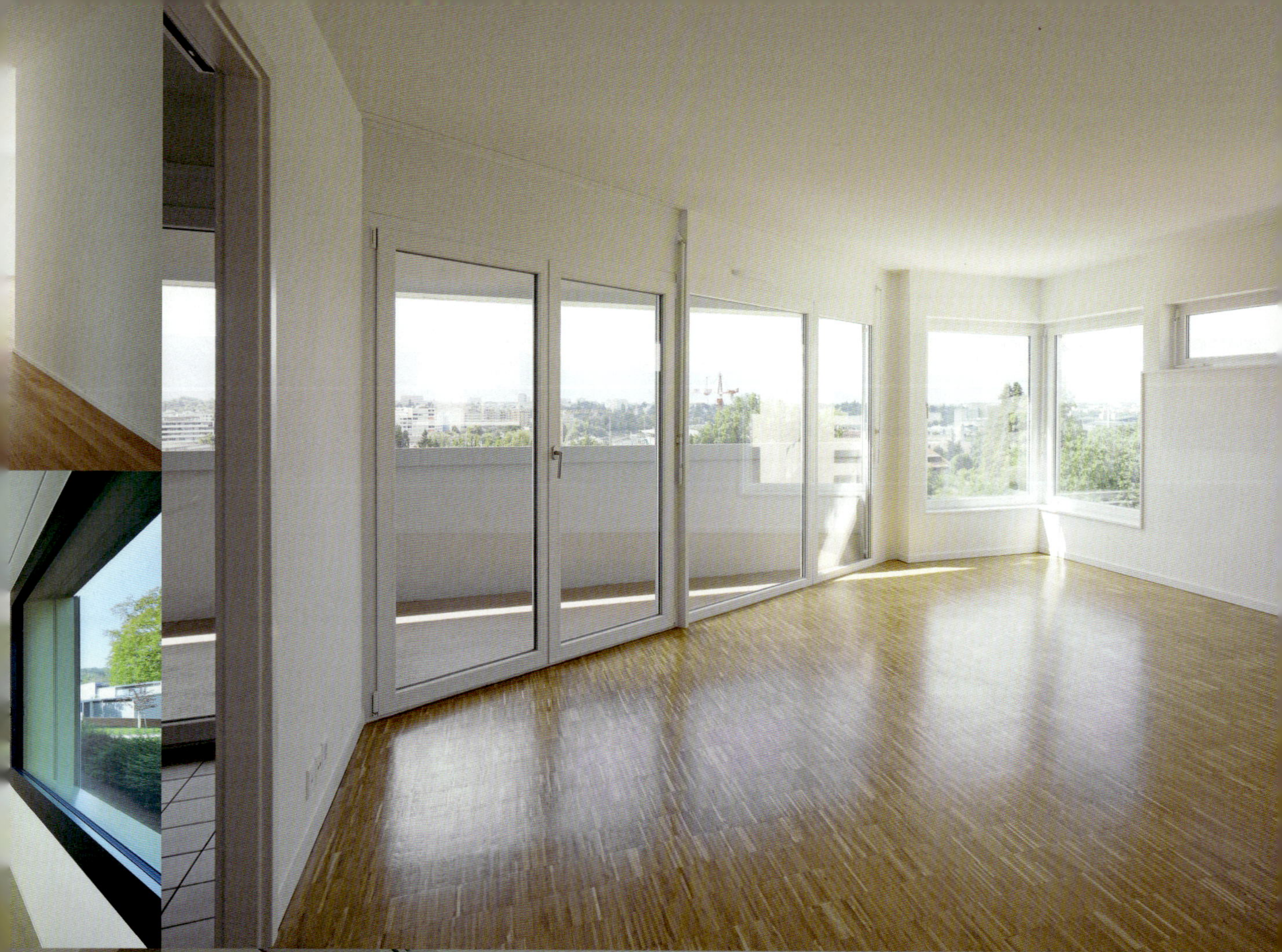

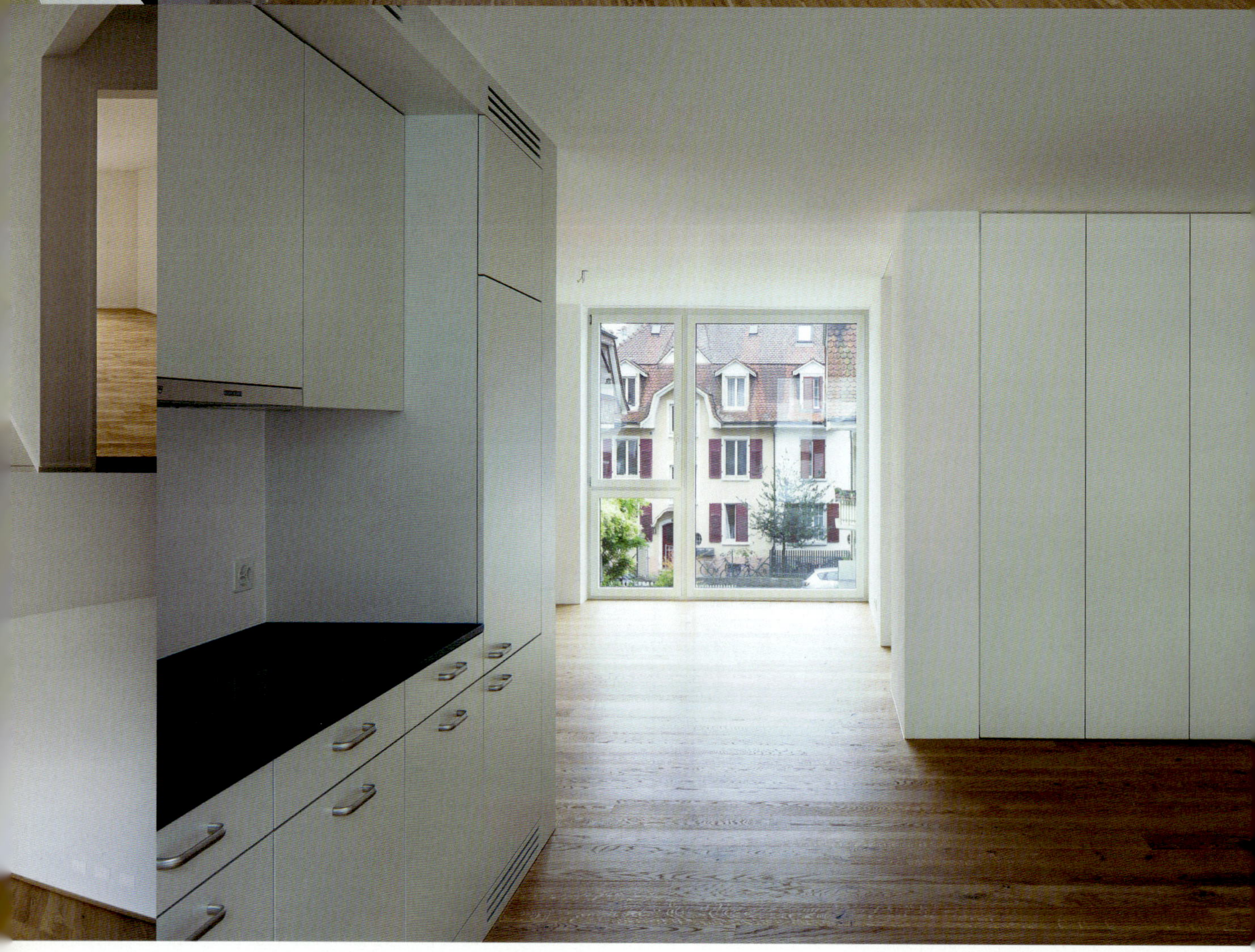

33

34

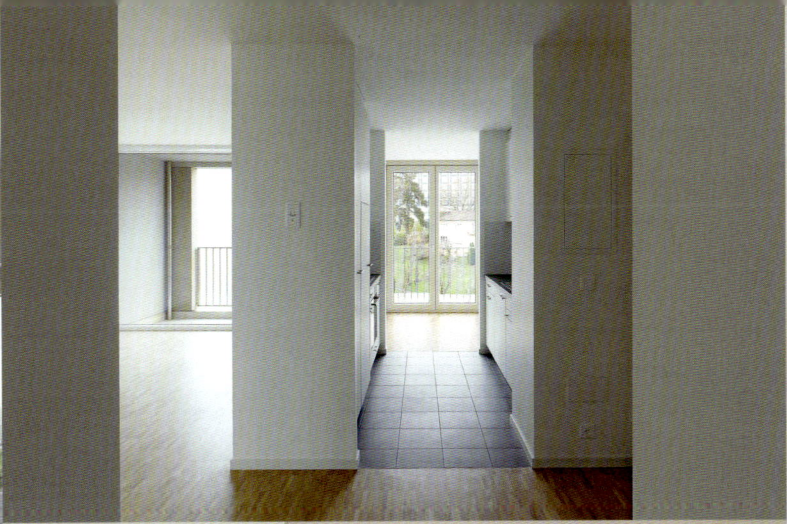
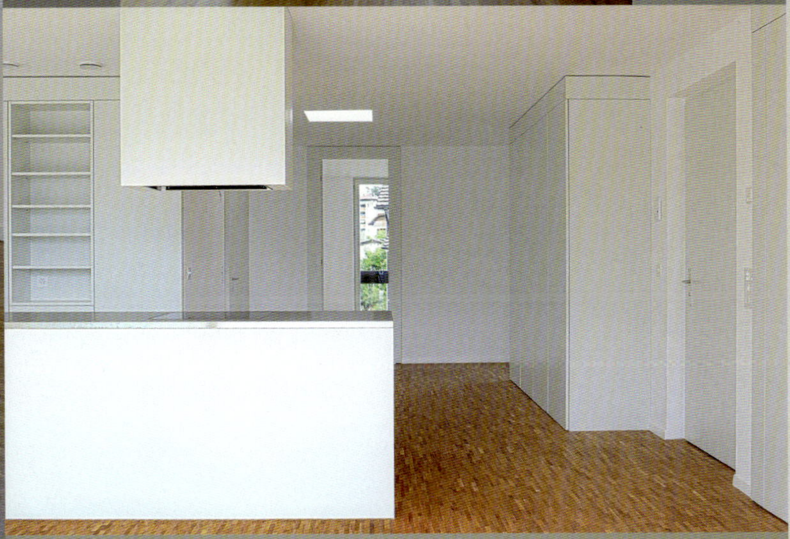
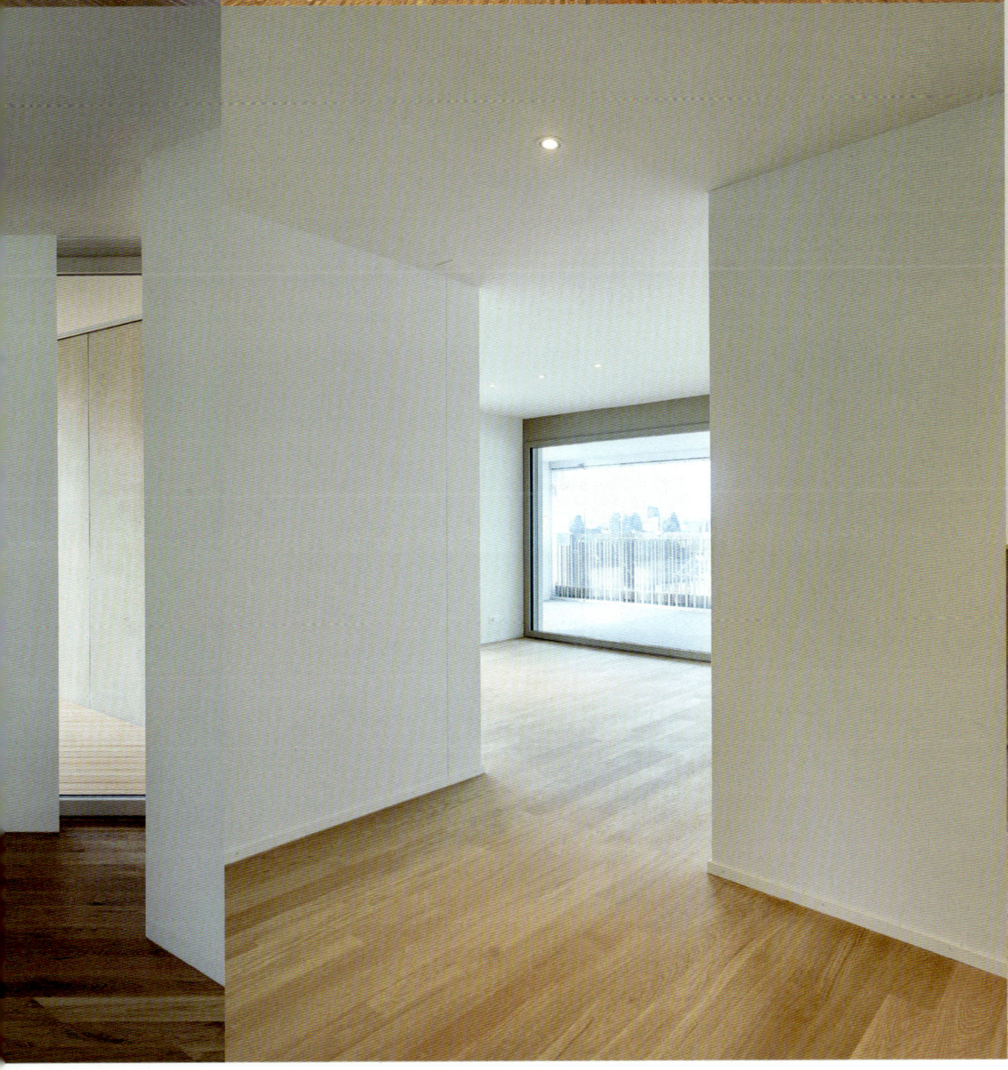

35
36

37

38

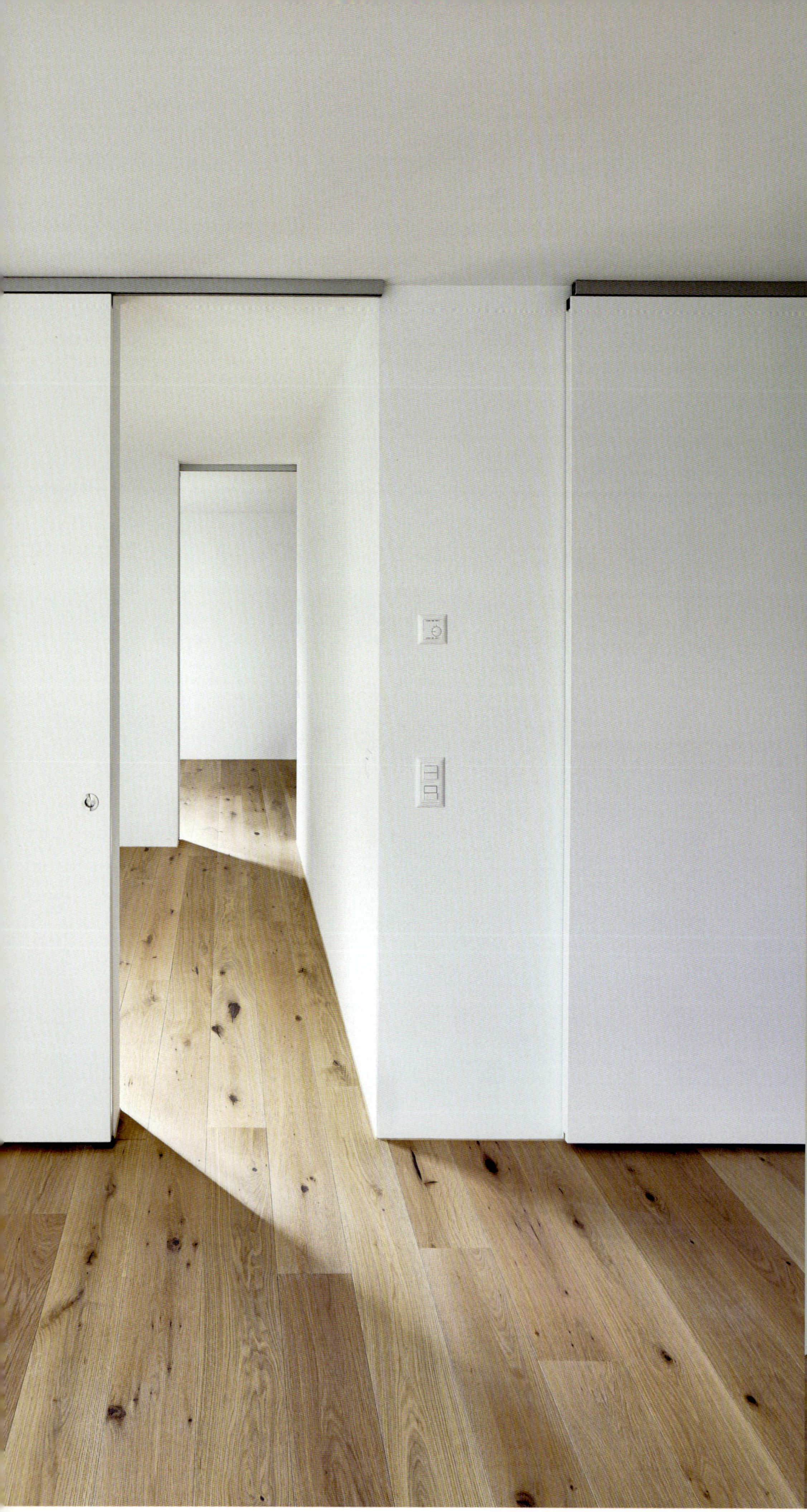

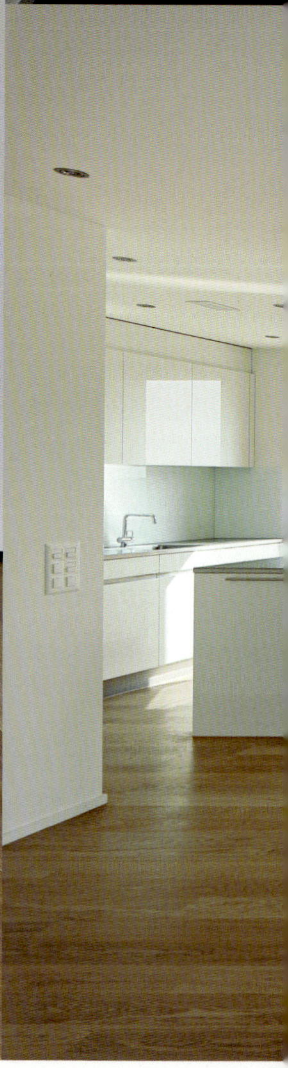

39

40

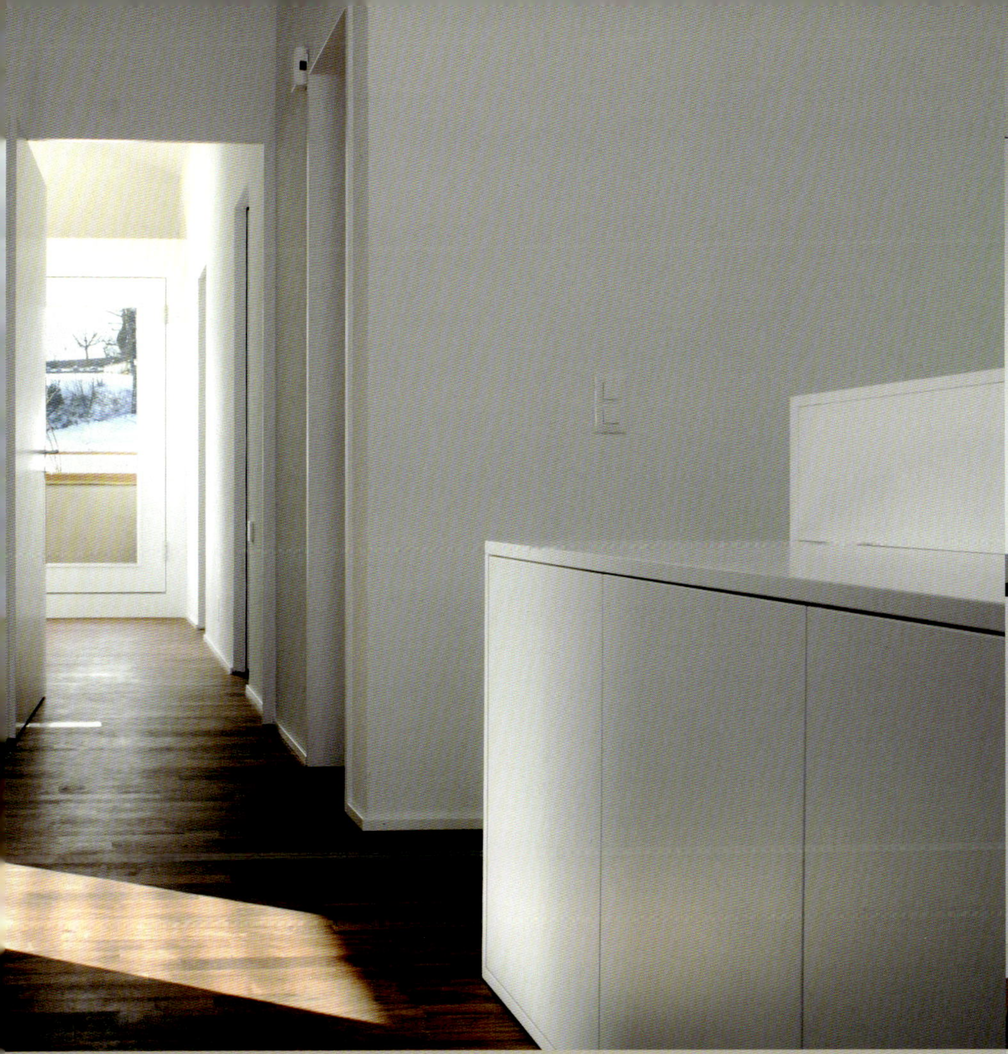
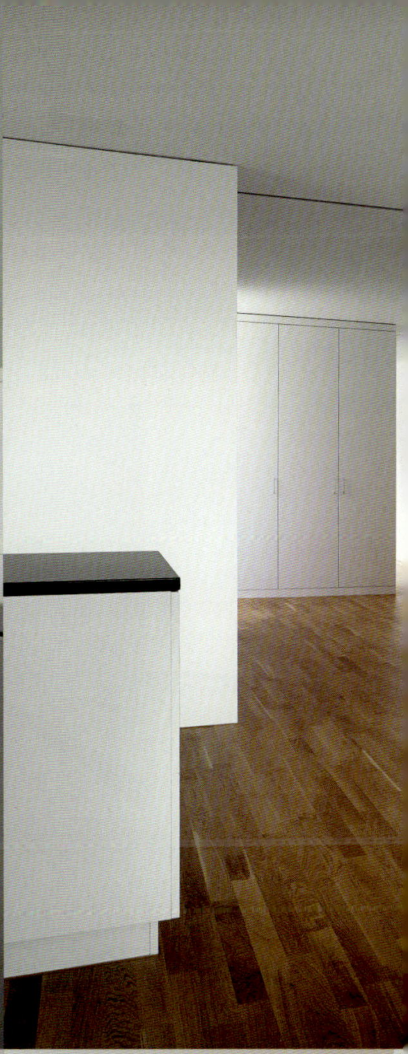
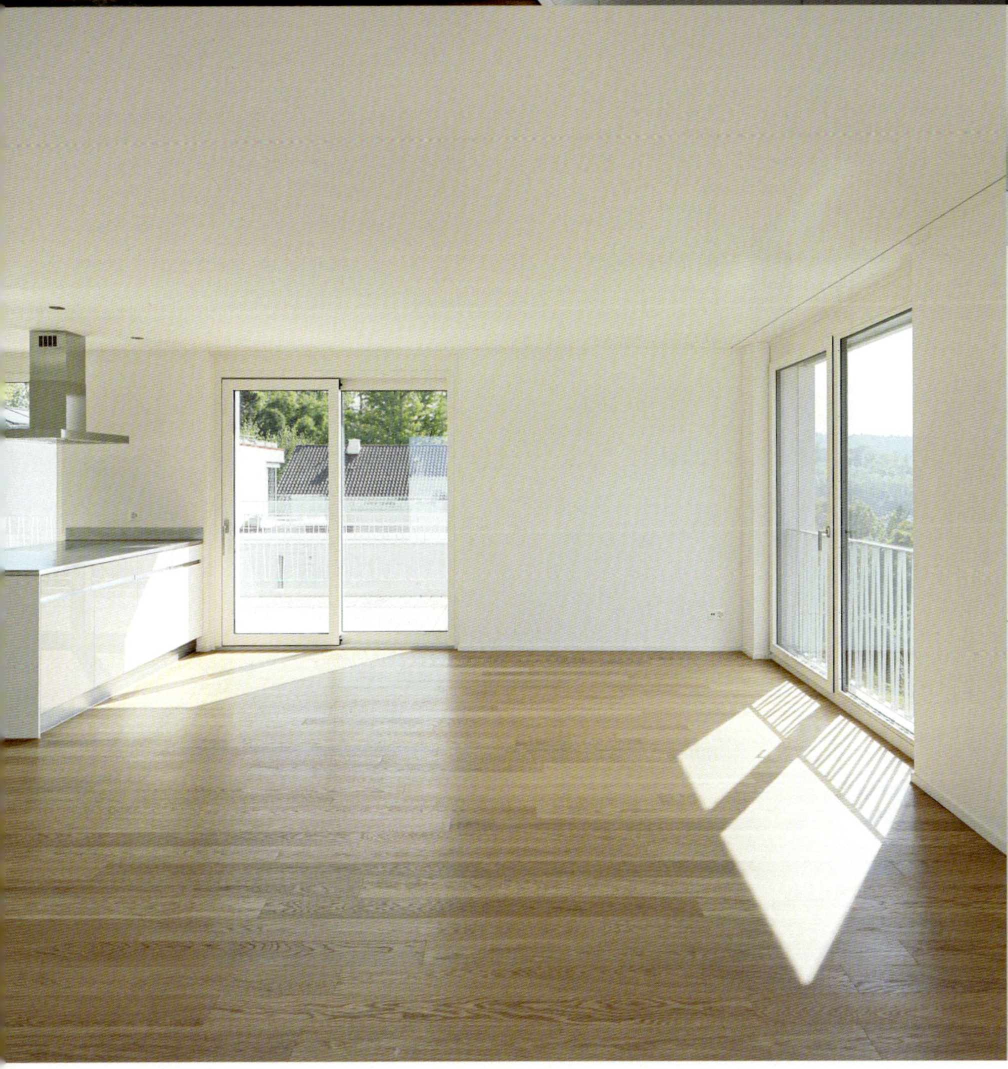

41

42

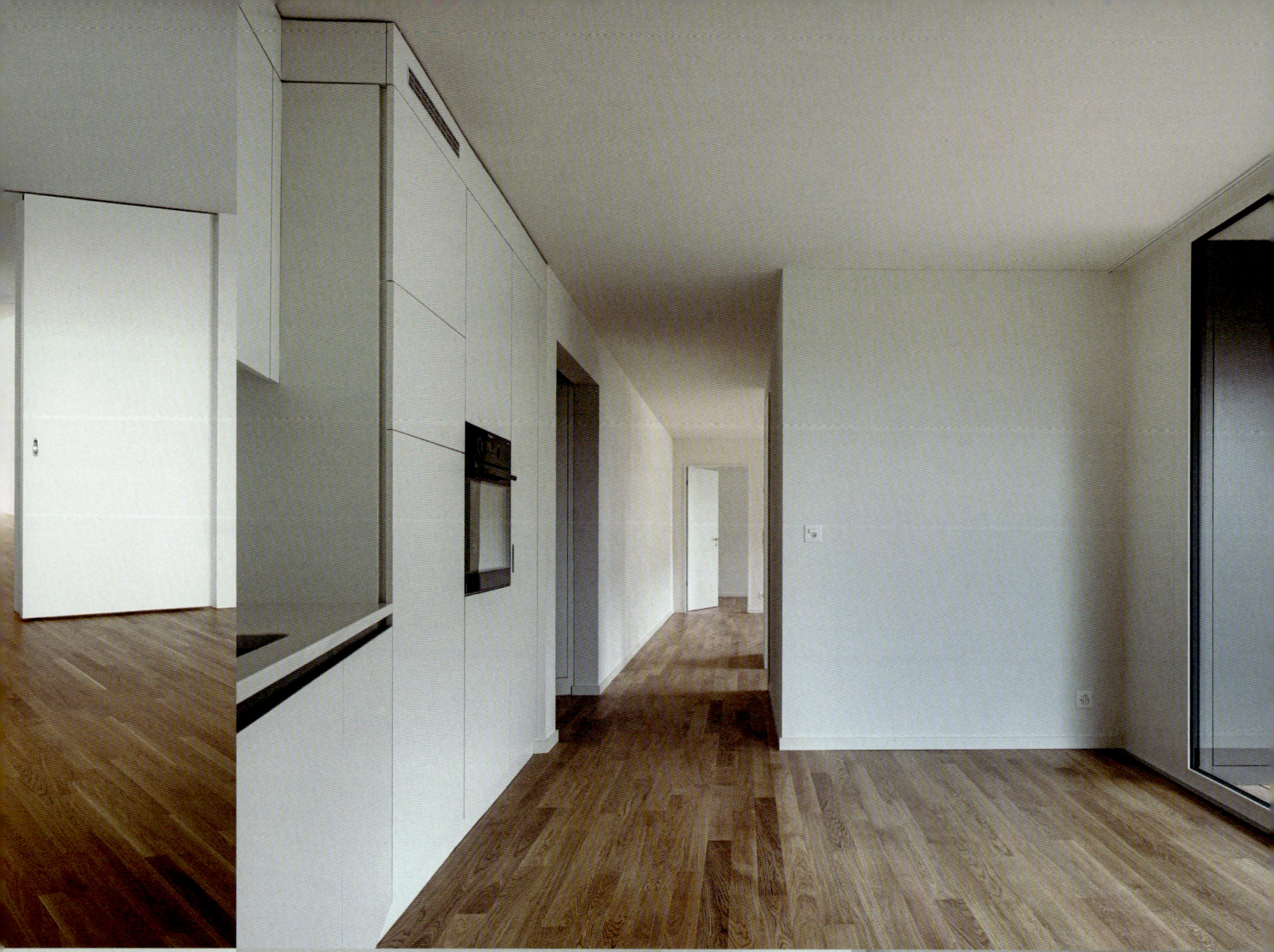

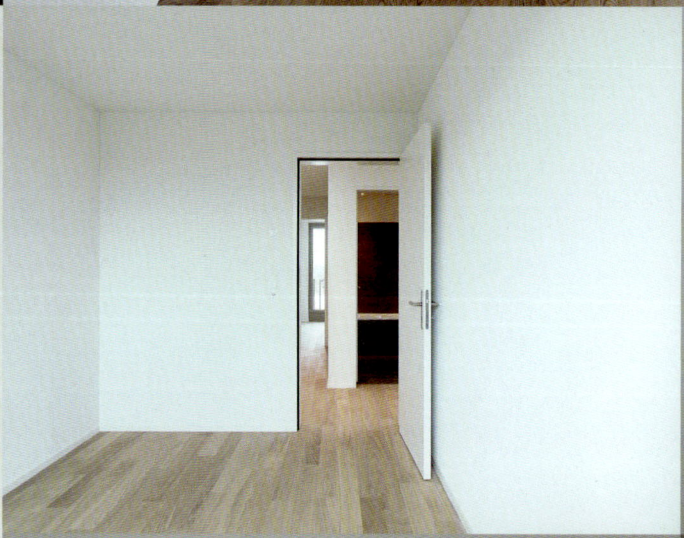

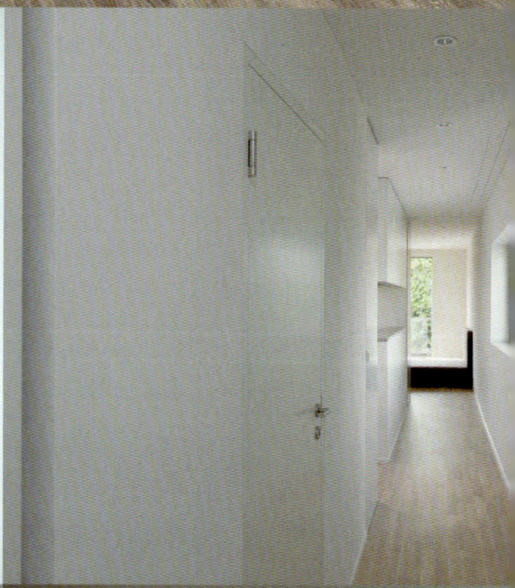

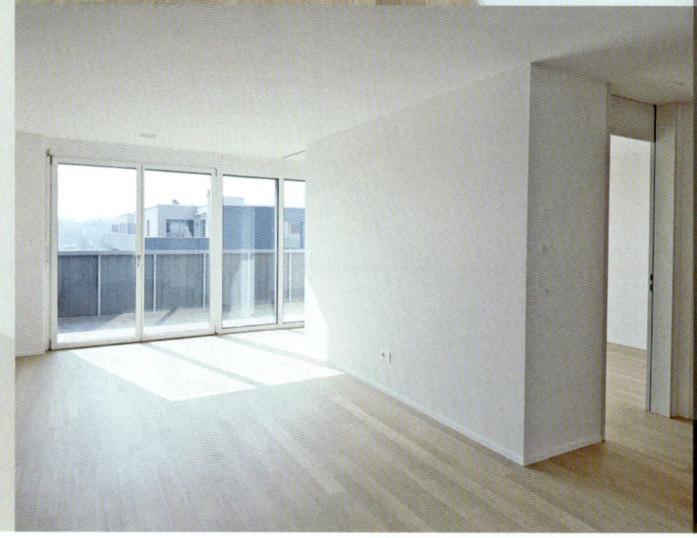

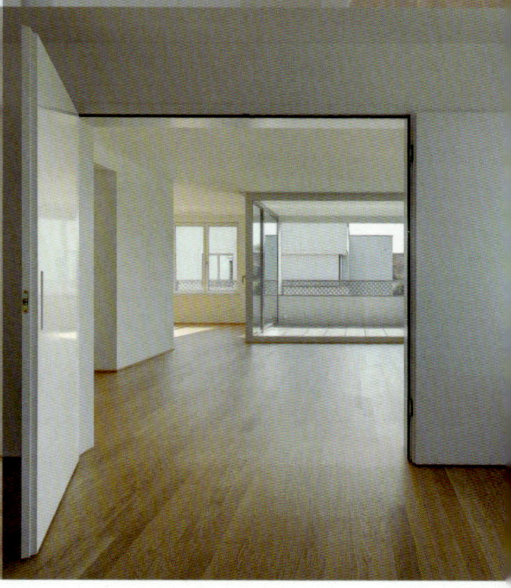

43
44
45

46
47

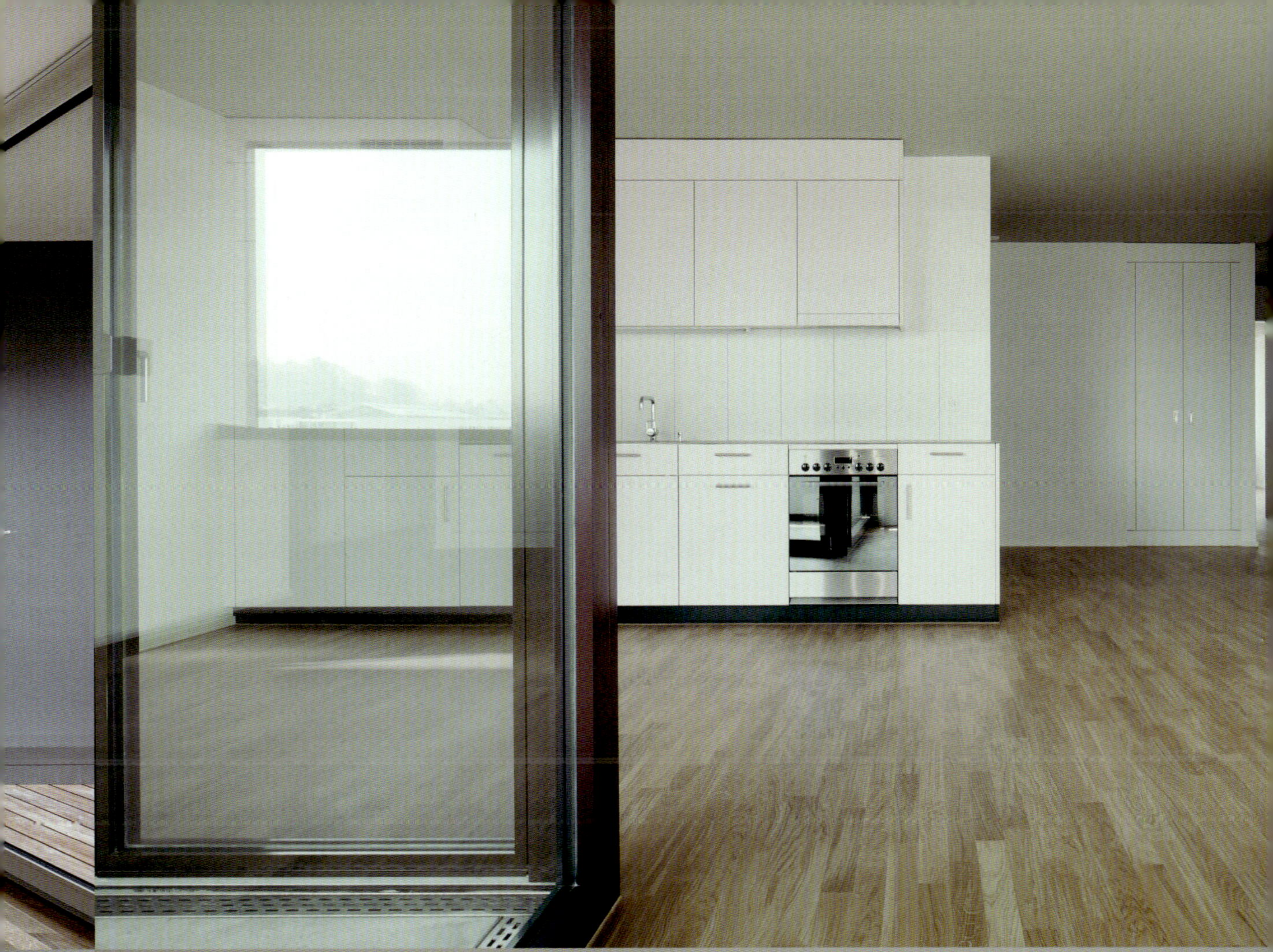

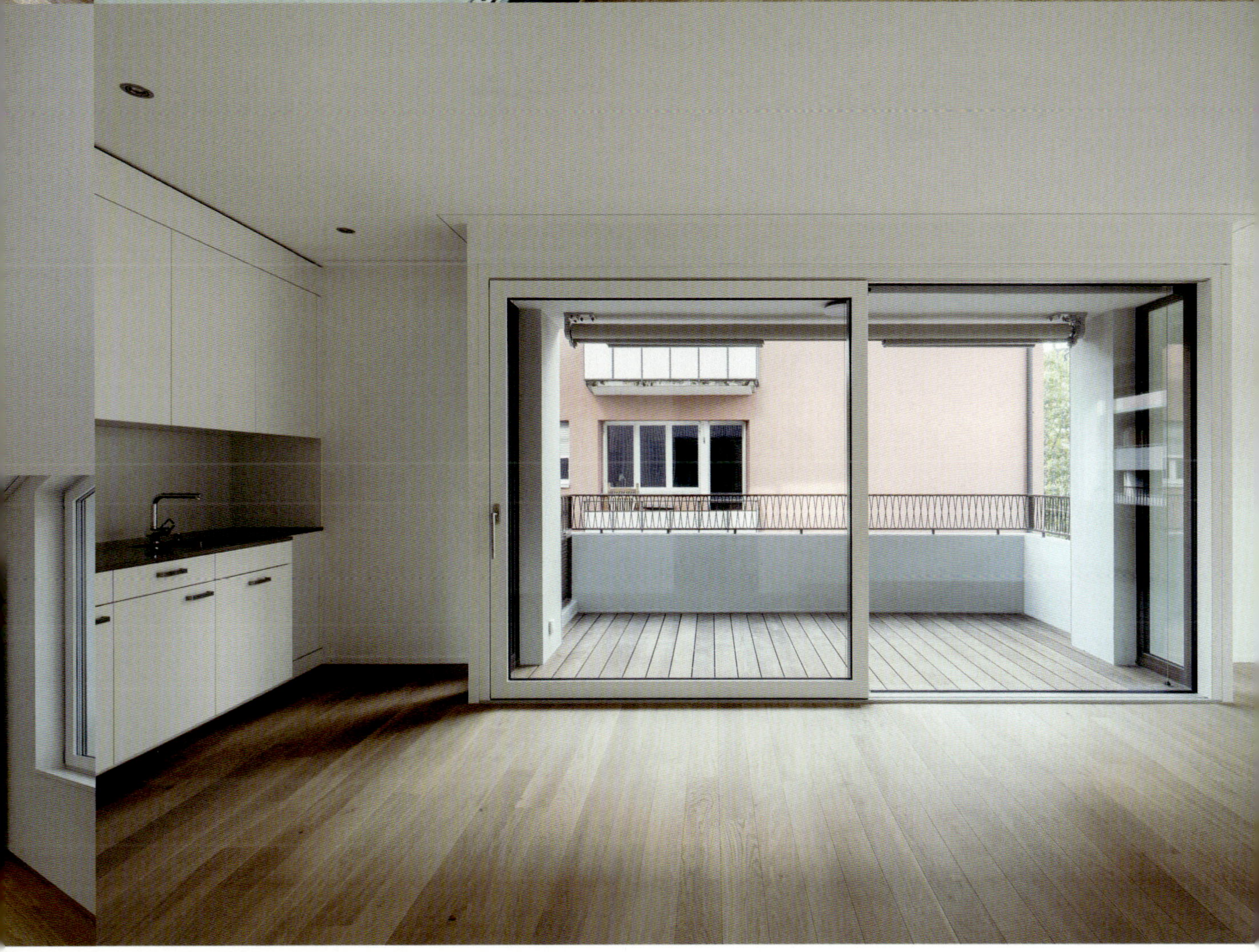

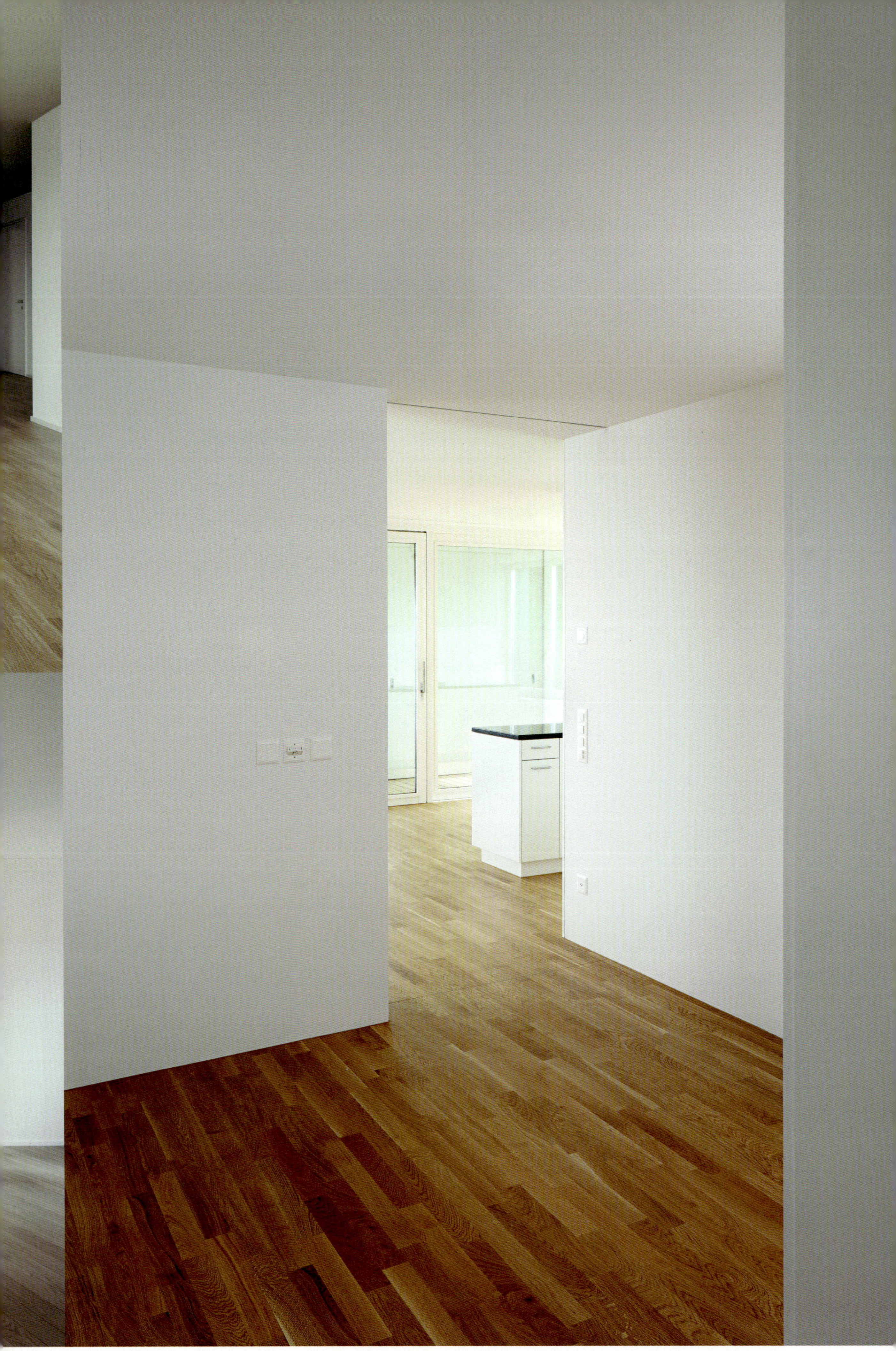

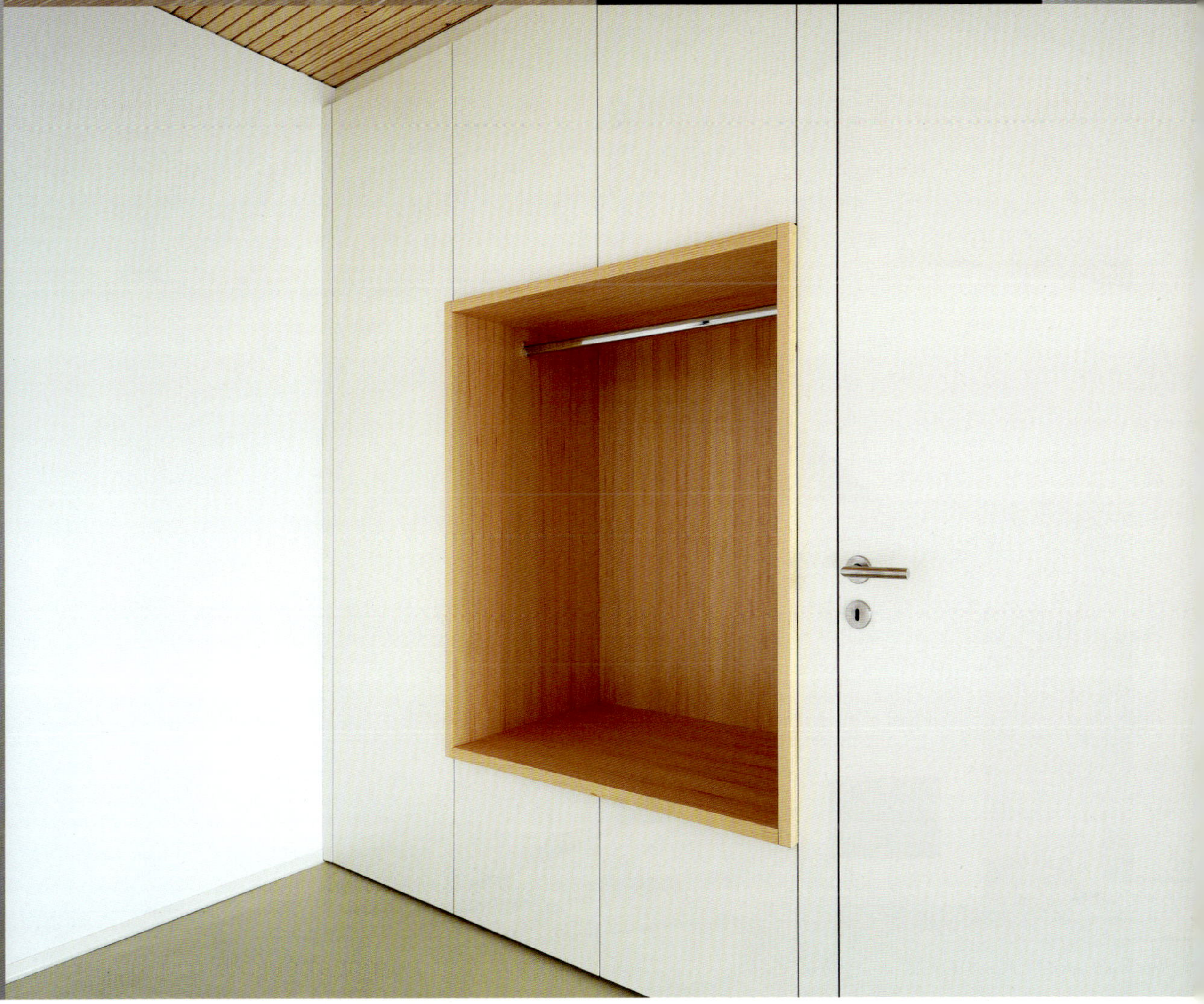

51

52

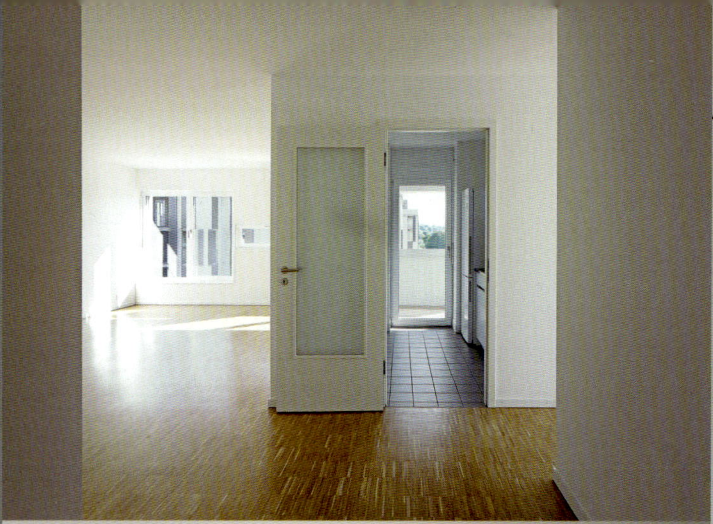
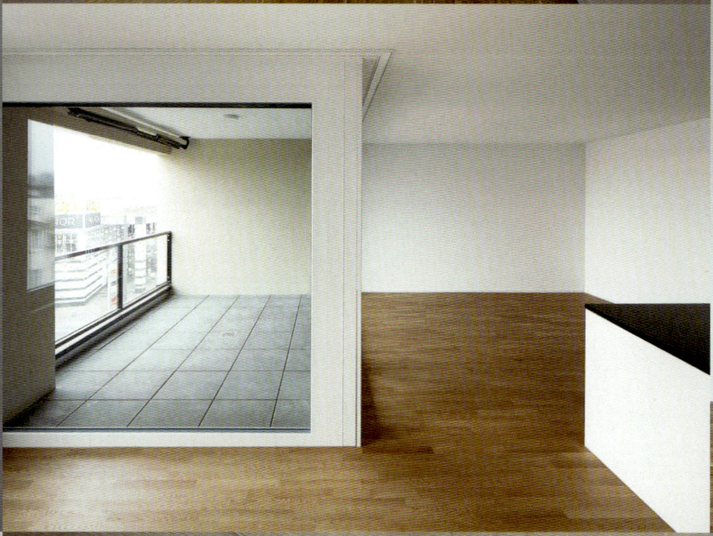
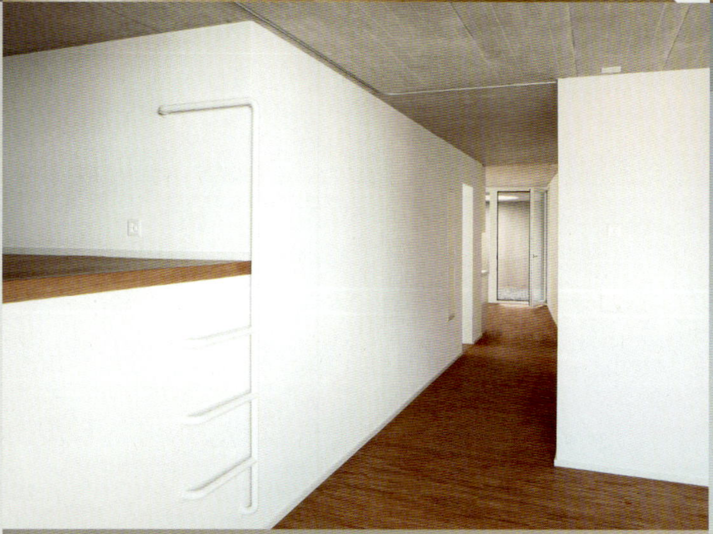
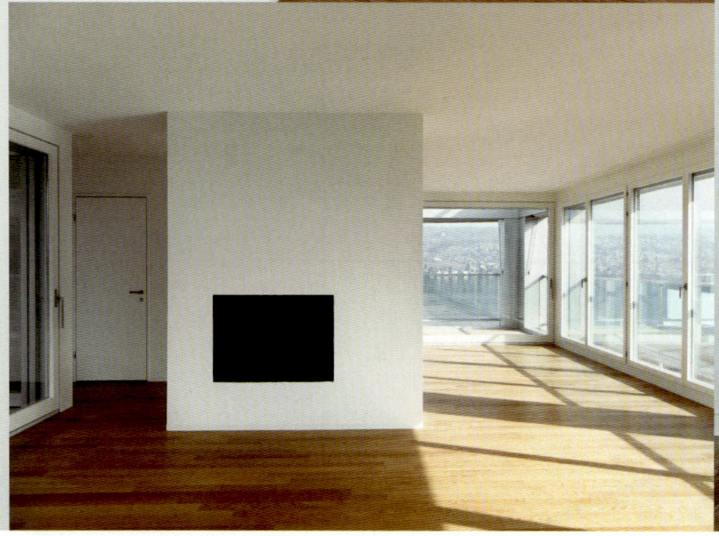
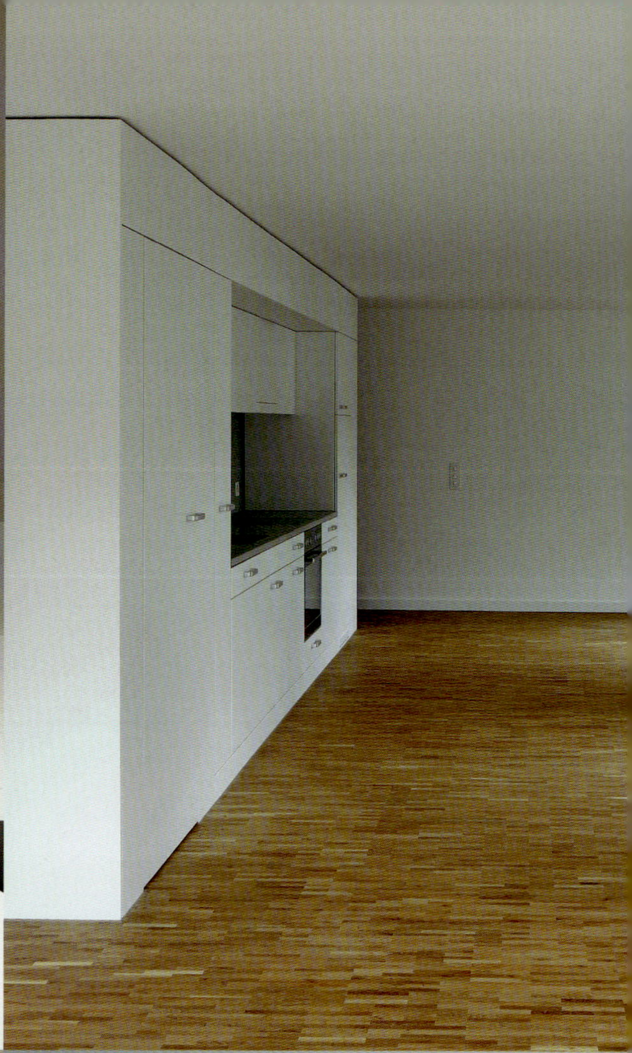
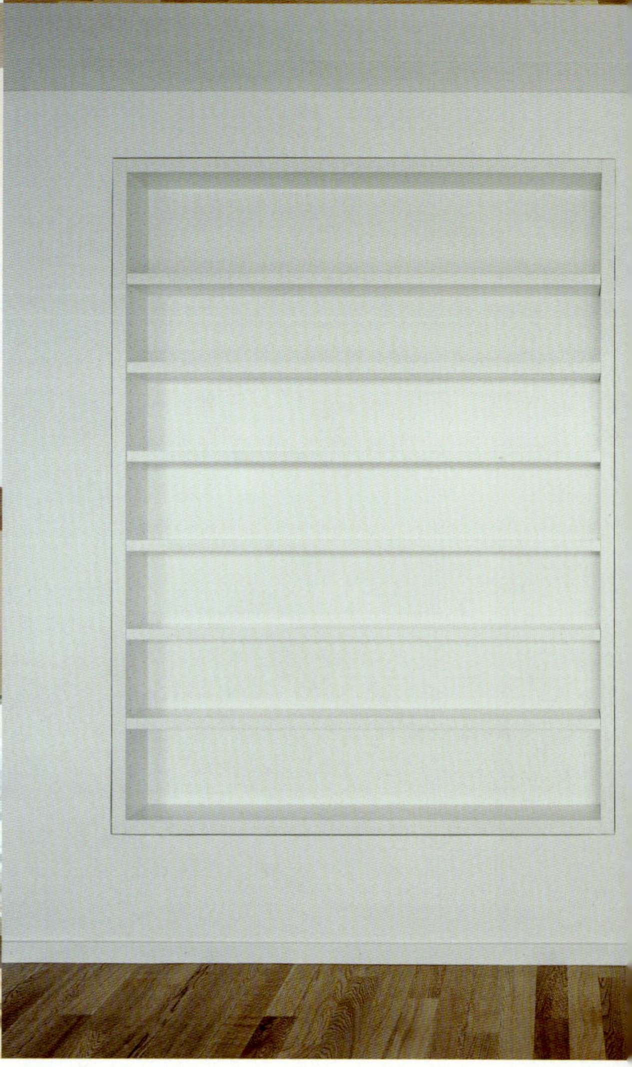

53
54
55
56

57

58

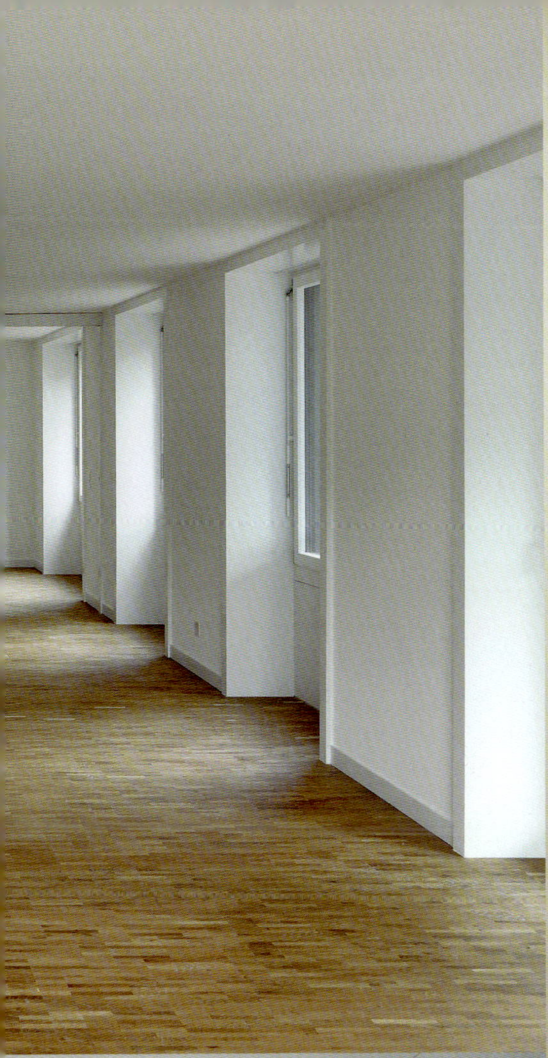
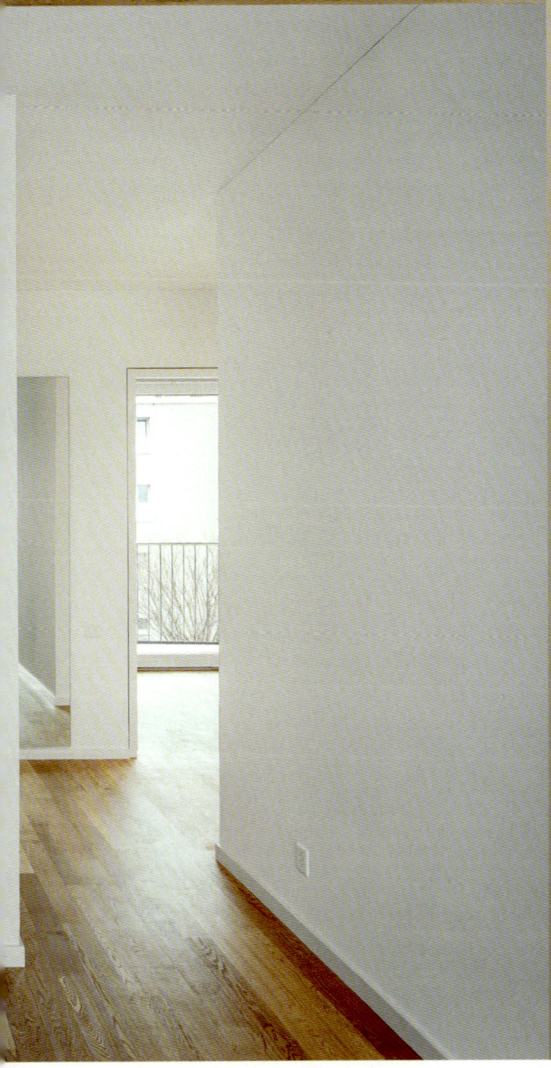
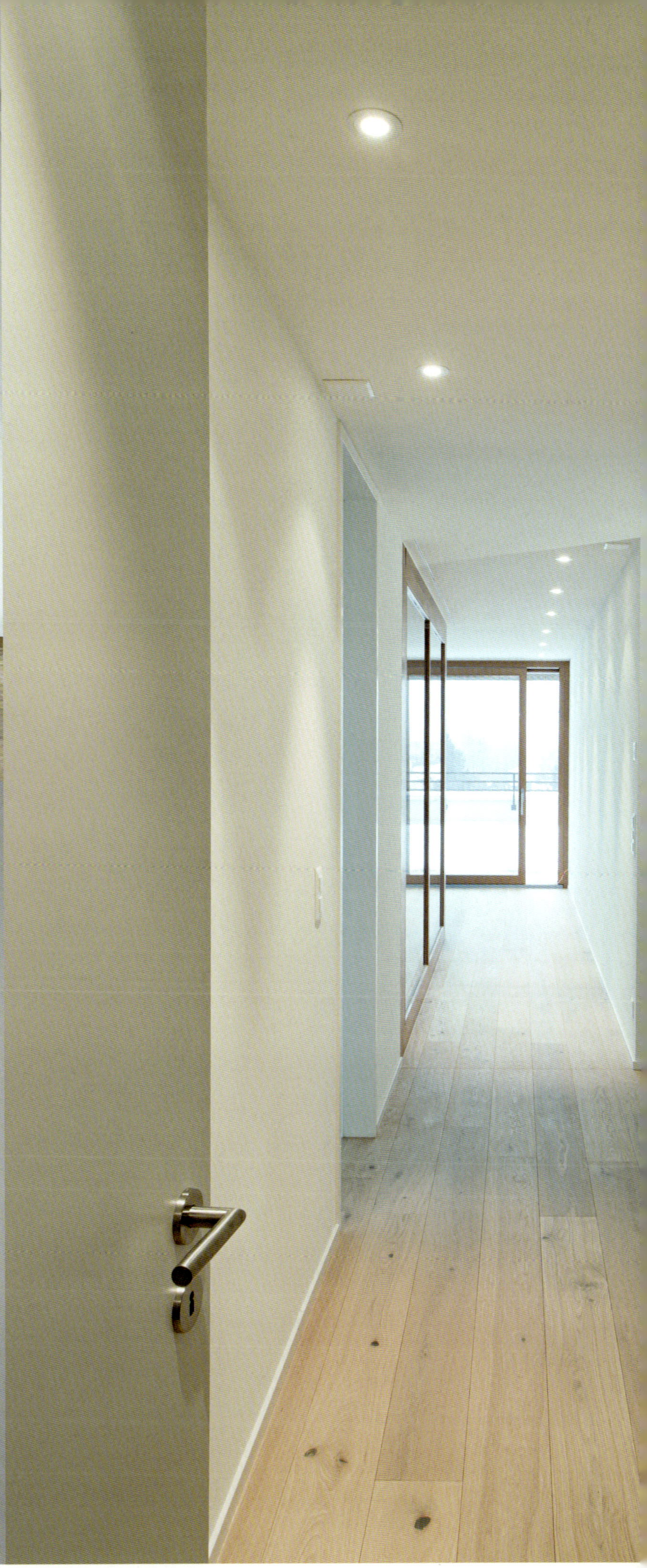

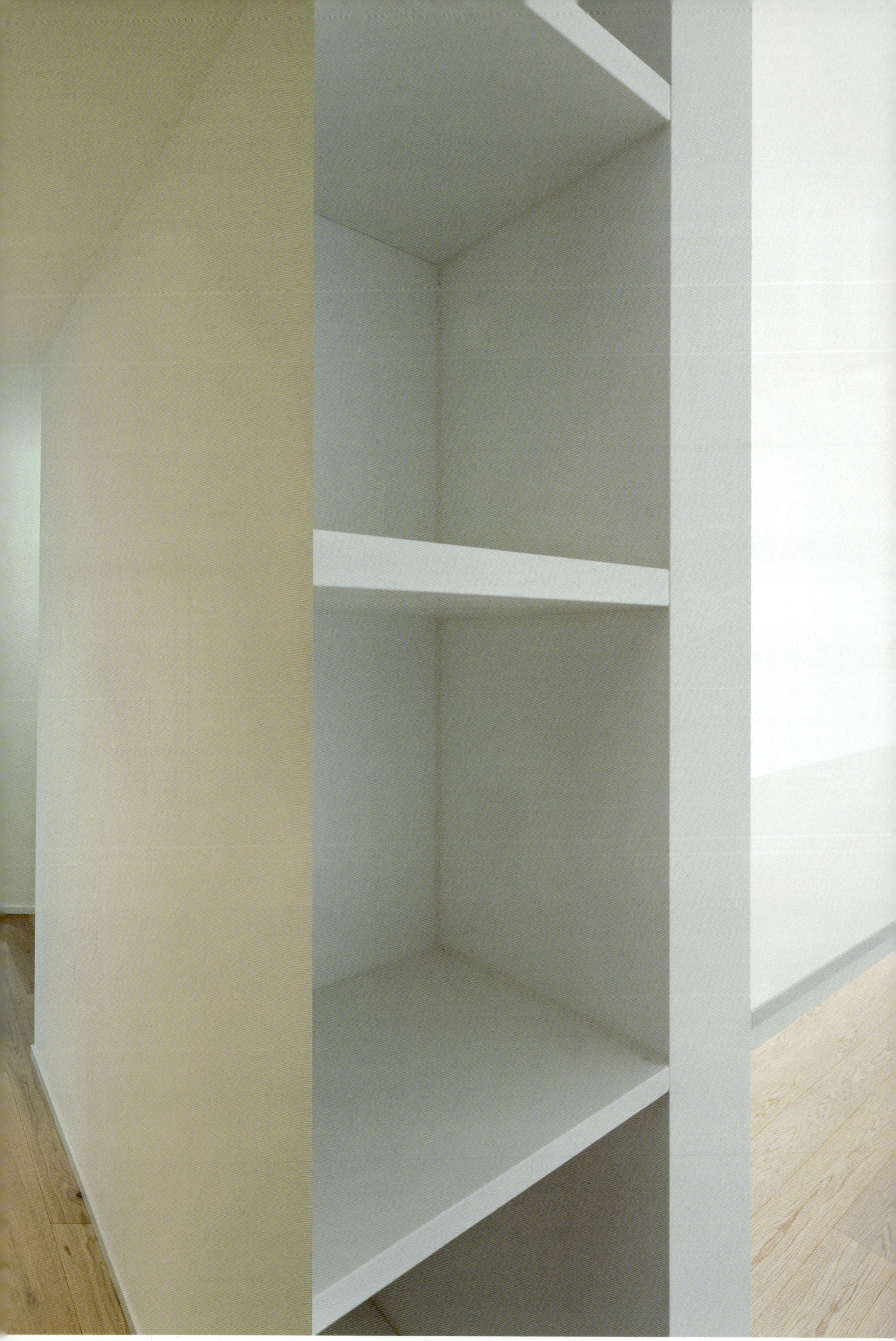

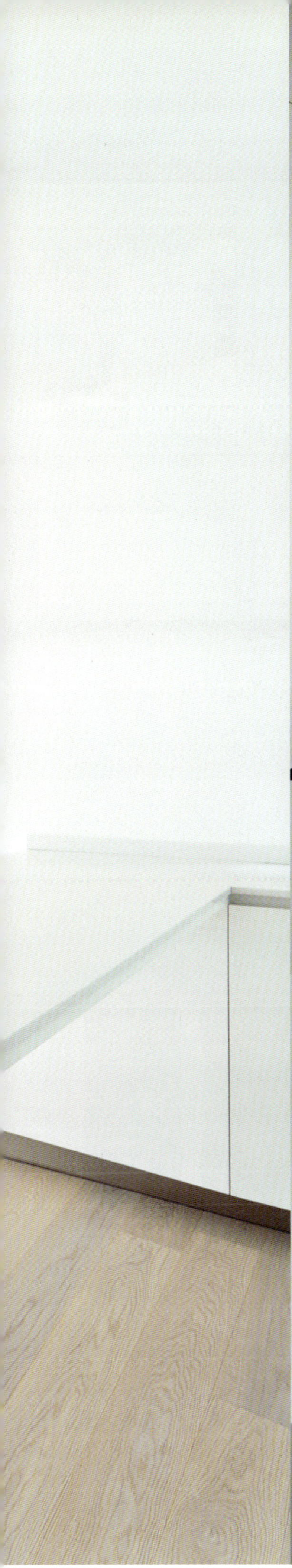

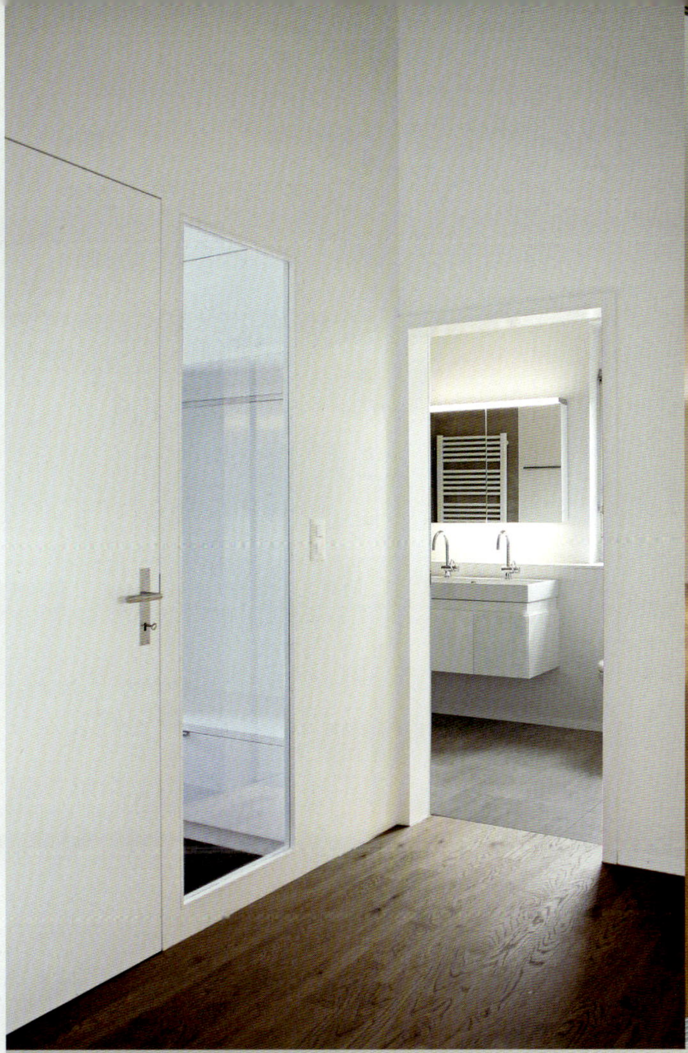

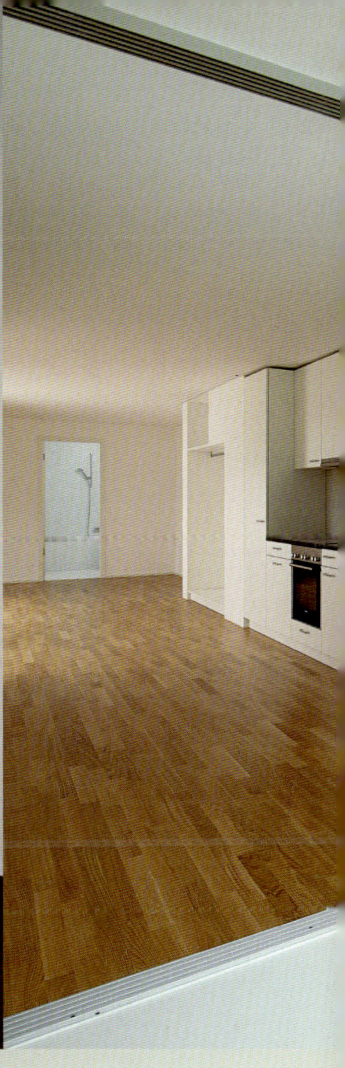

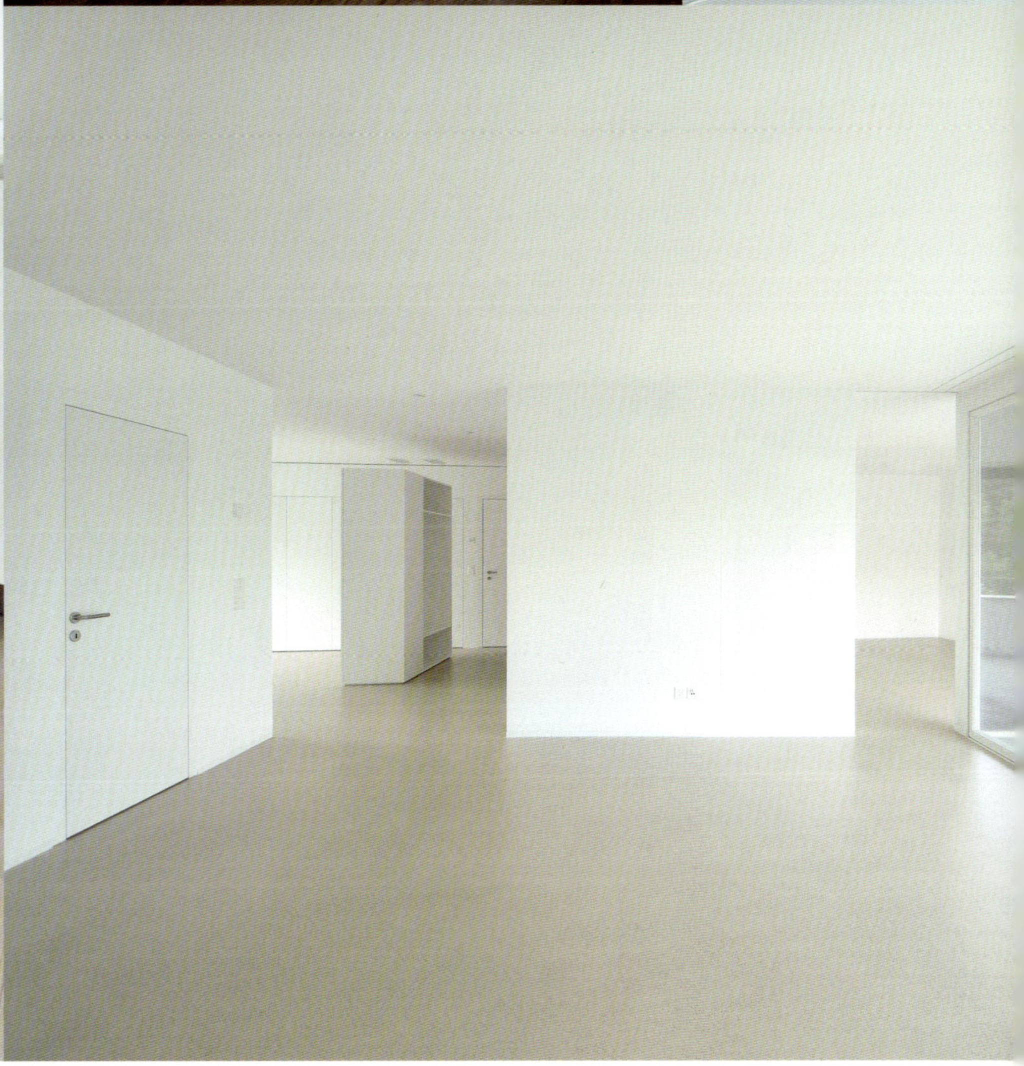

61

62

63

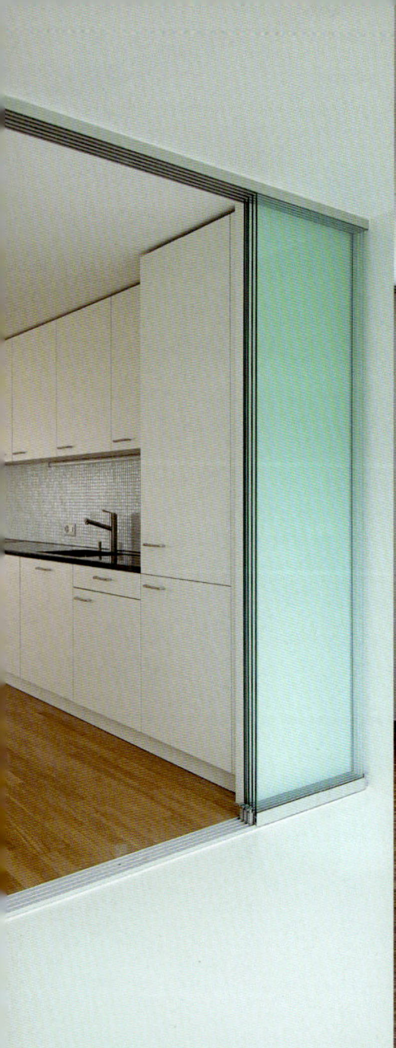
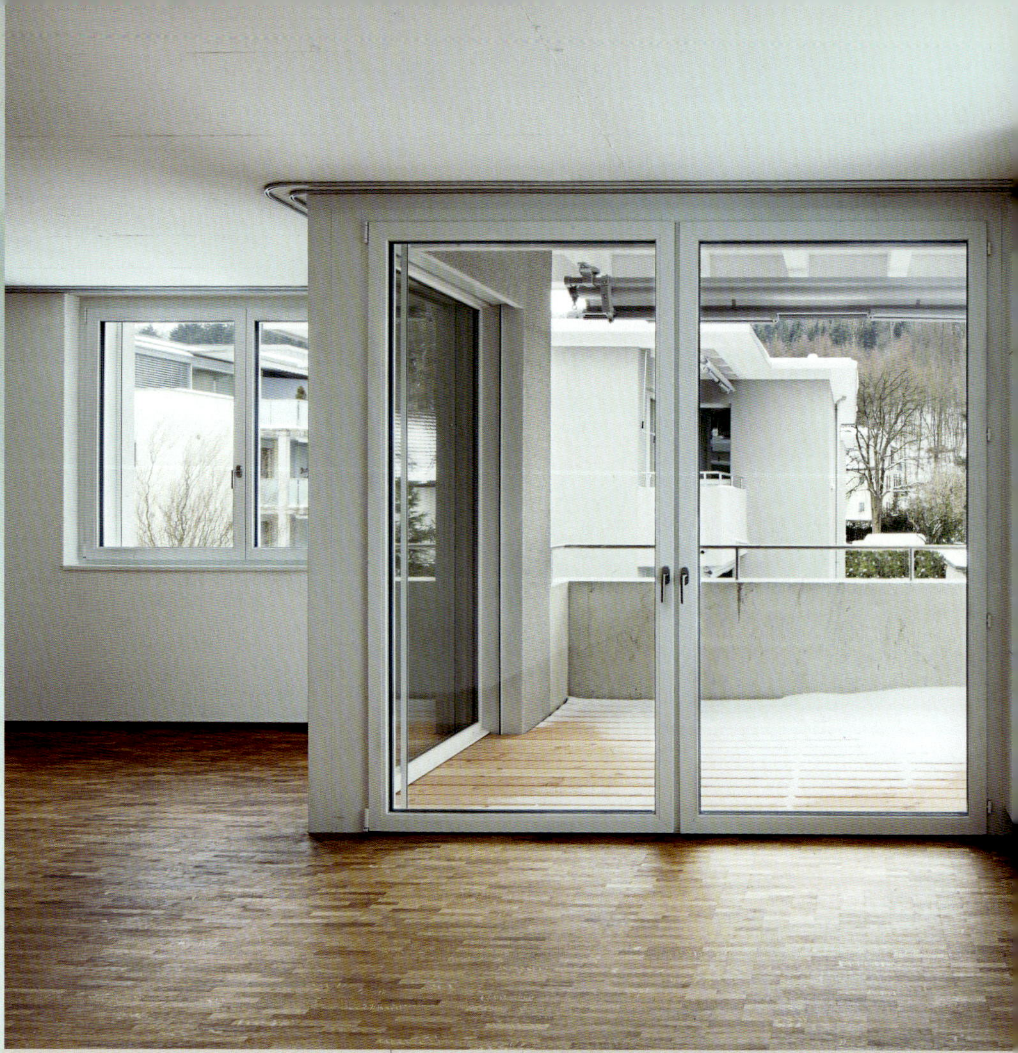
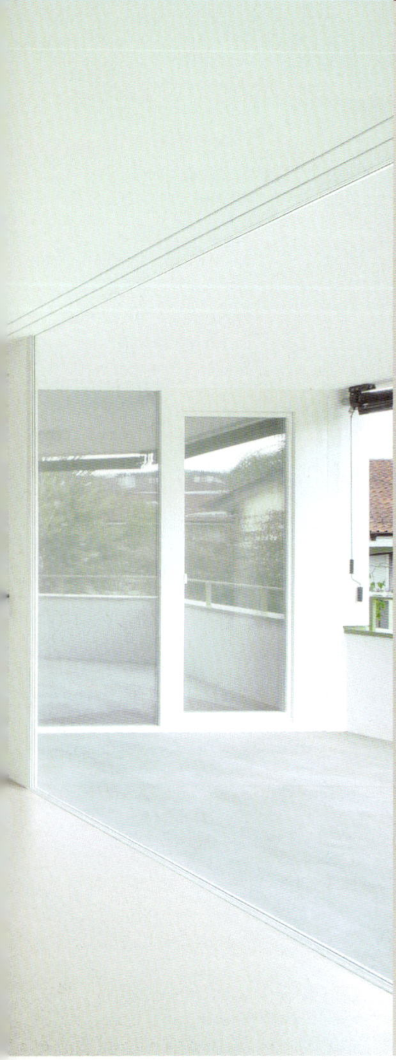
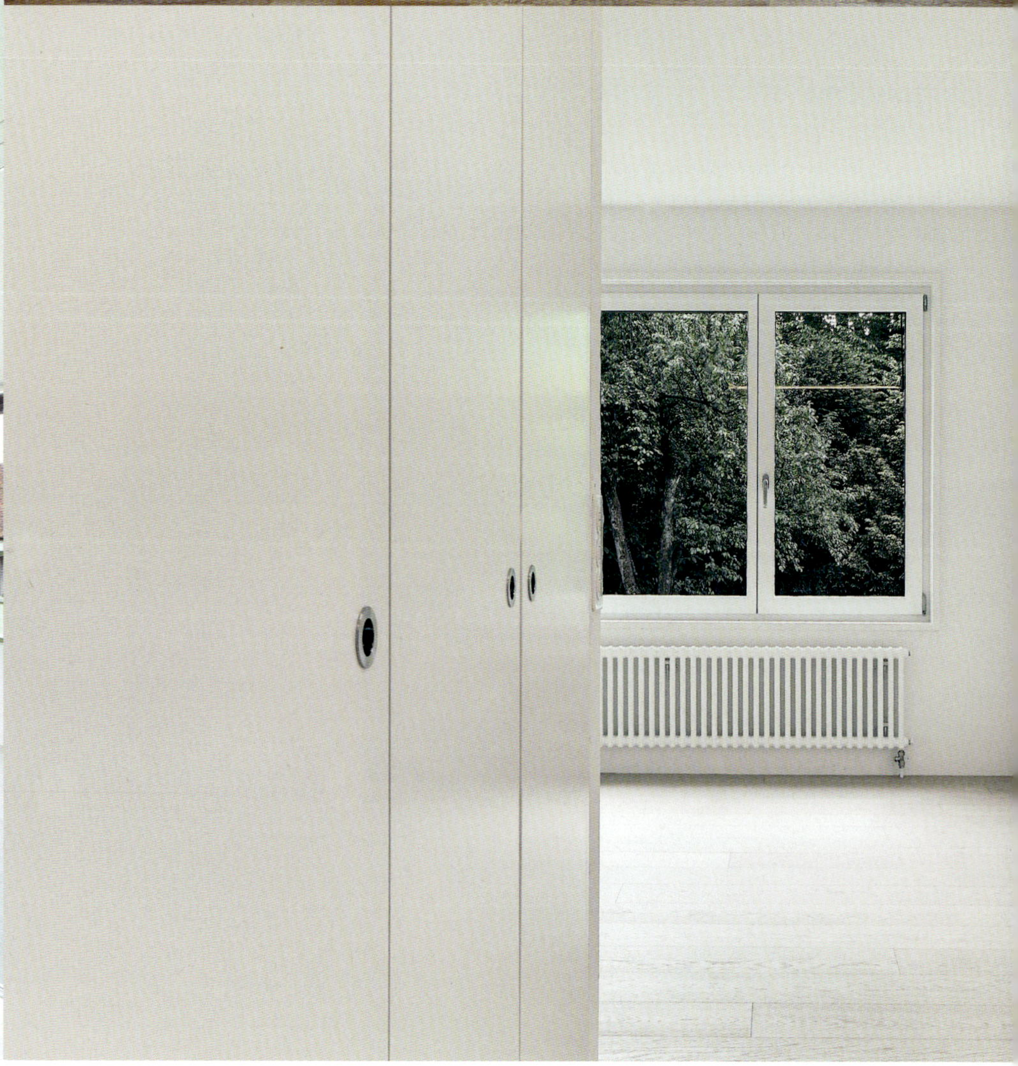

64

65

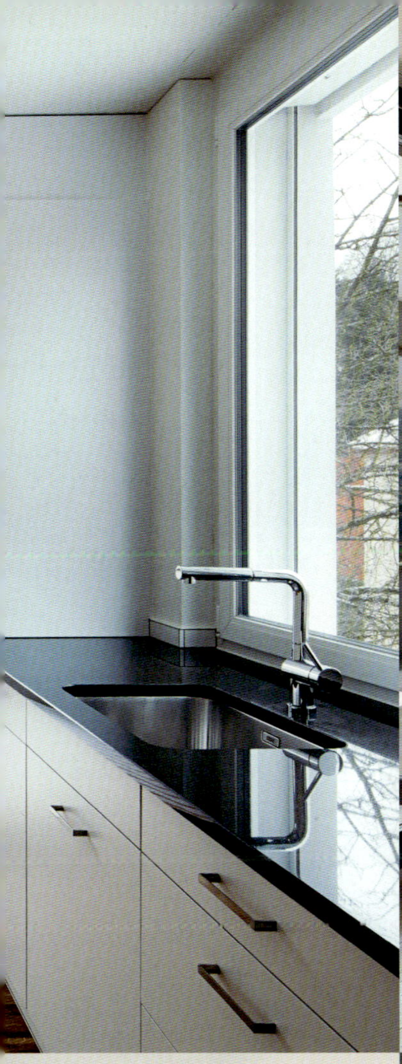
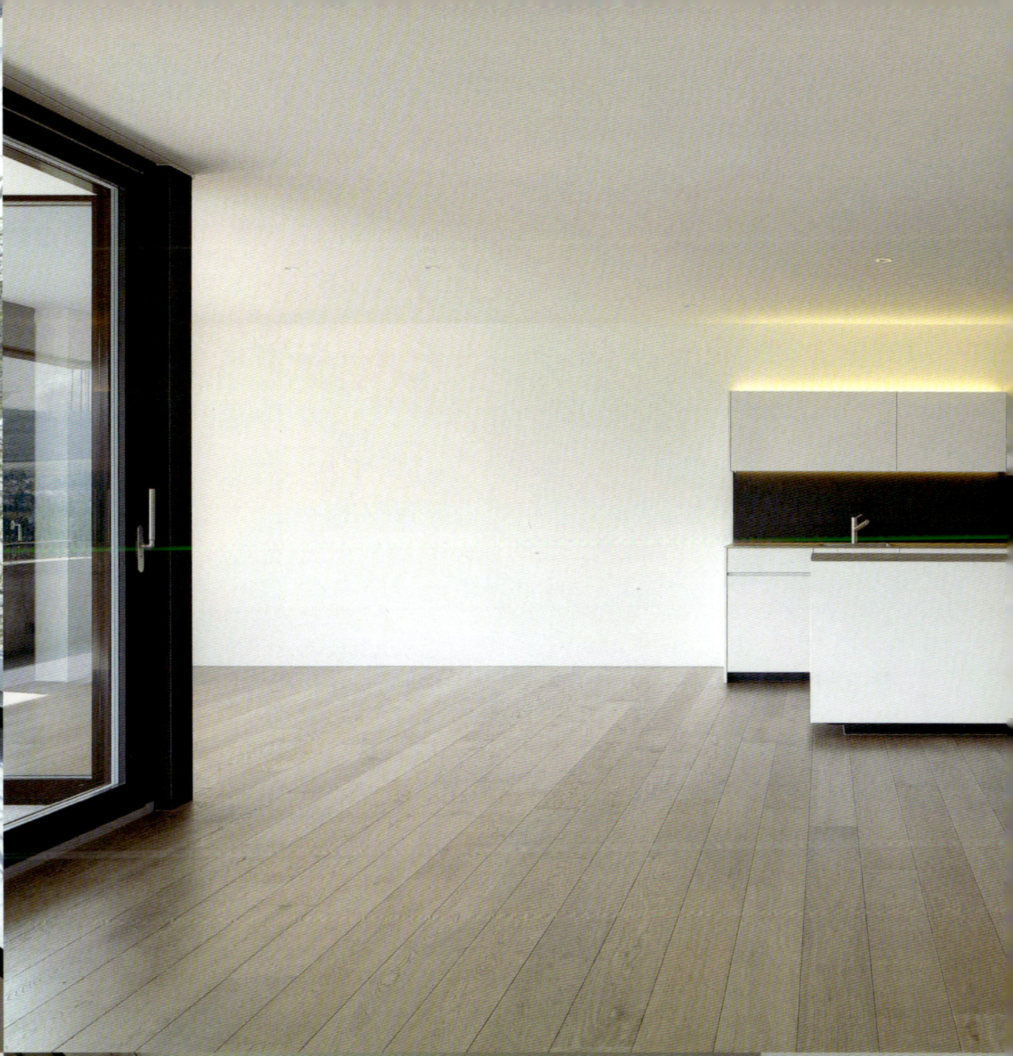

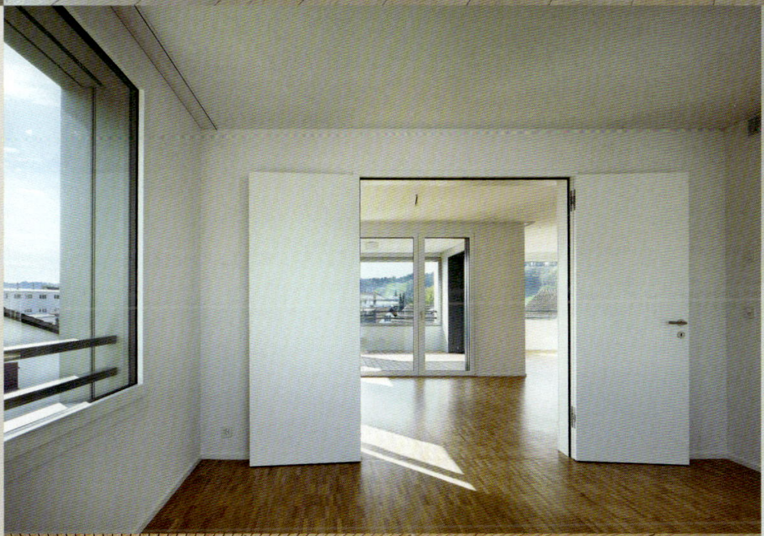
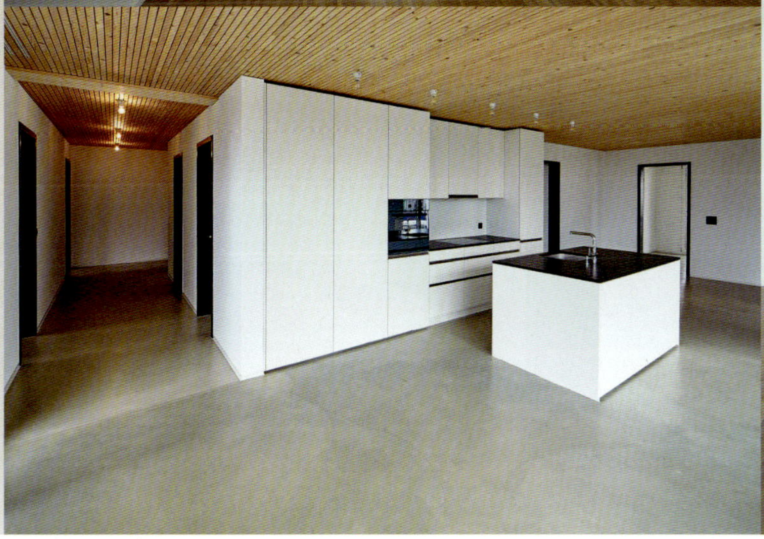

66
67
68

69

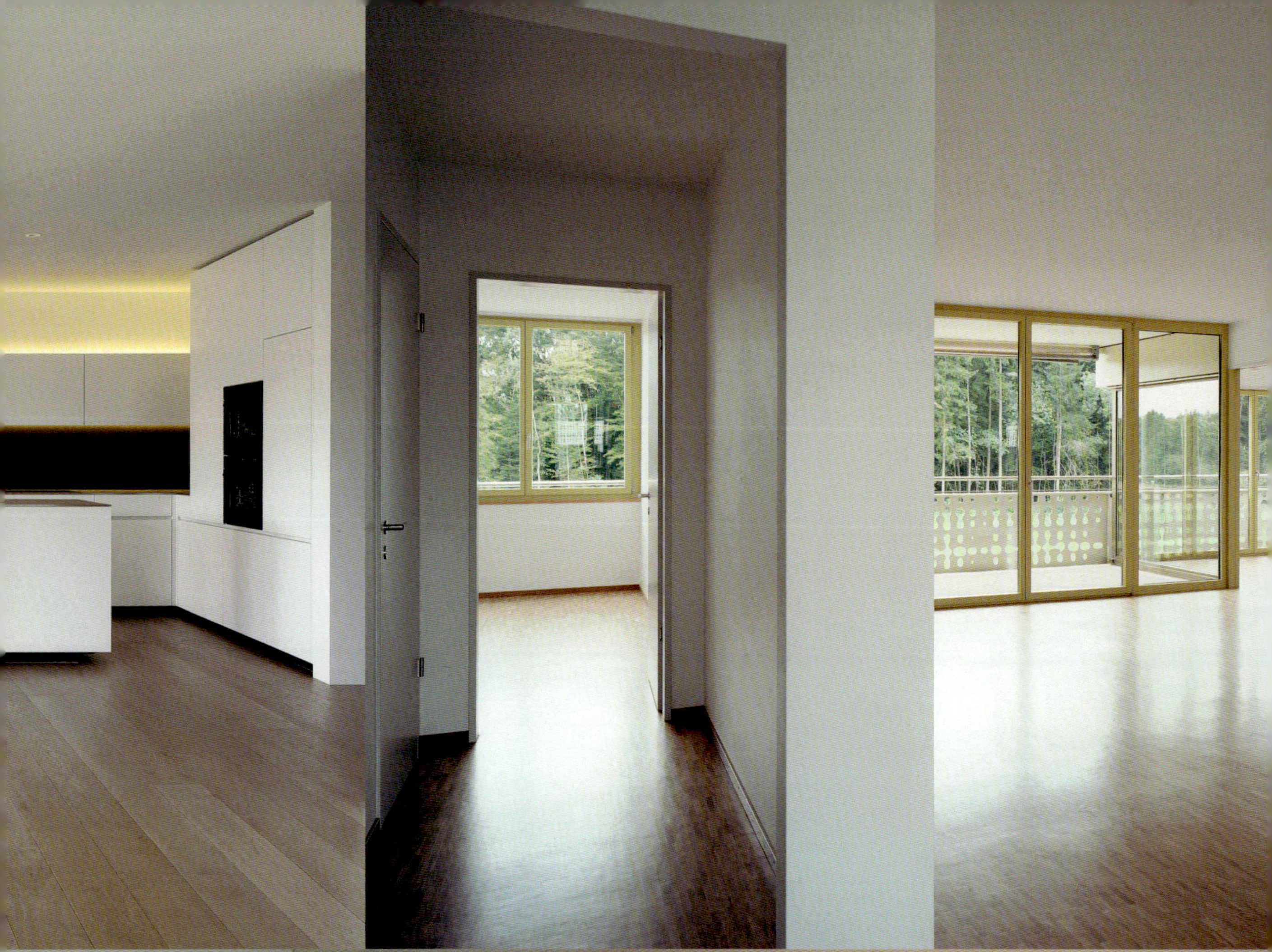

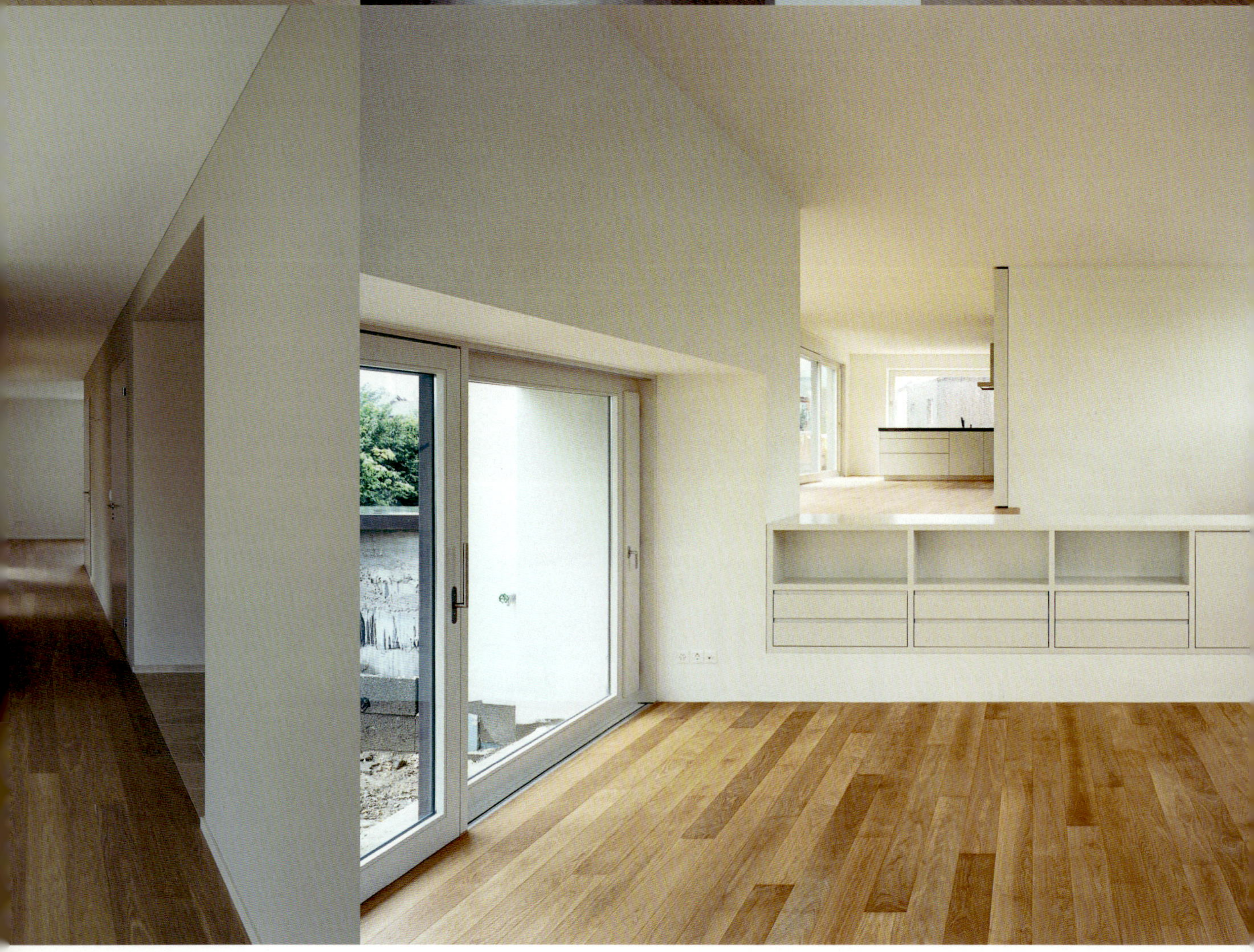

70

71

Kazuo Shinohara
Casas Houses
2G
Foto
dal finestrino

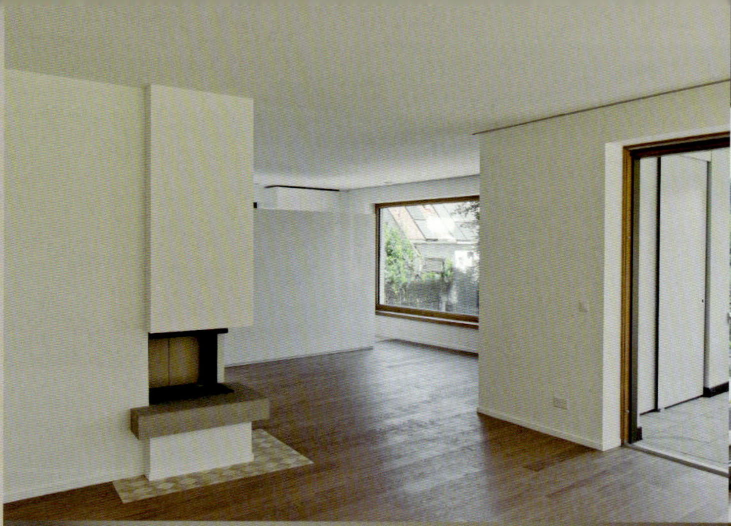

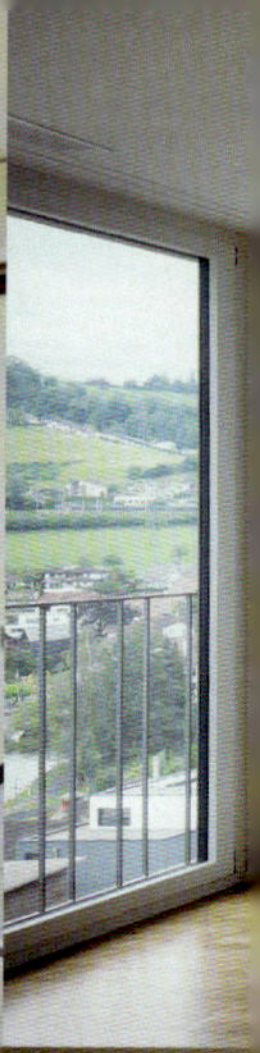

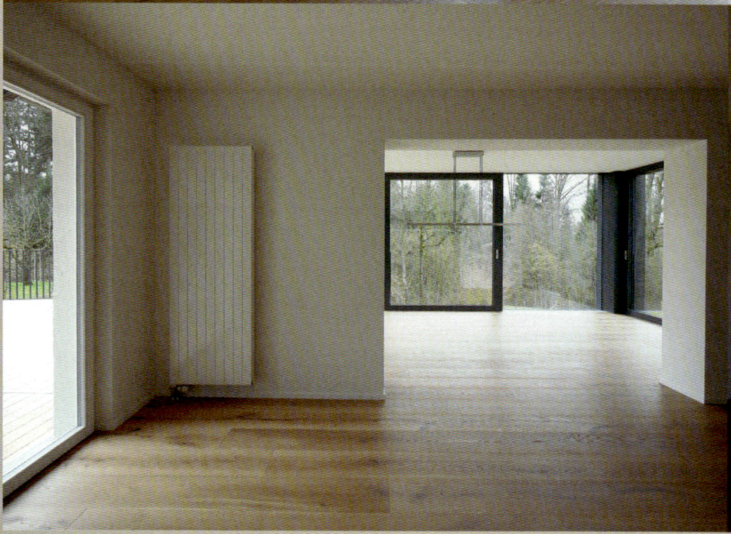

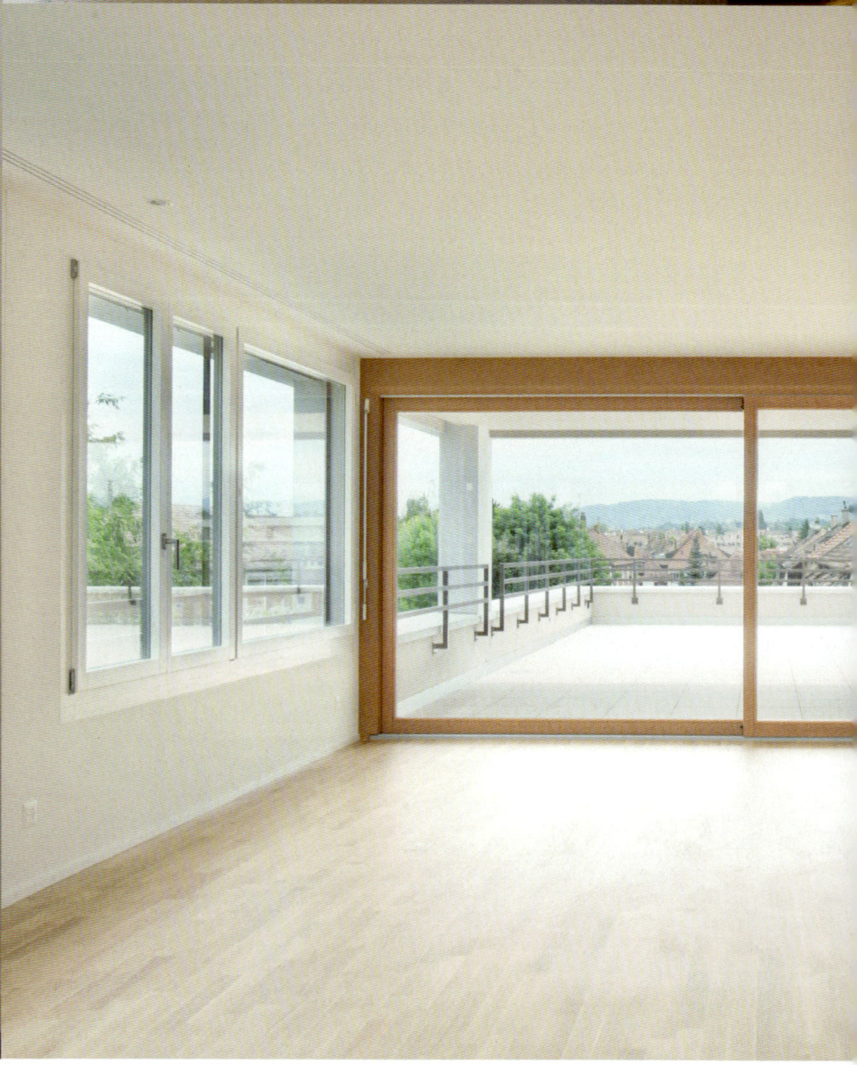

73
74

75

76
77

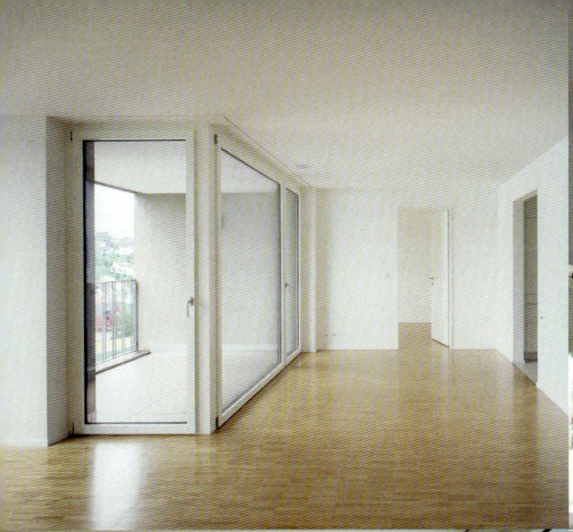
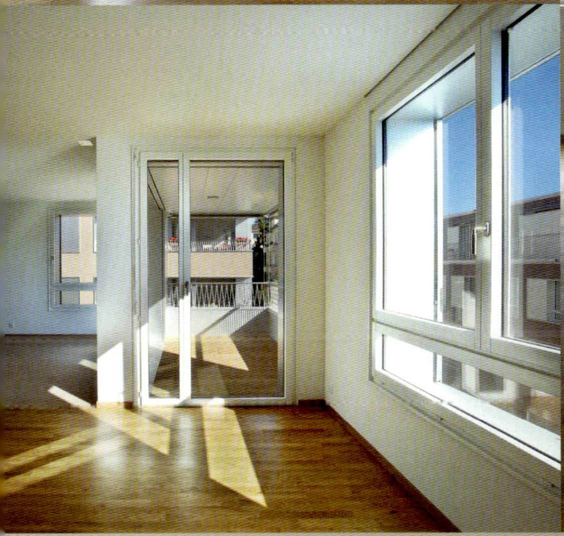
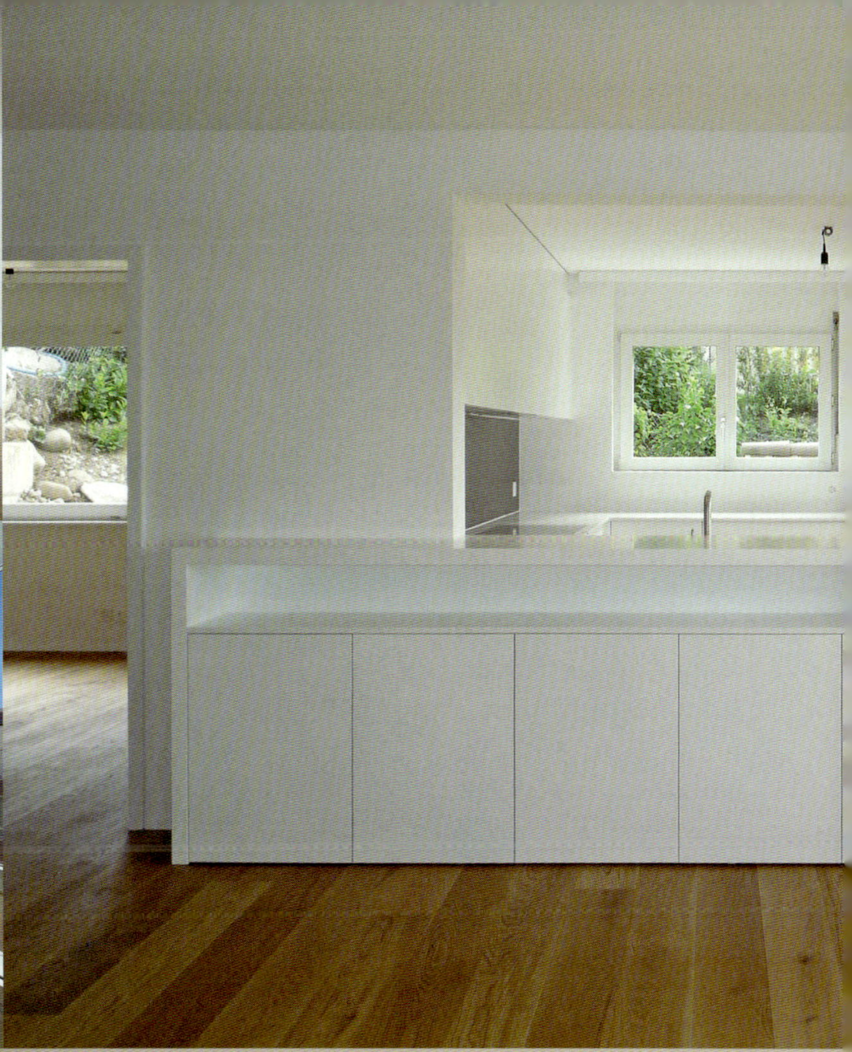
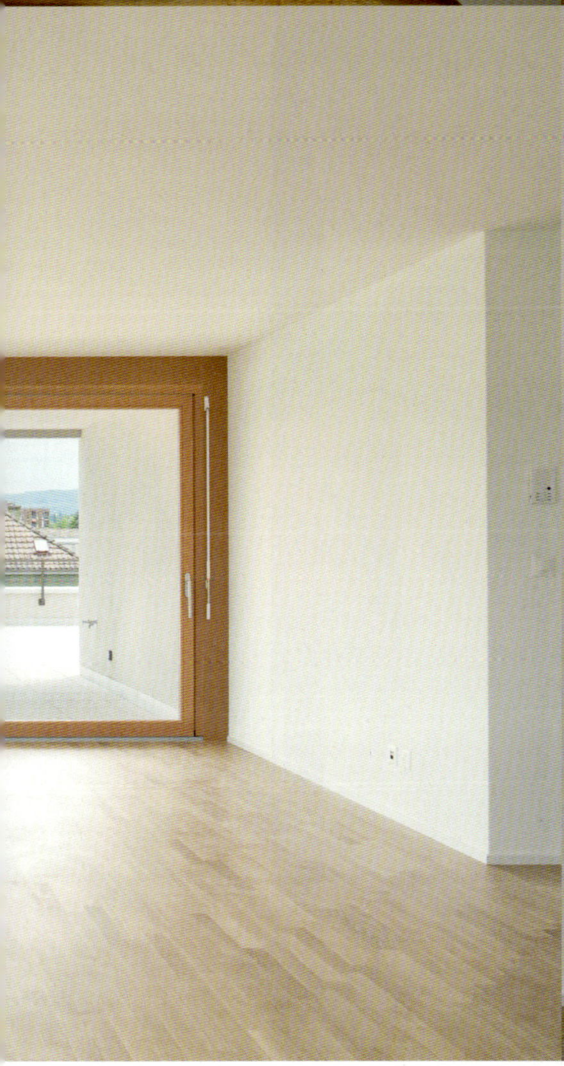
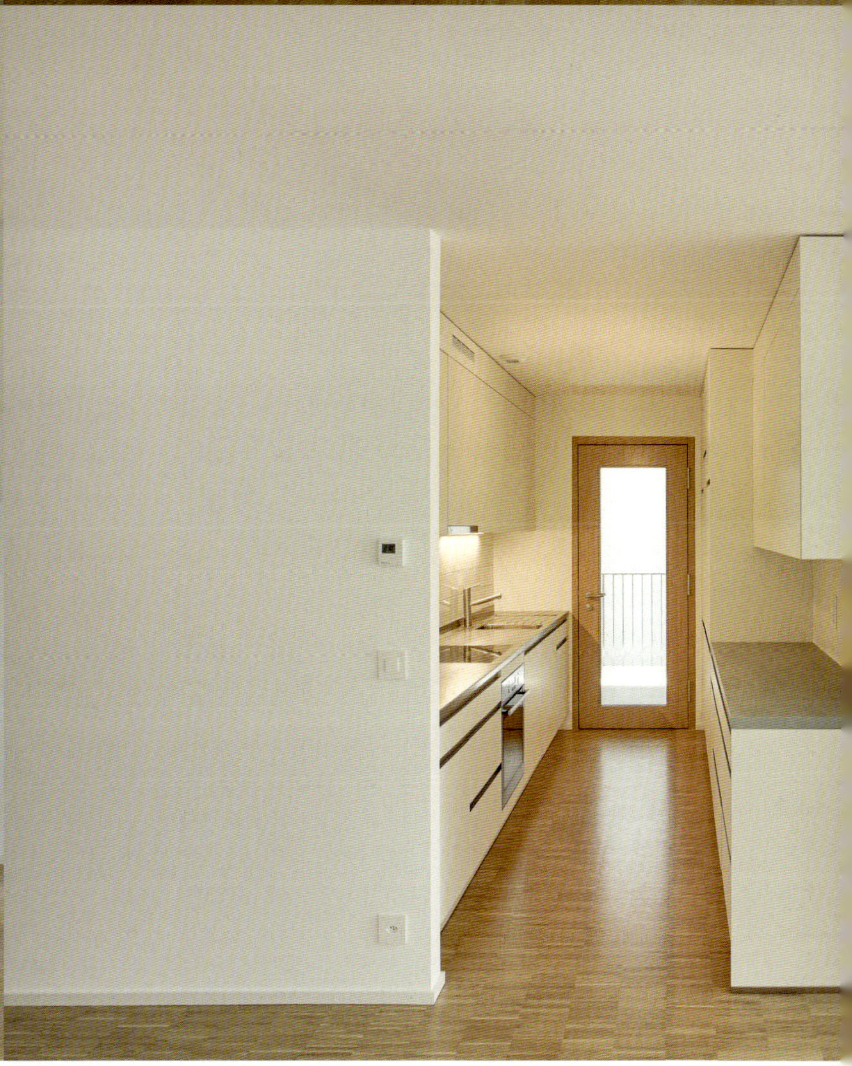

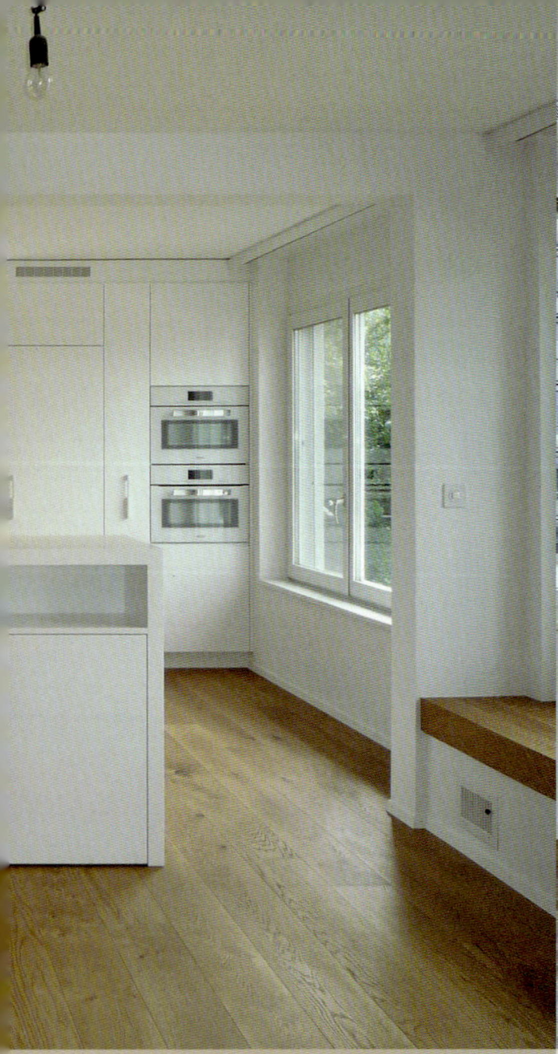

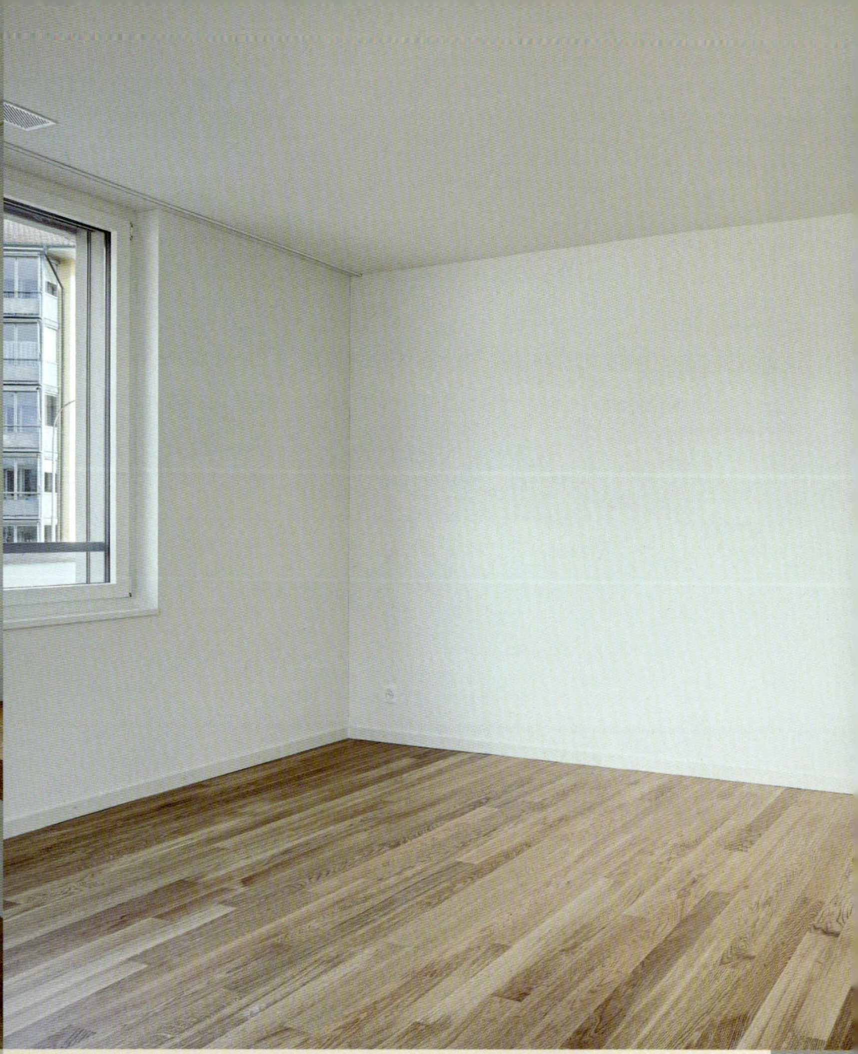

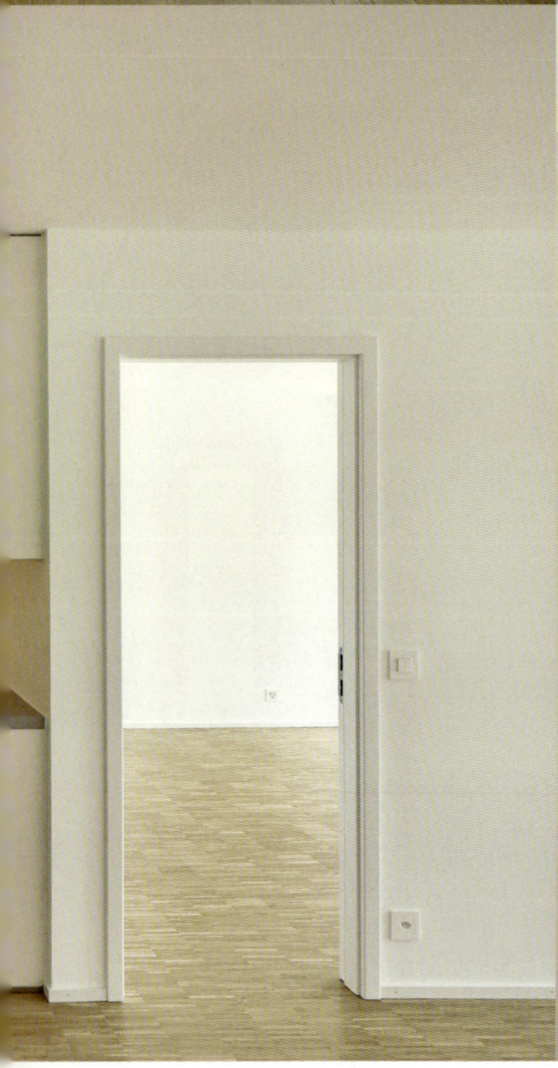

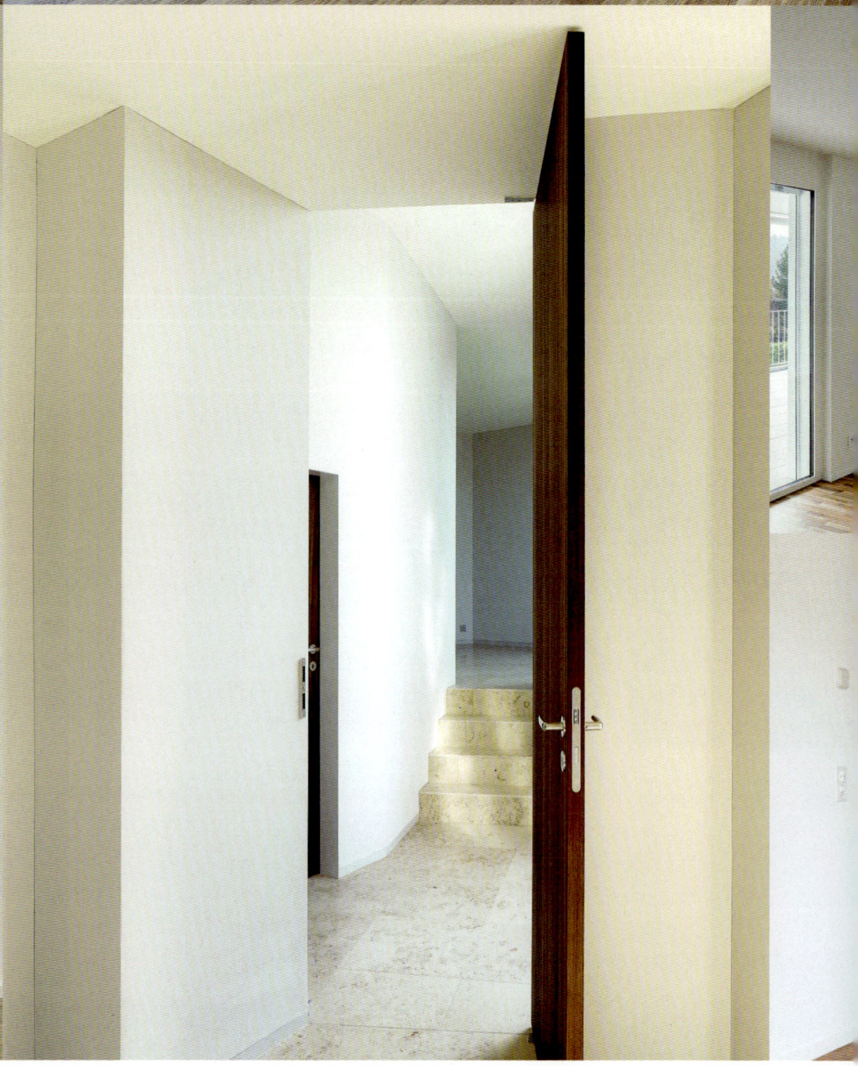

80

81

82
83

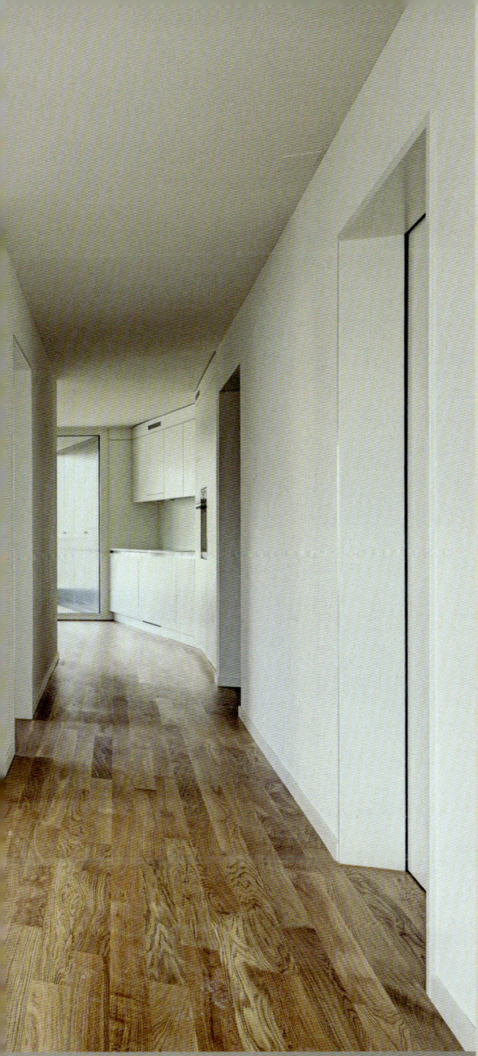

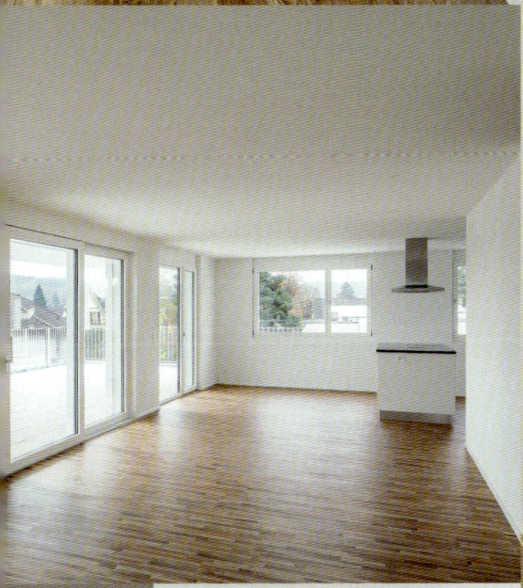

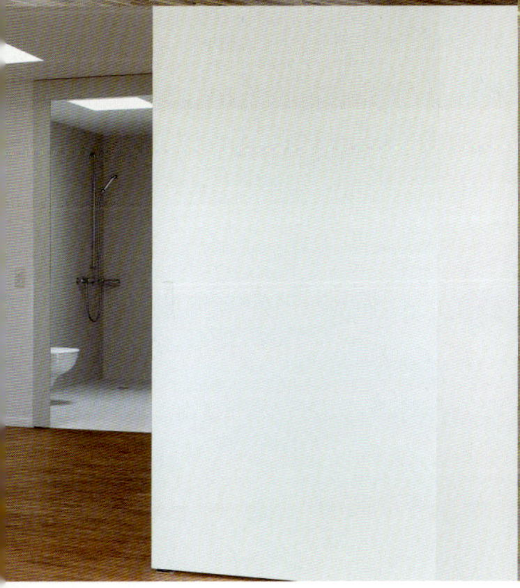

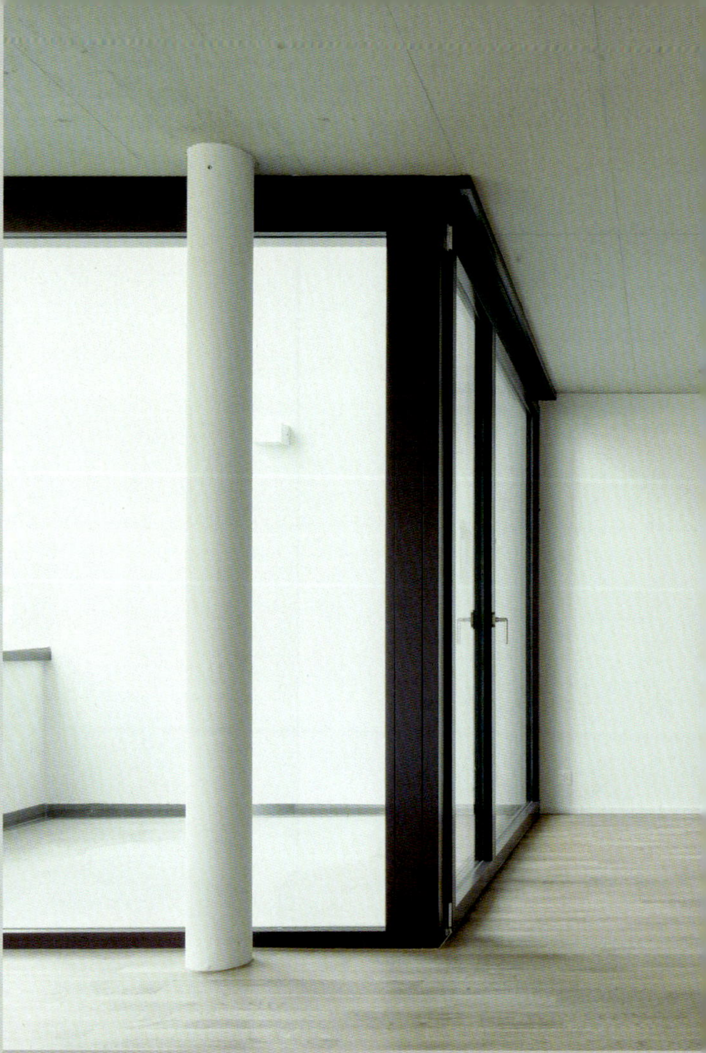

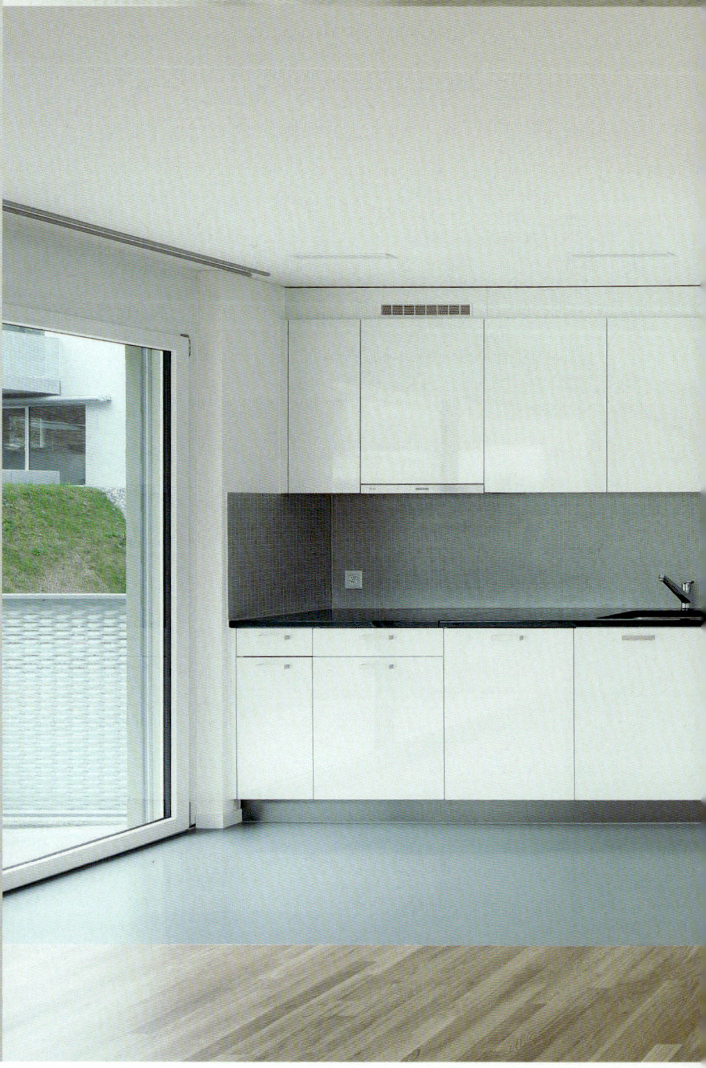

85

86

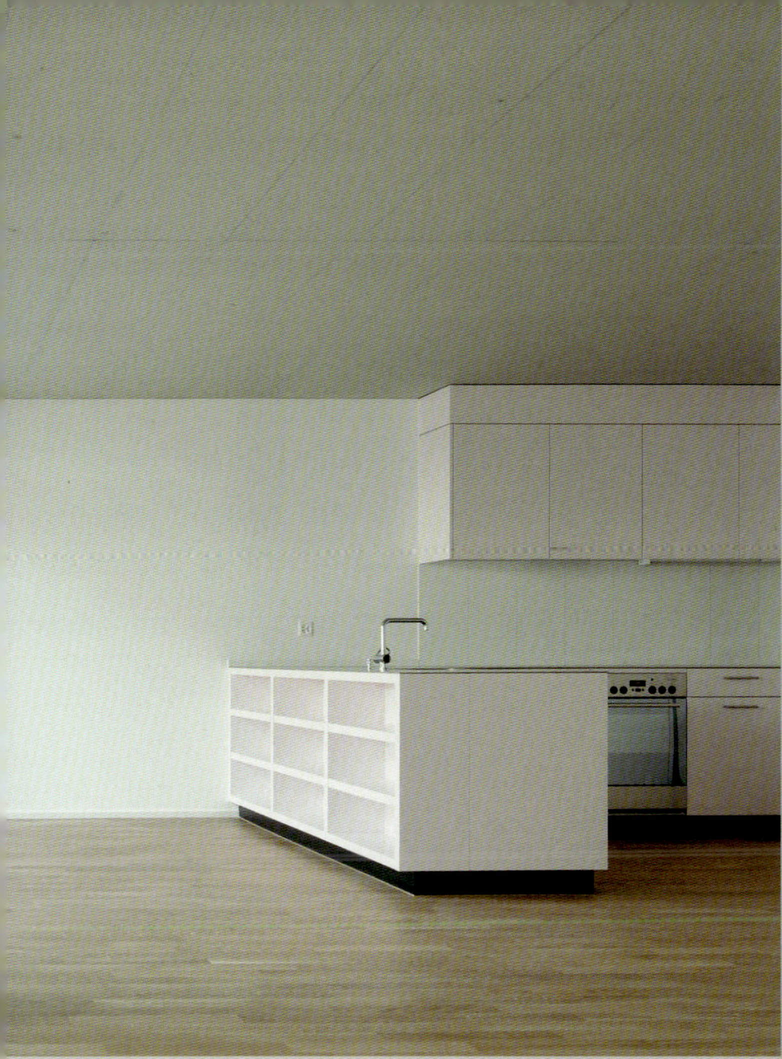
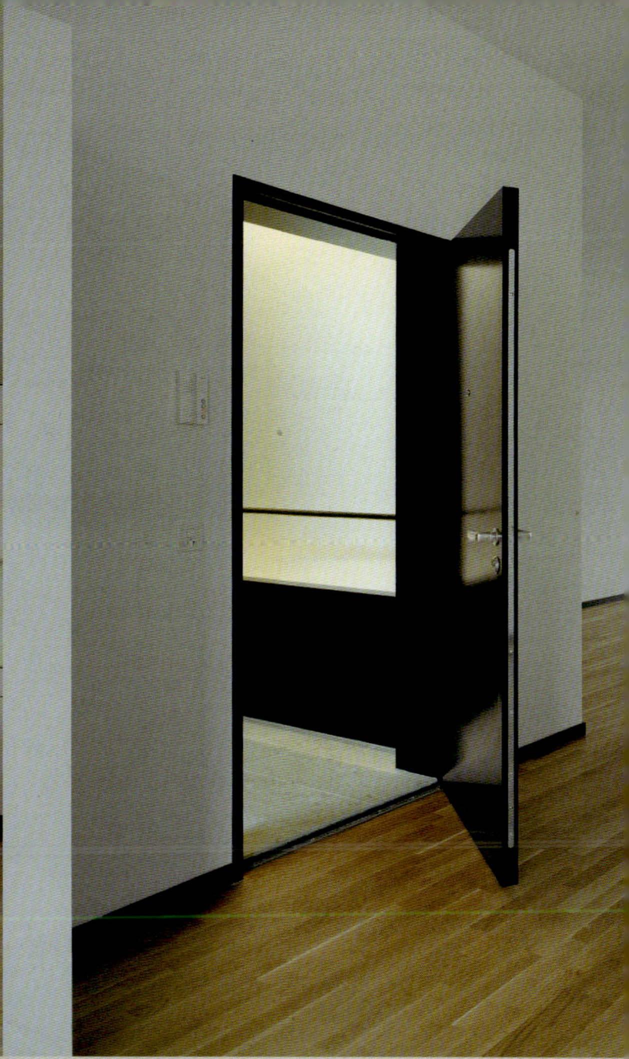
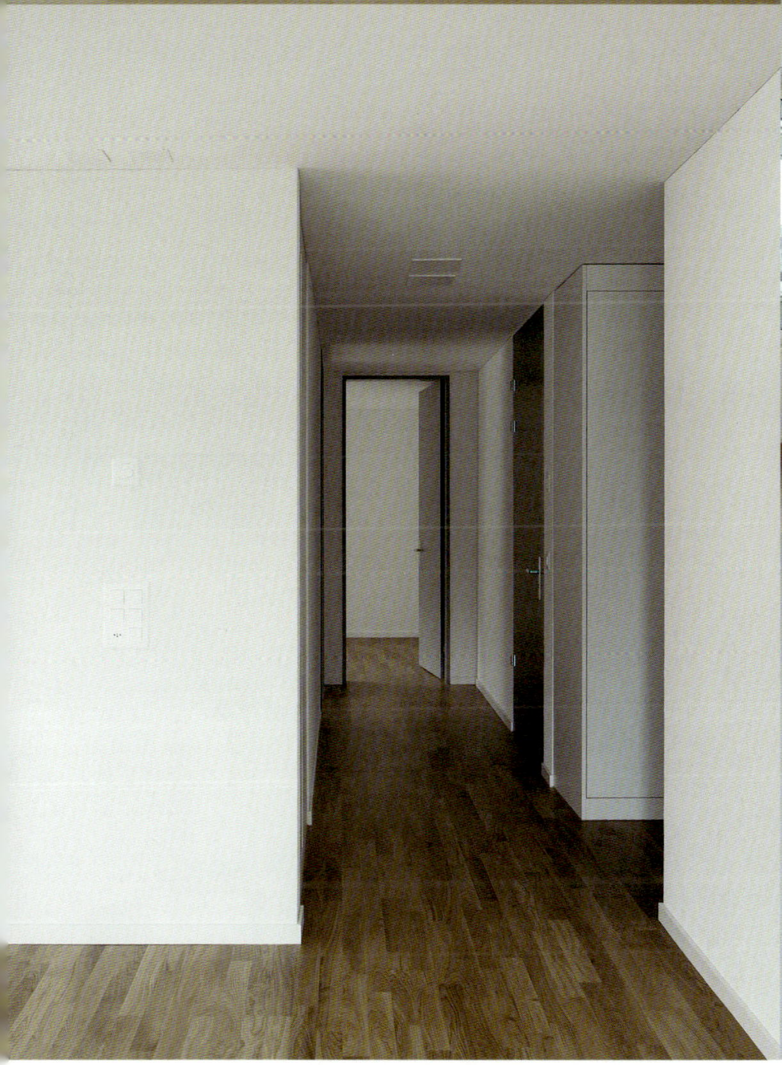
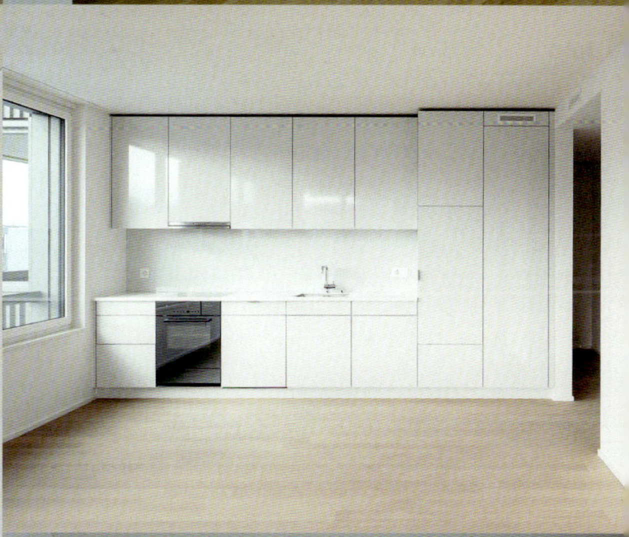
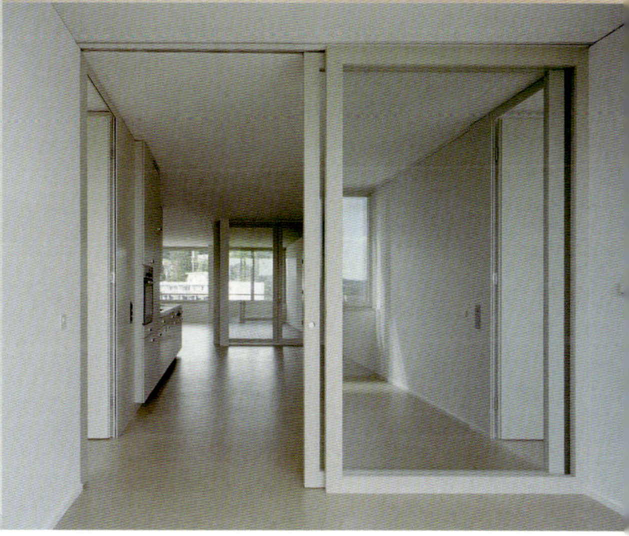

87
88
89

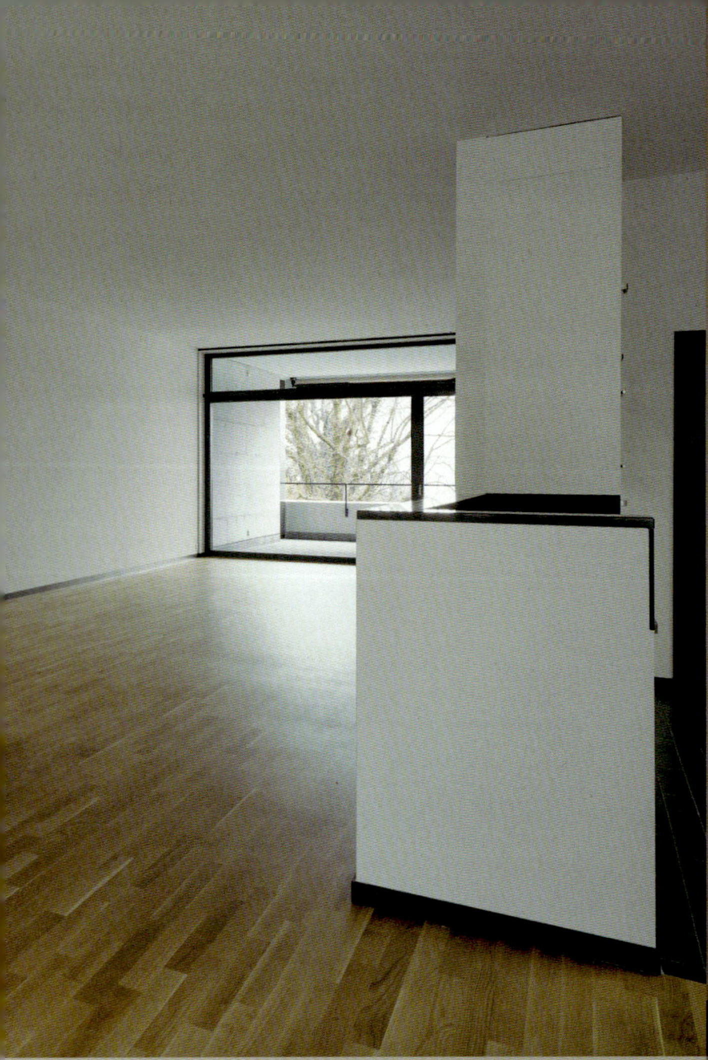

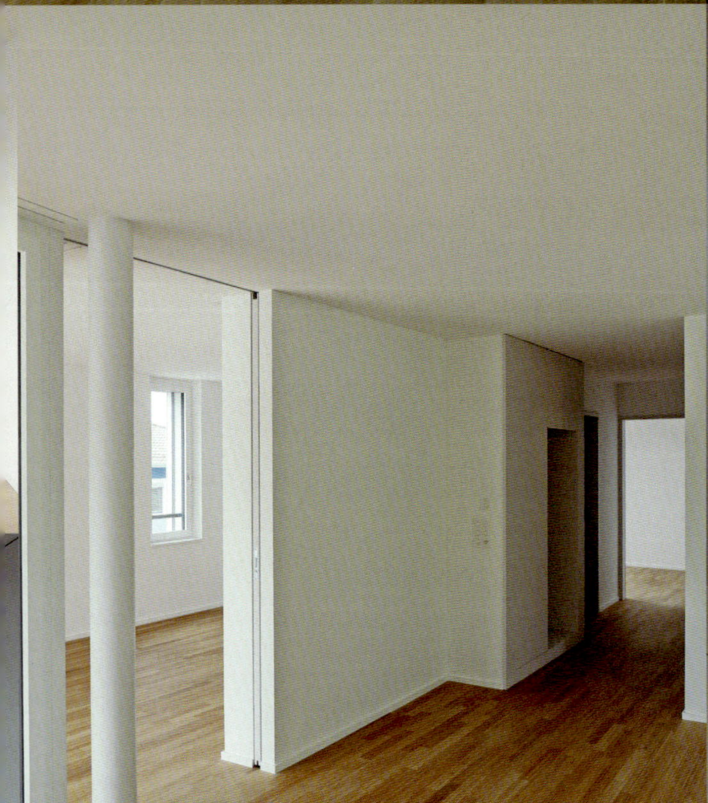
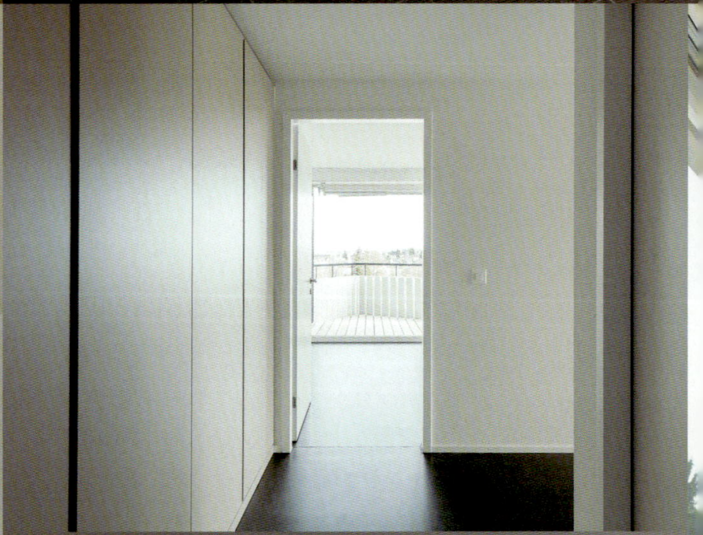
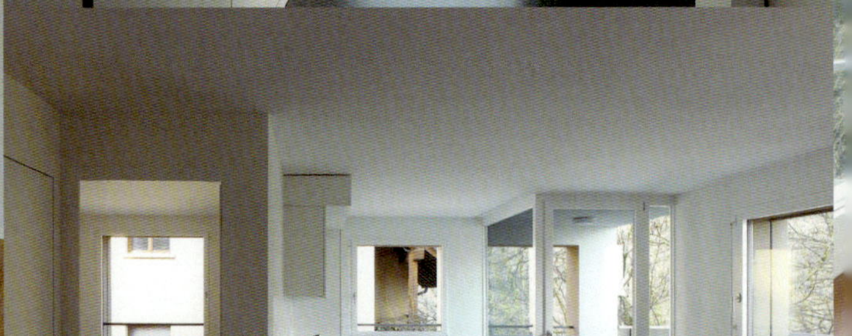

90

91
92
93

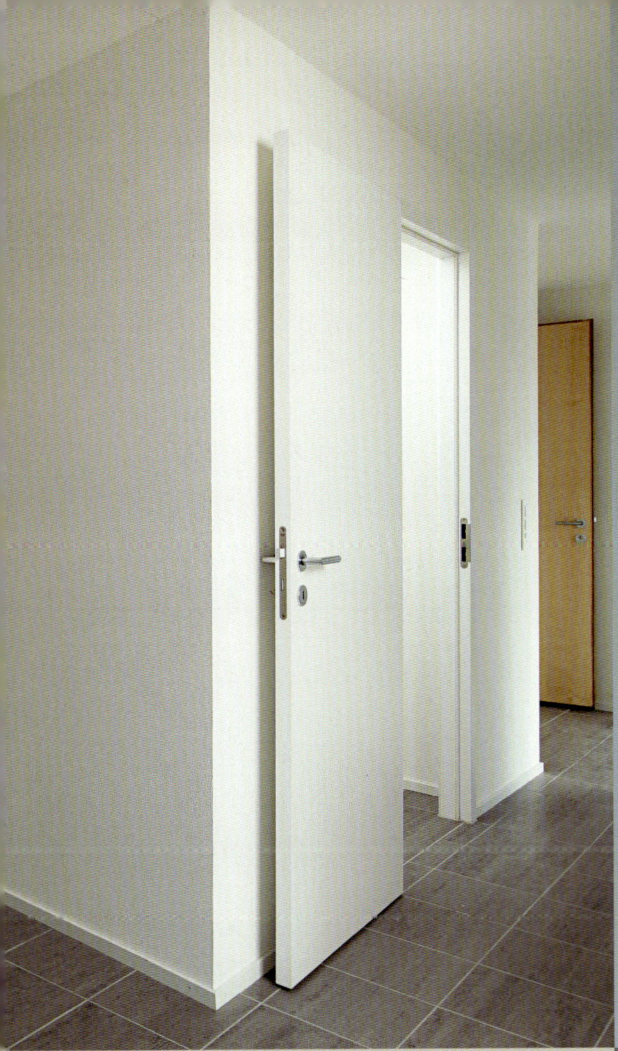
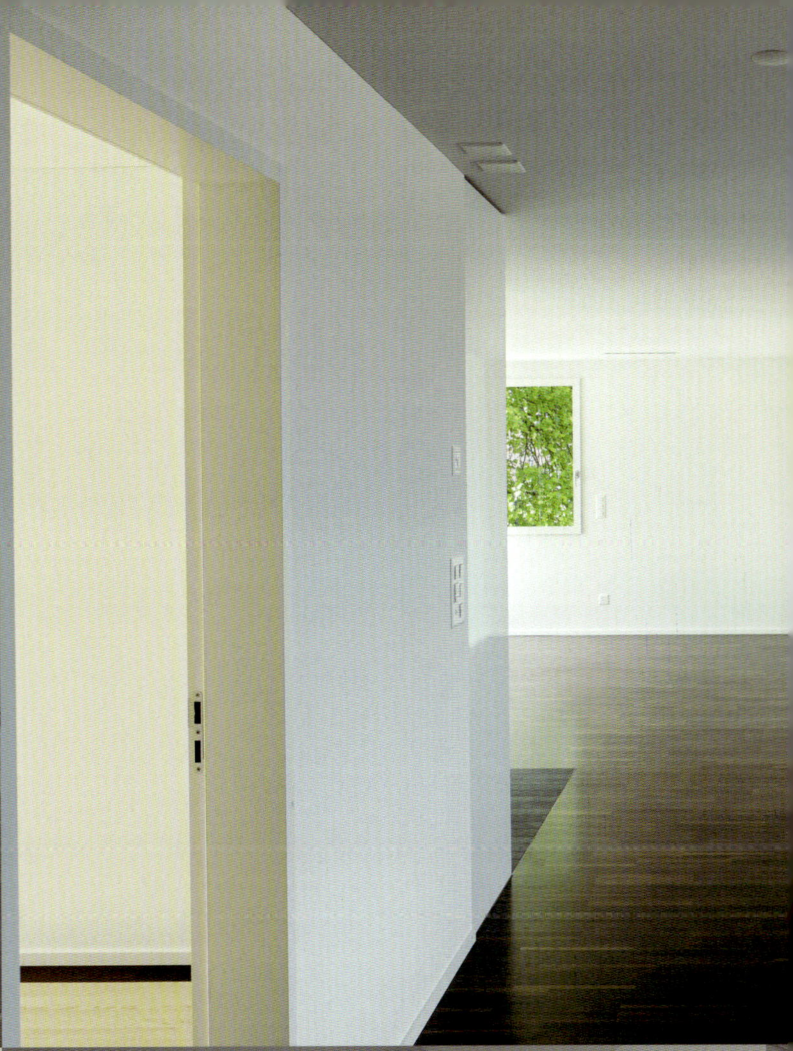
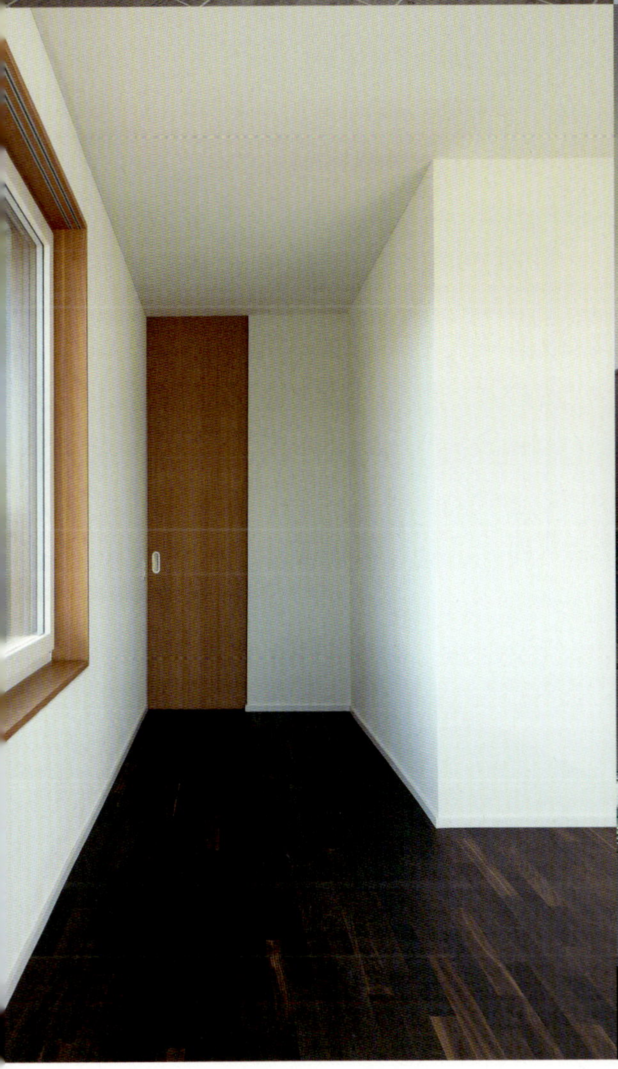
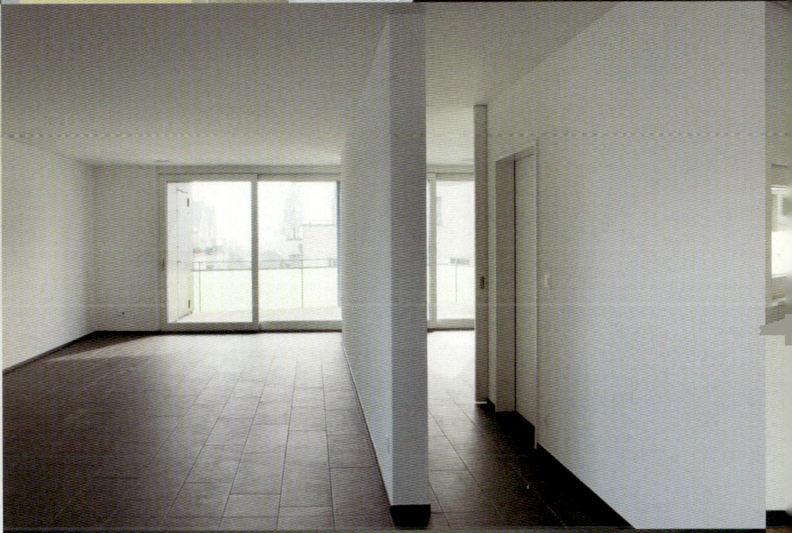
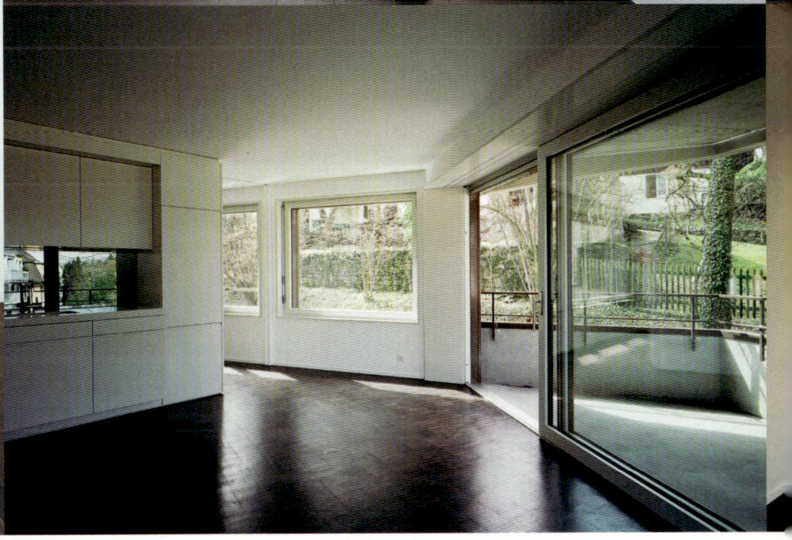

94

95
96
97

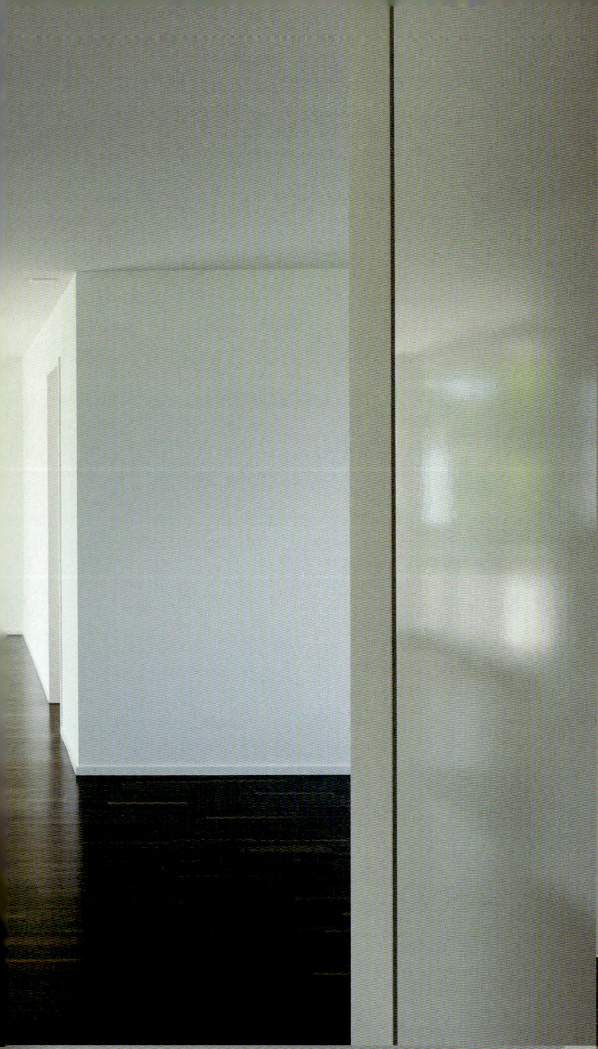
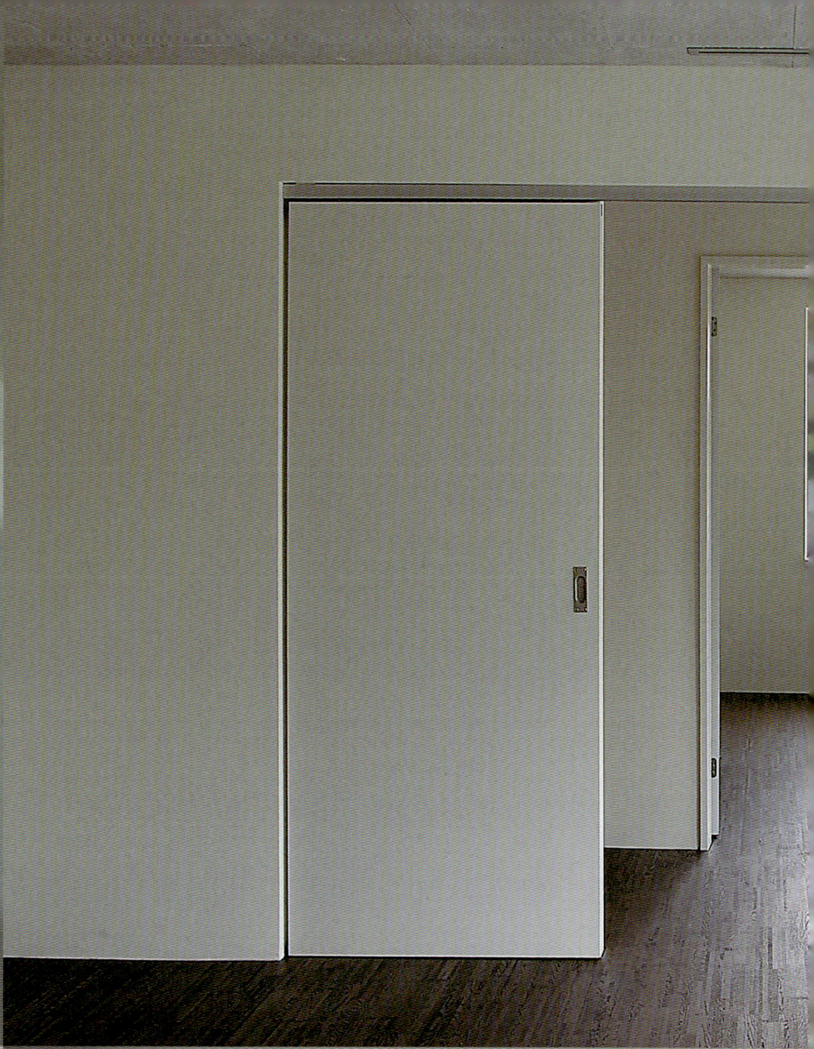
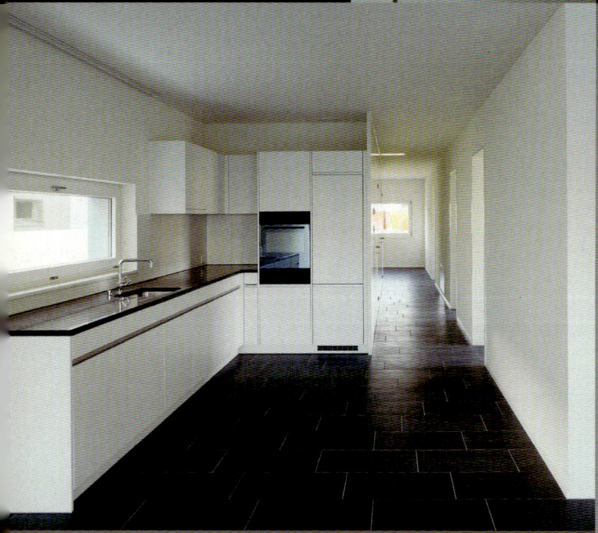
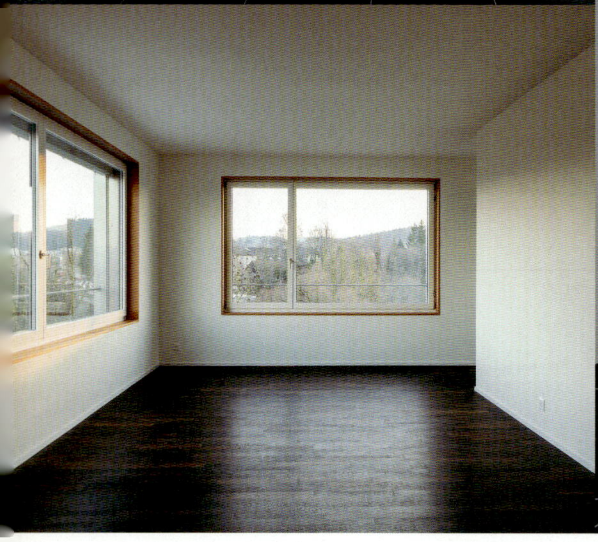
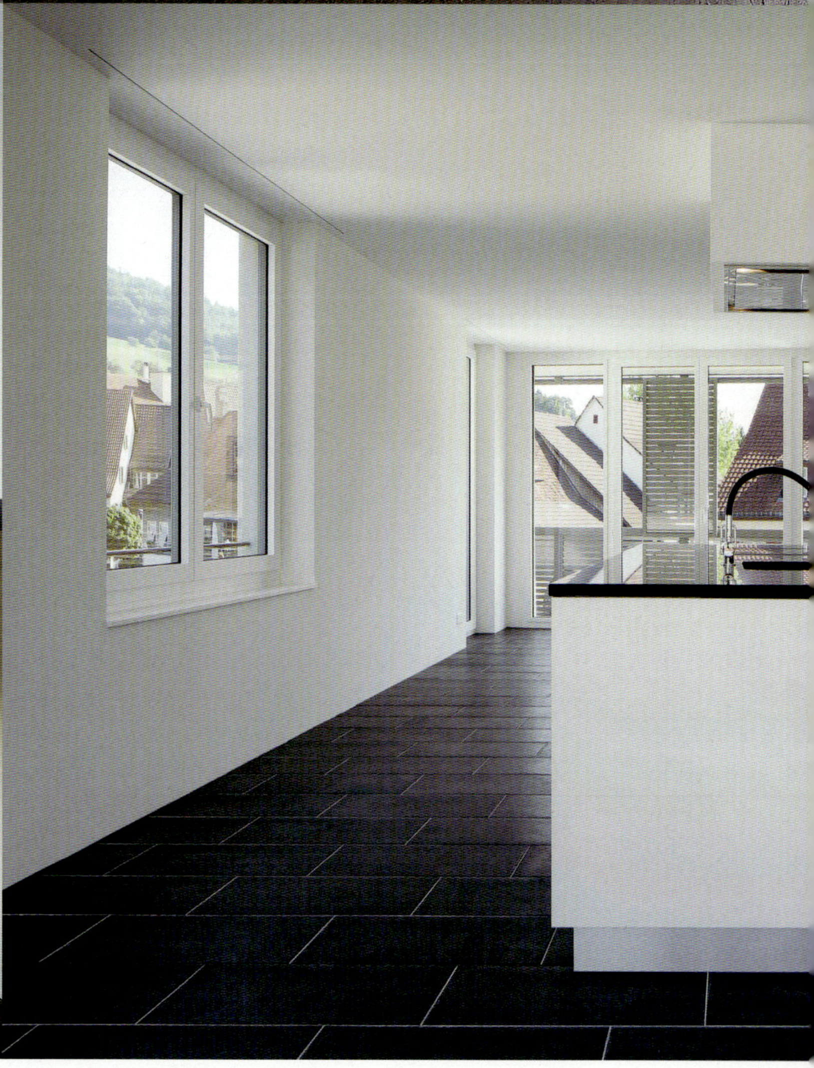

98
99

100
101

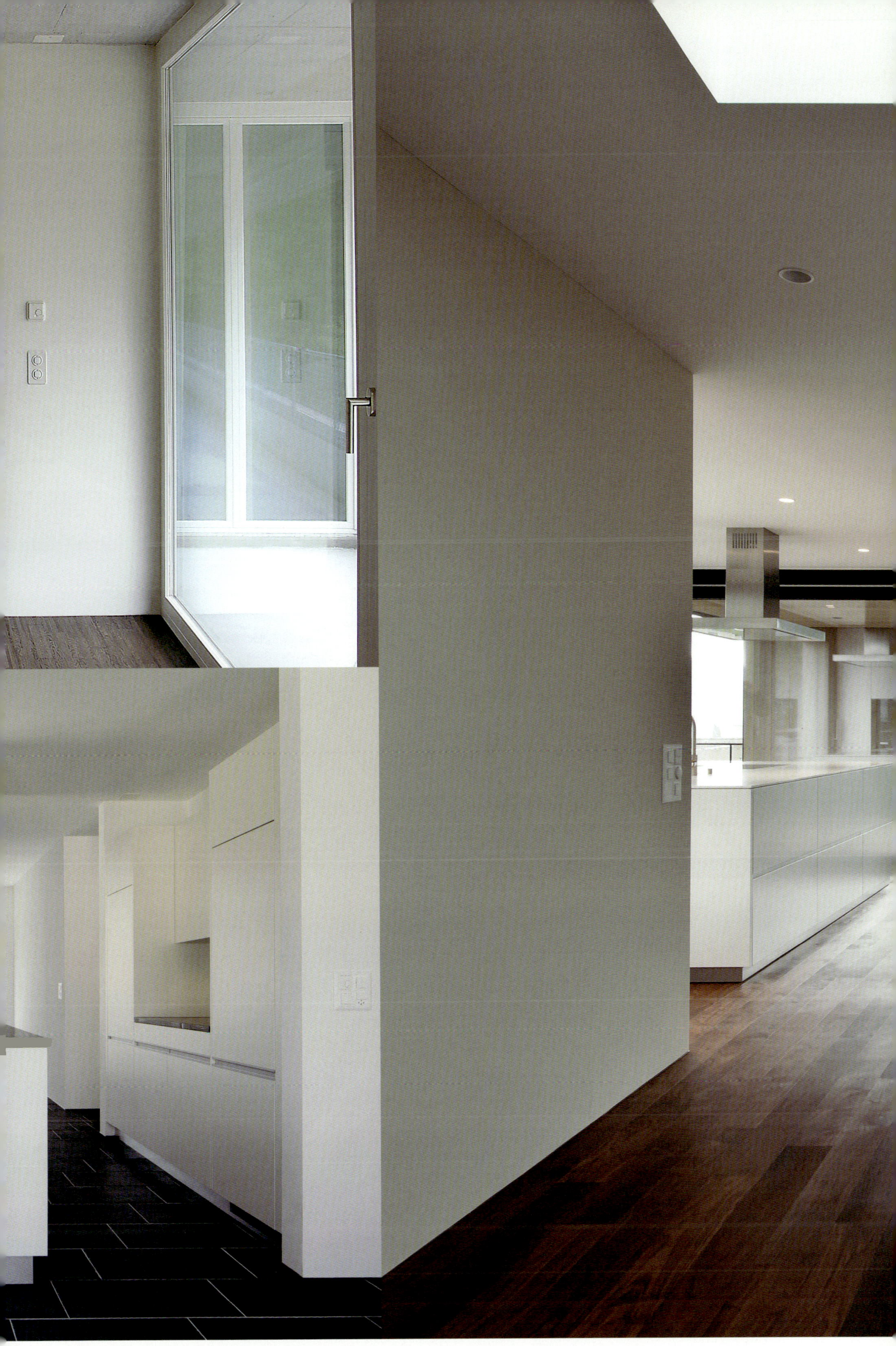

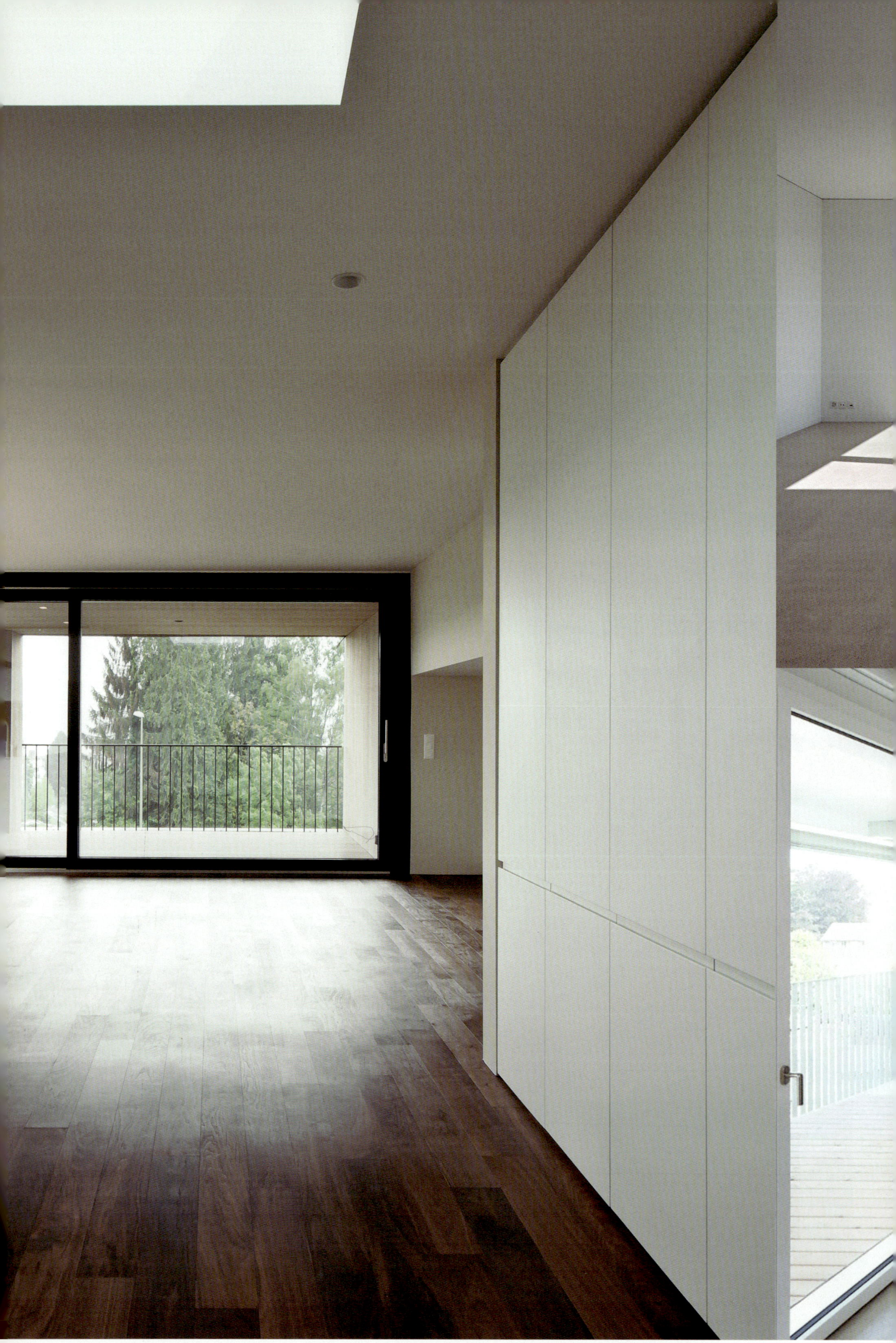

103

104

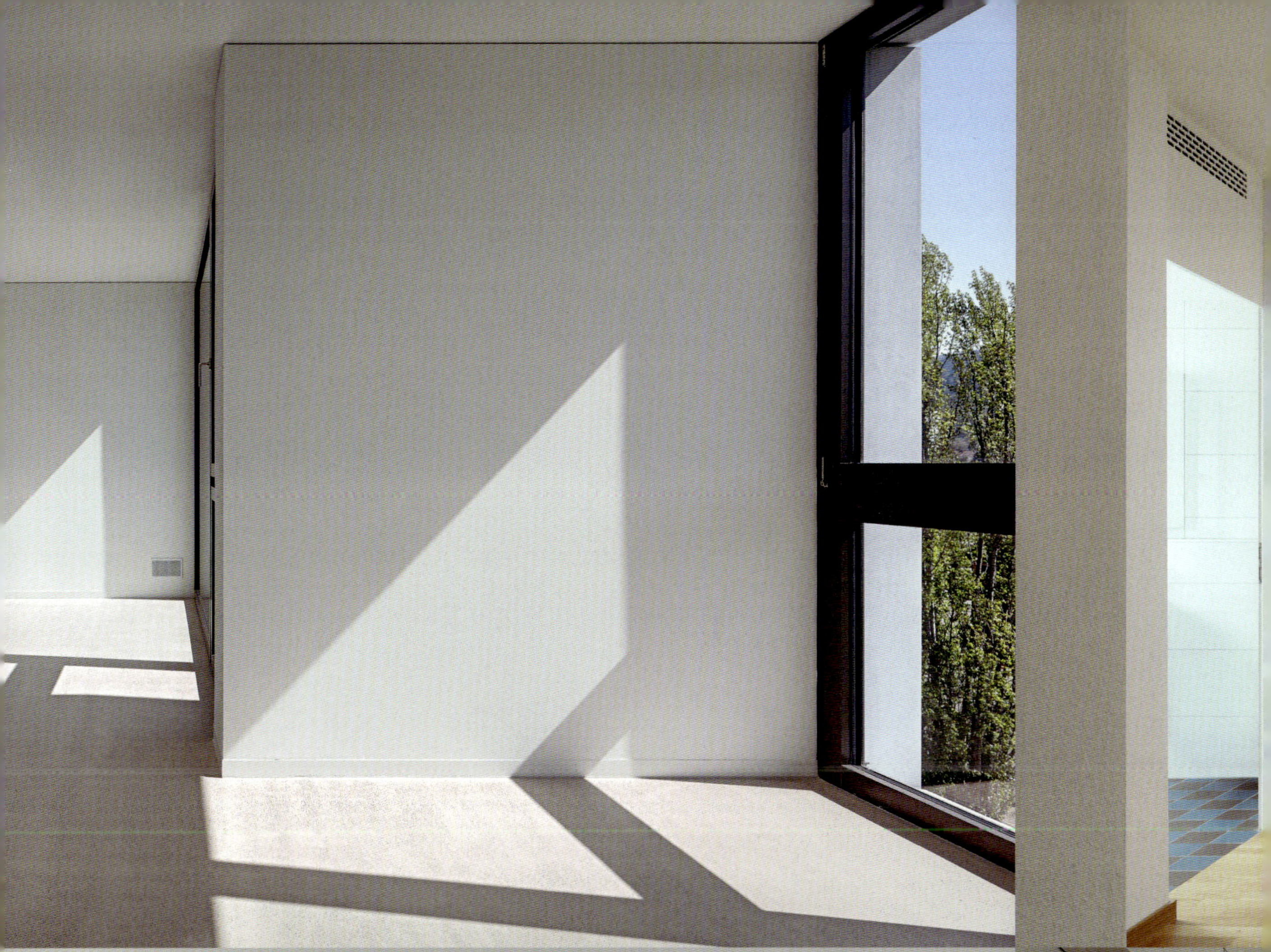

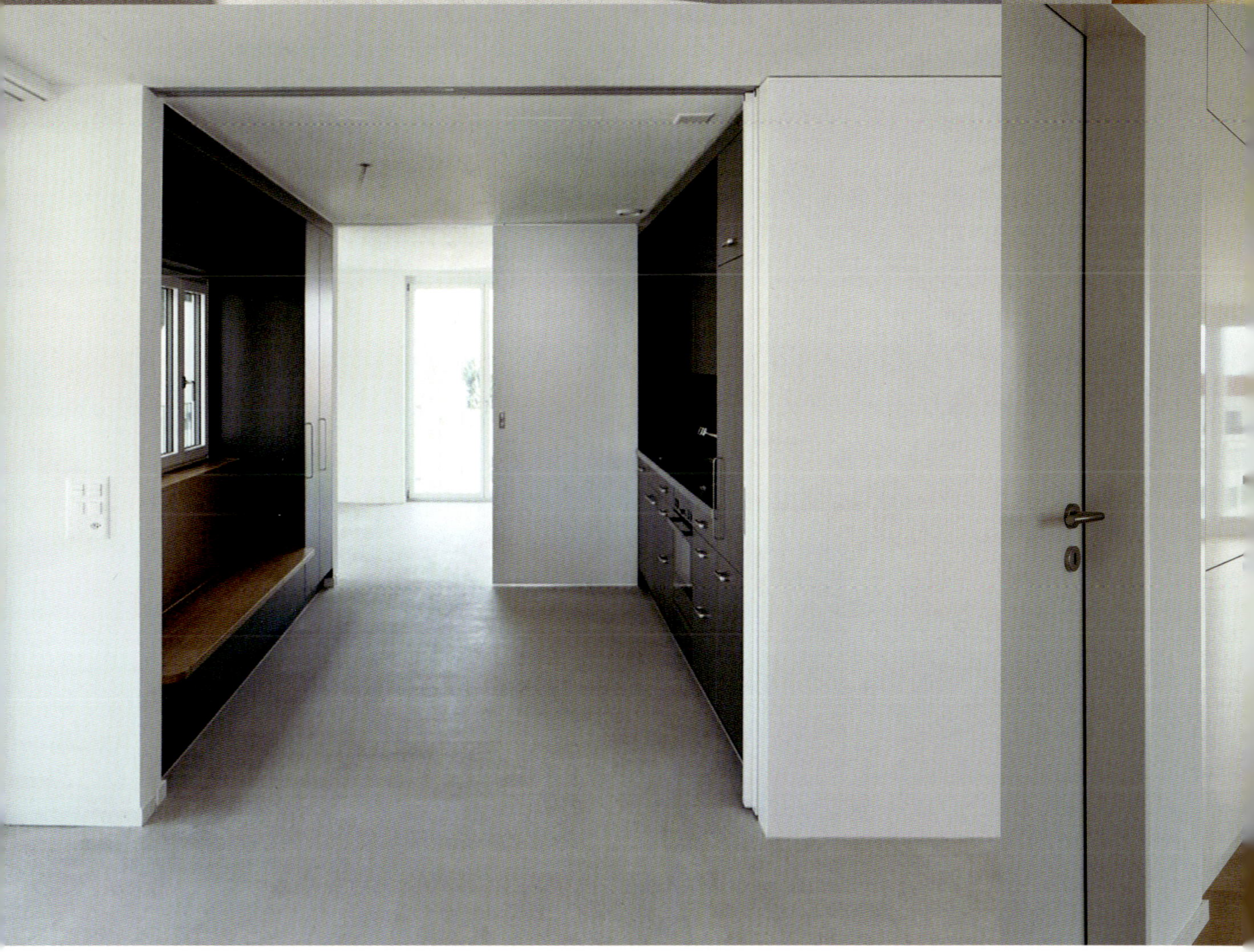

105

106

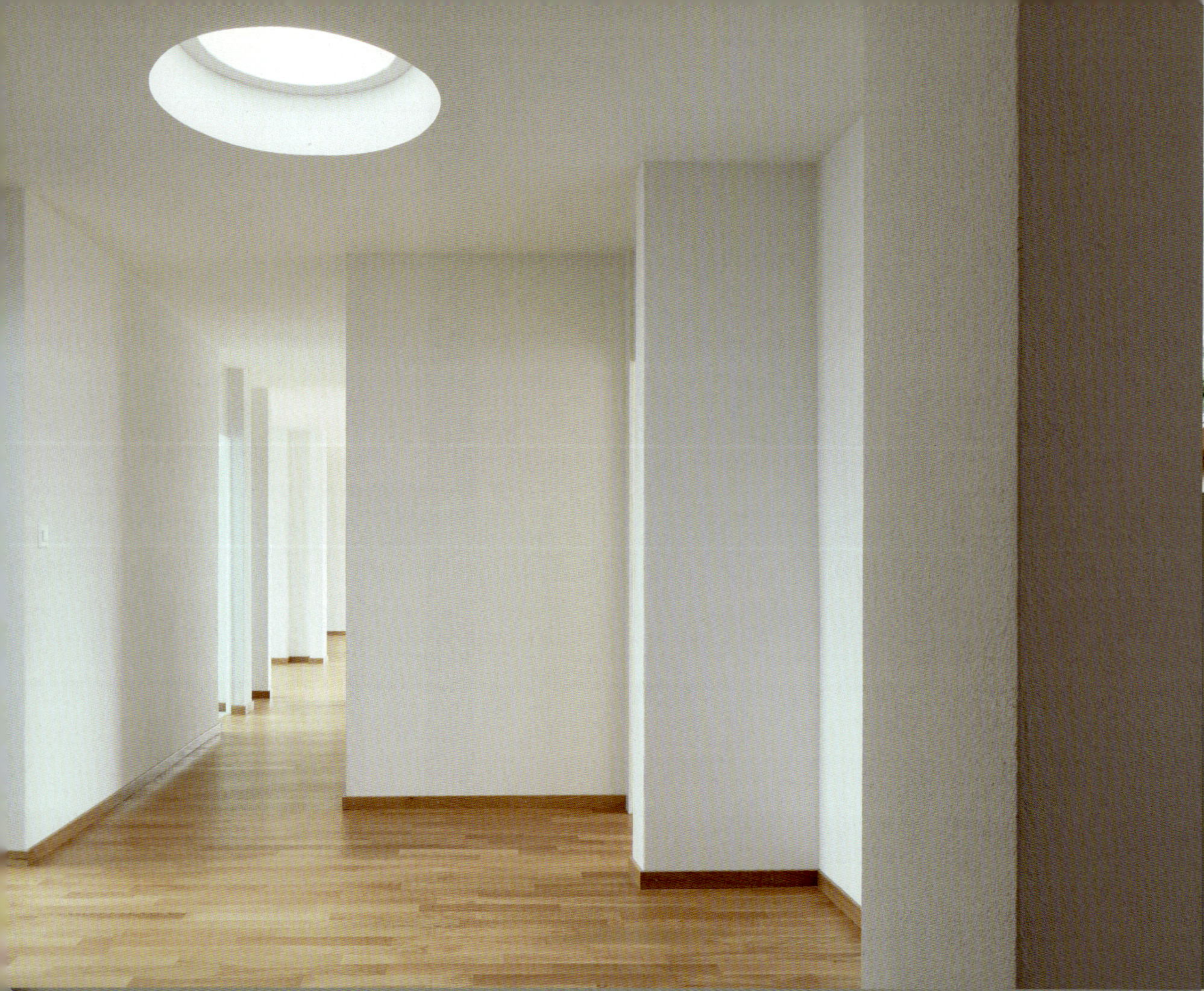
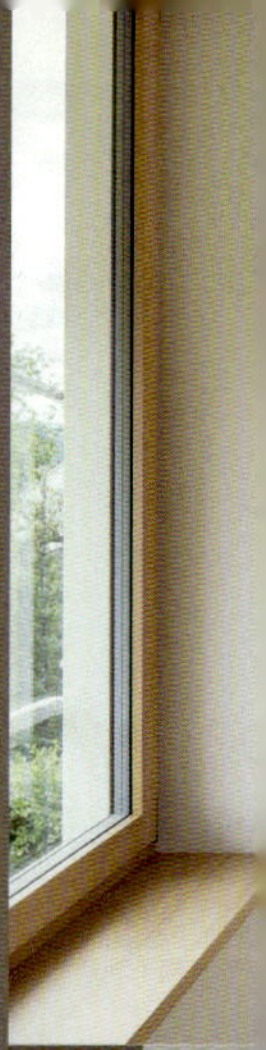
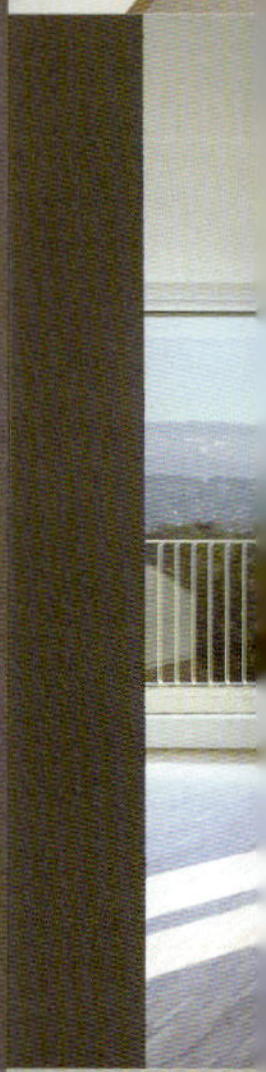
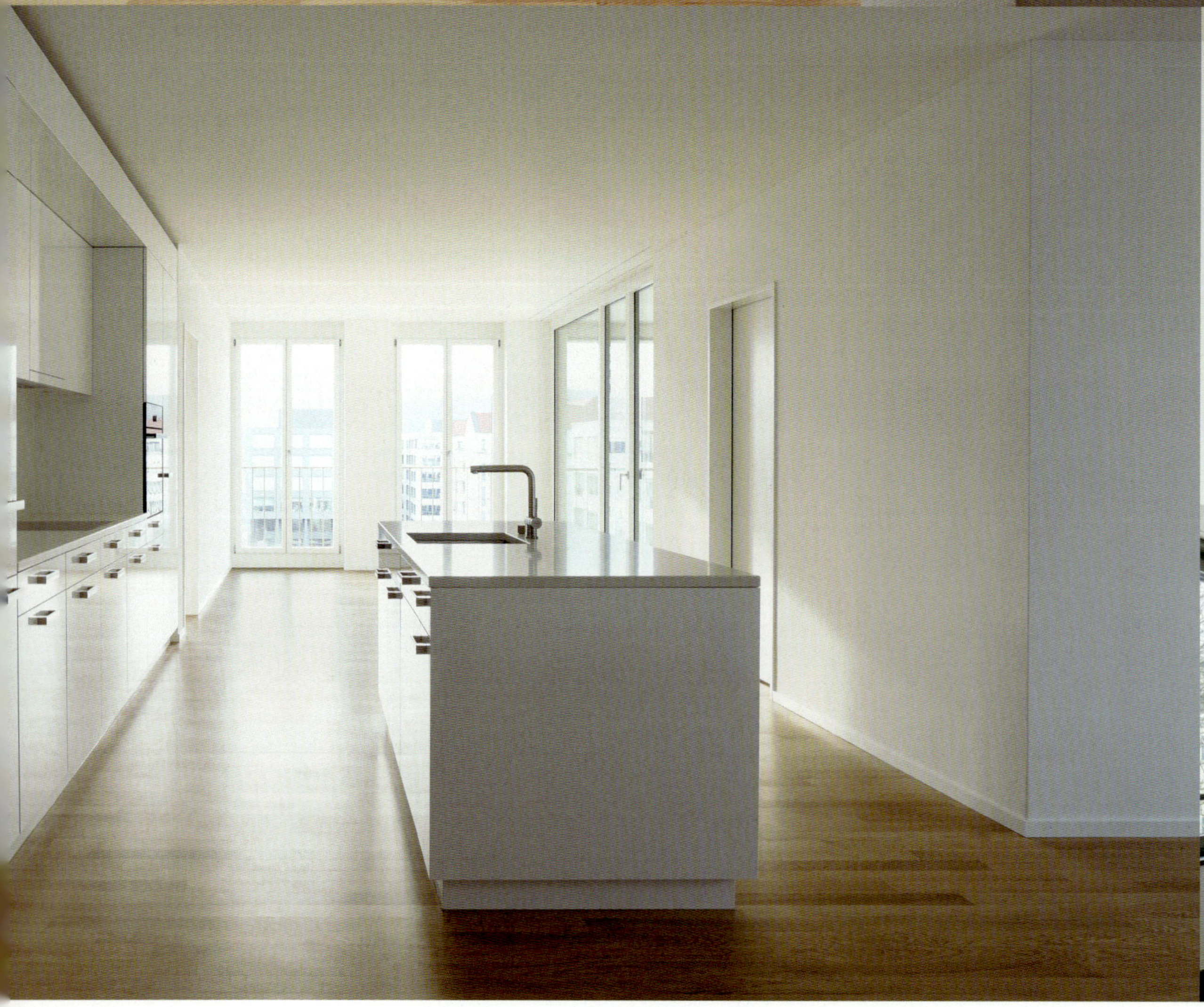

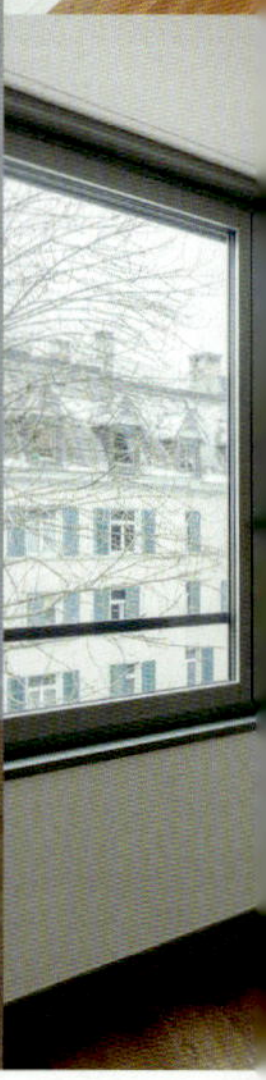

107
108
109
110

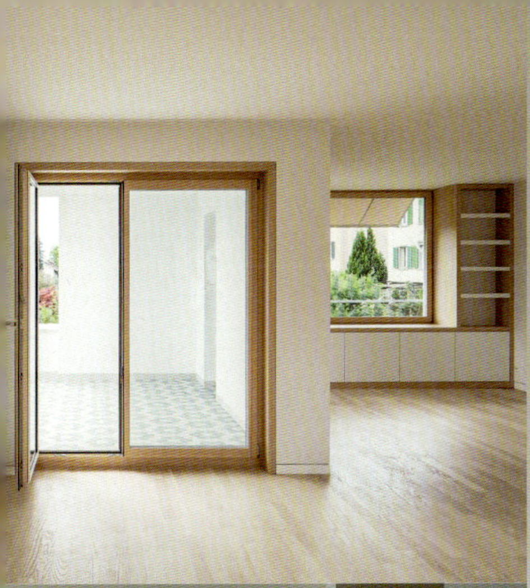

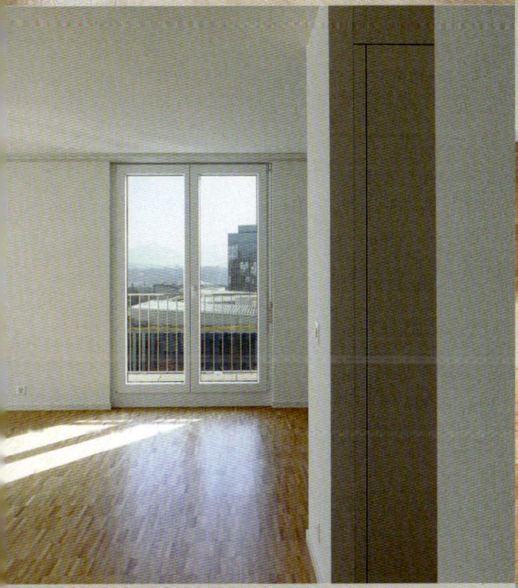

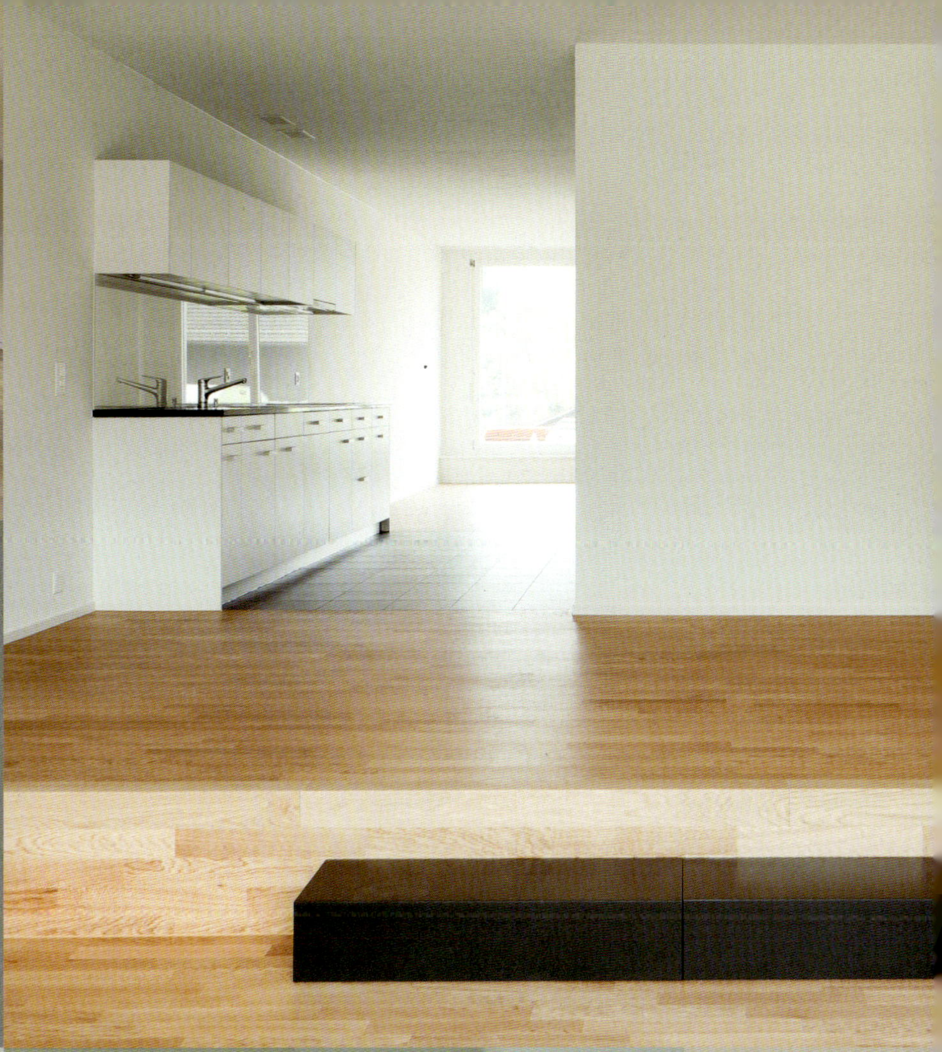

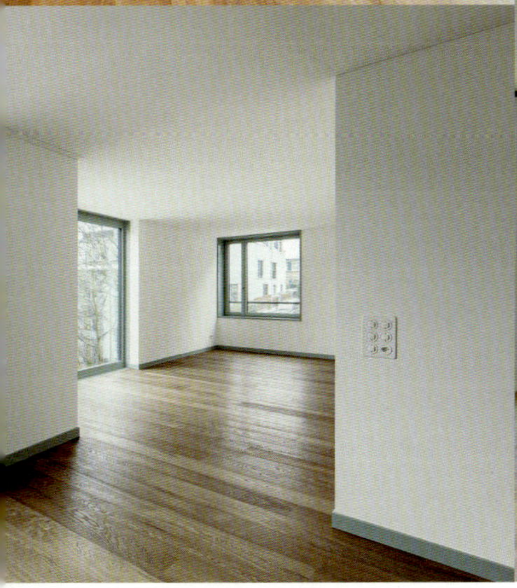

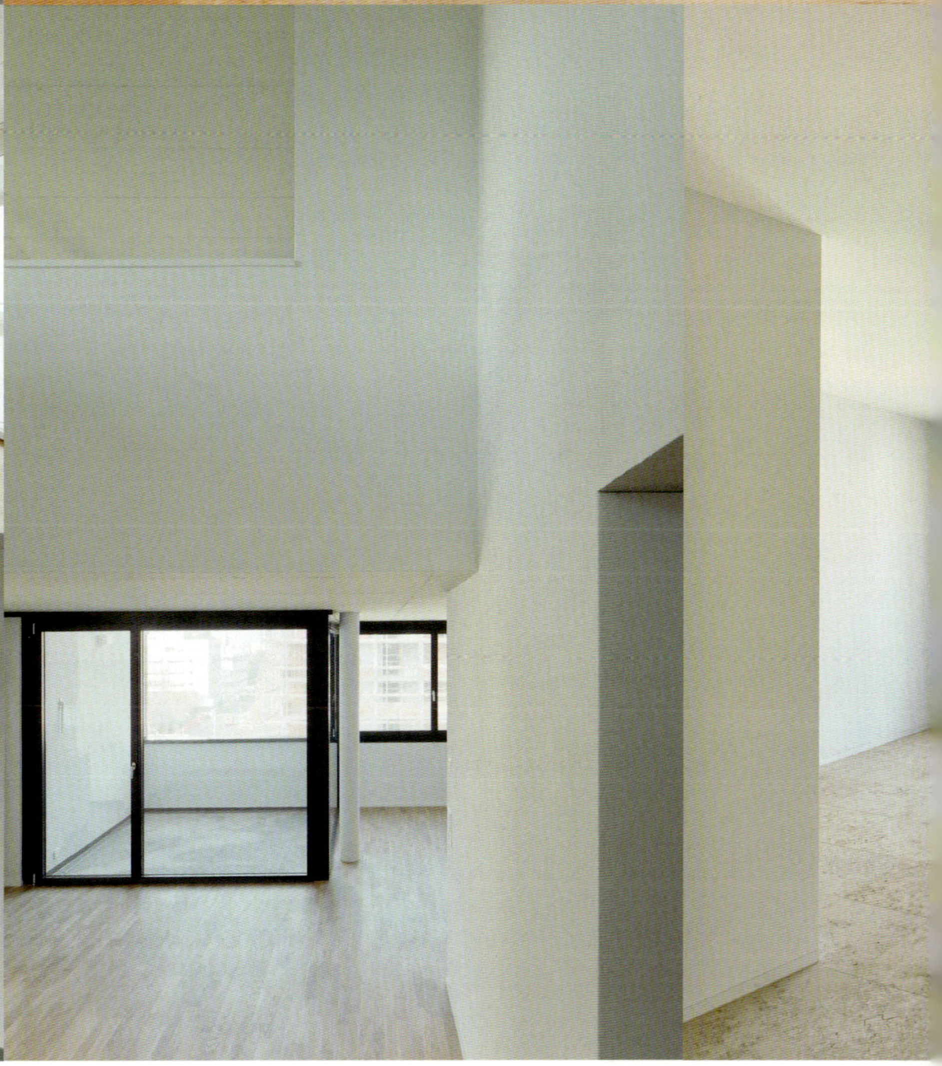

111

112

113

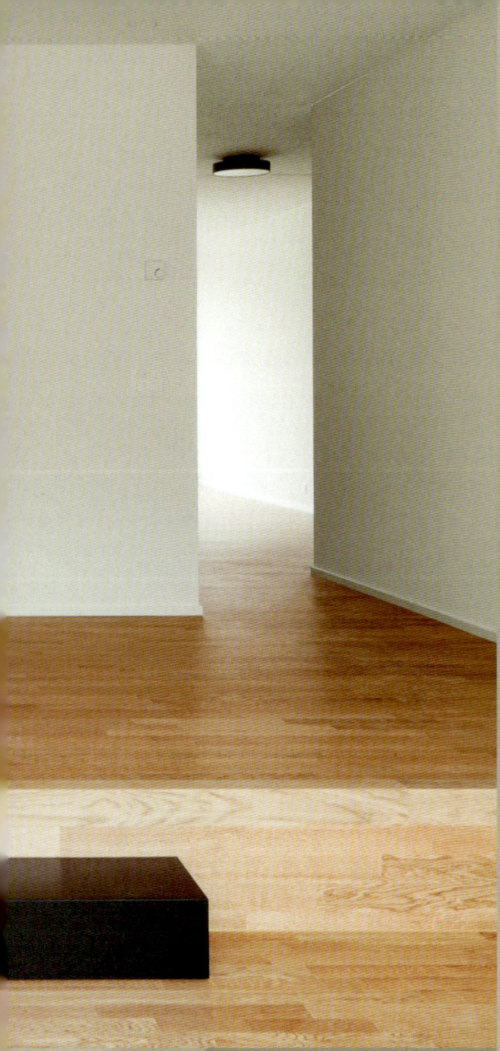

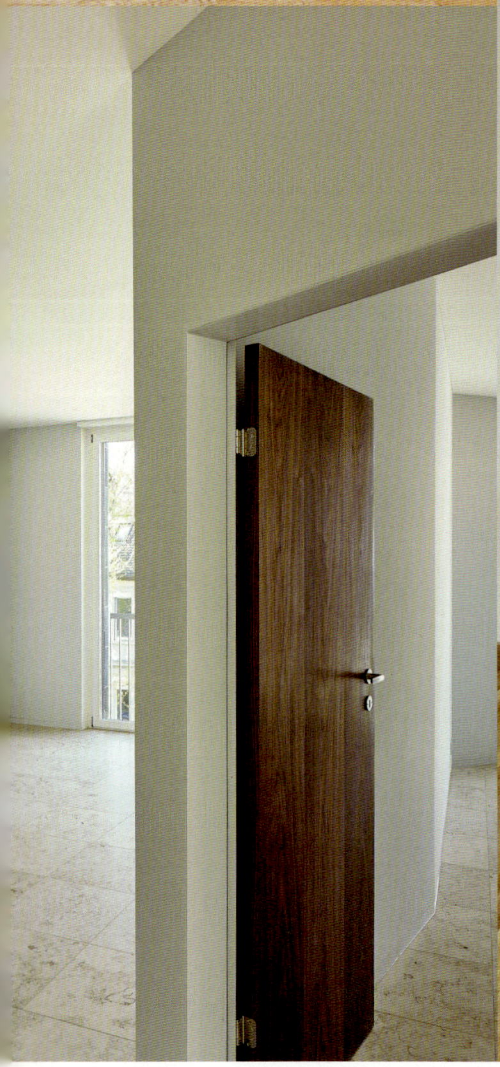

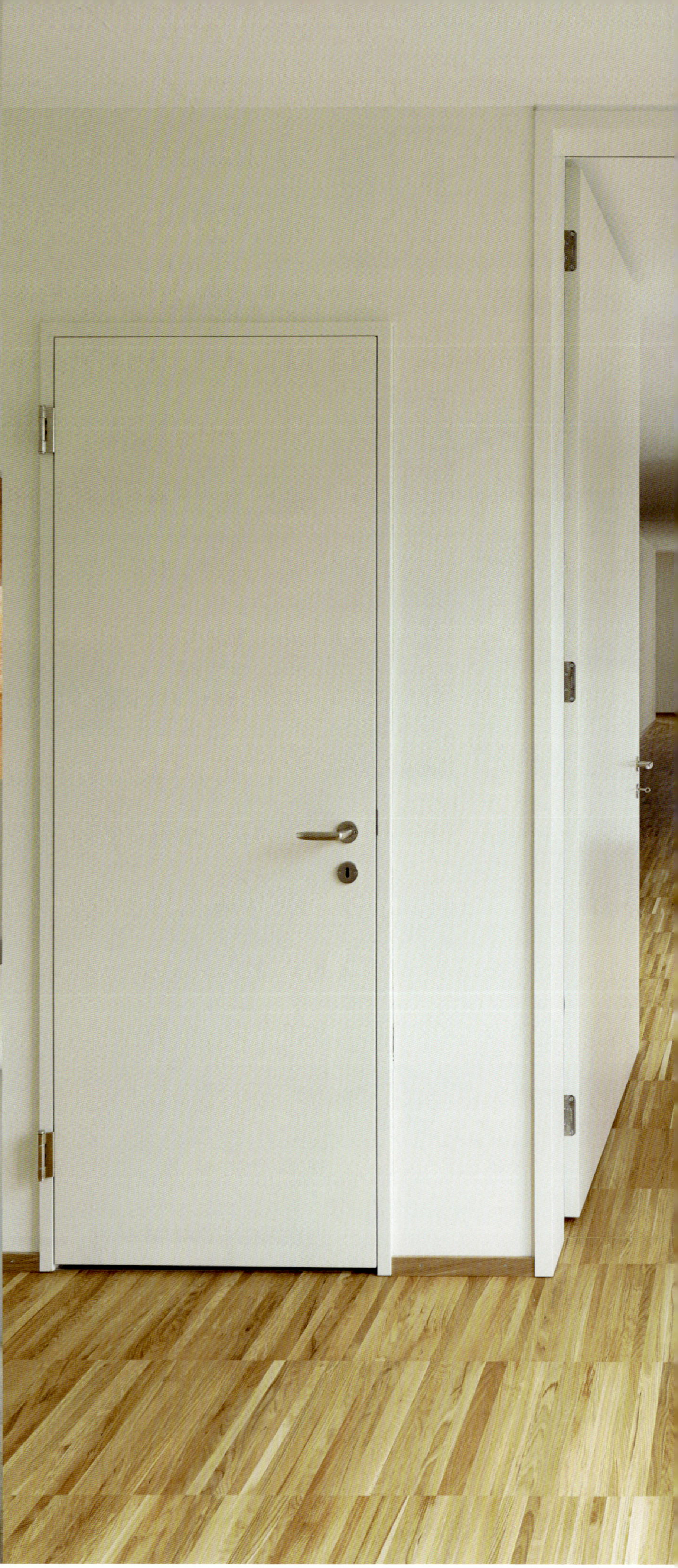

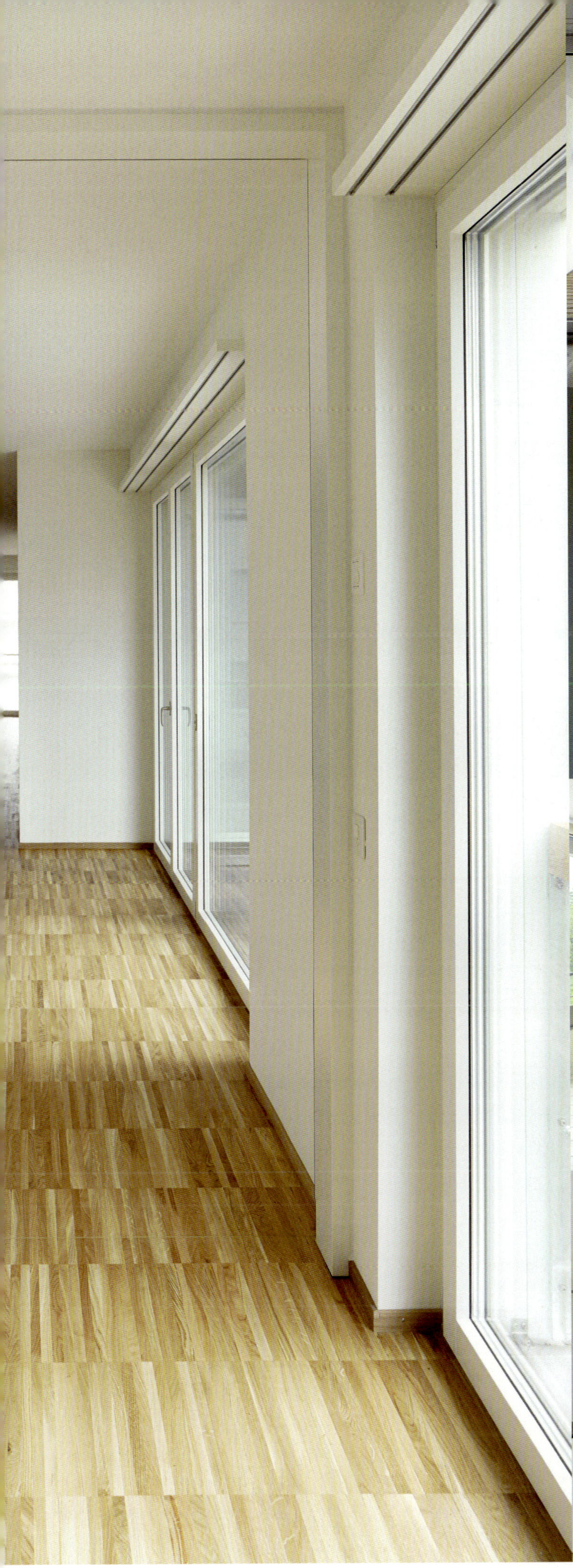

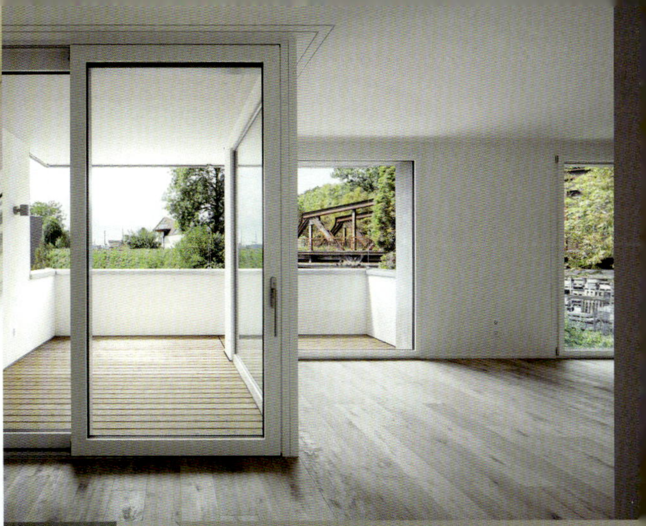

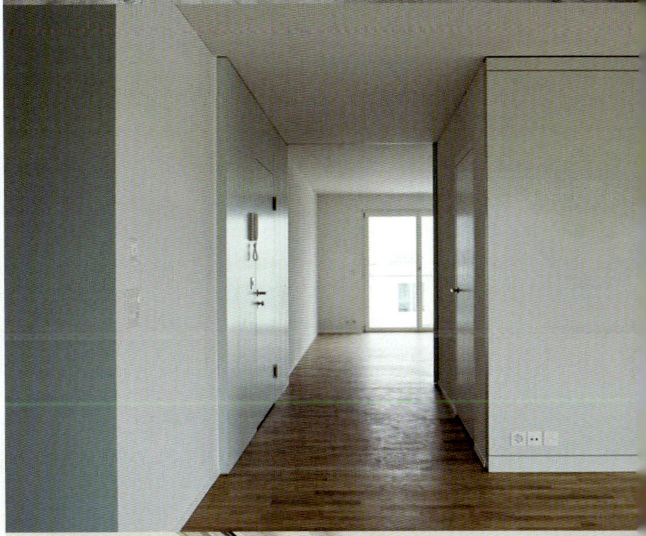

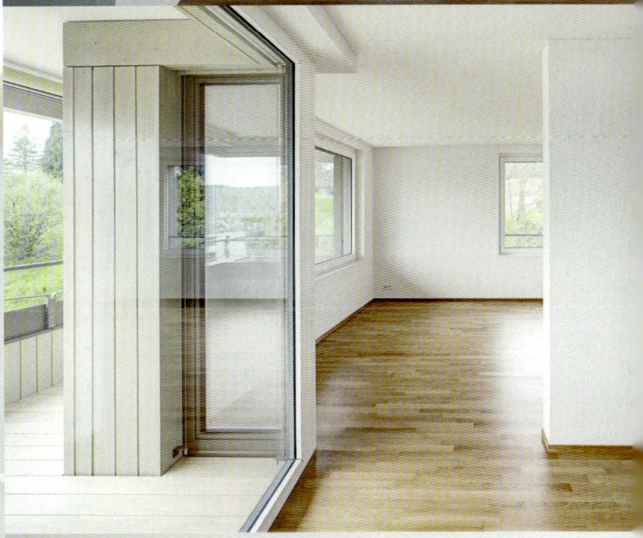

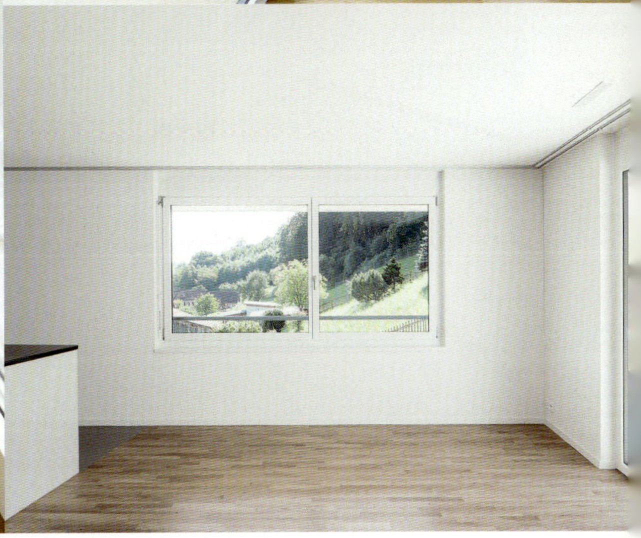

115
116
117
118

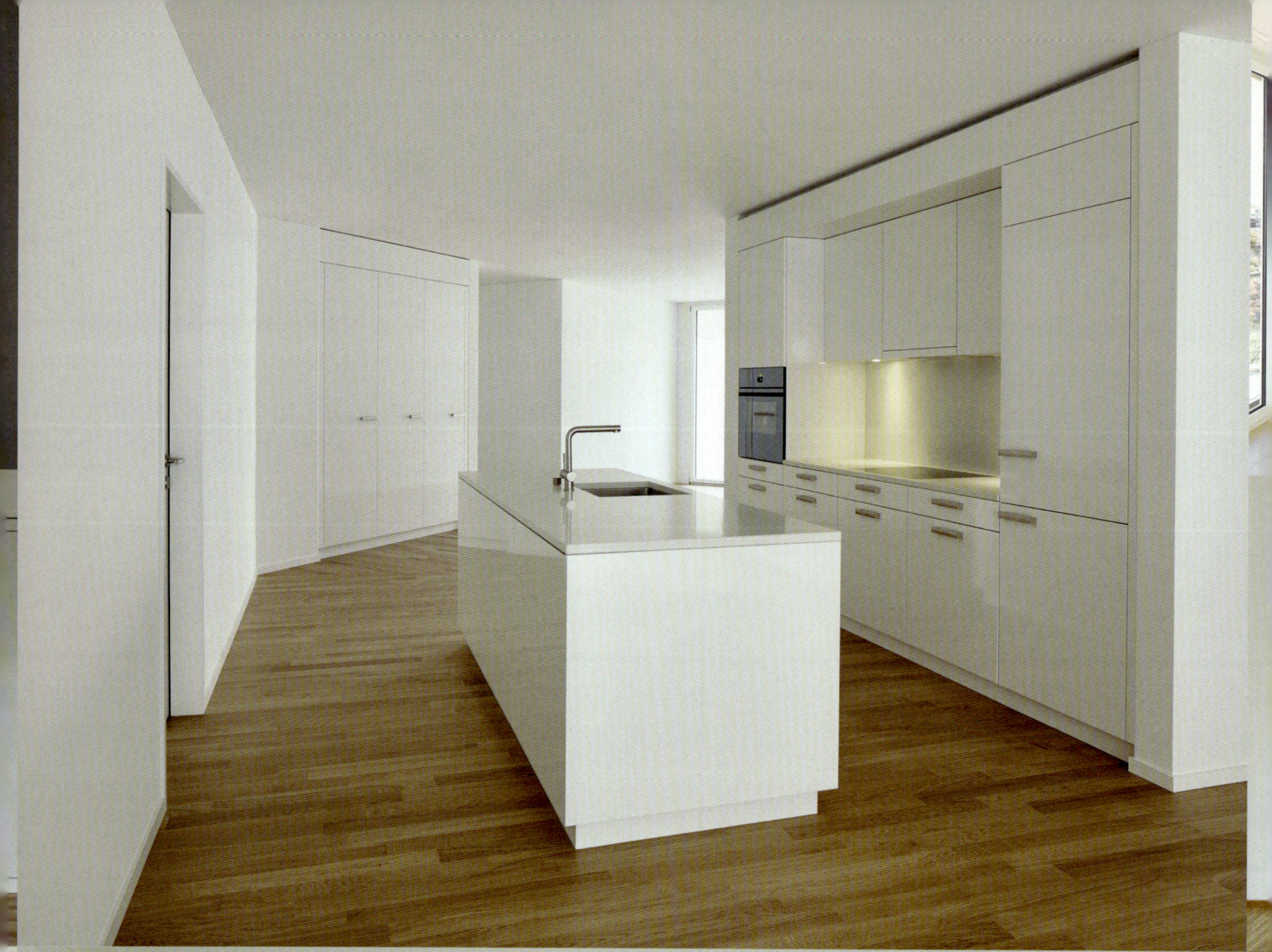

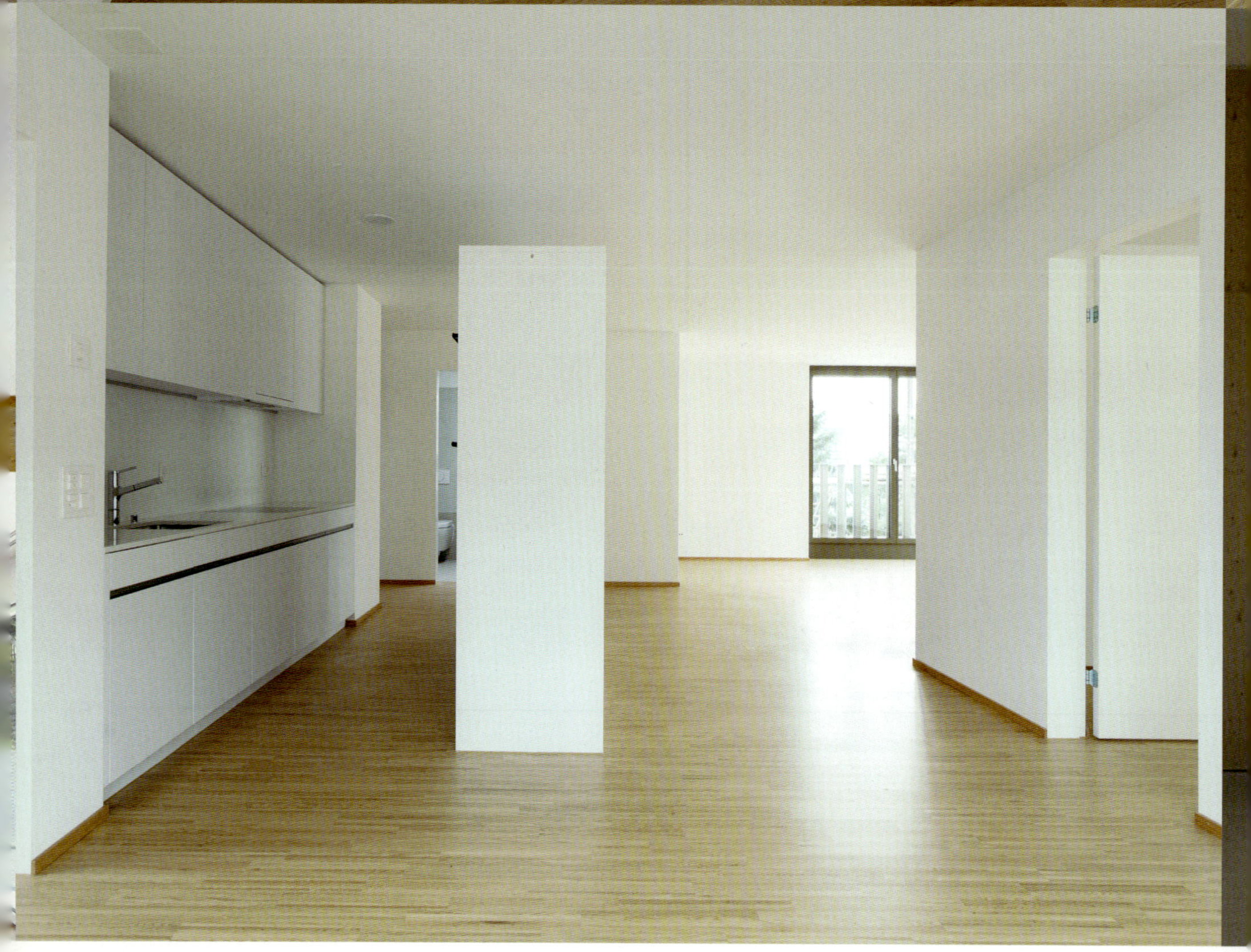

119

120

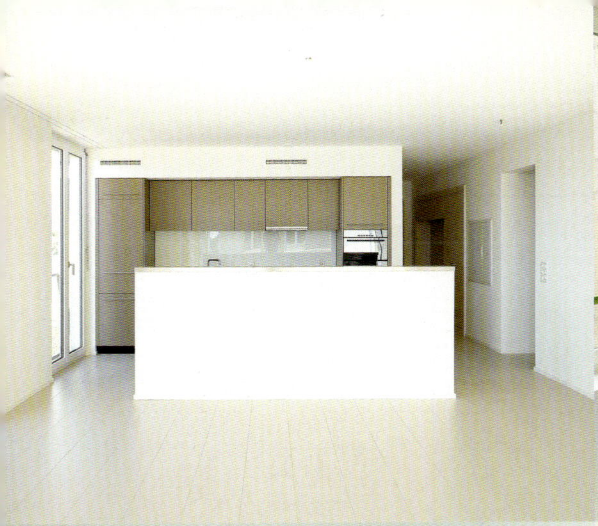
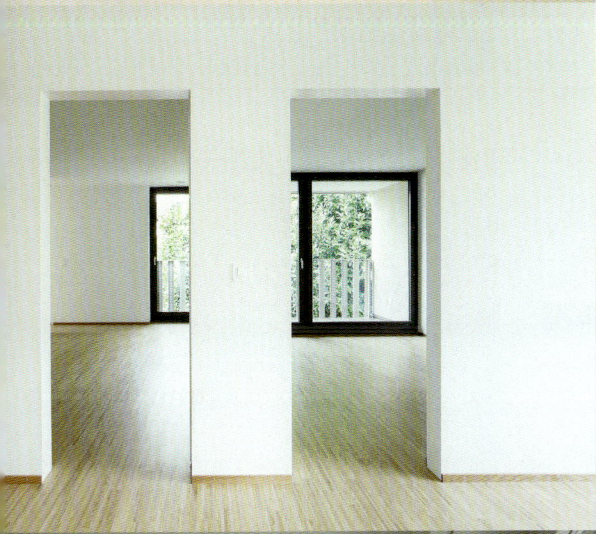
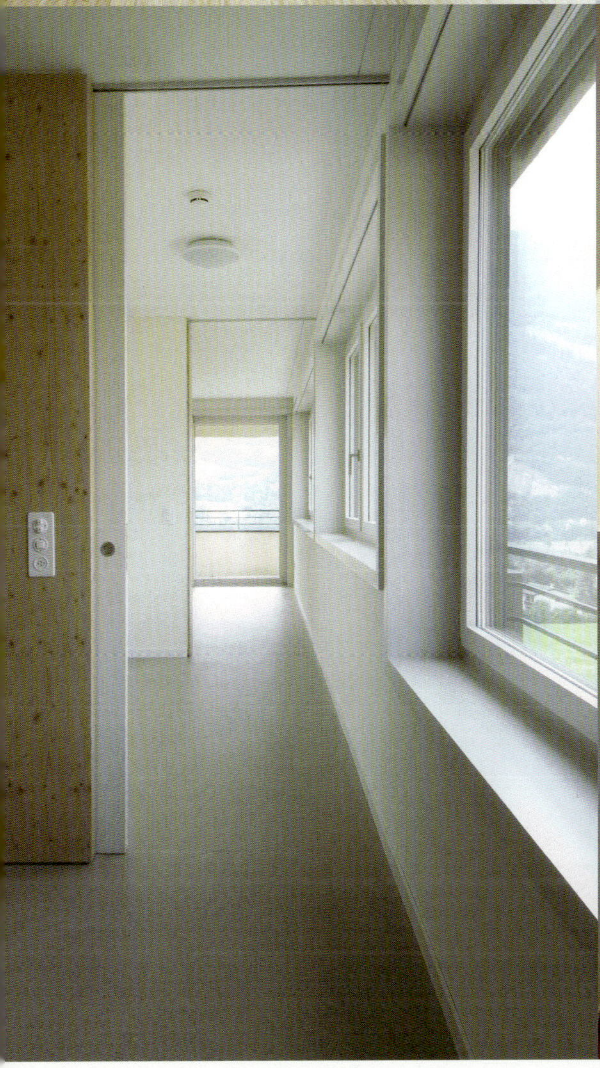
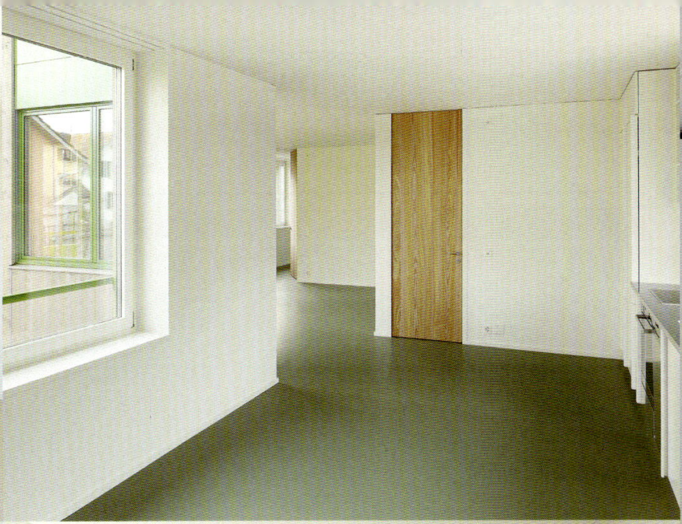
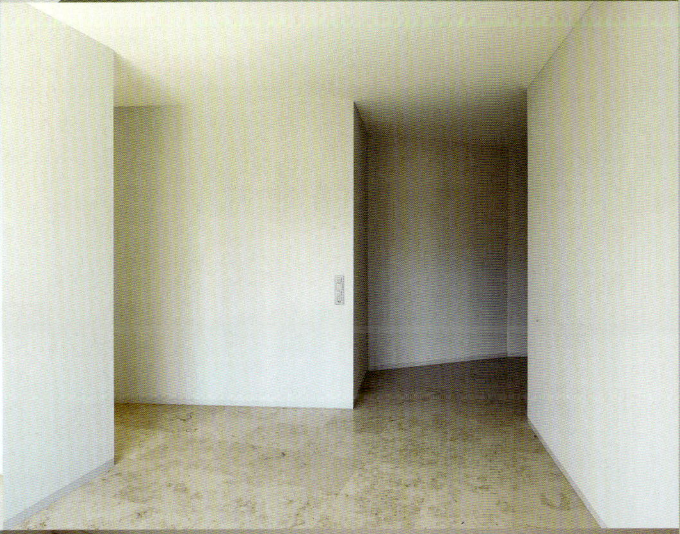
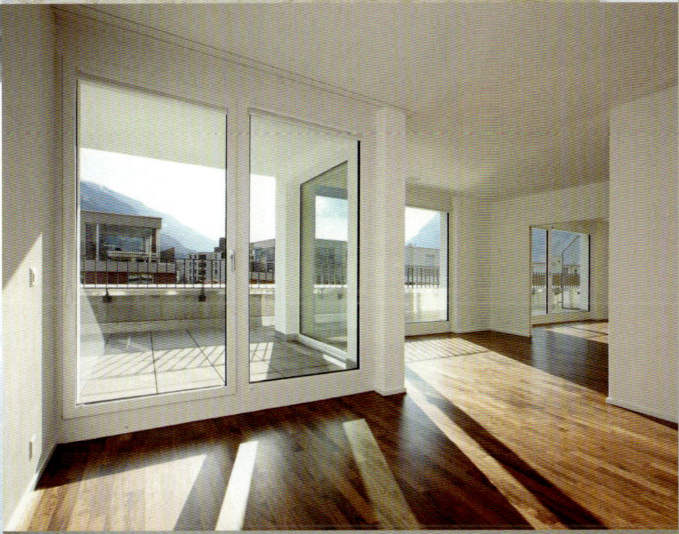
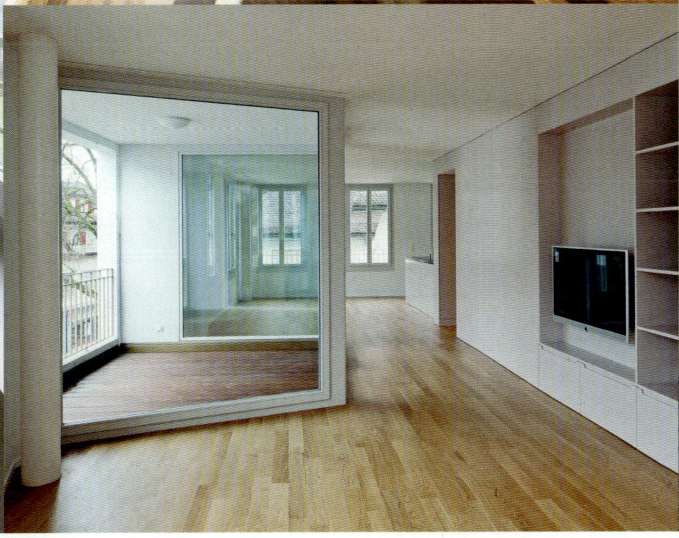

121
122

123

124
125
126
127

128

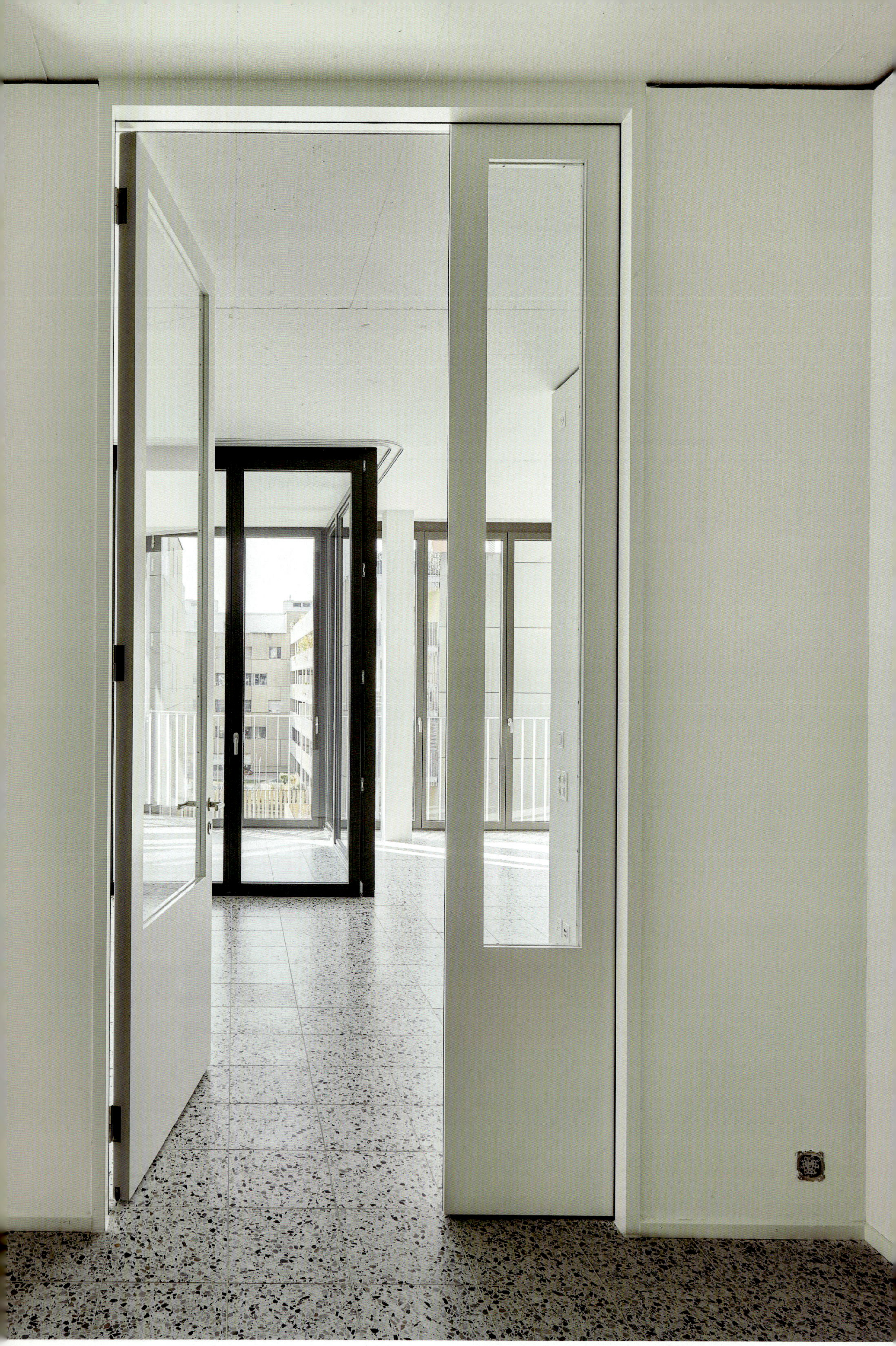

# House Tour:

Adam Jasper (ed.)

A project by
Alessandro Bosshard
Li Tavor
Matthew van der Ploeg
Ani Vihervaara

# Views of the Unfurnished Interior

PARK BOOKS

# Table of Contents

# White Lies: Bell Curves in the Bell Jar

Francesca Hughes

On a late spring morning you turn the corner of a familiar leafy street and see, at last, the lilac is in flower: that scent, the full stretch of summer ahead. The day is graced by the discovery of lilac's promise. But what of Adolphe Quetelet's day? Once Quetelet had perfected his algorithm for calculating exactly which morning the lilacs of Brussels would flower, could he still discover those first spring blooms in quite the same way? Can you even still truly *see* the lilac's first blossom, when you know already—you may even have known for several days—that its branches—in fact, all the lilac branches in the city—will erupt into flower on that particular day?

Prediction is a peculiar form of blindness. An event once predicted is, to some extent, as good as past. When it does happen, it no longer registers with the alacrity of the unpredicted because it has, at some level of existence, already registered. Surprise is not simply an element of tactical advantage; it is a prerequisite for being fully noticed, for counting on the horizon of the now. The partial blindness induced by prediction entails a strange negation of the present.Present existence is sharpened by that which never announces its estimated time-of-arrival, that which evades the many predictive systems that increasingly write our very next futures as they anticipate the spelling of the words we type, the snapping of the lines we draft, or our purchases, route home, love life and lifespan. In so doing, they are also eroding our sense of the present, rendering it as simply the moment in which past predictions are confirmed and new predictions are calculated. This present that already knows what it will see is thus increasingly blind, and it is a blindness not unrelated to our blindness when faced with the unfurnished interiors characteristic of contemporary Swiss architecture (the *House Tour* archive), whose very appearance, whose constant ceiling datum, whited-out materiality and integrated flattening of components, is all so predictable we simply don't see it, and certainly could never recall it. Could you even be sure in which of these spaces you slept the night before? These interiors are the product of and the vehicle for precisely this present: existence at the threshold at which the confirmation of past predictions meets the looping back into the previous present to generate predictions for the next. Thus the backstitch-like footprint of the inductive loop tracks our progress.

The perfect predictability of these domestic interiors is (predictably) delivered by the immutable alliance of smoothness (a longstanding signature of precision) and whiteness (a more recent signature of precision, but also of other things). David Batchelor describes in *Chromophobia* one of the now continuously burgeoning family of white interiors these interiors belong to:

> Inside this house was a whole world, a very particular kind of world, a very clean, clear and orderlyuniverse. But it was also a very paradoxical inside-out world, a world where open was also closed, simplicity was also complication, and clarity was also confusion. It was a world that didn't really admit the existence of any other worlds.[1]

Like all good predictive systems, from the Universal Languages of the Enlightenment of Francis Bacon and John Wilkins, to all pansophic or encyclopaedic systems since, these both predictable and predictive interiors must be hermetic, must deny any externality, in order to be exhaustive—and their conclusions thus be rendered universally valid. As Athanasius Kircher so concisely promised, this inside-out paradox entails *the reduction of all languages to one, the extension of one language to all.* The initial reductive impulse always prefigures expansive ambitions. That is, this interior-only predictive world, like the standardising systems that generated its many concealed components and eclipsing construction details, was not made *by* the architect; this is the world that has made many things, amongst them, the architect. Batchelor, via his reading of whiteness, comes to a parallel conclusion:

> Some would hold the architect responsible ... for the accusatory whiteness that was this great hollow interior, but I suspect that it was the other way around. I suspect that the whiteness was responsible for this architect and his hollow words.[2]

As Ian Hacking points out in *The Taming of Chance*, the sacred pansophic projects of the Enlightenment were rendered profane in the nineteenth century by its fever for measure and counting, and what were the beginnings of statistics: prediction industrialised.[3] In considering these blinding interiors, two of the forty-six letters written by Adolphe Quetelet to the Grand Duke of Saxe-Coburg and Gotha *On the Theory of Probabilities as Applied to the Moral and Political Sciences* are important: *Letter XXXIII* on the algorithm by which to predict the blooming of lilacs in a Brussels spring, and *Letter XXII* regarding the distribution of "dwarfs"and "giants" in a given population. Written in 1845, in the concluding years of five decades that had seen the numericising of everything in search of quantitative regularities, they are symptomatic of a contemporary pathology (strangely immune to the effects of the dull) which Dickens parodied as "ditchwateristics".[4] They are also exquisite finger exercises in the data control that would master the colonies and then quietly underpin much of that which became infrastructural to the materialisation of modernism (material sciences, standards and specifications, and identicality in mass production, to name but a few manifestations).

In *Letter XXXIII*, Quetelet takes that most capricious of events, the arrival of spring, and apparently brings it to heel by measure:

> Even the flower, so modest as it is, is not the product of a caprice of Nature: its frail tissue requires favourable →

1 D. Batchelor, *Chromophobia*, London, Reaktion Books, 2000, p. 10.
2 Batchelor, p. 10–11.
3 I. Hacking, *The Taming of Chance*, Cambridge, Cambridge University Press, 1990.
4 Hacking, in a footnote on p. 61, refers to Dickens' parody of the British Association for the Advancement of Science's Statistical Section, 'Section F', founded by Charles Babbage and Quetelet in 1833, as 'Umbugology and Ditchwateristics'.

| DIFFERENCE IN TIME OF BLOSSOMING REFERRED TO BRUSSELS. | | | | | | |
|---|---|---|---|---|---|---|
| PLACES. | Syringa Vulgaris. | Sambucus Nigra. | Aesculus Hippoc. | Philadelphus Coronarius. | Digitalis Purpurea. | MEAN. |
| | DAYS. | DAYS. | DAYS. | DAYS. | DAYS. | DAYS. |
| Parma . . . | — 9 | — 10 | — 8 | — 11 | — 14 | — 10 |
| Venice . . . | — 9 | — 2 | ... | — 14 | ... | — 8 |
| Alais . . . . | — 44 | — 16 | — 16 | — 22 | ... | — 24 |
| Geneva . . . | — 2 | + 8 | — 5 | ... | ... | 0 |
| Paris . . . . | — 7 | ... | ... | ... | ... | — 7 |
| Valognes . . . | + 7 | — 4 | ... | ... | — 8 | — 2 |
| Liége . . . | + 1 | ... | ... | + 3 | — 2 | 0 |
| Ghent . . . | + 3 | — 2 | + 1 | + 2 | — 5 | 0 |
| Bruges . . . | + 6 | + 3 | ... | ... | ... | + 3 |
| Ostend . . . | + 9 | + 10 | + 9 | + 7 | + 1 | + 7 |
| Environs of London | + 8 | ... | + 5 | ... | + 15 | + 9 |
| Do. of Cambridge | + 11 | + 10 | + 11 | + 9 | ... | + 10 |
| Vucht (Sr Brabant) | ... | ... | + 9 | — 6 | ... | + 2 |
| Utrecht . . . | + 9 | + 12 | + 8 | + 12 | + 9 | + 10 |
| Lochen . . . | + 12 | ... | + 6 | ... | ... | + 9 |
| Joppa, Deventer . | + 10 | ... | + 7 | ... | ... | + 9 |
| Groningen . . | + 14 | + 13 | + 17 | + 19 | + 7 | + 14 |
| Prague . . . | + 12 | + 11 | + 7 | + 15 | ... | + 11 |
| Munich . . . | + 10 | + 23 | + 15 | + 32 | + 8 | + 18 |
| Jever . . . . | + 26 | + 29 | + 14 | ... | + 33 | + 25 |
| Rochester, U. S. . | + 16 | ... | + 17 | ... | + 27 | + 20 |
| Epoch of Blossoming at Brussels . | 28 April | 22 April | 1 May | 19 May | 4 June | |

❶ The relative advance or retardation of the epoch of lilac blossoming in relation to that of Brussels.
Quetelet, *On the Theory of Probabilities*, p. 169.

| | |
|---|---|
| Extraordinary limit in excess . . | *Giants.* |
| Ordinary limit in excess . . . | *Large men.* |
| Limit of probable error in excess / Limit of probable error in defect } . | *The ordinary size.* |
| Ordinary limit in defect . . . | *Small men.* |
| Extraordinary limit in defect . . | *Dwarfs.* |

❷ Ordinary, extraordinary and monstrous variations in the heights of man.
Quetelet, *On the Theory of Probabilities*, p. 101.

> conditions for its development;
> and to arrive at its full bloom,
> it follows laws as stable as those
> which preside over the progress
> of worlds.[5]

Picking up where Linnaeus had apparently failed for lack of precision, Quetelet set out to discover the law by which to predict blooming and, by radical causal reduction, make sense of this apparently erratic event, "this labyrinth where so many threads cross each other".[6] To this end, threads, or variables, are systematically cut out of the picture, including those of the observers, themselves "a new cause of error", each with their propensity "to mark the epoch of blooming later than another".[7] The flowering of *Syringa vulgaris* is (not without some eroticism) fixed as "that day on which the first corolla opens and shows the stamina". All plants observed are to be equally healthy, aged, vigorous, fed and positioned in nearly identical soil and conditions. After just a few springs (such is the miracle of statistics) he is able to declare by induction that all lilacs in Brussels flower when the sum of the squares of the mean daily temperatures since the last frost reaches 4264 centigrade. Quetelet's law of lilacs, while being of questionable fundamentality, like all fundamental laws comprises an equation plus a constant, and thus endowed—like all laws—in predicting when lilac will flower, the normative state, then sets out that which is deviant; tardy and premature lilacs abound.

The ambitions of this normative paradigm are themselves colonial (as Kircher's reduction turns to expansion). Brussels becomes the prime meridian of global lilac blooming. ❶ Other cities in the world are defined in terms of being in retardation to, or in advance of, Brussels' zero. However, to Quetelet's evident irritation, the new map of the world as defined by lilac behaviour is unfortunately irregular:

> The line which may be drawn
> through the globe, through all the
> places where a plant may flower
> on the same day (the isanthesic line),
> is not necessarily parallel to the
> line which passes through the places
> where this plant flowered ten or
> twenty days earlier.

If the law is to better meet deviation, it will need to admit more variables or remain reductive while cunningly devising new architecture of variation.

Enter the genius of the bell curve, Francis Galton's "Procrustean Bed of the Law of Error", with its (apparent) tolerance of deviation.[8] In *Letter XXII: Ordinary and Extraordinary Events—Monstrosities*, Quetelet performs with scale what he performed with time in the case of his lilac analysis, this time seeking not the absolute resolution of the longitudinal line but the negotiated largesse of the bell curve ❷. Again the measuring impulse fast becomes corrective, as he reminds us that "I seek to give more exact appreciation to things to which everyone, according to his caprice, gives the most arbitrary values."[9]

The *Svizzera 240: House Tour* in the Swiss Pavilion presents us with a series of subtle shifts in scale, recalling the Victorian games of mathematician Charles Dodgson's Alice with her drink-me potion, but also our use of the zoom function to drag ourselves through the interior-only spaces of CAD models, enlarging the rooms we wish to enter and, by corollary, shrinking those we wish to leave behind. While Alice's scalar zoom operates on the subject, as she grows and shrinks to travel across the bell curve of the heights of man Quetelet had published two decades earlier, in this installation it is the spaces that grow and shrink around us as we walk through their scalar reenactments at 2:1, 1.5:1, 1.3:1, 1.2:1, 1.1:1, 1:1, 1:1.1, 1:1.2, 1:1.3, 1:1.4, consecutively.

Just as he had with Linnaeus, Quetelet is again recircling over the eighteenth century, this time updating Buffon's range for the heights of man from 2'6"-8' to 1'5"-9'3", generating a new mean size of 5'4". But nineteenth-century desires were quite different to those of the eighteenth. Whereas the latter's precision sought exactitude, that of the former sought the agreement lent by the clustering of values, rather than the singularity of the absolute. As Hacking points out, for the army of measurers and counters of the nineteenth century, the more numbers collected, →

5 A. Quetelet, Letters addressed to H.R.H. the Grand Duke of Saxe-Coburg and Gotha, *On the Theory of Probabilities: As Applied to the Moral and Political Sciences*, trans. Olinthus G. Downes, London, Charles and Edwin Layton, 1849, p. 156.

6 Quetelet, *On the Theory of Probabilities*, p. 157. Research on the blooming of the gooseberry, willow and birch in Linneas' *Aménités Académiques* was abandoned as no conclusion could be drawn from it. In Quetelet's assessment, there were "inexplicable discordances" in his numbers, and the question was not "sufficiently precise". Quetelet, p. 166.

7 Quetelet, p. 158.

8 Hacking, p. 184.

9 Quetelet, p. 102.

the more regularities appear and the more inductions are possible. Within the architecture of Quetelet's model, the normal height of man is bounded by the two limits of probable error, demarcating values greater or lesser than the normal range which itself corresponds to the probability of a ½. In this simple move, the "normal" is redefined as only ever comprising half a population:

> Thus we use with advantage the limits of probable error, which are very narrow, since they include but a half of the entire number of observations: we may take them as including *ordinary* cases. Beyond these you have cases which, without being extraordinary, give rise to the distinction of *great* or *small* in ordinary language ... Beyond these second limits are presented extraordinary cases, which are themselves limited by the impossible.[10]

This normal is itself a new interior state, an immaterial architecture of statistically fortified interiority; that is, the bell curve erects a statistical architecture that describes a hermetic interior whose external walls are made up of a series of layers, limits of excess, the outermost of which comprises the giants and dwarfs who patrol the borders to the monstrous (the impossible) and define the exterior of Quetelet's sample "as monstrosities all falling without these limits".[11] Whereas the tardy and advanced lilac-graced cities are defined by Brussels' zero meridian, the in-verse happens here as the upper and lower limits, the extremities that stake out a perimeter, define the normal, the mean-anchored centre ground of the interior:

> Thus, relying only on authentic documents, we know Frederick the Great had a Swedish bodyguard whose height was eight feet and a half in Swedish measure or 8'3" in English. On the other hand, according to Birch, there has existed an individual, thirty-seven years of age, whose height was only 16". Bébé the noted dwarf (of the King of Poland) was taller. If we take 5'4" as the average height, the giant of the King of Prussia exceeded it by 2'11", and the dwarf mentioned by Birch was 3'11" below it.[12]

The clustering of values evidenced in both these statistically and materially rehearsed interiors becomes self-consolidating as they generate new centre grounds, new default configurations of the normal. Upon entering the reenactments of the Swiss interiors of the statistically defined normal, as we transition across the scalar shifts of their thresholds, passing from space to space, we find ourselves becoming here Quetelet's giants, then there his dwarfs, as we roam the extremities of the bell curve.

Should our scalar roamings broach the limits and cause the negative hallucination that is our prediction-induced blindness to momentarily collapse, allowing us to see what is before our very eyes, we would find that two contributors to normalcy remain nonetheless unchanged: the smoothness and the whiteness.[13] For the paint on these walls is not white, but is part of the monolith of whiteness itself, an ideology so successfully assimilated it has long become invisible, even when in full view. That is, it is not the white of plurality, the white that admits if not other colours then at least other whites—the white of Wittgenstein's house, itself originally a *blanc* very *cassé*, or as Bernhard Leitner describes it, "the silky sheen of white-ochre stucco lustro with some red added", [14] offset by the olive of the ironmongery—but the white of Batchelor's bleaching action: "There is a kind of white that is not created by bleach but that is itself bleach ... It did its work on everything around it."[15] This whiteness then is an eraser, not unlike, hence their successful alliance, the censoring action of smoothness.

Some ten years before Wittgenstein was adding red to his white, Adolf Loos tells a story in "My First Building" about a porter's lodge he was building on Lake Geneva and of receiving a notice from the authorities, asking what he, a foreigner, was doing "desecrating the beauty of Lake Geneva. The house was much too plain. Where was the ornamentation?"[16] Loos immediately wrote back invoking the very smoothness of the lake as his precedent and justification: "On calm days

10 Quetelet, p. 101.
11 Quetelet, p. 103.
12 Quetelet, p. 102.
13 In Freudian terms, negative hallucination as an active erasure of perception produces a gap in reality.
14 B. Leitner, *The Wittgenstein House*, New York, Princeton Architectural Press, 2000, p. 129.
15 Batchelor, p. 10.
16 A. Loos, 'My First Building', 1910, in A. Opel and D. Opel (eds.), *On Architecture*, trans. M. Mitchell, California, Ariadne Press, 2002, p. 70.

the lake itself was smooth and unornamented and still people found it quite nice."[17] The smooth surface of Lake Geneva evidently gets under his skin. That same year, in an essay simply entitled "Architecture", Loos writes of it again:

> May I take you to the shores of a mountain lake? The sky is blue, the water green and everywhere is profound tranquility. The clouds and mountains are mirrored in the lake, the houses, farms and chapels as well. They do not look as if they were fashioned by man, it is as if they came straight from god's workshop, like the mountains and trees, the clouds and the blue sky. And everything exudes an air of beauty and peace.[18]

In the virtual image that is the reflection on the lake's surface, the complex topography of the alpine landscape is flattened and rendered smooth.[19] Like the virtual digital images to come, for all the illusion of depth, this image is defined by its smoothness at the surface in which all, be it made by god or man, is equally there, equally faithfully transcribed, in uniform resolution. Loos's Lake Geneva is a trope and a strategy: a surface treatment that helps you forget what lies behind it, what is necessarily fashioned by man.

The period between 1800 and 1850—when everything was measured and counted, the numericising of the Baconian sciences—is named by T. S. Kuhn as the second Industrial Revolution; Hacking reframes it as the first Information Age. Quetelet's eradication of caprice is, for his partner in arms, Charles Babbage, the filling of the Granary of Science. While Babbage's data harvest was to be stored for future use, Quetelet's was for present application or, to be more precise, for the prediction of present futures. Both paved the way for the new interiors of the new normalcy of the second Information Age: saving big data for the end.

The denuded interiors faithfully recited here are certainly the enduring legacy of Loos's Lake Geneva and Wittgenstein's whited-out walls and absent capitals and everything that makes up modernism's fetishisation of precision. But under their collective surfaces also lies an older debt: they are also statistical models, clusterings of data sets, bell curves that first construct and then dictate the claustrophobic space of the normal; life in the bell jar, the logical legacy of the nineteenth-century project of nascent social sciences, of what was called "moral statistics". The endeavour to measure all, in order to be able to predict all, has come home to roost. These interiors are for life in an inductive loop, once steam-powered, now seamlessly delivered in real time by that new paradigm of measure, big data—itself still measuring the past in order to predict and ultimately correct the future. Under this regime we are increasingly already existing in our very own customised futures.[20] We know the lilac will be in bloom even before we turn the corner. These interiors are *perfectly* contemporary. They have been predicted for us. They knew we were coming. ■

17 Loos, in *On Architecture*, p. 70.
18 Loos, in *On Architecture*, p. 73.
19 We are reminded of Massumi's warning: "Nothing is more destructive for the thinking of the virtual than equating it with the digital." B. Massumi, 'Line Parable for the Virtual', in J. Beckmann (ed.), *The Virtual Dimension*, Princeton Architectural Press, New York, 1998, p. 309.
20 Quite literally, we cannot make a spelling mistake in an SMS, spot it, and then go back and correct it; it is now, courtesy of predictive programming, corrected before we even make it.

# Then Add Colour

Nicholas de Monchaux

White Rooms

"[D]esigners face the ultimate test ...", proclaimed the marketing of a 2012 offering from the American cable television juggernaut HGTV, "... an empty white room."[1] ❶

Two things, then, have something in common. On one hand, the many hundreds of images collected and collated for the *House Tour* archive. And on the other hand, the far larger edifice of spatial representation, and consumption, represented by the multibillion-dollar global infrastructure of home-renovation television.

Beauties and Uglies

"We've found that our viewers' appetite for real estate and renovation programming is ... insatiable", concluded Steven Lerner, senior vice president of HGTV and its associated DIY Network, in 2013.[2] In 2016, HGTV overtook CNN to become the United States' third-most watched, after ESPN (sports) and Fox News.[3] As of this year, Scripps Network Interactive—owner of HGTV and DIY Network—has a market capitalization of nearly twelve billion dollars, and up to forty-six million separate viewers per week of the HGTV channel alone. Yet there's at least one essential difference as well. The white rooms in architectural culture are presented as the end-product. But in the world of televised home renovation, whiteness is only a awkward beginning, or, as it is called on set, a matter of "the uglies", instead of "the beauties".[4]

The two—more formally "the ugly shots" and "the beauty shots"—constitute together the home renovation show's most enduring element: the Reveal. Beginning with a "tease" immediately prior to the shows' last

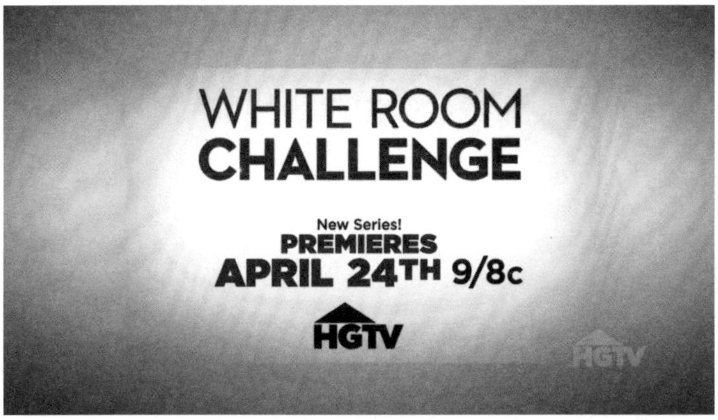


❶ *White Room Challenge,* which aired in 2012 on Scripps Networks' HGTV.

commercial break (showing a homeowner's reaction to the renovation, without the architecture itself), the Reveal is the climax and reward for an hour or half-hour of dedicated human life. Structurally, the sequence pairs the beginning "uglies" against the concluding "beauties", each filmed from the same angle and position in the space under consideration. These shots are also designated the "four corners", panning shots taken with a wide-angle lens from the far quarters of each space under consideration. Repeated as both "uglies" and "beauties", the shots are cut together to enact the final transformation.

This performance of architectural transformation involves other shots as well, related more explicitly to the position of an observer. First are "POV" shots, recording in wide angle the perspective through the home along the scripted path taken by the homeowner during the last-act Reveal. These are intercut onscreen by the "reaction" shots of the homeowner along the same journey. In fact, the two are filmed separately; the mechanics of cameras, booms and lighting mean that the filming of furniture and people are mutually exclusive, and the space the homeowner is reacting to is likely most remarkable for the way a burly assemblage of cameramen, booms and lighting have substituted for furniture.

## White People

The English word "stereotype" originally described a thin, metal casting of a platen of movable type combined with relief-engraved illustrations carved in wood. Such wooden carvings, usually in boxwood glued together on its end grain, had been combined with movable type by the English printer Thomas Bewick as early as the late eighteenth century. Allowing pictures, for the first time, to be easily combined with letterforms on the same printing bed. This process was revolutionised in turn by the economical stereotype, a thin plate cast from the flat platens of movable type and boxwood-carved image, then bent around the cylindrical drum of a rapidly automated steam-driven printing press. The technology allowed mass-consumption of printing to take place for the first time. The economics of the press room, however, led printers to re-use the wooden image blocks nearly as often as they did their massed legions of interchangeable letterforms. And so our visual culture gained a new word for a single image, or collection of them, repeated over-much.[5]

Where stereotype is cast, satire follows. In 2017, the premiere of the ruthlessly parodic *South Park* compressed the home-renovation oeuvre into a two minute micro-drama: *White People Renovating Houses.* ❷ The irony being that, while the stars and homeowners on display in this universe are overwhelmingly Caucasian, almost nothing else ends up white. Indeed, one reality-TV producer summarised the design imperatives as follows: "Add colour. Then add colour." Which has less to do with trends in decor →

1 HGTV, *The White Room Challenge,* https://www.hgtv.com/shows/white-room-challenge, (accessed 1 March 2018)
2 Scripps Network Interactive, 12/6/2013 Press Release, *HGTV set to premiere three new series in January,* http://www.scrippsnetworksinteractive.com/newsroom/company-news/HGTV-set-to-premiere-three-new-series-in-January/, (accessed 1 March 2018)
3 G. Smith, 'HGTV Will Never Upset You: How the Network Beat CNN in 2016', Bloomberg News, 28 December 2016, https://www.bloomberg.com/news/articles/2016-12-28/hgtv-will-never-upset-you-how-the-network-beat-cnn-in-2016, (accessed 1 March 2018)
4 For these and other insights on the filming of home-renovation television I am grateful to several cameramen and producers who allowed themselves to be interviewed for this piece.
5 R. Benson, *The Printed Picture,* New York, The Museum of Modern Art, 2008, p. 22.

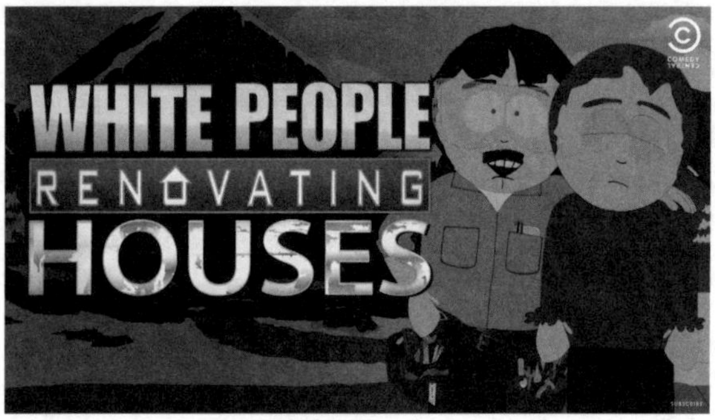


2 *White People Renovating Houses*
An in-episode series on *South Park*, series 21, episode 1, first aired 13 September 2017.

than the inherent dynamics of television. Marshall MacLuhan appropriately judged the medium to be "cool". But the colours it favours are not. Aside from brightly coloured surfaces, the remaining architectural imperative to renovation television is one shared, completely by the images of the *House Tour* archive. Within the brief, 120-second span of *South Park's White People Renovating Houses*, only one design decision is invoked, repeatedly: "We're going to take out the wall between the kitchen and living area and go for an open concept." And, indeed, of all the images in the *House Tour* archive, more than a third highlight the spatial connection between living space and kitchen.

## Open Concepts

*Open Concept* is now itself the title of an HGTV show starring Texan decorator-sisters Whitney Garnier and Ashley Turner. But it was originally very un-global Canadian slang for "open plan", only entering the larger lexicon through the breakout success of another pair of TV siblings: twins Jonathan and Drew Scott of the HGTV juggernaut *Property Brothers*. Currently viewed in more than 150 countries worldwide, the show originated with a low-budget, thirteen-episode series filmed in Toronto and aired on the Canadian W network, before being purchased by HGTV in 2013. The franchise now includes seventeen shows under development or in production, including *Buying and Selling*, *Brother Vs. Brother*, *Property Brothers: At Home*, *Property Brothers: At Home on the Ranch*, and *Property Brothers Take New Orleans*. Like the tendency towards pattern and colour, the "open concept" is in part a mainstay of TV decoration for the way it plays on camera; when juxtaposed the Reveal, the camera's eye is quite literally liberated. The "open concept" is essential, too, for the way in which it combines the directives of mass-market television with that of modern architecture.

## *L'Architecture d'Aujourd'hui*

In 1930, the editor of Paris' *L'Architecture d'Aujourd'hui*, André Bloc, commissioned the twenty-six-year-old Belgian director Pierre Chenal to make a film for general European audiences about the new avant-garde in French architecture—including the newly French Corbusier, who had taken citizenship that year. Corbusier dominated the production. In the end, he contributed not only the script and his brother Albert's music, but also his buildings and urban proposal as the focus of much of the film, titled *L'Architecture d'Aujourd'hui*.

The first eight of the film's eighteen minutes, featuring buildings by Corbusier's mentor Auguste Perret and his rival Robert Mallet-Stevens, are rarely shown. Several frames of the film's Corbusian core are by contrast famous, including a presentation of the Voisin plan: the erasure of a rectangle of historic fabric with a black grease pencil, Corbusier's hand conjuring details of a large-scale model of skyscrapers and highways. The portion of the film focusing on Corbusier's villas Stein-de-Monzie at Garches and Savoye at Poissy bears particular mention here, both for a remarkable comparison to the images of the *House Tour* archive as well as, equally, to reality TV.

Whether in Garches, Poissy or the lesser villas that make brief appearances, the focus throughout the film is on the interconnected quality of interior space, depicted through a series of wide-angle pans, "four corners", before the fact. Shared, too, is the quality of lighting, produced (as Corbusier's intertitles proclaim) "without [apparent] recourse to artificial illumination".

While not literally depicting apartments, the film is instead an extended argument for the construction of them. After celebrating the open plan of Garches and Savoye, the film moves to the exterior of Corbusier's only contemporary multi-unit housing, at Pessac (shown, however, *sans* interiors).

Then Voisin is presented in its grandeur, rendering the film's argument clear: only through such bold planning might all occupy the same miracles of space and light as now reserved to a privileged few. And arguing for these "beauties" are the requisite "uglies", underexposed, poorly stabilised shots of Paris' mediaeval Marais. ❸

As with today's reality television, much has been made of the film's sexual subtext. In the film's extended sequence treatment of Garches, the house's divorcée-occupant and children are shown, but with an abundantly present Corbusier replacing the paterfamilias at the family's core. At the villa in Ville d'Avray, a male instructor takes two women, clad in high heels and little more, through a set of gymnastic exercises, emphasising the association with health and hygiene of white walls (and yes, white people). And finally, in Poissy, a faceless woman is shown moving, in a series of counter-posed shots, through and up the houses' central ramps. As memorably observed by Beatriz Colomina, as the sequence ends, " just at the moment when she has turned and could face the camera (there is nowhere else to go) ...". Instead, "she vanishes." [6] ❹

*Vacuum Domicilium*

There is no on-screen protagonist in Corbusier's female-adorned tour of Savoye for the same reason there is no protagonist in the collected images of the *House Tour* archive—and indeed for the same reason there is no person shown in the central "uglies" and "beauties" of the reality-show Reveal. The protagonist is the viewer themselves and, it is likely imagined, a man, as in Drew Scott's explanation of the *Property Brothers'* success. "The shows are not so foofy that guys don't want to watch, kids want to watch because we're goofy and women appreciate it because you're getting real design knowledge." [7] Women are improved, kids are distracted, and men amused—particularly in the absence of a quality the gratifyingly exhaustive dictionary *Gay-2-Zee: A Dictionary of Sex, Subtext, and the Sublime* defines as "homosexual". [8] For such a subject, to own is to control the presence, or even more importantly the absence, of others.

In 1630, John Winthrop, founder of the Massachusetts Bay Colony, wrote of the legal principle by which native lands were expropriated beyond his original royal grant: "Being thus taken and possessed as *vacuum domicilium*", he would proclaim, "gives us a sufficient title against all men." The legal phrase means, quite literally, an "empty house". [9]

True Colour

Mass-produced images, as often as not, perpetuate seemingly necessary fictions; see the tautness of bodies or the flawlessness of female skin. In the case of the empty apartments currently on view, it is the myth of ownership by their architect-authors. The photographs preserve, indelibly, a fleeting inflection. The architect is proprietor as long as the dwelling is incomplete; yet the long-laboured-for completion brings with it mostly loss, above all, of control. Here, colour is essential through its absence. White, traditionally prized in kitchens for the observed absence of contamination, here serves for the hygienic absence of architecture's true consumers and owners.

We see a flamboyant shadow of this in the visual language of the Reveal. A central fiction of the sequence is that the furnishings shown will belong to, or are to be used by, the renovated homes' owners. In fact, they are generic, and temporary, just like (and often drawn from) the warehouses of furniture used to "stage" real-estate listings across America. The presence of actual possessions, and the human traces they contain, discourages the viewer, or potential homebuyer, from entering the space fully in their own imagination.

We might dwell a little longer, in this context, on two things seemingly missing from the *House Tour* archive—yet abundantly present in our larger visual culture: sex and colour. *The White Room Challenge* distills particularly the underlying dynamics. Its designer-contestants actually do not decorate dwellings, but one of an enfilade of white rooms facing a single stage set, devoid of architectural function. And instead of installing even faux-real furniture, the set pieces involve such assuredly, but more ephemerally alluring →

6 B. Colomina, 'The Split Wall: Domestic Voyeurism', in B. Colomina (ed.) *Sexuality and Space*, New York, Princeton Architectural Press, 1992, p. 103–104.

7 Drew Scott quoted in K. Rosman, 'They Have a Hammer', *The New York Times*, 11 May 2017, p. D1.

8 D. F. Reuter, *Gay-2-Zee: A Dictionary of Sex, Subtext, and the Sublime*, New York, St. Martin's Press, 2006, p. 79.

9 John Winthrop, quoted in David Grayson Allen, 'Vacuum Domicilium: The Social and Cultural Landscape of Seventeenth-Century New England', in Jonathan L. Fairbanks and Robert F. Trent (eds.), *New England Begins: The Seventeenth Century*, vol. 1, Boston, Museum of Fine Arts, 1982.

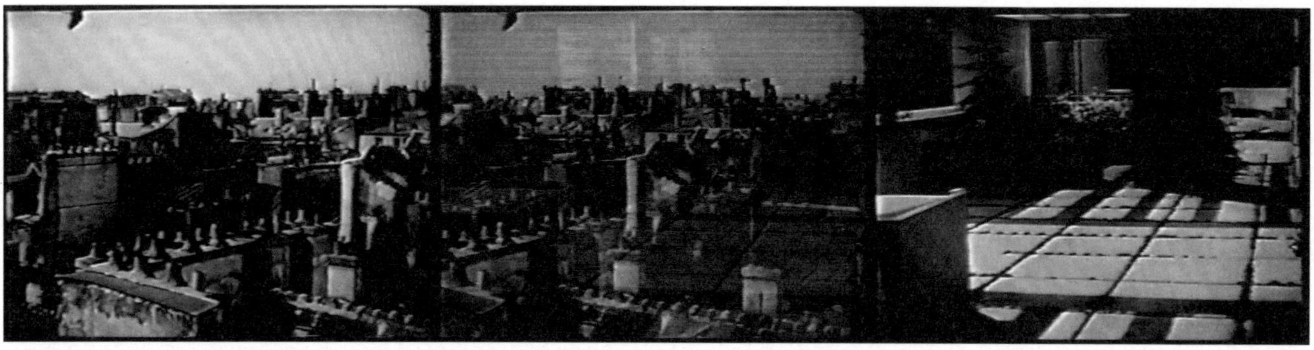

3 A pan/fade in Pierre Chenal and Le Corbusier's *L'Architecture d'Aujourd'hui*, 1931, showing "ugly" rooftops and "beauty" terrace by Corbusier.

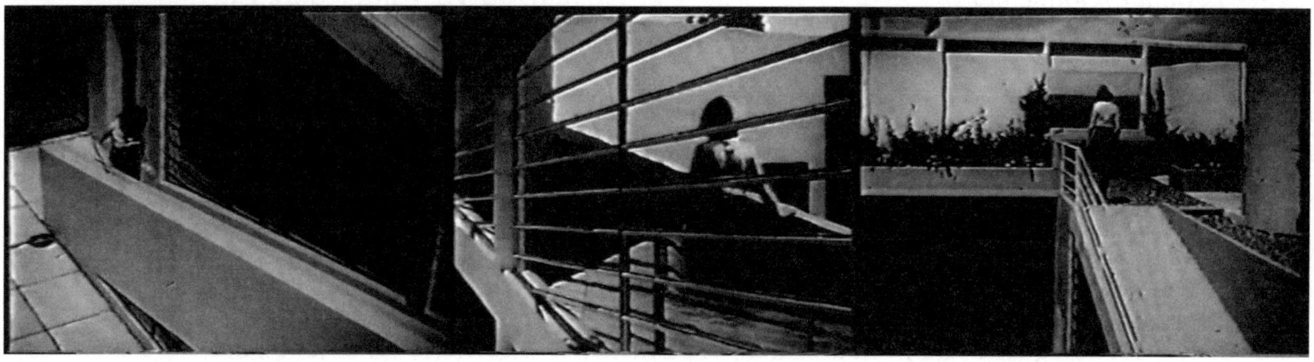

4 The storied sequence of the Villa Savoye from *L'Architecture d'Aujourd'hui*, 1931.

and reliably colourful elements as "delicious candy" and "exotic flowers". Architecture not lived, but consumed.

Contrast this with the profoundly un-Corbusian entrée of the kitchen's space of labour into the current open-concept reality. Not only are the food-preparation areas of Corbusier's free-plan villas hidden in his cinematic gaze, but they are in plan utterly blockaded. Just as Beatriz Colomina interprets the horizontal mullions that bisect the filmed and faceless female of the Villa Savoye, they are not free plans, but prisons.

Despite their first fame in black-and-white reproduction, it is probably essential to point out here that Corbusier's villa interiors were not actually white, but adorned with planes of cubist colour. Their kitchens, though, were not. Places of work and cleaning, not comfort, they are some of his only interior spaces truly without colour, veering claustrophobically to today's vernacular: white tile and stainless steel.

As machines for living, Corbusier's villas were less airplanes than submarines, their commanding terraces belying the machinery of labour below. By contrast, despite their airplane metal and handleless cupboards, the kitchens of the *House Tour* archive provide some of the most frequent, and profound, intimations of humanity and presence.

A century of effort, marked in the distance from Corb to the contemporary interior, has brought the traditional domestic sphere of women into apparent equality with the traditionally masculine ideals of comfort and rest. We are going to take out the wall between the kitchen and living area and go for an open concept. But kitchens still hide truths. It turns out that while the reality-TV recipients of renovation are often fine with exchanging bright interior colours for fleeting fame, they are just as frequently fixed on the idea of a kitchen in white—following not just fashion, but centuries-old sentiment of hygiene. In this room, apparently, they must most frequently be persuaded into a "less suitable" colour that will befit the screen. In its present of absence, white remains ideal. ▪

# Framing and Deframing[1]

Georges Teyssot

Summary: from the perspective space to our screens, how can we think of the gaze as it defines itself when it passes through different vision devices, considering that vision is not always discreet. To see, to glimpse, to look, to consider: it is indeed a matter of framing. Consequently, the frame offers mediation between the interior and exterior, the public and private, the manifest and hidden. A theoretical analysis of several "framing forms" will be undertaken, which does not rule out the possibility of thinking about deframing modalities. In such a hypothesis, the junction of different frames builds up the facets—faces, facades, surfaces, interfaces—whose massing allows for the laying out of inhabited spaces. Walls and partitions become membranes, bringing into play endosmosis and exosmosis, producing intermediary zones between intimacy and extimacy.

Behind the Victorian or Haussmannian conception of private and public lay a topography upon which the juridical existence of habitation was based. Thresholds, sheltered by a variety of custodians and janitors, thus became complex filters, sieves that let the outside in and vice versa. During the first half of the nineteenth century, the expression "wall of private life" assumed its legal and social significance. The French term *intérieur* no longer referred to the interiority of the human heart or soul but to what, in its midst, guaranteed the conditions for happiness and comfort; as Jean Paul wrote, "Only at one's place does one find back one's totality."[2] Thus, as a philosopher from the Biedermeier period, the ideal thing for Jean Paul was to be "at one's place". He went on, exclaiming: "How all disorder of feeling dissipates and gets in order

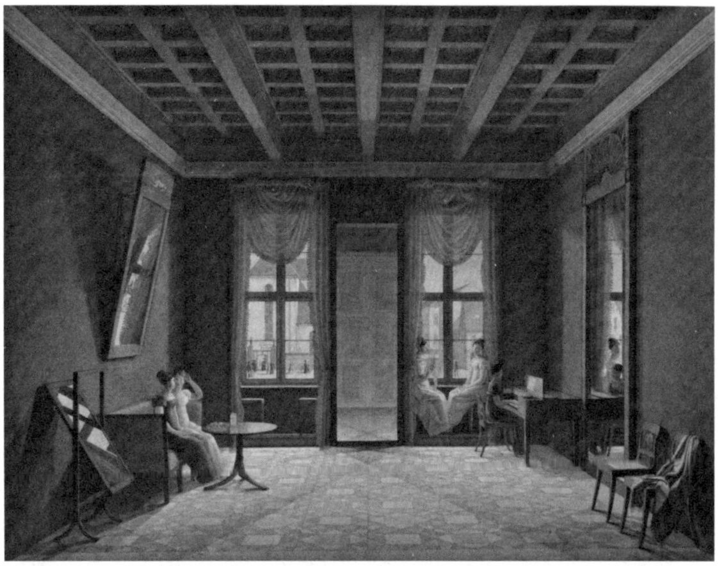

1 Johann Erdmann Hummel, *Berlin Zimmer,* 1820–25, pen and ink and watercolour, Museum für Angewandte Kunst, Frankfurt am Main.

when one returns from abroad and finds back one's four walls!"[3] Such a mindset is testament to the *Stimmung* (German; harmony) to which the culture of that time aspired. The desire for well-being in everyday life stands out in Johann Erdmann Hummel's watercolour interior view entitled *Berlin Room (Berliner Zimmer),* circa 1825. This kind of painting was called *Zimmerbild* in German. In such a room, mirrors and windows acquire the same luminosity and chromatic weight, becoming the same kind of objects within the painterly representation. Pictorial treatment turns windows into mirrors, while mirrors—which, in this pictorial fiction, reproduce the interior view at different angles—become windows through either their infinite reflection or the windows' own literal one.

Yet in Hummel's painting, there is a clear division between the interior and the world of things outside, a world that is almost excluded, rubbed out by the reflective veil of the glass surfaces. This room is like a box, on one side of which is situated the viewer. The mirror, centred between the two windows, reflects the closed door opposite, on the wall where the observer (or painter?) should be. But the observer is absent. The viewer of the painting looks into a room that looks back at him through a mirror. To the extent that he is not represented in it, it is as if the viewer were *part* of the room. Reflection along the central axis emphasises the general symmetry of its almost cubical, box-like aspect. Meanwhile, manifold reflections between the different mirrors highlight their interiority (German *Innerlichkeit*), which thus become autonomous and self-referential. Windows have become mirrors, maybe because the exterior is an illusion and there is no outside world; or the outside world is but a kind of representation. The five feminine figures sitting in this *Berlin Room* 1 are governed "by the principle of mirroring and doubling", as Ulrike Brunotte pertinently remarked.[4] These feminine characters exist only within this *Innerlichkeit*; they are here in their daily existence alone, yet they are not recluses, because such an interiority offers an efficient opening through art or fantasy, revealing itself as a sort of waking dream. Likewise, Jean Paul, a friend of the Schlegel brothers, saw a dream in his home:

> The dream opens to us the world's mirror where we only used to watch, and we (the spectator) multiply, by our presence, its (the spectacle's) inconsistent images.[5]

→

1 This text is a revised and expanded version of the chapter 'Windows and Screens', in G. Teyssot, *A Topology of Everyday Constellations,* Cambridge, MA, MIT Press, 2013, p. 266–72.
2 Jean Paul, *Être là dans l'existence,* trans. P. Deshusses, [Original title: Ideen-Gewimmel] Paris, Payot et Rivages, 1998, p. 31.
3 Jean Paul, *Être là dans l'existence,* p. 31.
4 U. Brunotte, 'The Inside as Exile and Abyss: Images from the History of Seclusion,' *Daidalos,* no. 36, June 1990, p. 62–71.
5 Jean Paul, *Être là dans l'existence,* p. 23 (parentheses indicate modifications by the author).

Before long, the new media of communication—books, newspapers, magazines—moved into domestic spaces and the tendrils of a planetary knowledge penetrated those sedate rooms, even before the spread of technologies such as the telephone and electricity.[6] As the home became the place of conflicting passions, it emerged as the fortress of English "privacy" (French *intimité* or German *Gemütlichkeit*) while conversely also becoming a microcosm crisscrossed by mobile borders. In domestic spaces, the public and the private engaged in confrontations, a state of warfare that led to André Gide's famous exclamation in 1897: "*Families*, I *hate* you! Shut-in homes, closed doors, jealous possessions of happiness."[7] The dividing line between the public and private spheres formed an active battleground that was constantly shifting and readjusting as society's norms evolved. For example, the telephone was perceived as an unbearable infringement by a certain "difficult man" in Hugo von Hofmannsthal's 1918 comedy *Der Schwierige*,[8] while at the same time ushering in personalised and individualised information—the tendrils became tentacles. In "The Telephone", a text from *Berlin Childhood around 1900*—a series of articles published in 1933–35—Walter Benjamin presents the domination of technology and the marks of alienation that can result from it. A signal of the invasion of the public sphere into the private, the telephone also reveals itself to be a symptom of children's anguish and parental conflicts, as Benjamin recounts: "Not many of those who use the apparatus know what devastation it once wreaked in family circles."[9] Its noise, when it rang, disturbing the father's nap, did not fail to cause a cataclysm in the whole household. The resounding aggression would thus expose a much more formidable aggressor in the person of the father:

> Disagreements with switchboard operators were the rule, to say nothing of the threats and curses uttered by my father when he had the complaints department on the line. But his real orgies were reserved for cranking the handle, to which he gave himself up for minutes at a time, nearly forgetting himself in the process. His hand, on these occasions, was a dervish overcome by frenzy.[10]

Obliterating the child's senses, the telephone ring multiplies the terrors of the bourgeois household. Conjunction of technology and the worrying world of adults, the telephone seemed to amplify familial conflicts.

Today, thresholds rarely constitute a barrier to public space, if they ever did; nor are they conceivable as an obstacle to permeability. For clues to this broader condition, one has to reread Georg Simmel's 1909 essay "Bridge and Door" ("Brücke und Tür"), in which he asserts that human nature is constituted by both separation and unification:

> The image of external things possesses for us the ambiguous dimension that in external nature, everything can be considered to be connected, but also separated ... Only to humanity, in contrast to nature, has the right to connect and separate been granted, and in the distinctive manner that one of these activities is always the presupposition of the other ... The formula according to which both types of activity come together in human undertakings, whether the connectedness or the separation is felt to be what was naturally ordained and the respective alternative is felt to be our task, is something which can guide all our activity.[11]

This separate-reconnect duo, describing a strictly human condition, resembles the two banks of a river which are separated, only to be reunited by a bridge:

> In the construction of a bridge ... the human will to connection seems to be confronted not only by the passive resistance of spatial separation but also by the active resistance of a spatial configuration. By overcoming this obstacle, the bridge symbolises the extension of our volitional sphere over space. Only for us are the banks of a river not just apart but "separated".[12]

It is not just a matter of connecting, but also of reconnecting what had been separated.[13] Paradoxically, a human being is an inhabitant of confines, a creature living enduringly on

6 See P. Ariès and G. Duby, eds. *Histoire de la vie privée*, Paris, Seuil, 1985–87, and in particular, M. Perrot *De la Révolution à la Grande Guerre*, Paris, Seuil, points histoire, vol. 4, no. 263, 1999, p. 15, 281, 284–6, 563.

7 A. Gide, *Les nourritures terrestres*, Paris, Gallimard, 1897. Translated as *Fruits of the Earth*, trans. D. Bussy, New York, Knopf, 1949.

8 H. von Hofmannsthal, *L'homme difficile: comédie en trois actes*, trans. J-Y. Masson, [Original title: Der Schwierige], Lagrasse, Verdier, 1992.

9 W. Benjamin, *The Work of Art in the Age of Its Technological Reproducibility, and Other Writings on Media*, eds. M. W. Jennings, B. Doherty and T. Y. Levin, trans. Edmund Jephcott et al., Cambridge, MA and London, The Belknap Press of Harvard University Press, 2008, p. 77–78.

10 Benjamin, p. 78.

11 G. Simmel, 'Bridge and Door', trans. M. Ritter, *Theory, Culture & Society* 11, 1994, p. 5–6.

12 Simmel, p. 6.

13 L. Charbonnier, *Cadre et regard: Généalogie d'un dispositif*, Paris, L'Harmattan, 2007, p. 38–39.

the frontier, yet, at the same time, has no secure limits by which to enclose himself. It is the human prerogative to decide, in the face of nature, whether to bond or to cut oneself off, and one way of acting will always presuppose the other in reverse. This binominal entity of union-separation is best compared to the two banks of a river: separate, only to be united by a bridge. Overcoming this separation, the bridge also symbolises the extension of human willpower in space. By crossing a bridge, one connects, and reconnects what was separated. A human being inhabits thresholds; the door offers the means to settle within, but also permits one to step out, by crossing the border.[14] As regards to theory, it is fruitful to consider the thematic of lodging by measuring it to the antithetic thematic of nomadic dislodgment—which comes down to saying that the separate-reconnect duo must include the laying-out and moving-out alternatives.

Simmel had previously mapped reciprocal states of unity-exclusion in his 1902 essay "The Picture Frame: An Aesthetic Study" ("Der Bilderrahmen: Ein ästhetischer Versuch"), a seminal investigation on the nature of framing an artwork:

> The essence of the work of art, however, is to be a whole for itself, not requiring any relation to an exterior, spinning each of its threads back into its own centre ... The work of art closes itself off against everything external to itself as a world of its own. Thus its boundaries mean something quite different from what one calls boundaries in a natural entity. In the case of the natural entity, boundaries are simply the site of continuing exosmosis and endosmosis with everything external; for the work of art, they are that absolute ending which exercises indifference towards and defence against the exterior, and a unifying integration with respect to the interior in a *single* act.[15]

Here, the frame, by the very materiality of its border, is thought of as a device that helps the painting to exclude anything exterior while allowing for a concentration in its interior. The frame isolates the artwork; it guarantees it the possibility of an autonomous existence by forbidding the possibility to be in perpetual trade with the outside, which biological phenomena would allow (like exosmosis and endosmosis in a cell):

> What the frame achieves for the work of art is to symbolise and strengthen this double function in its boundary. It excludes all that surrounds it, and thus also the viewer as well, from the work of art, and thereby helps to place it at that distance from which alone it is aesthetically enjoyable ... For only to the extent to which a being is self-enclosed does it possess that sphere into which no one can penetrate, that existence for itself with which it can protect itself from every other sphere.[16]

For Simmel, nothing should battle with the secondary position of the frame in relation to the painting. Instead everything (matter, colour, form and shape) should maintain the frame as a *parergon* (in Greek, a subordinate work or an accessory), a probable echo to Immanuel Kant's considerations on the status of the painted work (in Greek, *ergon*, main work, master work): "That is why the frame, through its configuration, must never offer a gap or a bridge through which, as it were, the world could get in ..."[17] Frame-object, the object of the frame, must reinforce the closure of the painting's object. Any attempt to weaken the essence of the framing—by opening up the encircling border, by transforming the frame into a piece of furniture, or by using the shape of architectural elements (such as pilaster or pediments) to build the frame—is condemned, in as much as it would abate the frame's *parergon* quality. This evokes Jacques Derrida's treatment in *The Truth in Painting* (1978) of the *parergon* as a crutch or prosthesis in Kant's argument: "There is always a form on a ground, but the *parergon* is a form which has, as its traditional determination, not that it stands out but that it disappears, buries itself, effaces itself, melts away at the moment it deploys its greatest energy."[18] Because it occurs posteriorly to a primary closure operation that is indispensable to the artwork, the →

14 The elaboration of an infinite network of reciprocal relationships, or of interactions *(Wechselwirkung)*, is one of Simmel's fundamental concepts.
15 G. Simmel, 'The Picture Frame: An Aesthetic Study', *Theory, Culture & Society*, trans. Mark Ritter, London, Sage, 1994, vol. 11, p. 11.
16 Simmel, p. 12.
17 Simmel, p. 12.
18 J. Derrida, 'The Parergon', in *The Truth in Painting*, trans. G. Bennington and I. McLeod, Chicago, University of Chicago Press, 1987, p. 61.

frame-object comes second. Any subversion or inversion of this hierarchy would be the outcome of a stratagem or of a choice made by the artist.

This happens because the frame, like the door, is in an unstable position, acting as an intermediary between the painting and its surroundings to which it is both connected and separated. For Simmel, the picture frame must be thought of as a metaphor for a border between social groups, thus showing that the true function of framing is "closing" the object "off against the surrounding world and holding it together."[19] In his essay about the picture frame, Simmel analogises the simultaneous wholeness of an artwork—per se and inclusive of its harmony with its surroundings—to the difficulties encountered by collective social entities, whose members have the contradictory aspirations of both belonging to a group and laying claim to the status of autonomous individuals. To conclude, Simmel's work offers a complex theory of the passage and the border that will influence his pupils, such as Georg Lukács, Ernst Bloch and Siegfried Kracauer, as well as Walter Benjamin's work on dialectical images. For both Simmel and Benjamin, the border—be it a limit or a demarcation—reveals itself through an "in-between" condition, like a middle ground, literally speaking. Any threshold or marginal zone induces a reciprocal state, offering two joint perspectives.

At the end of the nineteenth century, with the electrification of houses and the proliferation of telephone lines, energy itself invaded the interior. Transparency was not so much a matter of making use of metal and glass in constructions as it was a question of how energies would be figured and represented: hence the vital force's concretions, engendered by the "line as a force" of Henry van de Velde, who incorporated invisible factors such as vibrations or X-rays. Around 1900, the concept of ether was understood as the imponderable medium that would fill all space and serve as the vehicle for the transmission of electromagnetic radiation. In the popular imagination, ether was synonymous with space.[20] The interior was now a permeable space where bodies could act within forcefields. Henceforth, architecture's scope would provide both separation and permeability, becoming what biology has termed a "membrane". In the cell, the surface membrane permits the organism to find a balance between solidity and permeability (that is to say, a fluid balance) that insures the conditions for processes such as osmosis.

In 1926, following this logic, Bauhaus student Siegfried Ebeling published a work entitled *Der Raum als Membran* ❷ (*Space as Membrane*), in which he introduced his concept of the house designed as a multicellular hollow space whose surfaces were free from anything that would impede the flow of metabolic energies.[21] Ebeling, a friend of Marcel Breuer who also had Ludwig Mies van der Rohe as a patron, was the one to understand that, thanks to new materials and technologies, the wall could now be understood as a permeable membrane, both transparent and insulating.[22] Ebeling defined what he called "air radiation" from both a physical and physiological reading of the environment. The habitat was no longer conceivable as a place regulated by laws of geometry, but as a multicellular space surrounded by a membrane unsteadily balanced between the background and the climate's external conditions—described as "the spheres' subtle forces"[23]—and an interior environment regulated by equipment ensuring heating, ventilation and light, even providing medical-use radiations, and fitting out, lastly, homes equipped with radios and television sets.[24]

Le Corbusier and Paul Artaria ❸ / ❹ discoursed on the comparative advantages of traditional upright versus "lengthwise" windows.[25] Likewise, Mies's famous Resor house project (1937–39) ❺ found an apt depiction in a collage mixing different media such as perspective, technical drawing, photography and painting. A reproduction of Paul Klee's *Bunte Mahlzeit* (*Colourful Meal*, 1928) ❻, which was in the Resors' collection—is also included.[26] The collage brings forth the visual concretisation of a superposition of generic surfaces: the surface of the perspective view through the vast panoramic bay onto the surrounding landscape; the surface of the technical drawing showing the constructive

19 G. Simmel, 'Soziologie des Raumes', in *Aufsätze und Abhandlungen 1901–08*, Frankfurt AM, Suhrkamp, 1995, p. 138 (author's translation); G. Simmel, 'The Sociology of Space,' in D. Frisby and M. Featherstone (eds.), *Simmel on Culture: Selected Writings*, trans. M. Ritter, London, Sage, 1997, p. 137–70, 141.

20 L. D. Henderson, 'Vibratory Modernism: Boccioni, Kupka, and the Ether of Space', in B. Clarke and L. D. Henderson (eds.), *From Energy to Information: Representation in Science and Technology, Art, and Literature*, Stanford, Stanford University Press, 2002, p. 126–49.

21 S. Ebeling, *Der Raum als Membran*, Dessau, Dünnhaupt, 1926; S. Ebeling, *Space as Membrane*, trans. P. Johnston and A. K. Schoefert, London, AA Publications, 2010.

22 C. Asendorf, 'Bodies in Force Fields: Design between the Wars', in Clarke and Henderson (eds.), *From Energy to Information*, p. 195–212.

23 Ebeling, *Der Raum als Membran*.

24 C. Asendorf, 'Bodies in Force Fields: Design between the Wars', p. 201–03; see also: Laurent Stalder, 'Air, Light, and Air-Conditioning', *Grey Room*, no. 40, summer 2010, p. 84–99.

25 P. Artaria, *Vom Bauen und Wohnen: ein Bilderbuch für Laien und Fachleute*, Basel, Wepf, 1939, p. 12.

26 L. Mies van der Rohe, *Collage für den Entwurf des Hauses Resor*, 1937–39, in Horst Bredekamp, et al. (eds.) *Das technische Bild: Kompendium zu einer Stilgeschichte wissenschaftlicher Bilder*, Berlin, Akademie Verlag, 2008, p. 231, fig. 6.

structure; and the surface of Klee's painting, exhibited without a frame but framed within the ultrarational space. Ultimately, the horizon is created by the interlocking of different types of framings accompanied by a series of deframing operations: the section, the window, the painting, the partitions, the walls. The different panels composing the Resor house are as if compressed into an abstract unique surface forming a filtering membrane between the interior (the *Innenräume*) and the outside world (the *Außenräume*).[27] Mies's Resor project could be both the archetype and prototype of contemporary "interior architecture" where surfaces become generic, sliding upon each other, without any apparent joints.

In *What is Philosophy?* (1991), Gilles Deleuze defines affects and percepts as composed of blocs of sensations. But they are not the perceptions or affections of those who feel them. Affects and percepts are beings that carry their own value. But the compound needs to stand on its own; it is a monument. Disserting about material, Deleuze claims: "All the material becomes expressive. It is the affect that is metallic, crystalline, stony and so on ..." He goes on: "The landscape *sees* ... The percept is the landscape before man, in the absence of man." And it is what makes the landscape visionary. For Deleuze, we are not *in* the world as phenomenology would want it, but we become with the world, we become by contemplating it: "Everything is vision, becoming. We become universes. Becoming animal, plant, molecular, becoming zero." Art is indeed "the language of sensation" whether it passes through words, minerals, plants.[28]

For Deleuze, the three axes forming our becoming are the body (or the flesh), the house and the cosmos. Thereupon, the question is to understand what is conveyor of becoming in art in general and then, from there, in "architecture" specifically. Architecture is conceived through the place in which we live, namely the house. The house is defined by "sections" made of diversely oriented planes forming its armature, like a skeleton. Horizontal, vertical, front/back, left/right sections: "These sections are walls but also floors, doors, windows, French windows, and mirrors ..." or plate-glass windows, giving the power to stand on its own "within autonomous *frames*." The hardest is to know how to join planes. Through every possible mode, the house-sensation is "the joining of planes in accordance with a thousand orientations".[29] The third element (or axis) of our becoming is the cosmos, the universe. Not only does the house open upon the landscape through a window or a mirror, but even the most shut-up house spiritually opens onto a universe: Deleuze lists Monet, Matisse, Van Gogh, Gauguin, Bacon, Yves Klein's blue, symbol of infinite, of a shift, or jump, into the unknown.[30] Whether with abstract painting (Mondrian, Kandinsky, Kupka, Klee) or the abstract northern line of Gothic architecture (Wilhelm Worringer), the object of painting is to "paint forces", to unveil invisible forces, "of gravity, of heaviness, of rotation, of the vortex, of explosion, of expansion, of germination",[31] to reveal within the emptiness of ether the potential of magnetic waves, for instance. It is a matter of making cosmic forces perceptible. Such an attempt is apparent in abstract art that tends towards "an architectonic plane of composition" becoming a purely spiritual being, but also in conceptual art, in which dematerialisation is implied through a generalisation capable of neutralising the reality of represented things.[32] Robert Smithson's *Nonsite* (1968)[33] comes to mind as an example.

When one conceives the body (L., *corpus*), one thinks of the set of techniques and know-how that one learns to incorporate, such as the corporal hexis and the habitus. When one refers to the experience of the flesh (L., *carnis*), one is torn between a Christian version of incarnation and the condemnation of pleasures (or the "confessions") of the flesh, to follow Michel Foucault.[34] Incorporation or incarnation: art does not belong exclusively in the field of body sensations or in the field of the experience of the flesh. Since Giorgio Vasari, the *disegno* gives the matrix to all arts, and art begins with the house. From painting to sculpture or cinema, architecture is the first of all visual arts. For Deleuze, "the most knowledgeable architecture endlessly produces and joins up planes and sections",[35] making it possible →→

27 D. Mertins, ed. *The Presence of Mies*, New York, Princeton Architectural Press, 1994, p. 105–07; C. McAfee in P. Lambert, ed. *Mies in America*, New York, H. N. Abrams, CCA, Whitney Museum, 2001, p. 162–80.
28 G. Deleuze and F. Guattari, *What is Philosophy?*, trans. H. Tomlinson and G. Burchell, New York, Columbia University Press, 1994, p. 169, 179.
29 Deleuze and Guattari, p. 179.
30 Deleuze and Guattari, p. 180.
31 Deleuze and Guattari, p. 181.
32 Deleuze and Guattari, p. 198.
33 R. Smithson, *A Nonsite*, Franklin, NJ, 1968, painted wooden bins, limestone, photograph, Museum of Contemporary Art, Chicago.
34 M. Foucault, *Histoire de la sexualité, IV: Les aveux de la chair*, Frédéric Gros (ed.), Paris, Gallimard, 2018.
35 Deleuze and Guattari, *What is Philosophy?*, p. 186.

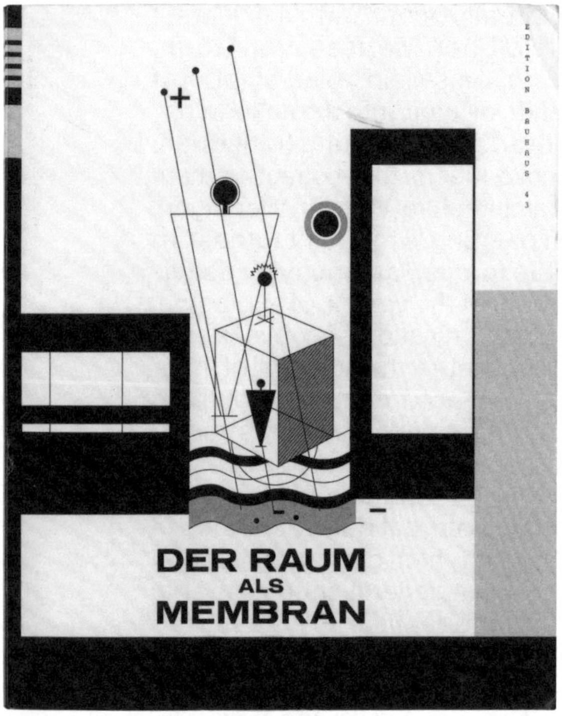


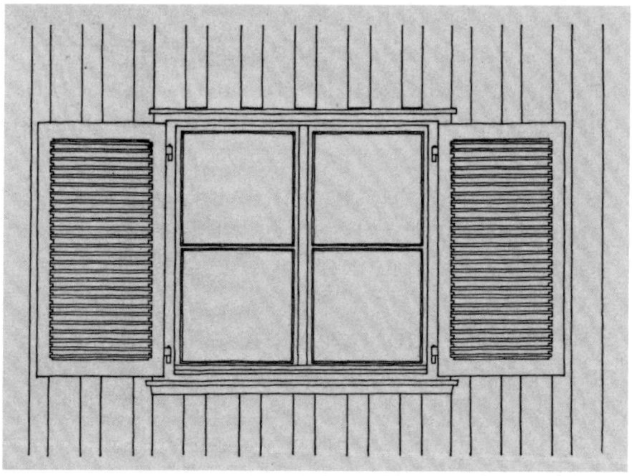

❸ Detail of the window of a small house in Grenzacherhorn near Basel, Switzerland; in P. Artaria, *Vom Bauen und Wohnen. Ein Bilderbuch für Laien und Fachleute,* Basel, B. Wepf & Co., 1939.

❷ Siegfried Ebeling, *Der Raum als Membran,* Dessau, Dünnhaupt, 1926, cover.

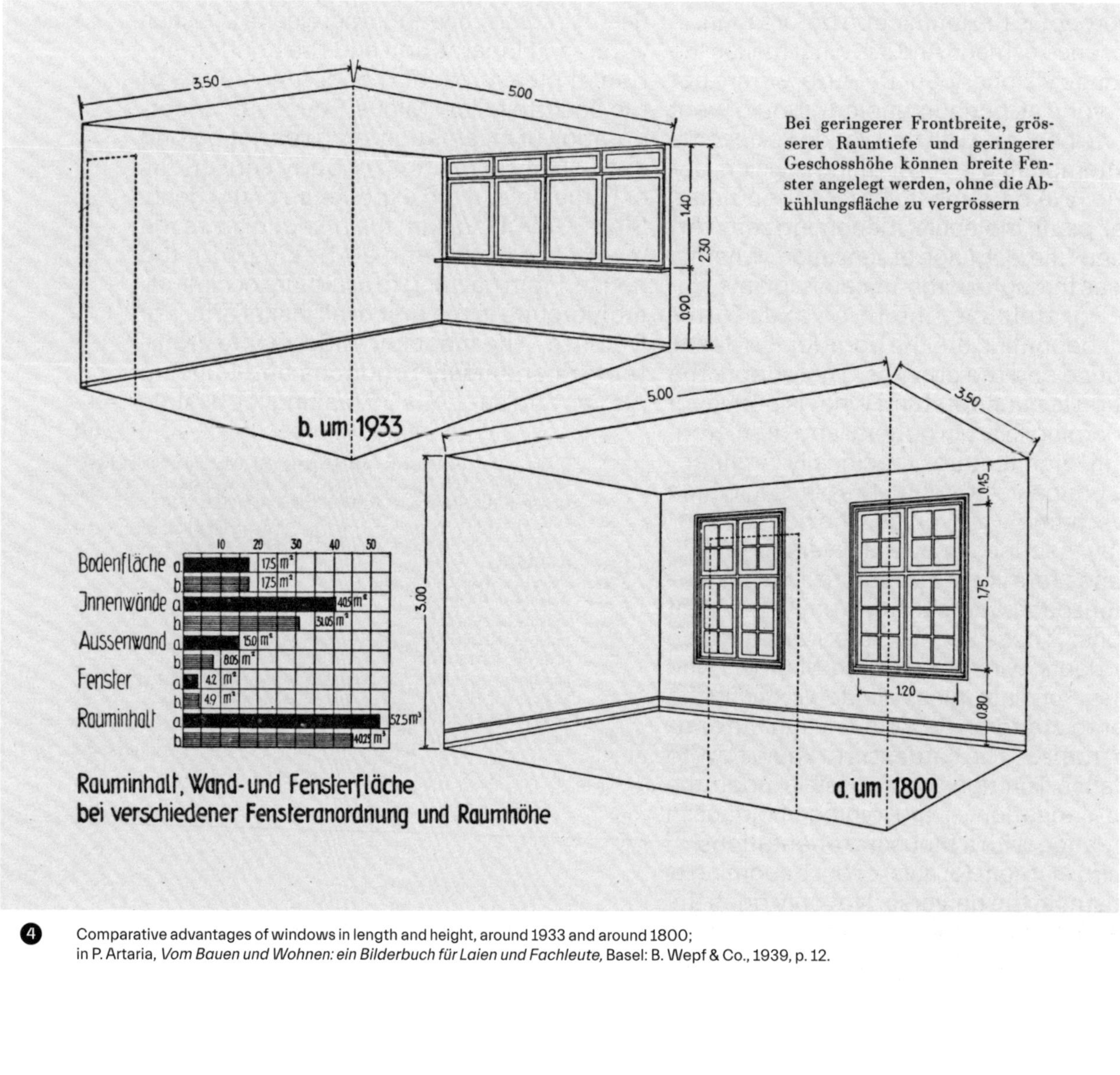


❹ Comparative advantages of windows in length and height, around 1933 and around 1800; in P. Artaria, *Vom Bauen und Wohnen: ein Bilderbuch für Laien und Fachleute,* Basel: B. Wepf & Co., 1939, p. 12.

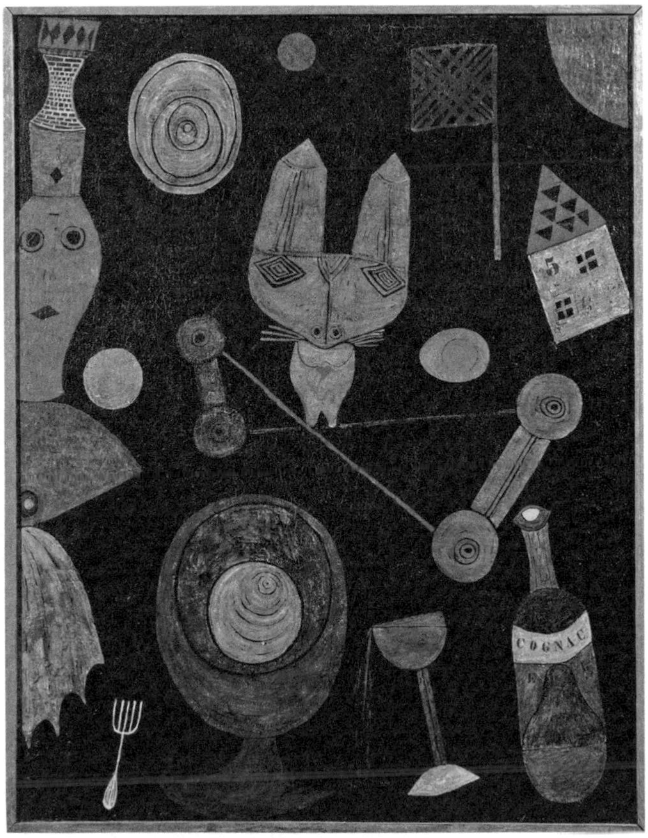


❺ Paul Klee, *Colourful Meal* (*Bunte Mahlzeit*), 1928, oil on wood, belonging to the Resor collection.

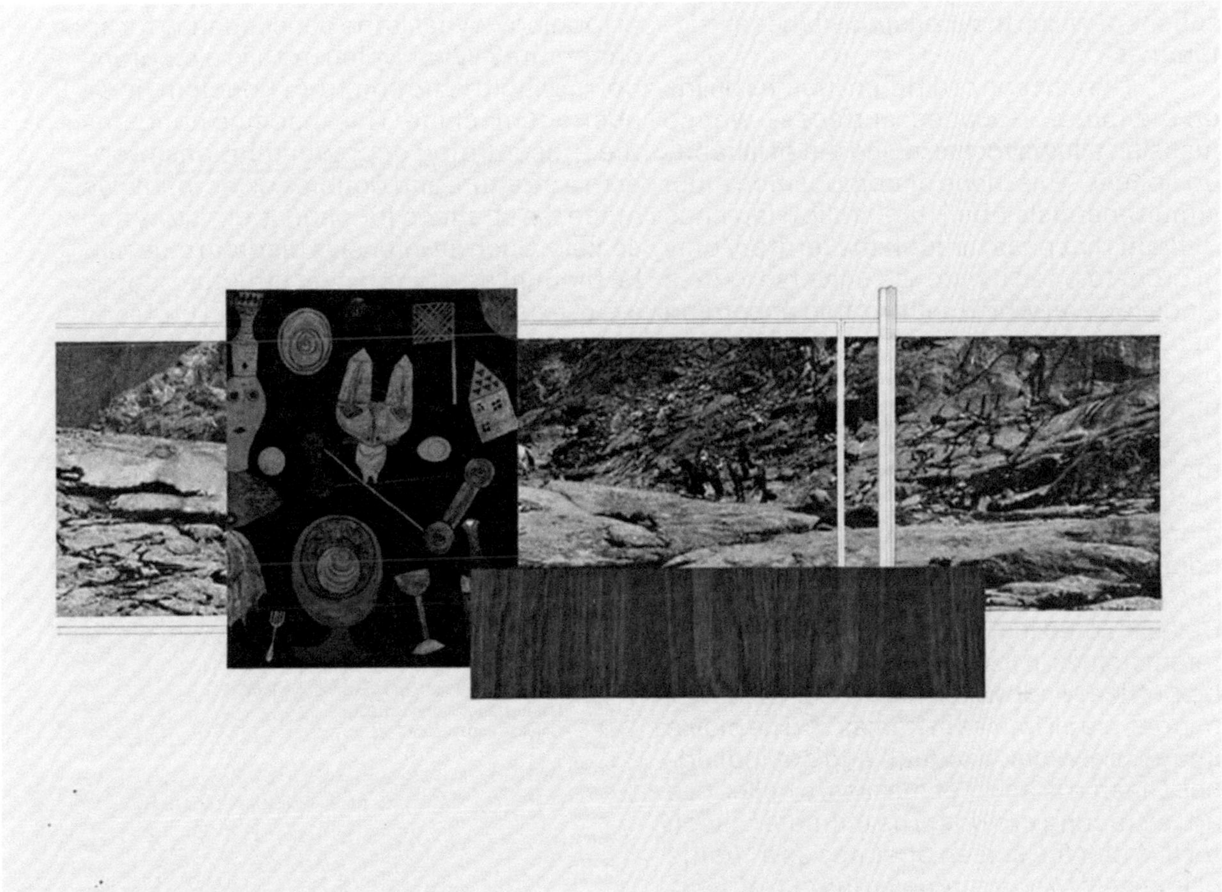

❻ L. Mies van der Rohe, *Living Room Collage, Landscape View*, one of the collages made between 1937 and 1939 for the design of Resor House on Snake River, WY.

to define the latter by "the 'frame', by an interlocking of differently oriented frames."[36] Henry van de Velde presented the prehistory of the painting as passing through the fresco in the frame of the wall, the stained-glass window in the frame of the window, the mosaic in the frame of the floor: "The *frame* is the umbilicus that ties the painting to the monument of which it is the reduction."[37] Citing Bernard Cache's *Terre Meuble* (1982), Deleuze enumerates enframing forms: "The wall that cuts off, the window that captures or selects, the ground-floor", letting corporal trajectories run wild, "the roof that envelops the place's singularity".[38] "Interlocking these frames or joining up all these planes—wall section, window section, floor section, slope section—is a composite system rich in points and counterpoints." Deleuze goes on: "The frame and their joins hold the compounds of sensations, holds up figures." Architecture is a compound of interlocked frames, offering various planes of sensation. Open/closed, up/down, front/back, inside/outside, manifest/hidden, soft/hard, hot/cold, opaque/transparent, full/empty, illuminated/obscure, straight/bent, intimate/extimate, nomadic/sedentary, smooth/striated. Deleuze adds: "Frames or sections are not [geometrical] coordinates" because "they belong to compounds of sensations of which they constitute faces and interfaces".[39]

The junction of different frames builds up the facets—facades, surfaces—whose massing allows for the laying out of inhabited spaces. This plane of composition must simultaneously open itself following lines of flight that pass through the territory only in order to open it onto the universe, onto a landscape on which vectors fold according to abstract lines. Following the enframing operation, a sort of *deframing*[40] must be operated. Deleuze draws his inspiration from Pascal Bonitzer's articles ("Cahiers du cinéma", 1978), highlighting new relationships between the "disjointed, crushed or fragmented" planes, thanks to which cinema becomes an art and by producing new affects.[41] In *Cinema. 1: The Movement Image* (1983), Deleuze noted that there are always many different frames in the frame: "Doors, windows, box-office windows, skylights, car windows, mirrors, are all frames in frames".[42] The movie image is always "dividual" and not individual. Cinema is an art of masses, a collective art, attracting crowds. The ultimate reason for it is that the screen operates as a "frame of frames."[43] And then comes the out-of-field. All framing determines an out-of-field.[44] So, as with painting, one must free oneself from the frame, disjoining planes by "a deframing power that opens it onto ... an infinite field of forces."[45] The artwork never stays within the frame. One could think of Fred Sandback's threadlike structures, Hans Haacke's, Piero Pascali's or Jan Dibbets' first pieces. There is indeed a plane of composition, a 'house'" made of interlocked frames. At the same time the plane of composition involves sensation in a deterritorialisation, a superior nomadic situation, "making it pass through a sort of deframing which opens it up and breaks it open onto an infinite cosmos."[46]

With the introduction of digital techniques, the project now addresses the status of the nomadic line, starting from Worringer's abstract northern line to that, inflected, of Klee, up to 2D/3D modelling splines. As defined by Deleuze (and Félix Guattari), the nomadic line circulates in an open and connected space (network or rhizome), becoming circulation and plastic transport. An extraordinarily thin topology is thus required—of the fog or mist type—which falls under smooth spaces. As an answer to the paradox of the exhaustion of genetic cycles it was proposed that three theoretical levels of complexity inspired by Deleuze's work would be introduced: thinking in terms of population (and not in terms of individual); thinking in terms of difference of intensity (thermodynamic and entropic); lastly, thinking in terms of topology. What is the consequence for architecture? What Deleuze calls a diagram, borrowing the notion from Foucault, is an abstract machine. This machine concerns the presentation of power relations proper to a stratum, and doubles on an intensive mode the stratified formations of history and society. Such an intensive diagram must not be thought as a permanent structure, nor as a pre-existing form, but as a virtual problem, a complex of forces. The diagram is not his-

36 Deleuze and Guattari, *What is Philosophy?*, p. 186.
37 H. van de Velde, *Déblaiement d'art*, Brussels, Imprimerie Monnom, 1894, followed by *Formules de la beauté architectonique moderne*, Brussels, Archives d'architecture moderne, 1979, p. 20, author's emphasis.
38 Deleuze and Guattari, p. 186.
39 Deleuze and Guattari, p. 186.
40 Deleuze and Guattari, p. 186.
41 Taken from: Pascal Bonitzer, *Peinture et Cinéma, Décadrages*, Paris, Cahiers du cinéma, 1985, 1987; Deleuze and Guattari, p. 187.
42 G. Deleuze, *Cinema 1: The Movement-Image*, trans. Hugh Tomlinson and Barbara Habberjam, Minneapolis, University of Minnesota Press, 1986, p. 14.
43 Deleuze, *Cinema 1: The Movement-Image*, p. 14.
44 Deleuze, *Cinema 1: The Movement-Image*, p. 16.
45 Deleuze and Guattari, p. 188.
46 Deleuze and Guattari, p. 188.

torical: it falls under becoming. Indivisible from its actualisation, the diagram is used for injecting “becoming” into all of the stratified reality’s points. The concept of diagram as an abstract machine permits to understand both the mechanical and biological reality of an institution, a device, or even a software program. The nomadic line henceforth adopts the model of the turbine and the fluid, taking into account a kinetic line. ■

# Space "in Itself": Notes on the Unfurnished Interior

Martin Steinmann

These notes were written following a conversation with the curators of the exhibition *Svizzera 240: House Tour.* The Volkshaus, where we sat around a small table, was packed and accordingly loud. I often understood only fragments of the discussion. The topic of the discussion—housing—is one I'm well acquainted with from my longterm engagement not only with its historical development in the nineteenth and twentieth centuries, but also with architectural design. For more than twenty years, I have focused mainly on teaching housing at the ETH Lausanne, from a point of view that I have only slowly come to regard as *phenomenological*. It is a type of design that values not only the feelings that the spaces and their characteristics arouse but their meanings as well. It seems to me that the exhibition is about these kinds of questions.

Serving as the starting point for these notes are photographs of recently constructed apartments. They document the current state of housing in Switzerland. The apartments are still unoccupied: there are no objects in the spaces, no people, nothing; they are simply spaces, empty spaces, with walls, doors, cabinets, windows. The ceilings are mostly white, even the baseboards; only the floors are made of wood or concrete—lending the rooms a certain realness—or, occasionally, a concrete ceiling or wooden window. Otherwise the photographs depict spaces in which emptiness—the nothingness between the walls—has, so to speak, solidified.

### Photographs

The photographs are taken in a way that gives the rooms the greatest possible sense of depth. There are few doors, or they are left open. This depth sets the eye—and, in a certain sense, us—in motion when viewing the photographs: space is, in the view of August Schmarsow, "a projection of the subject". Depth serves as its most important extension. "For the subject, it signifies the extent to which he can freely move around a given space, as necessary as looking ahead and walking."[1] The photographs remind me of the ball in Visconti's *Il Gattopardo* (1963), where the camera moves through the countless rooms of the palace in Palermo; only in that case, the rooms are full of people and voices while here they are empty and silent.

This empty space, what does it do? Does it promise that we can configure it however we like? That we can envision objects inside it—armchairs, for example, somewhere in the space? That we can imagine ourselves sitting in these armchairs? Does this space promise us freedom? Objects have a certain size, a certain function—an armchair offers a place to sit—a certain place. We can't just place it anywhere. It is part of a "geography". It's just that the empty space depicted in the photographs resembles Africa in the nineteenth century: a map with large blank spots. We don't have context to be able to envision where the chair goes. We know almost nothing. A door here or there, OK, but where do they lead to?

### Empty Space

Spaces serve purposes, for eating, for talking with one another, for reading, for watching TV, for sleeping. These activities are connected with objects that determine where they occur in the room. The relationship between objects and space is mutually interdependent. This what I mean by geography. Without objects, the room disappears from architecture. (Architecture is not free—it is grounded in functions, and objects are traces of functions.) So what is the *message*, what do the photographs *say* about empty spaces? One question contains another question, like with Russian dolls, namely: Who takes such photographs? Why don't they take photos of spaces with objects that provide a sense of meaning? Why do photographs of empty spaces appear in architectural magazines and on the architects' websites?

A recollection: fifty years ago, Dolf Schnebli remodeled a house for my parents in the Malcantone region. It's a good house; he wanted to publish photos of it but wasn't fond of the armchairs in the living room. The idea of photographing the spaces empty didn't occur to him; nobody was doing that at the time. Instead, his idea was to replace the armchairs and their English fabric with Eichenberger armchairs. (It was customary then to stage living spaces for photographs with the "right" objects, and maybe it still is. I'm thinking of the photographs of an apartment designed by EMI Architects—I'll come back to this later.) My parents did not like the idea and so the house was never published. →

1 A. Schmarsow, *Das Wesen der architektonischen Schöpfung*, Leipzig, Karl W. Hiersemann, 1894, p. 15–16.

This story offers a possible explanation for the empty spaces; unlike their renderings, architects have no say over how rooms are furnished, unless they happen to live in them themselves. As a rule, the objects do not reflect their ideas—or even the ways the rooms are inhabited—hence better to have spaces that are not yet compromised, empty spaces.

## Space "in Itself"?

But maybe it's about something entirely different. Maybe the armchairs that appeal to the architect even detract from the thing at stake, because this thing is the space "in itself", the nothingness between the walls. A.E. Brinckmann suggested making spaces imaginable by casting plaster models and turning them into physical forms. His goal was to provide a sense of "clarity regarding the effect of spaces" because it is easier to create a sense of sculptural form than it is of spatial form.[2] The attempt to grasp this nothingness is a futile one, I think, because the crucial thing is missing. We understand space only when we are part of it, or if something in it stands for us: a chair, for example, or the open umbrella Walter Mair used in his photograph of a flat.

Objects are signs, they signify how a space is used, whether or not that use is intended. They create a relationship between the space "in itself" and lived space. The space "in itself" is abstract; this is why it can only exist outside of architecture, as art. The empty spaces in the photographs are also unable to entirely rid themselves of a function: it is revealed—in addition to the doors—in handles, locks, hinges, switches, tracks, levers. An effort is often made to play down the reality that these components introduce as much as possible, via their white or gray or aluminium colour. So is it, in fact, about the space "in itself"? Are such photographs a means for capturing space in its ideal form, before reality—the occupant with his/her objects—takes possession of it? It would be the ideal form of a model made out of Forex, with white-sprayed figures providing scale.

These are assertions, this much is clear. But aren't they justified? Don't these photographs express a hidden longing that the viewer appreciate the space "in itself" as the real work of the architect? Objects inside an apartment are not part of this. The furnishings are the works—if you want to call them that—of the inhabitants. They allude to their life. They take the place of abstract space; they *are* the space, a different, concrete space determined by their actions. And that is more compelling than space "in itself". So let us consider photographs of inhabited spaces. Don't we see the objects in them before anything else, as traces of life, and of a particular mindset? Don't we see the Lehni bed as a sign of a "less is more" attitude, as the ads for this bed also suggest?

2 A. E. Brinckmann, *Plastik und Raum als Grundformen künstlerischer Gestaltung*, Munich, R. Piper & Co., 1922, p. 11.

### References

This brings us back to the house in Malcantone. For Schnebli, the—overly bourgeois?—armchairs did not match the spirit of *his* space. Let's consider a space that has been furnished by architects for the purpose of photographing it, inside the Avellana, a residential building designed by EMI Architects. The photographs don't really convey the impression that the objects therein are evidence of signs of life. They are references: for example, the Roth serving trolley, which also appears in a photo of another EMI-designed residential building. Thus, they bestow on the house certain connotations, akin to the way popular Moser chairs were used in a 1931 Wohnbedarf advertisement: liberated living.

In the photographs, time appears to stop; the spaces are like stage sets right after the curtain goes up. Something will happen momentarily—we are waiting for actors to enter and begin moving around the stage, giving it a sense of meaning through their actions. In the same way, actions also give an apartment meaning. Actions are typically associated with objects, and objects with locations. I repeat this is how they structure movements within the spaces. But how should one move around empty spaces? There are no instructions, for example, like those provided by a table that you have to manoeuvre around. But without movement, I assert tentatively, there is no space.

### How to Live?

Do empty rooms refer to the fact that architects shouldn't tell people how to live, as Peter Märkli asserts? This is not the case in housing, because architects don't know how people will inhabit the spaces. Maybe they'll only bring along a few items, perhaps many. Maybe they'll bring along a Casiers Standard, perhaps a baroque cabinet. The apartment should allow for both possibilities. Their appropriation of the space requires leeway. Even if they can't know, architects should still have an idea of how spaces are used and thus furnished. Without this understanding, designing an apartment isn't possible. It is not about the type of chair, but about the fact that objects in an apartment have certain places, out of necessity, and that the apartment must provide such places.

Paul Frankl was largely responsible for incorporating categories of function, space and movement into a single system. In his view, the shape that space takes is necessarily the result of the function it is intended to serve: "Formed space is thought of as the setting of specific actions. These actions define the very basis of perception. After this image has been reinterpreted into a representation of a ... space, it is possible to derive what function the whole serves from the form of the space, thus ... arriving at the meaning of the whole."[3] The function determines the movements of those acting within the space, but the form is the means for producing movements that correspond to the function.[4] Accordingly, Frankl writes that the function is the soul of the space. In his view—like Schmarsow's—dwelling is the true task of architecture. →

3 P. T. Frankl, *Die Entwicklungsphasen der neueren Baukunst*, Leipzig & Berlin, Teubner, 1914, p. 14–15.
4 P. T. Frankl, 'Raum und Zweck', *Die Raumkunst*, Vol. 11, 1908, p. 174.

## "Furnishings"

Space is therefore not defined solely by form: "The meaning of a space arises only through furnishing ...".[5] Frankl's remark seems to be a truism, because the "furnishings"—chairs, tables, armchairs and so on—are the signs of the function that a room serves. But they are also the end goal of movements: the table where the newspaper lies, the armchair where I read the newspaper; they give the space a functional structure by superimposing on the order of the walls an order of objects. This second order corresponds to the adapting of a space as both a functional and formal interpretation of its characteristics.

In this sense, dwelling means interpreting spaces via certain actions and their associated objects. It's just that empty spaces in photographs have no dimensions, so reading them—the way I'm using the word here—can only be done via objects which, in terms of shape and size, stand for the people who live with them. The openness that photographs claim turns out to be an illusion. Even a simple kitchen table and chair would provide the human scale needed to be able to adapt these spaces in the imagination. Many photographs deny this scale.

## Materials

The impression that we are dealing with space "in itself" is also owed to the colour white: it covers all walls indiscriminately. Functional elements such as light switches are also typically white, and seem as devoid of materiality as the walls. Only the floors provide a sense of their material; they are made of wood, or sometimes of concrete. The material injects a bit of reality into this empty space. And a bit of meaning: as a sign, it alludes to spaces where we've previously seen it used. It recalls the fields of thin strips of wood in our memories of cooperative flats of the 1950s. This defines the meaning of this material and the atmosphere of the space where it is installed.

The flooring thus becomes the haven of a design style that used to apply to all parts of a room. Just think of wallpaper that would set the tone for a space and its particular function. Or colour: in Goethe's house in Weimar, every room had its own colour, as was usual in 1800. So, for example, the breakfast room was painted a linden green as fresh as an early morning. Even in the limitations of the white space, however, material can be used to indicate different things, for example, when wood and the colour white are used to distinguish between doors and their function. Other materials also come to mind. In the apartments of the bourgeoisie, the door between dining and living rooms was typically glazed and designed to be pushed open, double-leafed, reminiscent of a theatre curtain. This not only means that the door itself is meaningful, but the way we open it is, as well.

5 Frankl, 'Raum und Zweck', p. 81.

Dimensions

This type of door is, of course, wider than 80cm. This brings me to another way of distinguishing the meaning of things in an apartment, even prior to any appropriation: their dimensions. In the case of a door, this means height and width. Our bodies give us a refined sense for the scale of things: certain dimensions are "normal" and others are not. Architecture has always taken advantage of this *physical* impression to create a response—just think of tall and heavy doors whose purpose is to intimidate. But let's stay with our apartments, which serve no social rituals anymore. Bedroom doors, a good 2m high and 80cm wide, we perceive as normal; doors for toilets or storage rooms can be narrower, doors to living rooms wider. And so they create a hierarchy of meanings expressed in how things relate to our bodies.

The spaces configured inside the Swiss Pavilion for the 2018 Biennale—abstract, like in some of the photographs—address this physical relationship to things; through smaller or larger shifts in scale, viewers are made aware of how matter-of-factly they register changes in what they perceive as "normal". The body has a gauge for deviations that are under or above, and these are loaded with feelings. A 3.5m door is not just tall, it is, as noted above, intimidating. This effect also depends on its material: a door painted white is less intimidating than a door made of oak or even bronze. But why would anyone coat such a massive door in white paint? Only someone who understands nothing of the fundamentals of architecture could do such a thing.

No normal apartment has rooms this height. Here the windows and doors within the 2.4m-high spaces provide a sense of scale that the title of the exhibition *Svizzera 240* alludes to. But it is an effective means for characterising these spaces, even before the objects do this in their own way, through the impressions they invoke as form—not as sign. In other words, these spaces reference one, two fundamental means of architecture—but only if the deviation from the 1:1 scale applies equally to all parts of a space. Thus, through differentiation, the exhibition avoids providing the—implied—apartments a geography that fits within the parameters that housing offers. But how could they? These aren't rooms in which people live, these are installations in which our perception of so typical a matter as an apartment should be made conscious for us: the sensations, and the consequent meanings, that the dimensions of the room call forth from us. And this brings them into the domain of art. ■

# Contemporary Swiss Housing: The Space Experiment

Christophe Joud
Lorraine Beaudoin

*To sleep, to wash, to cook, to eat, to meet…* Everyday housing is, first and foremost, a question of habits, whose most basic formula—rooms enclosed by walls and connected by doors—says nothing of the importance of what architects like to call *space*. Under the constraint of bureaucratic norms, industrial standards and housing shortages, "space" may seem to allow too little movement to be promising as a field of innovation; for most people in most places, experiments in the distribution of space probably remain an esoteric architectural topic. Against this general trend, mainstream Swiss architecture has placed spatial questions at the centre of housing, starting with its German-speaking regions, which have benefitted from an economic prosperity that reward ambition. Made of shadow and light, projection and depth, space has revealed its ability to generate sensation. Contemporary images of Swiss interiors provide evidence of an ongoing exploration, constantly renewing the capacity of domestic space to both connect and separate. Without marginalising the question of use—quite the contrary—this contemporary imagery unveils an investigative field where human scale gives singular influence to the most minute adjustment and slightest detail.

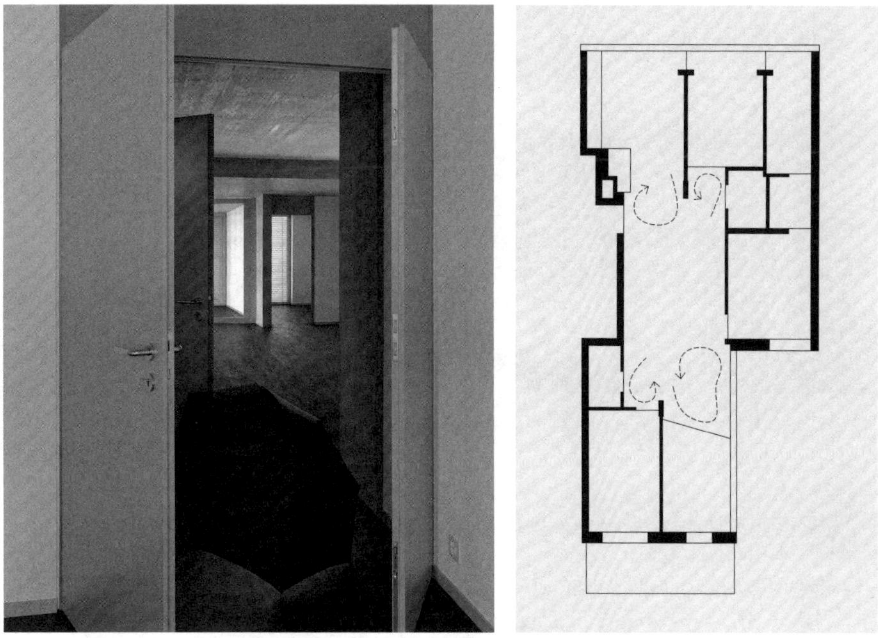

❶ The architects create irregularities to shape spaces for idiosyncratic use. Lutjens Padmanabhan, Herdernstrasse Apartments, Zurich, 2011–2016. Photo: Walter Mair, drawing: authors

> [...] every corner in a house,
> every angle in a room,
> every inch of secluded space
> in which we like to hide,
> or withdraw into ourselves,
> is a symbol of solitude
> for the imagination; that is to say,
> it is the germ of a room,
> or of a house.[1]
> —Gaston Bachelard

### 1. Angle, nook, alcove, interstice: places for immobility

*Place* comes first, and the idea has been rediscovered that creating it does not necessarily require its strict delimitation. This intuition may be responsible for the popularity of a type of plan much explored in recent decades, in which the dwelling's more social functions—kitchen, dining room, living room—form a continuum meandering between closed boxes—rooms, bathroom, loggia. These boxes participate in the space's subtle narrowing and dilatations which, without dividing the social functions into rooms, will nonetheless identify them with places. The first degree is the so-called bayonet plan, where a continuous open space consists of two main areas unaligned with each other; the simple shift provides both connection and separation. A higher degree of complexity appears when the open space develops a thinner constellation of niches and nooks integrating the entrance and bedroom hallway; the open space becomes a fluid space.

This new type abandons the formula of "space = room" and implies that the functions of living do not require strict limits to exist other than, perhaps, an out-of-the-way ending space, an invitation to settle. Pushing this intuition further, current plans attempt to shape spaces for idiosyncratic use. Lütjens Padmanabhan's interior views ❶ of the Herdernstrasse building in Zurich suggestively contain an umbrella and a guitar, to evoke the coincidences of everyday life. Through details such as the rooms' protruding "bay window" walls or abnormally skewed partitions, architects create irregularities that must be adapted to, but that also stimulate the evolution of domestic life. →

1 G. Bachelard, *The Poetics of Space*, trans. M. Jolas *[La poétique de l'espace 1958]*, Beacon Press, Boston, 1994, p. 136.

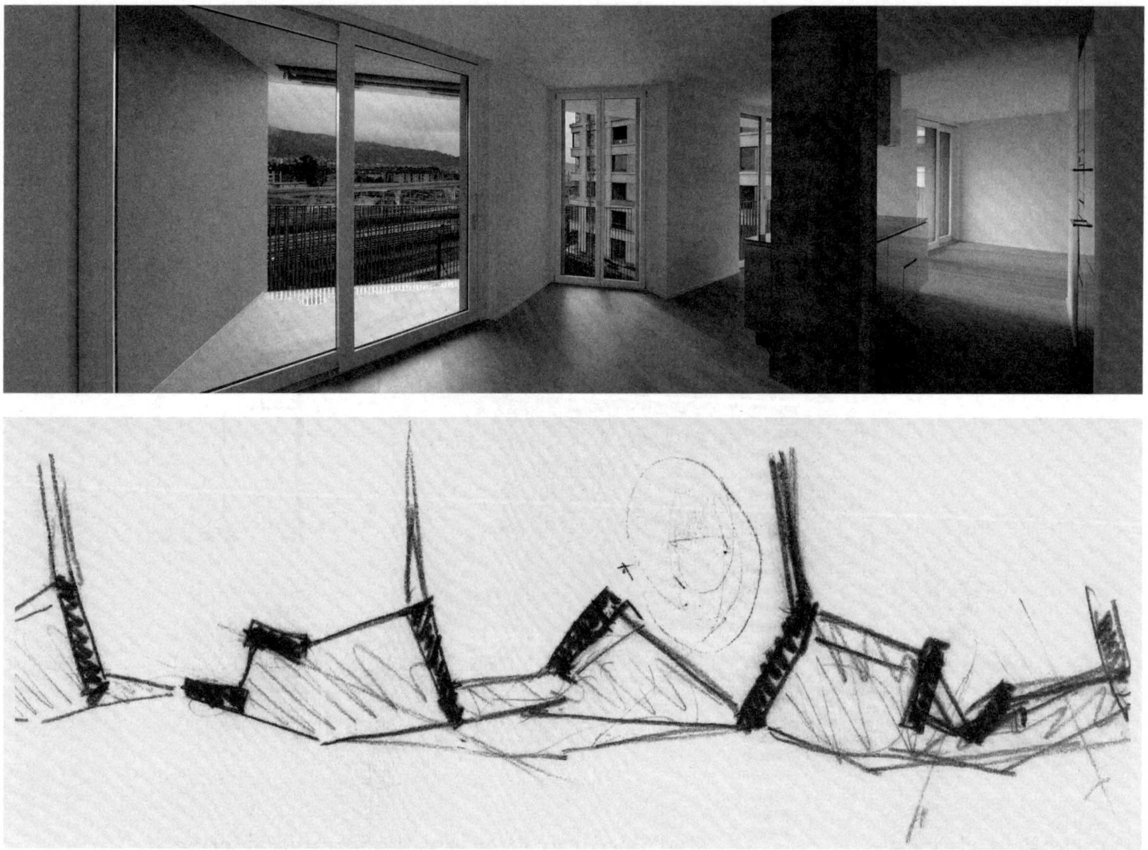

❷ Meili Peter, House A, City West Zurich, 2009–2014.
Photo: Walter Mair, drawing: Meili Peter

More recently, architects' experiments with geometrical distortion has liberated further possibilities, enriching the apartment's main living space with new protrusions and recesses. In City West's A buildings ❷, Meili Peter architects have designed a facade that shears at several angles, its twists and turns creating niches whose purpose is deliberately left open to interpretation. In these niches, one can imagine one's own reading spot, looking out onto the urban landscape, or simply a corner from which to reflect upon one's living space; in these niches, one extracts oneself from the centre, sitting outside the dining-room space, yet not quite inside that of the living room.

Such fluid plans are not the only way to achieve spatial continuity. They constitute the first step of a wider ambition to go beyond the open plan, where one finds precisely defined spaces that nevertheless possess the quality of an open ensemble. The solution to this paradox proceeds from a geometry that allows for a reconsideration of both the shape of rooms and their interconnections, as shown on the plan developed by Esch Sintzel for a development in Bern's Schönberg Ost district ❸. The architects offer a system of rooms that are assembled through angles to a central room whose chamfers highlight the diagonal relations. The centrifugal logic produces a radiating structure that is strengthened by the generous openings, making it possible to simultaneously see into several spaces. So, without suppressing partitions, the plan manages to make it possible both to appreciate the apartment's depth and to experience it as a whole.

## 2. Depth, perspective, opening, enfilade: the opening of the gaze

An attitude characterises the interior views architects present: leaving doors ajar, with a glimpse from one space to the other, as if to exhibit the width of the dwelling. In these images, the living space is not fully disclosed; rather, what is celebrated is the succession of interlocking plans, evidence of a complex interior that above all draws on the spatial relations enabled by the typologies.

As Meili Peter demonstrated with the Zypressenstrasse apartments ❹, there are many ways to conquer space through the gaze, even in the orthogonal plan. To the extent that the Zypressenstrasse apartments were to be inserted into the regular pattern of an existing industrial structure, Meili Peter chose to thwart the frontal aspect of the crossing "tube" by organising the apartments in a quincunx, S-shaped formation, so as

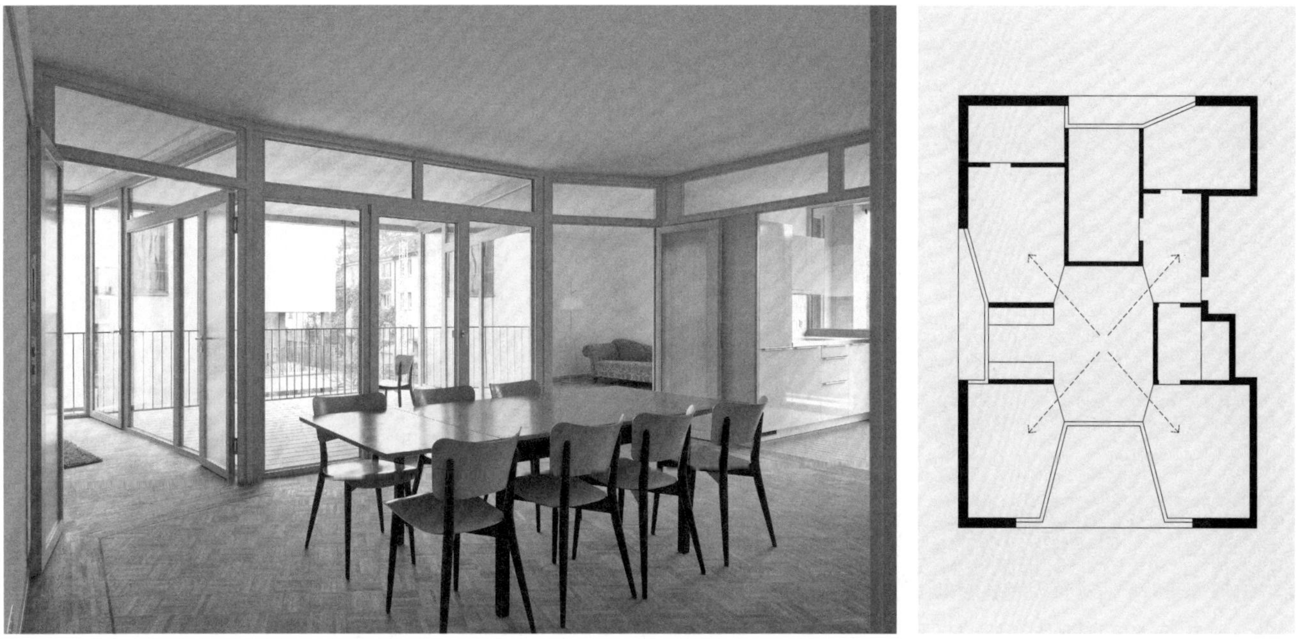

3 The centrifugal logic makes it possible to see into several places simultaneously.
Esch Sintzel, Schönberg-Ost Apartment Buildings Schönberg-Ost, Bern, 2010–2014.
Photo: Hannes Henz, drawing: authors

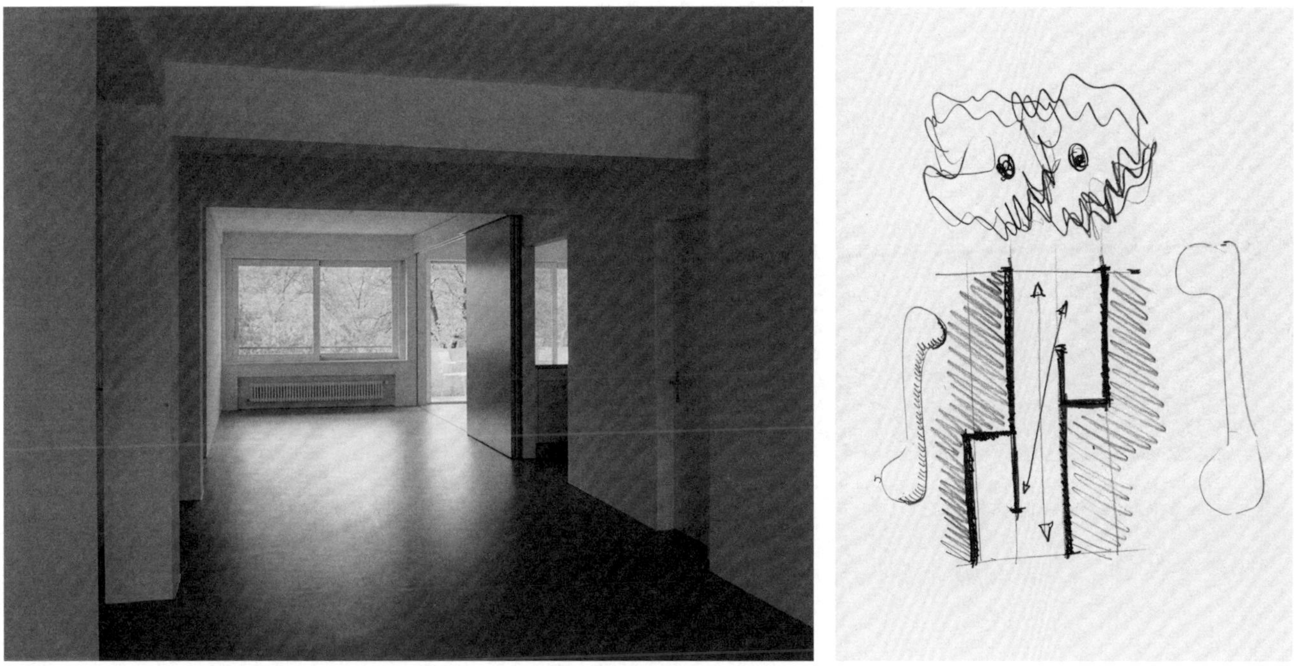

4 Meili Peter, Studio and Apartment House Zypressenstrasse, Zurich, 1994–1997.
Photo: © Heinrich Helfenstein; gta Archiv / ETH Zürich, Archiv Heinrich Helfenstein, drawing: Meili Peter

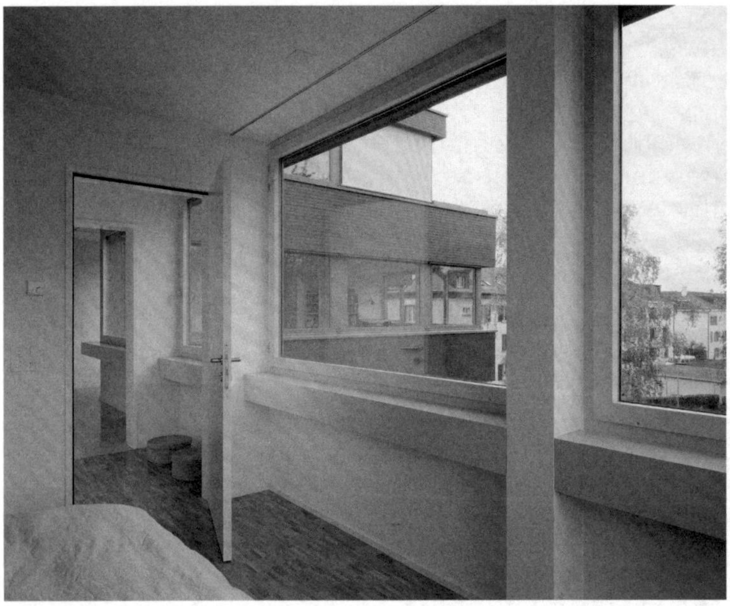

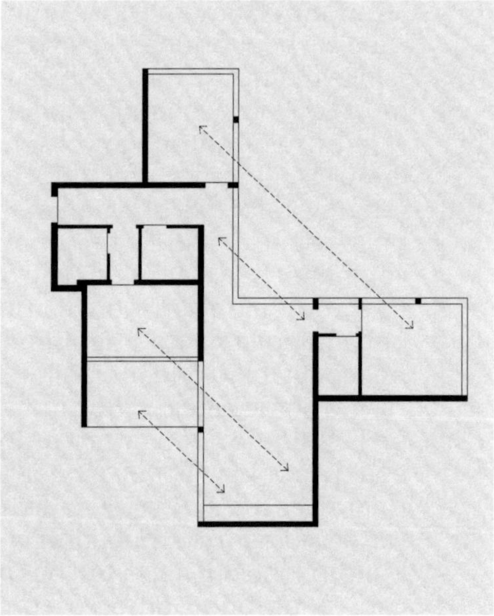

❺ Seeing part of the inhabited space from another part.
Adrian Streich, Lienihof Apartments, Zurich-Wollishofen, 2004–2007.
Photo: Adrian Streich, drawing: authors

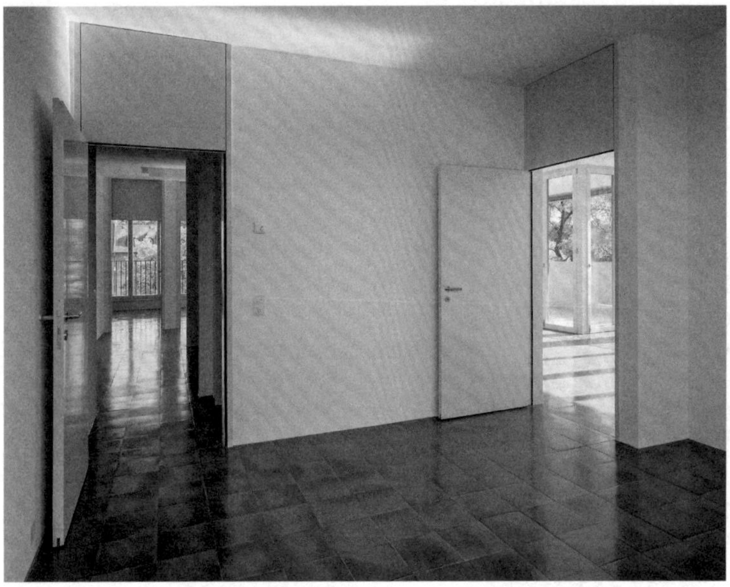

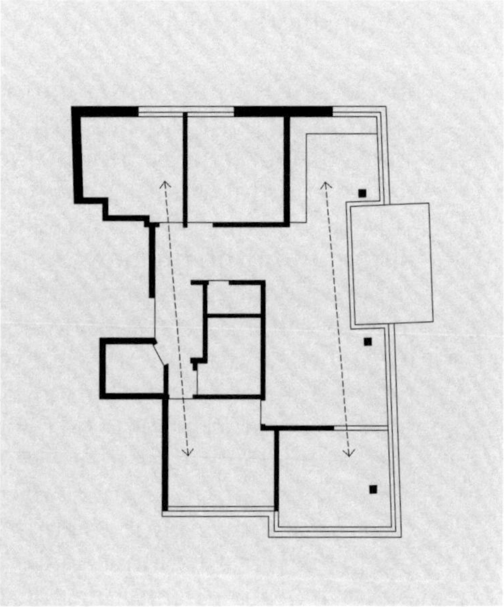

❻ Peter Märkli with Gody Kühnis, Hohlstrasse Apartments, Zurich, 2001–2005.
Photo: Roger Frei, drawing: authors

to create a diagonal dynamic. The elaboration of openings then comes into play, a permeability arises thanks to interior windows and sliding doors placed along the facades in order to favour oblique views.

Other attempts at maximising space go as far as placing the apartment on a reflex angle, so as to put the resident in the unusual situation of seeing part of the inhabited space from another part, through the facade. Adrian Streich's Lienihof housing development in Zurich-Wollishofen ❺ is a remarkable example:although organised in rigorous orthogonals,the apartments are arranged around the building's articulation points so as to repeatedly glimpse into each other. At the same time, the facade's modulation increases the interface between interior and exterior, and one experiences both inside and outside through the long horizontal windows' panoramic openings. The notion of depth here reaches a kind of climax.

In this pursuit of transparency and openness, one can glimpse the risk of producing a space that is more like a museum diorama than a home, too exposed for domesticity or comfort. Gradations of privacy, or thresholds, remain of paramount impor-

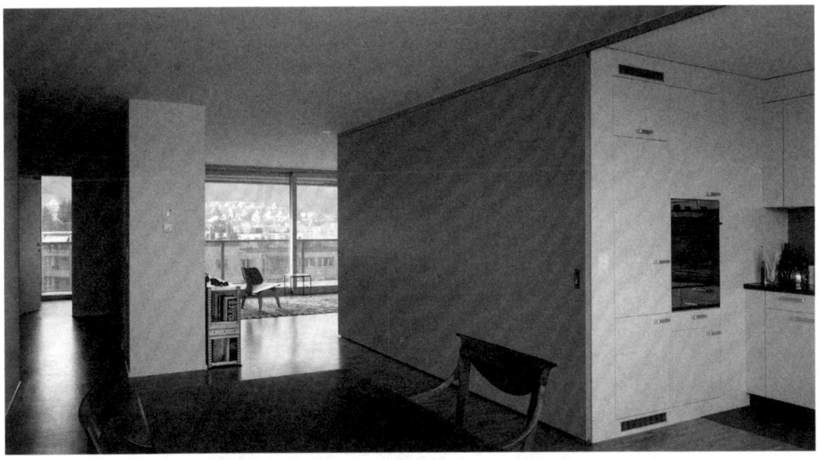
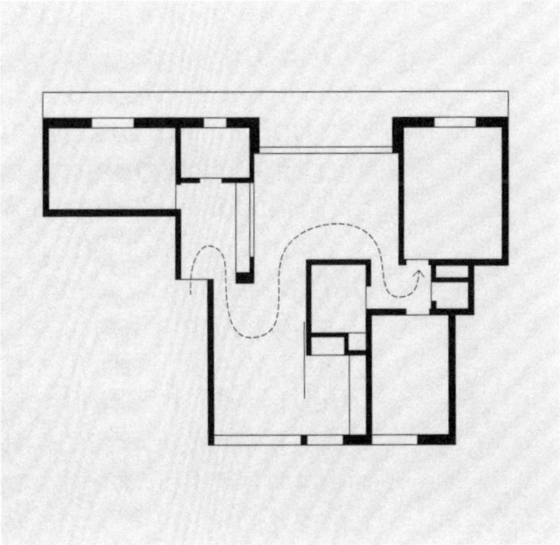

7 Sinuosity brings astounding amplitude to the experience of the gaze.
Baumann Roserens, A-Park Housing Complex, Zurich-Albisrieden, 2003–2008.
Photo: Andrea Helbling, drawing: authors

tance between the private and public spaces of the dwelling, and imply working on nuances, as well as typology. Peter Märkli explored this problem in the Hohlstrasse lodgings 6, as Barbara Wiskemann notes: "The interior spaces of the apartments are organised into sequences of opposing spaces: dark to light, compressed to open, etc. ... Along these windows, an open sequence of kitchen, balcony, living and corner rooms create a spectacular, albeit difficult to furnish, space. The architects describe the interior space as a topography of functionally undefined zones with varying degrees of privacy and openness."[2] The domestic spaces Märkli imagined establish favourable conditions for different degrees of privacy, without regimenting their use — a way of letting ambience suggest habitation.

## 3. Passage, detour, loop, meander: the space of movement

The emphasis on space also renews attention to the choreography of motion, and produces a remarkable range of gestures. A function in its own right, traditionally embodied by the corridor, circulation now tends to dissolve itself across the open space, giving it a new freedom.

This evolution started with the rise in the popularity of "core" typology in which circulation is distributed around a box—sometimes several boxes, usually including bathrooms—arranged in the plan. Although this type of plan is traditional in that it devotes some floor space to circulation, it also introduces new possibilities for continuous circulation by eliminating dead ends and widening the range of possible paths. Furthermore, thanks to the diffusion of light in such "unblocked" space, the atmosphere of the corridor improves.

It is only through the blurring of the separation of housing's diurnal and nocturnal functions that the corridor can dilute itself across the inhabitable surface. A singular situation results where static and circulatory spaces should blend but not interfere with each other. Baumann Roserens architects have remarkably resolved this difficulty in the plans they conceived for the A-Park project in Zurich-Albisrieden 7, where interior floor plans send us on a slalom-like route, successively from one facade to another. By revealing new spaces with each turn, sinuosity brings astounding amplitude to the experience of the gaze, while at the same time keeping the body at the centre of the plan, thus limiting the distance that has to be crossed. Instead of placing a monotonous linear corridor at the centre, the architects used a simple geometrical plan to give movement a shape. →

2 B. Wiskemann, 'Der Städtebau an der Ecke', *Werk, Bauen + Wohnen*, no. 10, 2006, p. 27.

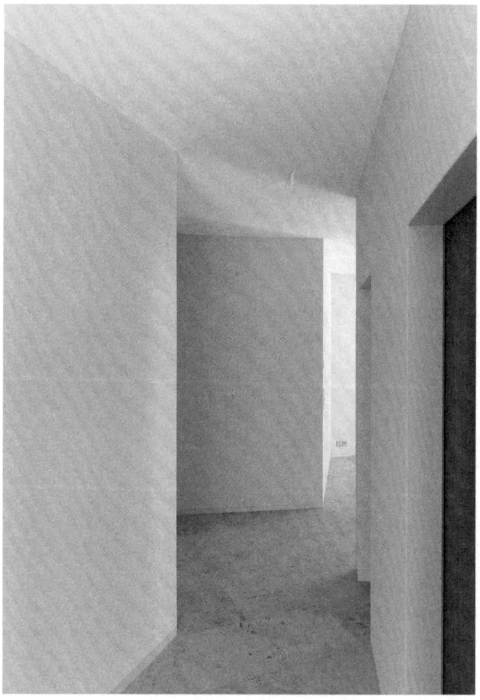

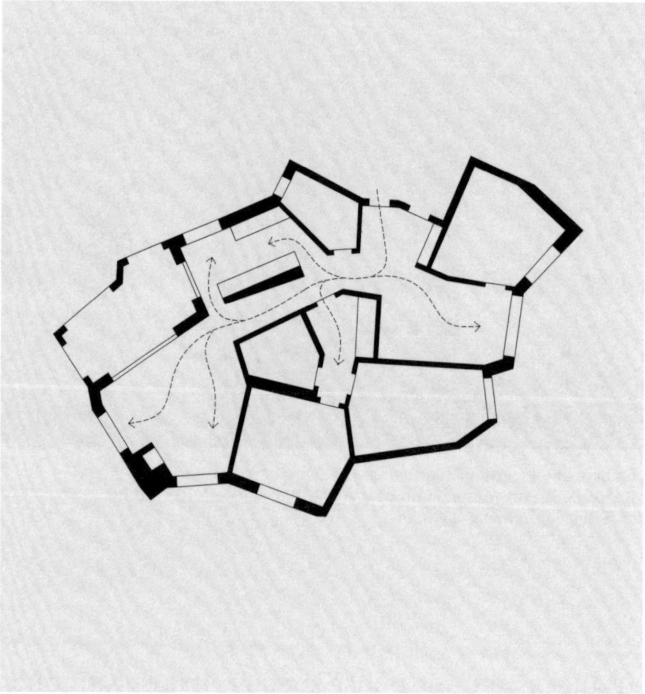

8 Within such meanders, one finds one's way only through the act of moving.
Edelaar Mosayebi Inderbitzin, Steinwies-/Irisstrasse Apartments, Zurich-Hottingen, 2011–2015.
Photo: Roland Bernath, drawing: authors

It has, however, become rare for a path through an apartment to lead us merely from one point to the other; the current trend is to try to develop the dynamic possibilities of motion. The multiplication of doors is an indication; it is quite common for a bedroom or even bathroom nowadays to have two doors, and offer itself as a space to be crossed, creating a loop that includes closed rooms. This fascination with alternatives clearly serves the desire to diversify the experience of movement in and through the apartment.

The Zurich-Hottingen project 8 by Edelaar Mosayebi Inderbitzin (EMI) suggests a fragmentation of distributive space by obstructing the view of the path the body will take, and by otherwise breaking up the feeling of continuity. The division of the dwelling's social functions in four rooms—kitchen, dining room, living room and loggia—all the same size as the bedrooms, creates the sensation of a profusion of spaces without hierarchy, which is already favourable to a certain confusion. Geometrical deformation then enhances this entanglement that architects define as "open" shape: "Like natural form, shaped by growth and decay, marked by constant change, it is distinguished by an 'unstable' state. It thematises time, and hence movement." [3] "Open" here means to free oneself from regular geometric shapes and to let the plan develop in accordance with surrounding constraints. If fluidity of movement results from obtuse angles and from the kinking of partitions, space is perceptible only in fragments, remaining hard to comprehend as a whole. Within such meanders, one finds one's way only through the act of moving. As in previous examples, movement is thematised here, but it takes on another value, beyond pragmatism: "It is no longer a matter of finding but of losing oneself." [4]

3 C. M. Inderbitzin, 'Model and Image', *Trans,* no. 19, 2011, p. 86–91.
4 On the same topic see: L. Beaudoin: 'Couloir: L'espace du mouvement' in C. Joud (ed.), *A l'intérieur: Les espaces domestiques du logement collectif suisse,* Cahiers de théorie, no. 13, Lausanne, PPUR, 2016, p. 43–59.

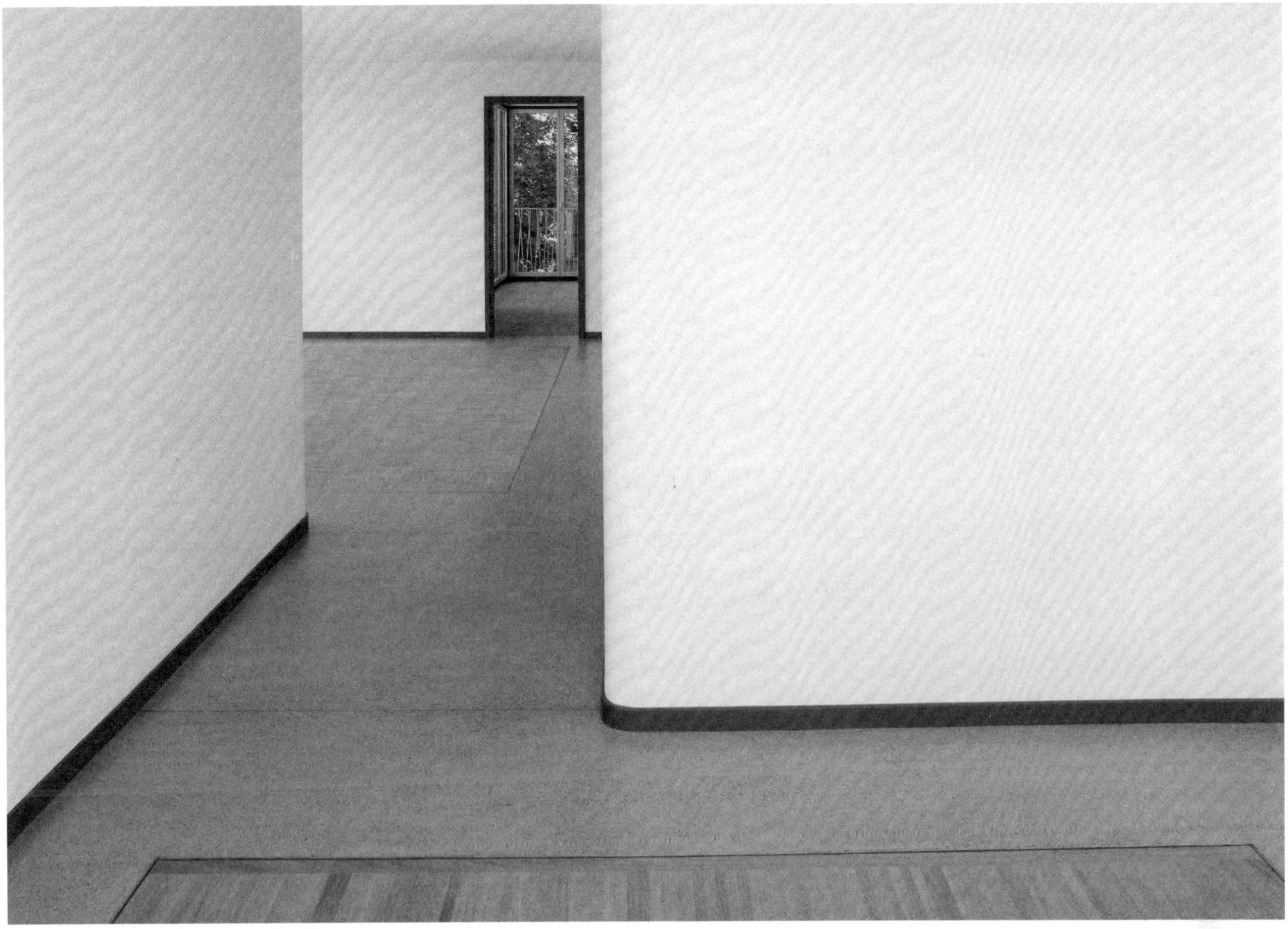

9 Loeliger Strub, Felix & Regula Apartments, Zurich, 2008–2012.
Photo: Francesca Giovanelli

### 4. Contour, frieze, threshold, frame: space for details

Be it in the materiality of floors, experimental expressive motifs, or carefully drawn carpentry details, these contemporary domestic interiors give architectural details pride of place, and thus go against a vision of neutrality as a supposed facilitator of use that was considered, until recently, common sense. Of course, it is easy to see here the appeal of decor, a way of reviving a splendour inherited from bourgeois interiors, at a time when the rise of the privative sphere was contributing to the development of domesticity. However, one can also argue in favour of this spatial exploration.

For instance, in the Felix & Regula buildings in Zurich 9, Loeliger Strub explored the effects of underlining. The eye is drawn to a thin black plinth that underlines the contour of each room, and even the frames of each doorway. This abstract line weaves from one space to the other persisting in our vision's different planes, so that it emphasises the feeling of spatial continuity. A frieze made of concrete completes the drawing of the floor plan, and delineates a wooden floor island at the centre of each room. The frieze even illustrates the thresholds between one room and the other thanks to overlapping walls with rounded corners that accentuate the feeling of fluidity. The architects evidently sought to highlight elements capable of expressing the apartment's spatial principles by drawing onto the floor precise places to settle, while suggesting the continuity of space.

→

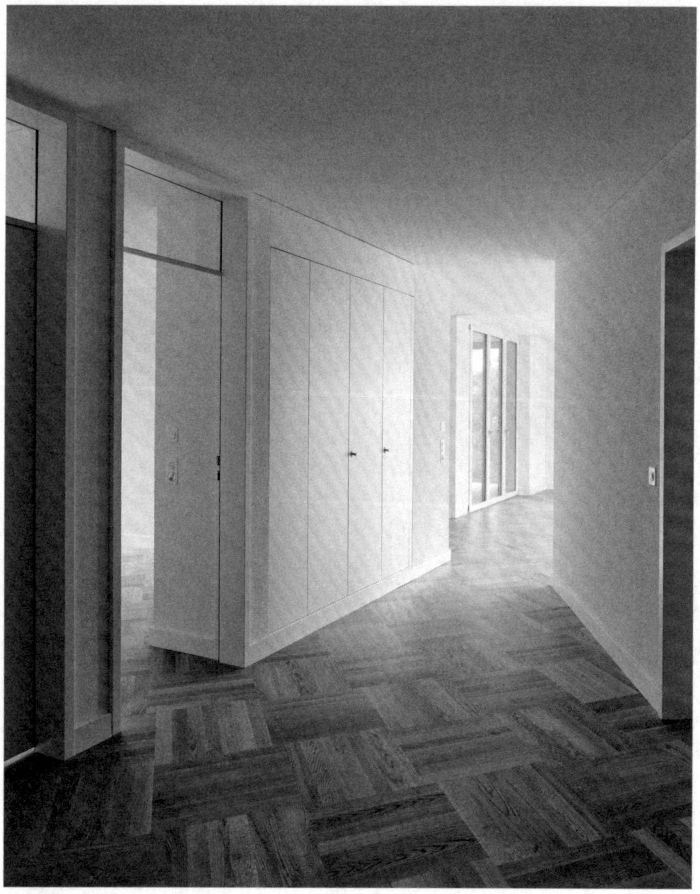

⑩ Edelaar Mosayebi Inderbitzin, Katzenbach IV, Zurich-Seebach, 2012–2015. Photo: Roland Bernath

The physical duality of the dwelling—opening and closing, mobile and immobile—invites us to look more closely at the subject of the door. As the apartment's mobile limits, doors permit us to act on the degree and nature of communication between spaces. Work on the doors' proportions allows for the establishment of a hierarchy, the pregnancy of which can be modulated through work on detail. Amongst the architects thematically rethinking the door are EMI, who consider the door to be, first and foremost, a "visual-scale landmark in space",[5] an "anthropomorphous" landmark at the scale of the body; that is to say, one that is capable of strongly inflecting a space's characteristics and the sense of privacy resulting from them. In EMI's Am Katzenbach IV building in Zurich-Seebach ⑩, the photograph of an apartment taken from the entrance shows the hierarchy—which has become quite common—they have established between access to utility rooms and to living spaces. Indeed, the rooms' high doors with transoms clearly contrast with the ordinary dimensions of doors opening onto wet-rooms. In addition, the absence of thresholds and the wooden floor's continuity reinforces the feeling of porosity already suggested by the light going through the imposts and into the corridor. The doors do not express privacy as dramatically as might have been familiar in the past, as a kind of hermetic withdrawal; but they do demonstrate how details may transform a room.

5 E. Mosayebi and C. M. Inderbitzin, 'La porte, une échelle de l'habitat', *matières*, no. 13, 2016, p. 86–97.

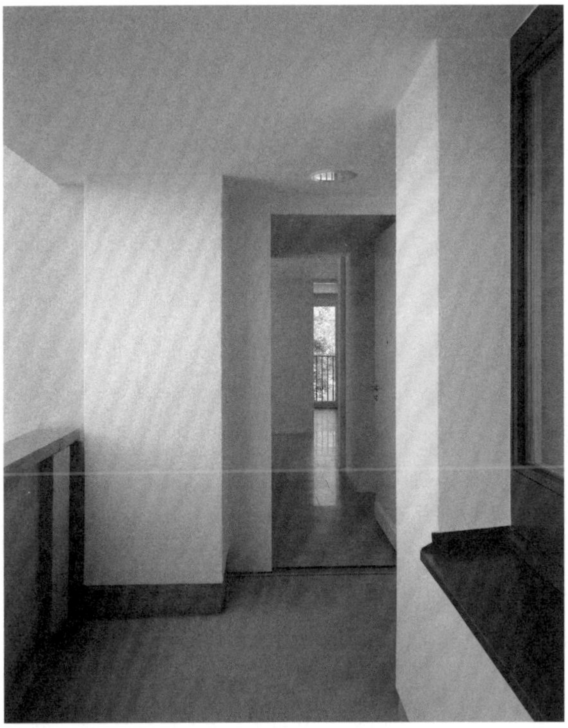

(11) Peter Märkli, Gutstrasse Housing Cooperative, Zurich, 2010–2015. Photo: Walter Mair

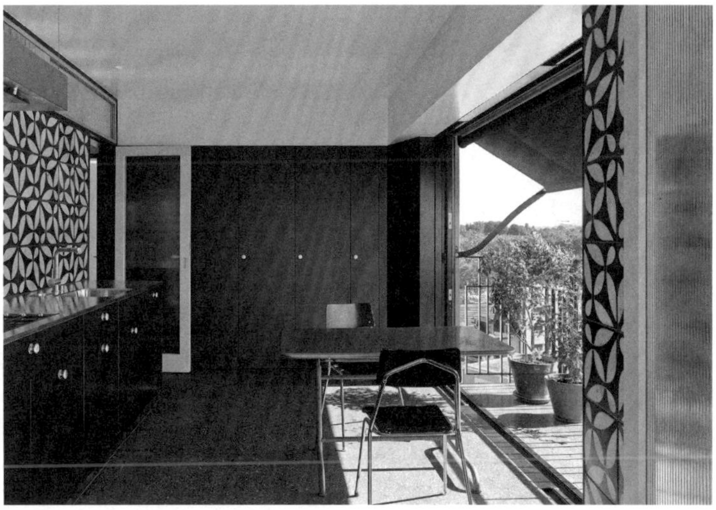

(12) Loeliger Strub, Hohes Haus West, Zurich, 2009–2013. Photo: Roland Bernath

## 5. Landing-vestibule, entrance-veranda, balcony-fireplace, kitchen-loggia: usage outside limits

> As the heart of the plan of each apartment is a void—the openness of the main living space.The smaller rooms are set around its edges… And across from the entrance is a window, so if you leave the door open and know how to use the hall, you can increase the space of your apartment.[6]

In this description of his design for a building in the Gutstrasse in Zurich (11), Peter Märkli refers to twisting the landing into a spare corner of the apartment, which can be used beyond its own limits. The extension of the inhabited space exceeds usage, since it is for everyone to imagine what it could ultimately become.

Granting spatial quality primacy over the standard determination of function ultimately permits an enrichment of the question of usage, giving us the possibility to rethink use in a more free way. With this in mind, one notices that the apartment's extensions are subject to designations taken from the lexicon of the house: the veranda, oriel windows, pergola, porch, etc. These precise domestic gestures allow for a diversification of the ambience in the social spaces and bring the atmosphere a little closer to that of a picturesque garden.

In Zurich's city centre, the Weststrasse highrise building (12) designed by Loeliger Strub illustrates this phenomenon. The architects explain:

> The rather restricted space conditions on the Weststrasse inspired us to build something à la Hohes Haus West. Thanks to the windows gliding sideways into the window frames, the kitchen can be turned into a veranda when it's sunny, and into a little aromatic garden-like balcony.[7]

→

6 P. Johnston (ed.), *Peter Märkli: Everything One Invents is True*, Lucerne, Quart Architektur, 2017, p. 187–193.

7 Loeliger Strub, 'Ganze Tage in den Bäumen', 2017, http://loeligerstrub.ch/gallery/ganze-tage-in-den-baeumen/, (accessed on 28 February 2018).

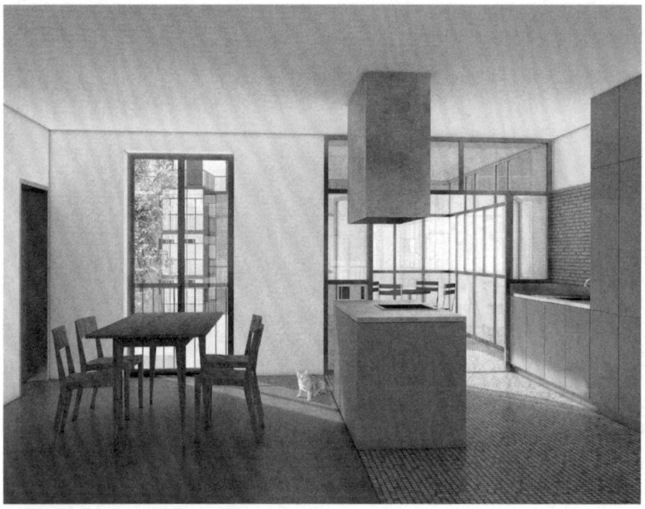

⓭ Knapkiewicz & Fickert, Im Stückler, Zurich-Altstetten, Competition, 2011. Rendering: Knapkiewicz & Fickert

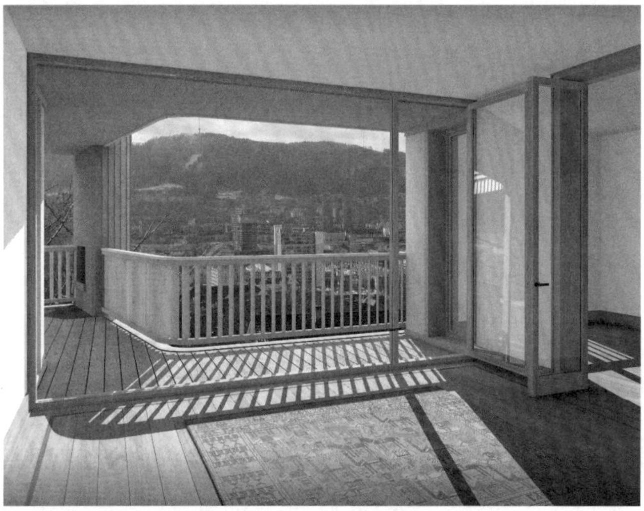

⓮ Edelmann Krell, Tièchestrasse, Zurich, Competition, 2010. Rendering: Edelmann Krell

The architects also speak about a *Kochloggia*, a kitchen-loggia, that transforms the functionalist image of the kitchen into a domestic room closer to the comfort of a garden terrace, with the patio door disappearing into the walls. Its atmosphere is based on details: black polished concrete screed is reminiscent of a soil floor, while earthenware walls and awning blinds evoke a holiday resort.

Should we take it that the traditional balcony and loggia are now obsolete? Seemingly under pressure from the interior space, contemporary balconies are progressively undermining the inside/outside binary traditionally determined by the facade's plane. Thanks to hybrid systems, a facade's cavities or projections develop into fully fledged exterior rooms able to influence the morphology or composition of the building. Closing elements are reconsidered through their capacity to manage proximity and relations to neighbours.

Knapkiewicz & Fickert give the veranda a twist in the Im Stückler housing development in Zurich-Altstetten ⓭. The veranda is a device one would rather imagine at floor level, but is here placed vertically in a surprising superposition. In addition to the evocation of a certain comfort, a warmth specific to the dwelling, the veranda is conceived as a spare room—a dining room projected into the courtyard—and acts as a filter softening the outlook onto the opposite building, thanks to a glazed-tile design.

In the Tièchestrasse project by Edelmann Krell ⓮, it is the hearth that is taken outside the limits of the apartment, acting as a structural column to a balcony that has become a balcony-fireplace. On one side it offers a wall corner away from prying eyes; on the other, it shapes a prodigious angle emerging from the building like a ship's prow.

### The Open-Up Experiment

Our five suggested themes treat the dwelling as a physical object designating and exploring space. This is not intended to marginalise the functional aspect—rather, it means that the trend is to manipulate space and its sensitive properties to create opportunities that usage will then take and implement. Working on space de facto encourages reflection on space occupation by giving the chance to project onto it different moments of domestic life—little satellite actions kept out of space's conventional schedule.

The opening up of the lexical field, essential to describing the diversity of potential interiors, points to a decompartmentalisation of traditional typological schemas. It has become standard procedure to blend several devices, to superimpose different ambiences, or to twist together references borrowed from history. This experience of an architectural "as well as"—present in all current practice—highlights the fact that Swiss housing escapes any univocal tendencies, other than that of experimentation along which new qualities are forever to be found, and which we call the constant opening-up.

Spatial emphasis and the quality of detail may build a sense of opulence, implying the coming of a new bourgeois habitat that we would perhaps only imagine as possible in a favourable economic context. There is no question that the intense typological exploration of recent years first appeared in the microcosm of German-speaking Switzerland; Zurich was the pioneer city due to architectural design competitions, exemplary property, and social policies through which architects gained an expansion of inhabitable surfaces; an abundance allowing for true work on space. All the same, the unavoidable focus on density makes ground optimisation a constant consideration, threatening a reduction of area that may reduce flexibility and, in the long run, diminish the emulation and elaboration of current ideas. Be that as it may, in the light of the opening up of domestic culture in the past decade, and the interest manifested by architects regarding innovations in housing, we remain confident in architecture's ongoing capacity to continuously adapt itself to new circumstances. ■

# The Cornice (A Recent History)

Emma Jones

In 1809, the Prussian architect Karl Friedrich Schinkel was asked to design a bedchamber for Queen Louise. ❶ The image he presented of the scheme contained, amongst other romantic fancies, a startling feature: an elaborate interior cornice capping the walls, festooned with owls taking flight, holding rings in their mouths on which the draperies were suspended to encircle her bed. The gilded cornice ran around the tops of the walls on all sides, and was brought substantially forward of the junction between wall and ceiling, not only to hide it, but also to allow the birds' wings to cast looming shadows across the receding gap behind. With this single interior detail, Schinkel introduced into the room the perceptual possibility of spatial extension; that is, the ceiling, as the plane hidden from view, seemed to possess the potential to extend infinitely beyond the confines of the walls, as if taking on the appearance of a dawn sky under which the queen might regally awake. Exposed to this endless sky, the queen's bed suddenly appears in the image as an object in a game of inversion, in which the room is as exposed as the public square; and the walls that enclose her appear as building facades topped, in classical fashion, by their customary cornices.

What Schinkel had manufactured through illusion was case of *Ortsversetzung* (imaginative transport); a characteristic aspiration of the art of his age that was to enjoy immense popularity in Prussia as the nineteenth century wore on. Its full emergence was to coincide with the increased state policing of public life after the withdrawal of Napoleon's troops from Berlin, aided by the

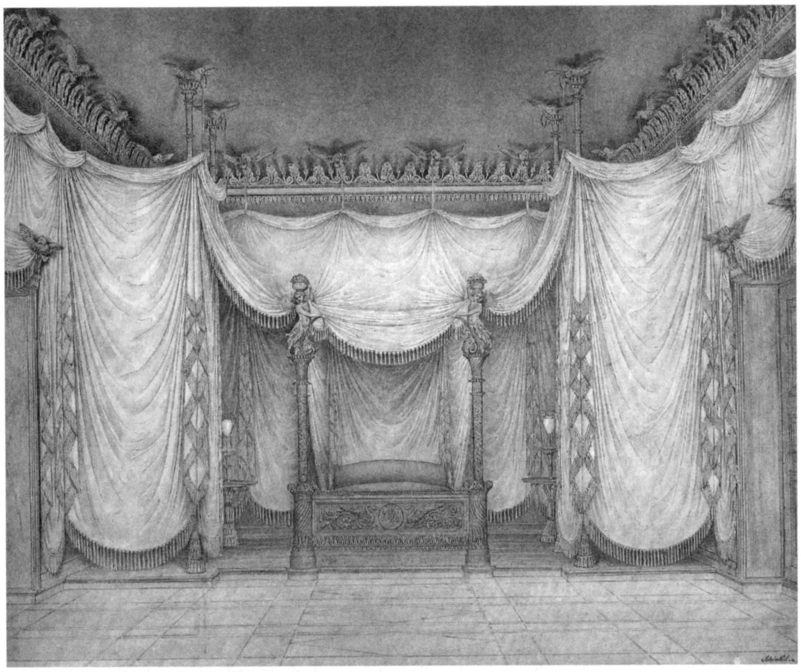

1 K. F. Schinkel, *Bedroom of Queen Louise in Schloss Charlottenburg*, 1809, ink and aquarell, 36 × 51 cm. Prussian Palaces and Gardens Foundation (SPSG), Schloss Charlottenburg, Inv. C.20a.

1814–15 Congress of Vienna peace talks. The Prussian monarchy was pressured by Austria at these negotiations to introduce a series of reactionary censorship and surveillance measures designed to control expressions of individualism and German nationalism in the population.[1] The practice of Ortsversetzung consequently responded to this state-imposed censorship of civic life by transforming the bourgeois Biedermeier interior into an idealised microstate: a fantastic, expansive realm of individual freedom. The illusions that created this interior *Gemütlichkeit* were spun largely in the interiors of either the theatre or the home, and were part of an overriding sentiment of withdrawal from public life, as both aristocracy and bourgeoisie were united in the aspiration to turn inward to the private sphere.[2] The same period was marked by a new restraint in the outward face of Berlin's public buildings, in stark contrast to the demonstrative ornamentation of earlier Baroque facades. Schinkel himself participated in this turn toward simple public architecture even as he continued, paradoxically, to play the fantasist in his designs for interiors.

Schinkel's identification of Queen Louise as the conduit for this interior escapism was no accident. She was not just Prussia's most beloved public figure, a patriotic symbol of moral fortitude, courage and grace in the face of French occupation; but also an active stateswoman who had pleaded with Napoleon, while in exile, for the restoration of Prussian peace. She and her husband were finally allowed to return to Schloss Charlottenburg in 1809, and Schinkel's design for her new bedchamber was rumoured to be in response to Napoleon's desecration of the royal palace; he had supposedly even slept in her bed. In keeping with Louise's status as a public heroine, Schinkel would thus, in a metaphorical sense, turn her private body "outward" through the inversion of her most intimate of rooms into a public square—though his design would never be executed. Queen Louise died only a year later, becoming nearly deified by her →

1 See R. Waissenberger (ed.), *Vienna in the Biedermeier Era: 1815–1848*, New York, Rizzoli, 1986.

2 Freyja Hartzell, 'Otherworldy Worldliness: Romantic Fantasy and Modernistic Desire in Schinkel's Berlin', *Centropa*, vol. 10, no. 2, May 2010, p. 80–105.

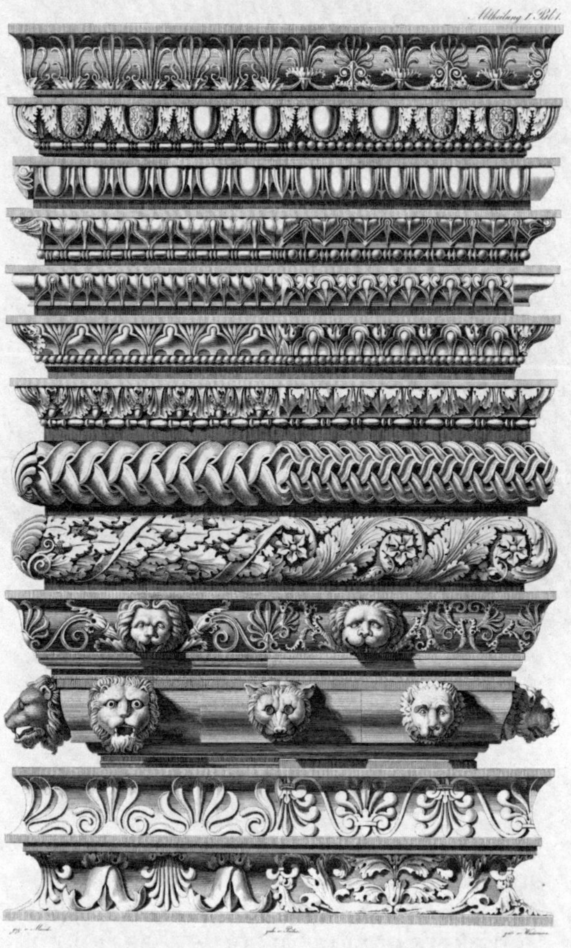

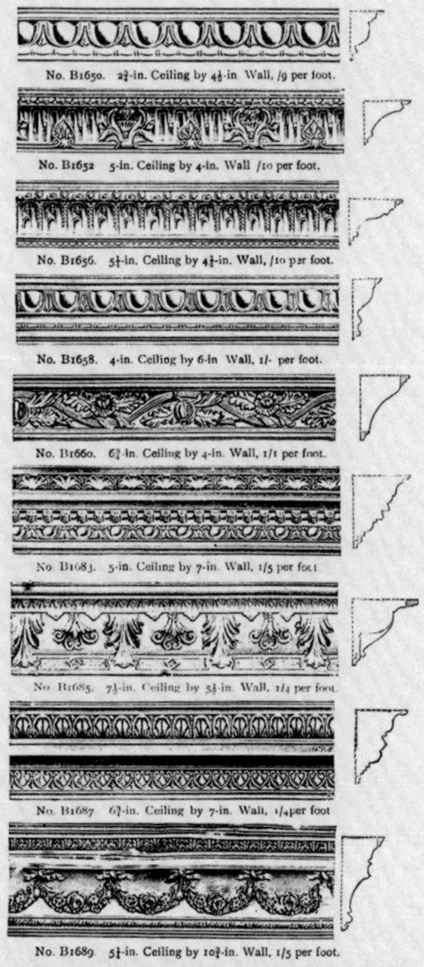


❷ Plate from *Vorbilder für Fabrikanten und Handwerker*, published by the Technische Deputation für Gewerbe (Schinkel and Beuth), 1821–1830. Part 1, Section 1, Plate 1: Examples of architectural cornices drawn from antique structures. Karl Friedrich Schinkel, inventor; Johann Mathäus Mauch, draftsman; A. Wachsmann, engraver; A. Prêtre, printer. Copperplate engraving and etching on vélin paper. Kupferstichkabinett, Staatliche Museen zu Berlin.

❸ Cornices to be ordered by the row: Young and Marten's Building Catalogue, 1898.

people as a symbol of heroic Prussian resistance. Schinkel's bedroom for Queen Louise expresses the idea of the interior becoming a sanctuary against a hostile civic life precisely through imitating it. It does so by using one particularly powerful, ubiquitous piece of ornamentation: the cornice (in German, *das Gesims*). His choice of accentuating the cornice in this interior is a pointed one, as its effect is that of repurposing the external visual language of the classical facade. In classical architecture, the cornice is an external moulding forming one of three principal members of the classical entablature, above the frieze and architrave. Crystallised and abstracted into pure decorative stone in Greece, the cornice nevertheless contains the visual traces of an original timber structure that would have served to throw rainwater off the face of a building. Because of its adherence to strict proportional rules, the cornice is an essential "finishing" to a building's outward presentation, a crowning feature without which the predefined proportional relationships of each part of the whole cannot work. By the eighteenth century, particularly in France, the cornice in this strict definition had been incorporated along with other emblematic classical profiles into a strict system of rules to be learnt by rote, on which the student or practising architect could rely when needing to imbue his building with a classical "correctness" of character. Yet despite the rather academic treatment of such profiles in architectural circles, the definition of the cornice nonetheless continued to expand from the Renaissance onwards to eventually refer to any horizontal continuous moulding that forms the projected crowning feature at the top of a wall, internal or external, or other architectural element—a door, window or pedestal. Taking advantage of this expanded definition in the popular sense, Schinkel toys with historic associations of the cornice as an intrusive feature into civic space in order to recast his interior in a new light.

The cornice Schinkel drew for Queen Louise was, naturally, a bespoke design. Yet the architect had by no means ignored what the future might hold for the manufacture of such items. In 1821 he edited, along with his friend, Prussian industrial statesman Peter Wilhelm Beuth, the first of a series of publications called *Vorbilder für Fabrikanten und Handwerker* (*Patterns for Manufacturers and Craftsmen*). ❷ The publication contained a series of illustrated plates for household items and interior decorations designed by Schinkel, like vases, picture frames, furniture and cornices. The aim of the handbook was not only to recognise the future industrialisation of the building trade as inevitable and even welcome, but also to affirm the role of the architect as creator of the design models that would best serve these processes. Schinkel's plates were therefore intended to be exemplars that could be copied by manufacturers, providing a minimum common standard accessible to the middle classes.

During Schinkel's career as an architect, Prussia did not yet have to contend with the processes of industrialisation that would eventually cause both the mass deskilling of the European manufacturing workforce, and a new and unprecedented demand for the supply of goods, including building materials. Yet having visited England in 1826, then the most industrialised country in the world, he had seen first-hand the extent to which building quality could suffer under the push toward mass-manufacture. In response, Schinkel intended his *Vorbilder* as a means of reaffirming some kind of quality control under the capitalist regime that would soon reach Prussia. He never lived to see this onslaught happen, nor, perhaps mercifully, to see his ideal of the architect as supreme creator of mass-produced models resolutely fail to materialise. He died in 1841, just before Berlin's full but belated induction into the industrial revolution that had begun eighty years earlier in England.

Indeed, for the cornice's induction into commonplace use—with the architect nowhere in sight—it is England we have to thank. The interior cornice has existed as long as builders have puzzled over how wall and ceiling should meet. The mass-produced cornice, on the other hand, is unequivocally connected to early industrialisation processes in England, to speculation, to the rise of the bourgeoisie and to the proliferation of suburban mass-housing to accommodate them. Early nineteenth century London saw—before the rest of Europe—the rise of the mercantile classes, political freedom and decentralisation, laissez-faire economic conditions and lax land-use laws. Speculators took advantage of these conditions, building rows upon rows of identical suburban homes to accommodate the growing moneyed middle classes. Demand for housing was so great that developers began to hire a cheap, unskilled workforce to meet it. Previously untrained in their trade, these workers relied on a new type of practical publication—the building manual—to learn quickly on the building site. The nineteenth century saw the explosion of the building manual in Europe; not only as a result of this large-scale development, but also due to the increasing affordability of publication, and new image-printing techniques and equipment, like steam presses and lithography. Rapidly increased literacy, which occurred quickly in England after the Education Act of 1870, was also a factor in their popularity. These building manuals were different from earlier wholistic pattern books of generic house designs, like J.B. Papworth's popular *Rural Residences, Consisting of a Series of Designs for Cottages, Small Villas and Other Buildings with Observations on Landscape Gardening* (1818).[3] Directed more at potential clients than builders, these earlier publications did not offer technical information and were not specialised or trade-specific like the later manuals were. →

3 Papworth's *Rural Residences* was exported across Europe as an example of fashionable "English-style dwelling", becoming especially popular in Prussia and other Germanic states.

In the new suburban developments, standardised decorative elements were used both inside and out to give houses a recognisable cultural currency. This gave rise to the "workaday cornice": fast, cheap, standardised and ready to be installed in the rooms of every developer-constructed home across the London suburbs. The medium that suited this decorative standardisation best was the building manual, which offered up the cornice not as symbol of the classical ideal, but of the ordinary. Such books of "shop knowledge" were not directed at architects or their aristocratic clients, but rather were written by craftsmen for craftsmen, and occasionally amateurs. Such building manuals became responsible for taking building knowledge out from under the protection of the guild system and making it freely accessible in books.

By the 1870s the suburbs around London had expanded to huge estates, and to cope with this volume of work the building trade shifted from using local materials and components made on site, to cheap off-site manufacture and imported goods. To the building manual could now be added the subgenre of the trade catalogue: a document allowing builders to order ready-made components to be assembled on site by unskilled workers. Young and Marten's popular 1898 catalogue of building samples ❸ contains, for example, rows of premoulded cornices to be ordered and fixed into place on site. In line with the increasing division of labour in the building trades and the emergence of factory-built components, information on specifications, prices, as well as specific product types and brands, were usually given in these catalogues for the aid of the builder.

One of the most popular manuals of the era is William Millar's *Plastering Plain and Decorative* (1897); ❹–❿ covering all aspects of the preparation and installation of plaster mouldings and finishes, it was disseminated widely throughout the trades and contributed greatly to the standardisation and normalisation of decorative elements, particularly the cornice. The manual reads as an extended general builder's specification document. It describes how to formulate different kinds of plaster; apply them to different foundation structures, like meetings between walls and ceilings, or casings for steelwork; and form decorative mouldings to cast plaster elements to ideal proportions and designs. Alongside text and diagrams, profiles and decorations are occasionally drawn at full scale to allow direct transference onto plaster elements or moulds. Details for nearly every ceiling condition are given.

A plasterer all his life, and a member of the National Association of Operative Plasterers—his membership is proudly displayed on the frontispiece to the volume, signalling his authority as author—Millar was no scholar, yet *Plastering Plain and Decorative* remains one of the most successful architectural books of all time. From the end of the nineteenth century to the present day, it has never been out of print—the most recent edition emerged in 2009—and has thus been responsible in large part for transforming domestic landscapes across the English-speaking world. The manual was exported to Britain's colonies, providing a blueprint for construction in line with the English model on the remotest of sites with the most rudimentary knowledge and tools. Its current use extends to preservation, repair and copying of plaster decorative elements in domestic restoration work, and it is used in distant locations like Australia to determine the correct plaster-repair techniques and patterns for Victorian-era housing stock.

By the end of the Victorian period, when Millar wrote his manual, there were vast numbers of small- to medium-sized detached, semi-detached and terraced houses on the outskirts of British cities that externally appeared homogenous, but inside could exhibit an almost infinite range of combinations of standardised details. This served to give the aspirational middle-class homeowner the "personal style" and individual character they were after, albeit with a limited budget. Houses like these could be built in an endless parade of interchangeable eclectic styles taken directly from house-building manuals: from Italianate to Elizabethan, Old English to Scottish Baronial, or French Gothic.

Millar's manual distinguishes itself from others in the genre, however, by an unusual section on the history of the plaster trade. It begins as early as Greek and Roman antiquity, proceeds to the rediscovery of the ancient technique of stucco-duro by Raphael in Nero's Golden House, and ends with a description of contemporary applications of lime-making processes and how they differ from those techniques described by Vitruvius. Millar, with the assistance of historian George Robinson, traced in this fashion an alternative history of architecture through material and technique. He also offered an inventory of plaster mouldings and profiles used in different historical periods, assembled comparatively on the page and thus able to be copied and reused in easy fashion. On a single plate, it thus becomes possible to trace the migration of cornice profiles from classical ruins to popular commerce; their forms reduced, refined and standardised until

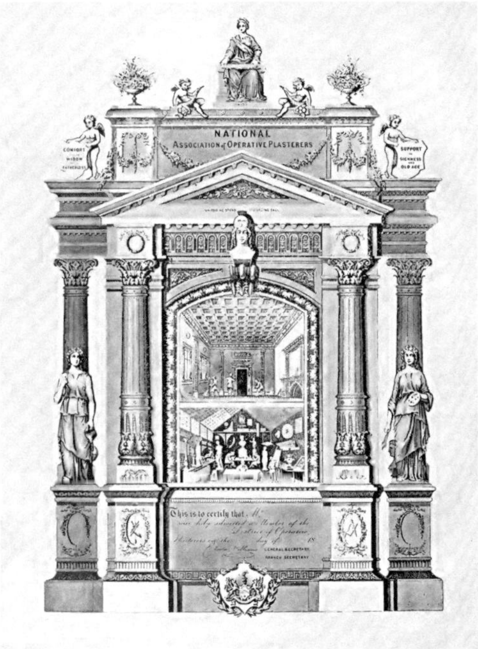


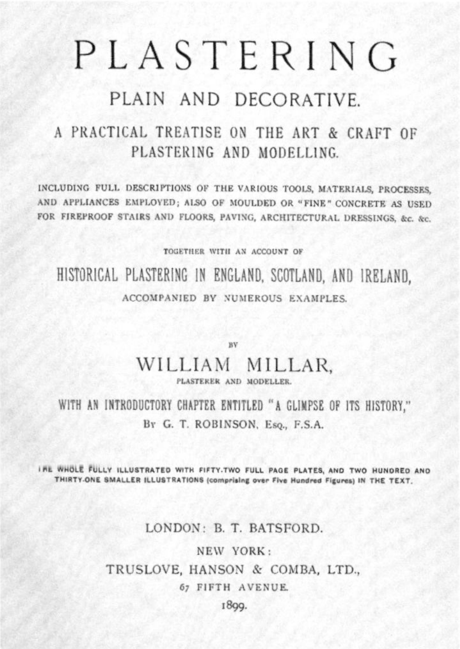
PLASTERING

PLAIN AND DECORATIVE.

A PRACTICAL TREATISE ON THE ART & CRAFT OF PLASTERING AND MODELLING.

INCLUDING FULL DESCRIPTIONS OF THE VARIOUS TOOLS, MATERIALS, PROCESSES, AND APPLIANCES EMPLOYED; ALSO OF MOULDED OR "FINE" CONCRETE AS USED FOR FIREPROOF STAIRS AND FLOORS, PAVING, ARCHITECTURAL DRESSINGS, &c. &c.

TOGETHER WITH AN ACCOUNT OF

HISTORICAL PLASTERING IN ENGLAND, SCOTLAND, AND IRELAND,

ACCOMPANIED BY NUMEROUS EXAMPLES.

BY

WILLIAM MILLAR,

PLASTERER AND MODELLER.

WITH AN INTRODUCTORY CHAPTER ENTITLED "A GLIMPSE OF ITS HISTORY,"

By G. T. ROBINSON, Esq., F.S.A.

THE WHOLE FULLY ILLUSTRATED WITH FIFTY-TWO FULL PAGE PLATES, AND TWO HUNDRED AND THIRTY-ONE SMALLER ILLUSTRATIONS (comprising over Five Hundred Figures) IN THE TEXT.

LONDON: B. T. BATSFORD.

NEW YORK:

TRUSLOVE, HANSON & COMBA, LTD.,

67 FIFTH AVENUE.

1899.

4 William Millar, *Plastering Plain and Decorative*, frontispiece and title page, 1897

they contain only the ghost of the examples from which they were derived. These numerous plates reveal the possibility of taking the vocabulary of classical architecture and stripping it of its past associations, making of it a popularised language.

In the technical section of the manual, Millar demonstrates how to make various types of moulds for standard groups of cornices, laying out sections and elevations of the moulds themselves. He also describes moulding tools for the "reverse running mould": an English invention that sped up the process of installing a cornice, whereby the mould was exchanged for a steel plate in the chosen profile, then affixed at the back with a handle. The plate was pulled manually along soft plaster, removing the excess to form the desired shape (this technique is still used in restoration operations). In a novel moment of demystification, Millar also presents an elevation of the back of a cornice cast, so revealing its hidden wood supporting frame and bracketing. On another plate, he describes visually the composition of an enriched cornice, breaking its elaborate form down into a series of easily cast pieces that are then fitted together. Such images give a sense of the fragility of these elements, of their absolute surface value, their gaudy theatricality and their role as a set dressing to the domestic sphere. This empty repetition of forms, derived from iteration upon iteration of an earlier ideal, marks the final subordination of ornament as an expression of culture to the spectacular forces of the market.[5]

The facades of European cities were once adorned with ornaments that, by virtue of their classical origins, served to endow architecture in public life with a familiar cultural lexicon. But by the nineteenth century, rapid technological progress had debased these ornaments in the collective consciousness and, by the twentieth century, almost banished them altogether. The cornice, in particular, became the target of scorn for those in favour of a rediscovery of architectural integrity. In 1930, architect Frank Lloyd Wright chose to recount a boyhood anecdote involving a cornice, by way of imparting a morality tale for modern architecture. On passing Capitol Square in Madison, Wisconsin, the young Wright →→

5 In 1974 the Italian architect Luigi Moretti notably attributed the reduction of profiles in the early twentieth century—cornice or otherwise—to an "empty repetition of forms" to a certain "academic neoclassicism" stripping these profiles of their original formal and expressive meanings. This academicism can, in fact, be traced back to the eighteenth century, particularly to French architectural education—although this is not the whole story, and perhaps attributes too much blame to academic developments. Moretti does not make mention of nineteenth-century industrialisation processes at the more "popular" level that I discuss here; for example, "good taste" no longer signified a proper set of architectural rules (including appropriate mouldings) as it did in the eighteenth century. Taste was simply a function of what was available on the market. I would argue that this phenomenon of market-level eclecticism in ornament led far more to modern architecture's rejection of profiles and mouldings than any sense of reductionism at the academic or expert level. Luigi Moretti, 'The Value of Profiles', trans. Thomas Stevens, *Oppositions 4*, October 1974, p. 109–39.

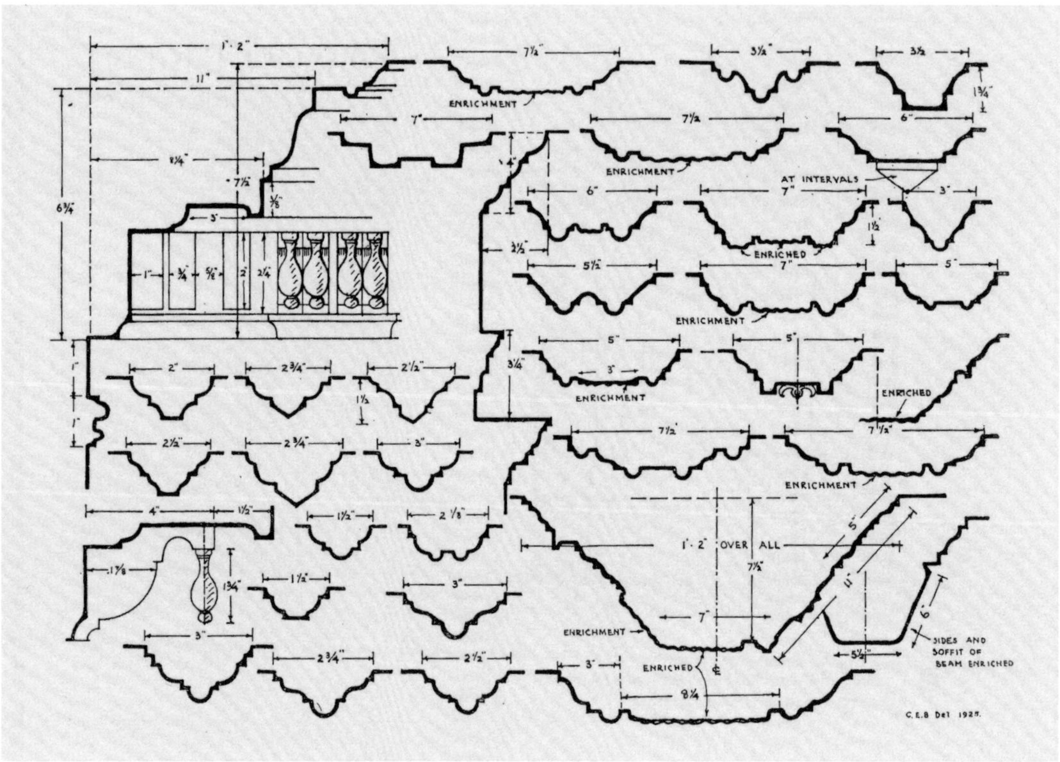

5 Variations of typical Elizabethan and Jacobean plaster mouldings.
From William Millar's *Plastering Plain and Decorative*, 1897

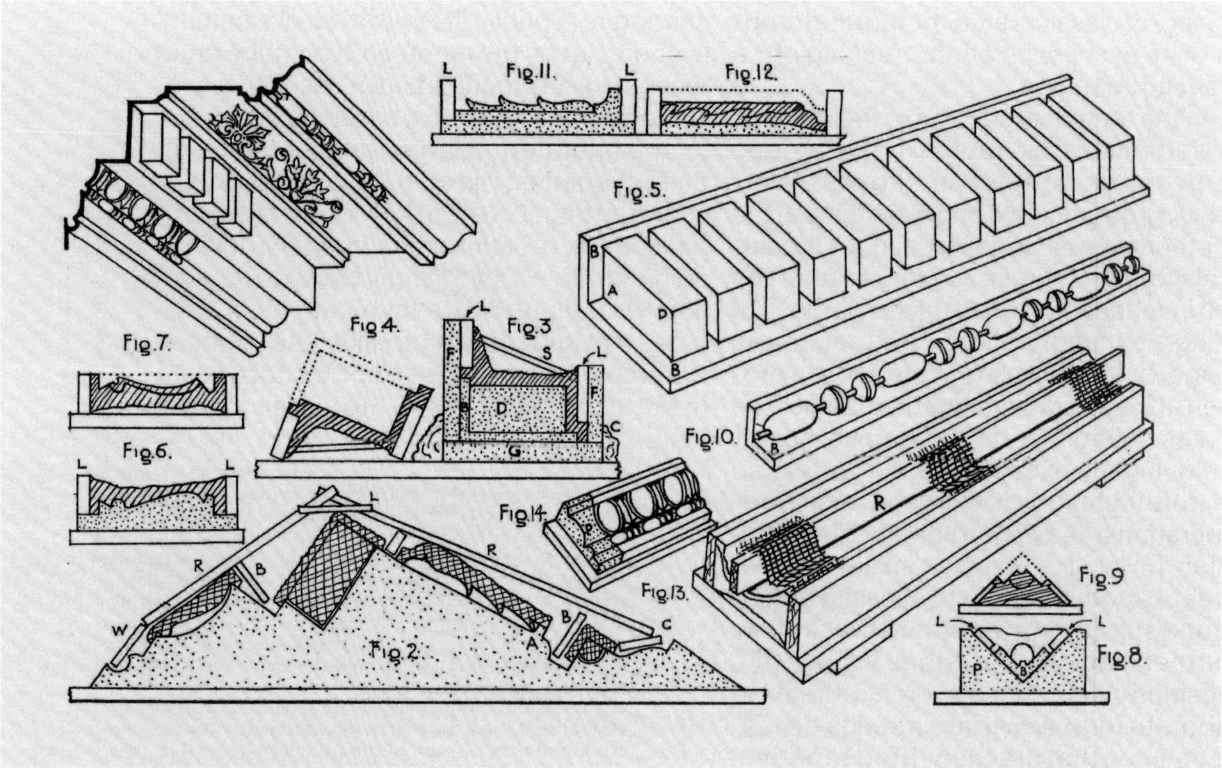


6 Casting complex cornices in segments.
From William Millar's *Plastering Plain and Decorative*, 1897.

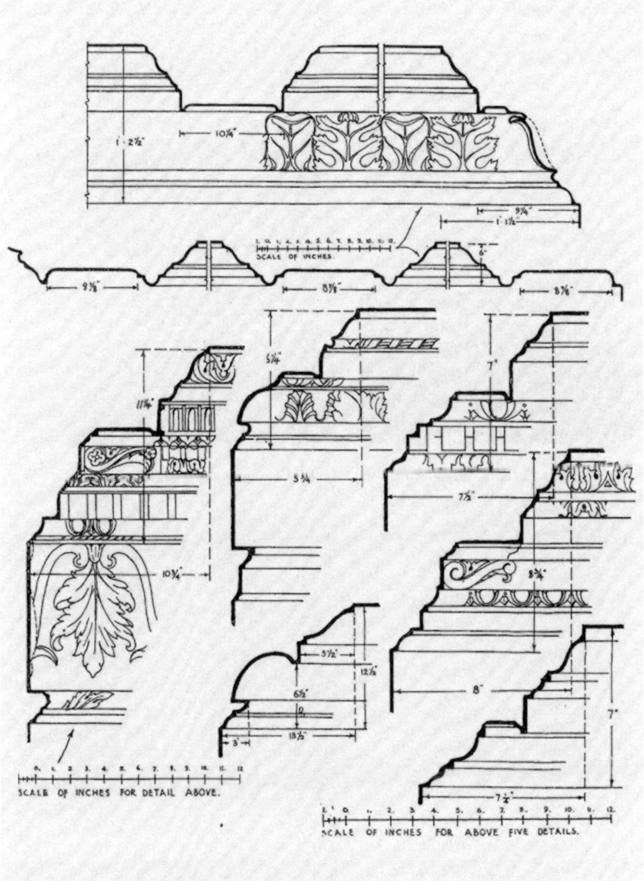


❼ Variations of typical late Stuart and Queen Anne plaster cornices.
From William Millar's *Plastering Plain and Decorative,* 1897.

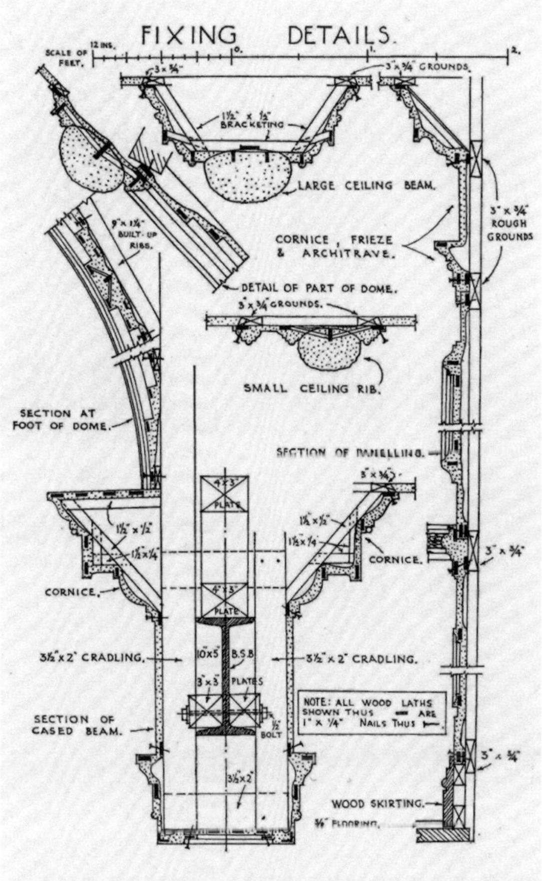


❽ Cornice fixing details.
From William Millar's *Plastering Plain and Decorative,* 1897.

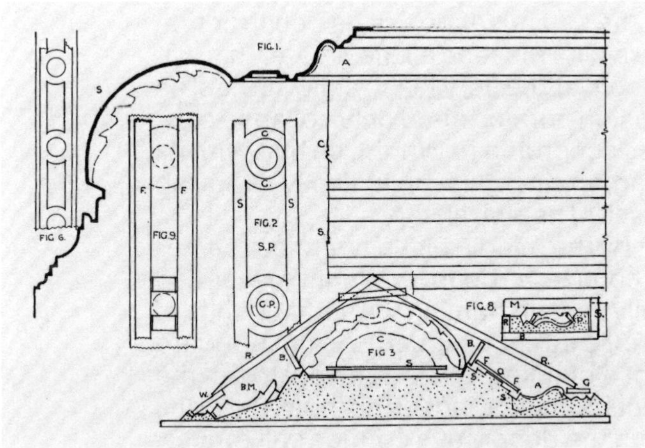


❾ Skeleton structure of the formwork system and mould of the cornice, with view from the back showing the reverse of the cast. Finished cornice occupies the corner of the plate.
From William Millar's *Plastering Plain and Decorative,* 1897.

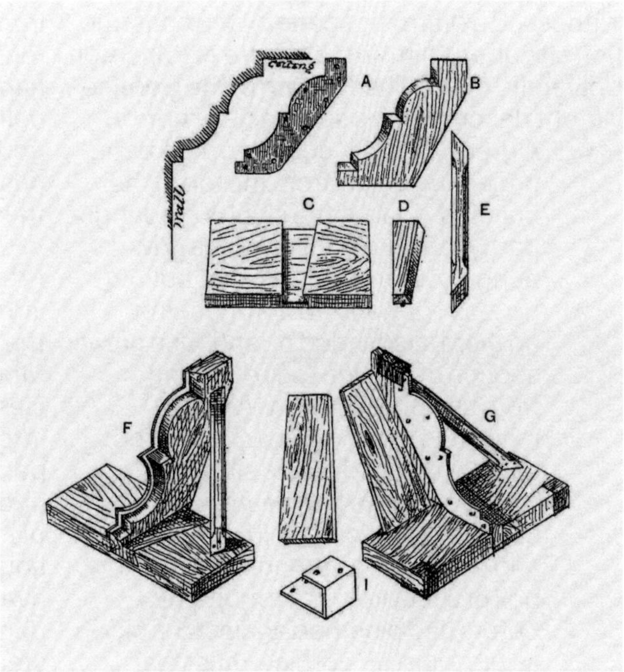

❿ How to make an English "running mould".
From William Millar's *Plastering Plain and Decorative,* 1897.

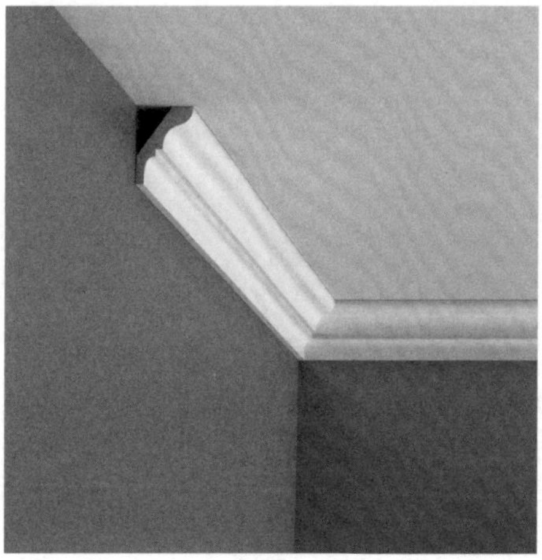
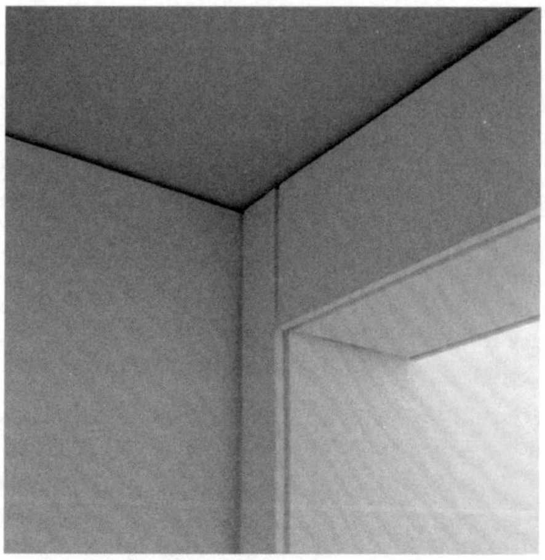

11 Progression of the decorative interior cornice.
Left: fibre cement contemporary cornice;
right: shadow gap;
bottom: no cornice
Images: EMI Architekten, Zurich

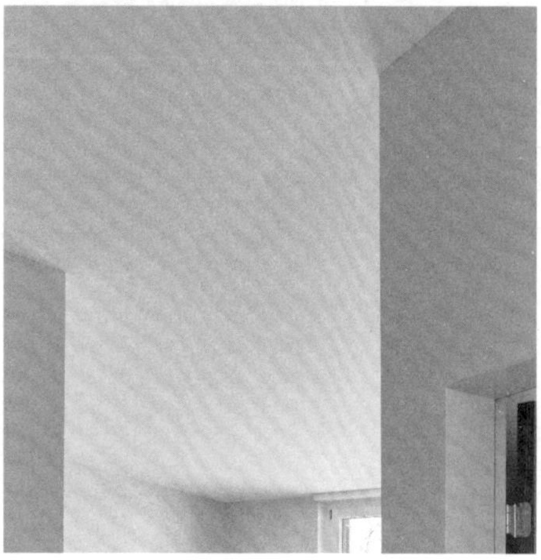

witnessed a dramatic scene on the construction site above him. In his lecture at Princeton University titled "The Passing of the Cornice", Wright described this spectacle of horror:

> A great "classic" cornice ... had been projecting boldly from the top of the building, against the sky. Its moorings partly torn away, this cornice now hung down in places, great hollow boxes of galvanized iron, hanging up there suspended on end. One great section of cornice I saw hanging from an upper window. A workman hung, head downward, his foot caught, crushed on the sill of this window, by a falling beam. A red line streaked the stone wall below him and it seemed as though the hanging box of sheet iron that a moment before had bloomed against the sky as the "classic" cornice, must tear loose by its own weight and cut him down before he could be rescued ...

This cautionary tale, about a man both literally and figuratively crushed by the weight of architecture's classical past, contains one further shame: the cornice itself is only a sham, like Millar's moulded offerings—only a stone skin folded over a supporting box of steel and iron—the sad falsehood of its construction rendering its menace all the greater than if it had been, at the very least, solid stone. The collapsing cornice need only collapse altogether, according to Wright, so that with its passing, architecture might finally be able to free itself of its own history.

By the middle of the twentieth century the cornice, no doubt to Wright's relief, had virtually ceased framing the vertical limits of the public street or square. As the outward face of a building, as its special crown, the classical cornice is indeed no more. But in the interior, the decorative cornice still thrives, particularly in those parts of the world still under the influence of the Victorian sensibility, or with large reserves of Victorian-era housing stock. The notion that Millar's plates, over 100 years old, might present only redundant techniques and forms is disproved by a step into the interior of nearly any new home or apartment across many parts of Europe, the US, Australia or Britain. A glance upward will reveal the same cornice profiles as those depicted in Millar's manual: covering pieces now often made from fibre cement rather than plaster, and screwed in place to hide a multitude of builders' sins.

Even in the architect-designed home with presumptions toward contemporary design, an acknowledgement is made of the symbolic role of the cornice in the form of the shadow gap, modernity's answer to the old ornamented cornice profile. The shadow gap—which involves inserting a metal angle or bracket between the covering materials of wall and ceiling, and thus separating them by a thin-shadowed recess leading, in Schinkelian fashion, to the potential infinite—remains one of the most difficult details in the domestic interior to execute successfully. Rather than acting as a stage set dressing or cover-all, the shadow gap asserts its superiority in modernist lore through its pretence of removing unnecessary ornamentation while maintaining the purity and separation of materials. The modernist ideal of pure and uninterrupted vertical and horizontal planes is perfectly encapsulated by this detail, which makes of each interior surface an isolated, floating prism, untouched and uncontaminated by the others that lie suspended in the ether beside it. The detail attempts to realise the great German modernist (and staunch Schinkel-admirer) Mies van der Rohe's famous collages of interiors, which superimposed cut-outs of walls, ceilings and floor plans over one another to form the semblance of a room, yet always maintained their isolated status as independent shapes, sliding beyond and through one another. In articulating the meeting of vertical and horizontal planes by leaving their collisions exposed, the shadow gap allows for very little tolerance in installation, being left vulnerable to imprecision and poor workmanship. The shadow gap is forever the builders' nightmare, the detail on which they will be judged, and usually found wanting: for every imprecision destroys the illusion of a wholesome material and formal clarity, bringing Mies' floating planes resolutely, and painfully, back down to earth.

The interior cornice can thus be seen as a motif revealing modernism's persistent failure to penetrate in any meaningful way the middle-class domestic interior, which still largely follows the arrangement of its Victorian forebears, and which continues to assert its status as a place of retreat from the modern world, in one way or another. In light of this fact, the pernicious absence of the cornice in the Swiss interior of today is shockingly radical and indeed almost rude, particularly to the foreigner not accustomed to such visions of unabashed nakedness. With no covering piece or shadow gap in sight, wall meets ceiling unceremoniously and without shame. This kind of exposure gives us no comfortable retreat, and no illusion of enveloping privacy. If Swiss architects and builders are unafraid of such exposure, is this merely a means to showcase the famed precision and expertise of the Swiss construction industry, for which the necessity of using a cover piece to hide any unfortunate detail might well become a source of embarrassment? Or is it associated rather with something deeper, more rooted in history? Switzerland has never undergone the same radical expansion of industry endured by England and Germany, nor has it had to contend with the same level of commodification of its built heritage. The familiar tropes of the nineteenth-century bourgeois interior, which crystallised elsewhere in Western Europe, may largely have escaped a foothold in Switzerland due to its isolation for much of that century. Not only that, but the motifs of the classical tradition are remoter here and less imbued in the cultural consciousness, which is rather more saturated with ideal images of the alpine vernacular than with Rome or the Renaissance.

Never before or since was the gulf between public space and private life so pronounced as in the nineteenth century, as urban upheaval was matched by the cultivation of comfortable domesticity. In Biedermeier Berlin, interior decoration was used as a form of resistance to the political and behavioural repressions of public life. In England, it had become an easy, commoditised means of introducing comfort and familiarity into a tumultuous urban environment that seemed increasingly alien to the pace of human life. Today, in an age when such repressions and discomforts have been drastically reduced in the European urban context, the domestic interior, with all its ornamental trappings, is no longer called upon to play such roles. Does this mean the perfunctory interior nakedness found in Swiss interiors has the potential to become the future norm? After all, these are not the interiors of modern architects' experimental fancies, but of everyday, mass-produced homes. And if the cornice truly is a thing of the past, how should architecture respond? Considering that the de-ornamentation of the public face of architecture has always been countered by the proliferation of standardised decorative elements in the domestic interior, might we now be approaching the reverse scenario? Could the current, radical de-ornamentation of the interior prompt architects to reconsider architecture's symbolic relationship to civic space? ■

# White Space: An Interior Monologue

Sandy Isenstadt

I believe in plenty of optimism
and white paint.[1]
— Elsie de Wolfe, 1913

In his authoritative review of modern English houses at the turn of the twentieth century, the German architect and writer Hermann Muthesius commented on the unadorned surfaces that he felt characterised his subject. Of a design by William Lethaby, Muthesius writes: "Apart from the carpet, colour is left out, walls and ceilings appear in plain white."[2] Throughout, simplicity was axiomatic. As Muthesius puts it, C.F.A. Voysey's Broadleys (1898) achieved "the greatest simplicity" while a design by Edwin Lutyens reached "the extreme simplicity of the peasant hut".[3] "Simplicity" turned out to be the name of an ideal that was then beginning to eclipse older notions of interior design that favoured the visual density of eclectic historical styles, exotic influences, bric-a-brac and the richly patterned surfaces characteristic of late-nineteenth century home design. It became a standard joining the spare, gauzy white interiors of Karin and Carl Larsson, working in Sweden, with the delicate motifs of Charles Rennie Mackintosh, in Scotland, to name just a few, however distinct their aesthetic sensibilities may have been otherwise. As historicist styles began to appear strained, simplicity presented a new and higher level of aesthetic insight if only, in the words of the popular American author Florence Morse, one could appreciate "the beauty of economy—that is, of the artistic value of sparseness, almost of bareness" that was relevant to any design approach.[4]

Of course, simplicity more than a century ago might not today be recognised as such. As the influential American interior designer Elsie de Wolfe wrote in 1913, "One thing you must have: simplicity! It may be the simplicity of a marble floor and tapestried walls and a painted ceiling, it may be the simplicity of white paint and muslin and fine furniture, but simplicity it must have."[5] However broadly it was conceived, simplicity was more than a formal trait. It was a leading indicator of so-called hygienic design—with clutter banished and surfaces scrubbed to create interiors allegedly inhospitable to germs and their cargo of disease. The simplicity of retiring profiles, plainer surfaces, subdued colours, and fewer decorative elements contrasted sharply with objects that, as de Wolfe put it, "litter the room", or pictures that "dot the walls". Simplicity drew attention away from separate objects and towards a more atmospheric apprehension of interior space.

In this, it had psychological effects as well. By diminishing visual density, simplicity was believed to ease the jarring effects of modern life, with its crowding and incongruous juxtapositions. What an editor of American shelter magazine *House Beautiful* called "The Tyranny of Things" lay in the frenetic scattering of attention among disparate objects; simplicity, in contrast, liberated the mind by submerging dissonant things in a harmonious background, which left to the autonomous self an open field of operation. "What we ought to aim at is freedom from any consciousness of either walls or furnishings, precisely as the well-dressed woman aims at obliviousness to her clothes", the editor continued.[6] A sense of repose, in other words, was the ultimate goal of simplified, spare interiors. "Simplicity and repose", as Frank Lloyd Wright said in 1908, must be the true metric for architecture.[7] By conjoining all in a unified sense of space, simplicity served self-sovereignty by unbinding the mind from the things that pressed upon it.

It was left for a subsequent generation of architects to forge these reforms in interior design into the abstractions of modernism. Walls washed white suggested virtues of honesty and purity, a visual cleansing that was tantamount to "*inner* cleanness", as Le Corbusier said, thus concluding that whitewashing walls was a moral act.[8] That austerity also represented a disciplined, even ascetic temperament, and thereby comported readily with the utilitarian and unsentimental approach to design that modernists touted and that contrasted so sharply with Victorian sensibilities. Modernists decried the bourgeois interior that teemed with things to testify to every tic of the owner's personality. Its abundance of goods announced the absence of personal depth. Considering the same overfilled rooms, Walter Benjamin described the poverty of an ersatz experience, which was the result of a world weighted by an "oppressive wealth of ideas" streaming incessantly from new media and roiling the time and mental space otherwise available for sustained and reflective engagement with the world.[9] For Benjamin, modernists—he mentions Adolf Loos, Paul Scheerbart and Le Corbusier—stripped architecture of its accumulated dead weight so that it could accommodate "the naked man of the contemporary world who lies screaming like a newborn babe in the dirty diapers of the present". The empty space of the modern home cradled this new man. The unyielding surfaces of modernism refused to bear objects; glass in particular was "the enemy of possession".[10] The modern interior, for Benjamin, was a first step in freeing oneself from the artefactual chaos of an unfettered industrial age that fostered the false equation of private possessions with personal prosperity. →

1 E. de Wolfe, *The House in Good Taste,* New York, The Century Co., 1913, p. 47.
2 H. Muthesius, *Das Englische Haus: Entwicklung, Bedingungen, Anlage, Aufbau, Einrichtung und Innenraum,* Berlin, Ernst Wasmuth, 1908, p. 152.
3 Muthesius, *Das Englische Haus,* p. 164, 194.
4 F. Morse, 'About Furnishings', in C. Wheeler (ed.) *Household Art,* New York, Doubleday, 1893, p. 181.
5 de Wolfe, *The House in Good Taste,* p. 176.
6 E. Matson, 'The Tyranny of Things,' *House Beautiful,* 36, September 1914, p. 113.
7 Frank Lloyd Wright, 'In the Cause of Architecture,' *Architectural Record* 23, no. 3, March 1908, p. 54.
8 Le Corbusier, *The Decorative Art of Today,* trans. James Dunnett, Cambridge, MA, MIT Press, 1987 [1925], p. 188. For an overview of all the ways that whiteness also helps to construct a white racial identity based on the absence or devaluation of other colors, see Nell Irvin Painter, *The History of White People,* New York, Norton, 2010.
9 W. Benjamin, 'Experience and Poverty', in M. Jennings, H. Eiland, and G. Smith (eds.), *Walter Benjamin. Selected Writings 1927-1934,* trans. R. Livingstone et al., Cambridge, MA, The Belknap Press of Harvard University Press, 1999, p. 732.
10 Benjamin, 'Experience and Poverty', p. 733–34.

Today's interiors clearly derive from these modernist precedents. Materials are few: plasterboard walls and ceilings (wood, laminate or tile is allowed as an accent); floors are wood or polished concrete. A glass wall is inevitable. Likewise, colours are spare: planes, panels and strips of white; a burr of black or red in contrast. Glass, of course, is no colour at all. Although minimalist in terms of visual density, the designs hint at a generous experience of space as planes recede, openings between rooms stretch wide, and perspective pulls the eye toward, through and then out past the wall of glass and into the view, which is often overexposed and reads as bright as a white foreground wall. Such images choreograph the integers of architecture carefully to suggest the play of one space tumbling into another rather than, say, refined surface effects, intricate details or luxurious materials, and certainly never so much as hint at complete enclosure. Nearly always, the interiors are pictured unfurnished.

Luxury dwellings subscribe to the same visual vocabulary as cheaper premises, making budgetary matters only one of several factors contributing to the style of contemporary housing interiors. In upscale conditions, that aspect of modern design demanding precision detailing to carry off minimalist visual effects comes into play and contributes to an air of sophistication, easy elegance and, possibly, an open-minded and progressive outlook. In these circumstances, the glass walls that surround, but do not enclose, the pictured interiors are less about a promise of spatial graciousness (such units are usually large in fact) than they are an emphasis on the desirable settings money can buy: an ocean panorama, a mountain vista or an elevated point of view. That is to say, the architecture—or, at least, the architectural representation—emphasises real-estate values as much as it highlights refined design.

For architects, challenges to their professional skills have always been motivating. Many mid-twentieth century architects, for example, took part in a discourse of spaciousness, an effort to engender a sense of depth despite difficult dimensional limits. They fostered visual mobility with diagonal planning, interior uses of glass in transoms or between rooms, mirrors, low partitions and level changes that help to define territory but without slowing the eye. As Elizabeth Mock wrote while she was the director of architecture and industrial design at New York's Museum of Modern Art: "Only the modern architect is ... *free* to give you at least a feeling of spaciousness if the actuality is unattainable." [11] Restricted designs that are nonetheless varied would thus testify to a high level of expertise. Clean lines suggest clear thinking; bright spaces bespeak a lucid mind: virtuosity in coaxing expressive potential with minimal means is an architectural virtue. As Wilfried Wang writes in regard to the work of the Zurich-based firm Gigon/Guyer, the best designs today achieve a kind of "variegated minimalism", a shared austerity that, upon closer inspection, rewards the attentive viewer with subtle variations on otherwise constrained themes. Such designs rehearse the certainties of earlier minimalisms but now with "minor irregularities" that bestow a degree of personality, and "seemingly monochromatic surfaces" turn out to be "subtly varying" and can even include projects where strong colours are judiciously employed. While the problem of housing preoccupied modernists as much as it does present-day architects, Wang differentiates historical minimalism, with its emphasis on the clarity and autonomy of the architectural object, from variegated minimalism, which reflects the many contexts architecture is inevitably imbricated within. It favours discrepancies rather than strict uniformity, and defers to circumstances early modernists might have preferred to expunge. It gestures towards conventional compositions and welcomes readily purchased or prefabricated solutions. It is practical rather than resolute, and cleaves to capricious realities rather than to a singular ideal. Wang cautions against over-generalisations but still grants a striking consensus regarding such a "return of the minimal".[12] Architects' sustained attraction to this distinctly modernist provocation—less is more—no doubt further helps to explain the continued appeal of a particularly widespread interior design ideal.

11 E. Mock, *If You Want to Build a House*, New York, Museum of Modern Art, 1946, p. 17.

12 W. Wang, 'The Variegated Minimal', *El Croquis*, vol. 102, 2000, p. 25–27.

The allure of undemonstrative interiors hints at another lingering connotation of modernist design that tantalises a profession strongly marked by a concern for social justice. As Corbusier writes, "Whitewash is the wealth of the poor and of the rich—of everybody." [13] Today, a widened franchise for a formal approach available to nearly all and, no less important, desirable across social classes, validates an egalitarian aspiration that is still vital and, if one reads the newspaper, desperately needed. An emphasis on flowing space rather than relative size, expensive fittings, or custom furnishings might turn out to be a solid foundation for a democratic society. Creating a sense of deep space within a shell of shallow space can help to diminish class differences in housing. Architect Maria Zurbuchen-Henz, based in Lausanne, admires the open planning of Zurich-based Adrian Streich, for example, for just this reason. His housing designs create "free spatial figures that interlock like the pieces of a puzzle" and that consequently have the power "to bridge the distance between the aristocratic *hôtel particulier* and the workers' lodging house, between ideas of the minimum existence and bourgeois sequences of living spaces". [14] An emphasis on space, in other words, portends and, in our own moment of political retrenchment, protects ideals of egalitarian society.

Compared with the American practice of staging—the custom of installing domestic props that guide a potential home buyer toward generic notions such as comfortable-place-to-sit, decorative-object-that-displays-good-taste, or charming-place-to-gather, but without risking the specificity that might evoke an actual person with different preferences—austere interiors are, in their off-the-shelf components and unfurnished exposition, a kind of anti-staging. They do not hint at how one might occupy a space so much as they evince a kind of authenticity. Rather than a dreamy presentation of what might be, these interiors offer a sharp-focus rendering of what is, the specific features that comprise the sturdy foundation upon which a good domestic life can be built. They present the underlying facts about a place from which emerges a reasoned generalisation about one's own tenancy. In other words, with their emphasis on verifiable facts about a place, including responses to contextual contingencies, today's interior images aim to engender trust. Trust, in turn, entails a degree of transparency.

This new sense of architectural transparency is distinct from the literal transparency of seeing through a glass wall or, as Colin Rowe and Robert Slutzky tell it, the phenomenal transparency of implied dimensions and layers that can thicken spatial experience in modern design.[15] Rather, today's white-surfaced simple interiors herald the transparency of the honest broker, someone presenting an unadorned story, without gimmicks or hype, the exact opposite of the huckster's fevered come-on. It is an image of confidence and strength: the design stands on its own merits, without the support of soft pillows, framed photos →

13 Corbusier, *The Decorative Art of Today*, p. 192.

14 M. Zurbuchen-Henz, 'Kleine Netze. KraftWerk 2 in Zürich-Höngg von Adrian Streich', *Werk, Bauen + Wohnen*, no. 4, 2012, p. 14–19. English translation provided by the magazine. The original German suggests that Streich's rethinking of housing typologies provides a rare opportunity to find correspondences between aristocratic and workers' homes. The emphasis on spatial continuities, a mainstay of modernism, remains prevalent in recent years. To take only one example, see P. Esch and C. Kerez, 'Der Raum Selbst', *Werk, Bauen + Wohnen*, no. 5, 2004, p. 24–33.

15 In their famous essay, Colin Rowe and Robert Slutzky, 'Transparency: Literal and Phenomenal', *Perspecta* 8 (1963), p. 45–54.

of indistinct subjects, or an over-scaled floor vase of pampas grass plumes obscuring an ill-conceived corner. A forthright image says: "Fact: the basics of bodily comfort and domestic and spatial accommodation are assured here and require no further proof or elaboration."

Of course, this version of transparency may be its own form of hype and certainly cannot guarantee good design. In today's world of media illiteracy, anti-staging might simply be the latest twist in conventional staging, but it is very much in keeping with a contemporary notion of transparency in other areas, or, more precisely, a familiar image of transparency. In this, visions of uncluttered white surfaces in dwelling interiors have less to do with representational traditions of modernism than they do with the ubiquitous white surfaces we encounter every day across so many websites on our monitors, pads and phones. As study after study has shown, people trust "white space" in promotional situations. In contrast to the visual noise of dense or wordy advertisements, a field of white space with a limited graphic palette suggests that the things pictured can stand on their own; their publicity consists of simply appearing before a public, which is thereby enabled to make its own decisions based on demonstrable merits. They require no dramatisation to underscore their usefulness or to adorn their desirability.[16] In this way, white space in websites is akin to the early modernists' efforts to clear the interior from the clutter and detritus of indifferent accumulation; "All the sacrificial offerings of the past", as Benjamin puts it.[17] It presents a nearly blank page that seems to silence the mayhem of the marketplace to create a respite, an all-but-empty space that suggests sustained experience is possible even in a media-saturated environment.

Meaning is promiscuous in the modern world, migrating among and between different goods and, of course, goods and people. The significance of white space is one such meaning on the move. White surfaces in recent housing design might recall modernist interiors of the 1920s and 1930s, but their meaning has changed as the world around them has. Their lineage is overcome—whitewashed, in a sense—by contemporary circumstances. Today, as British architect John Pawson puts it in regard to a minimalist aesthetic, of which he is no small advocate, "Emptiness allows us to see space as it is, to see architecture as it is, preventing it from being corrupted, or hidden, by the incidental debris of paraphernalia of everyday life."[18] In this formulation, architecture not only outlasts the coming and going of everyday people, along with everyday life, it also hints at something one can rely on, as if emptiness were the stable reality beneath the erratic residue of so many distracted lives. Pawson was surely thinking in historical and cross-cultural terms.[19] But the spare, white-surfaced spaces of today must also be understood in the context of the constantly churning consumer society in which they appear. However much it resonates with representations from a century ago, the white-walled interior so often now pictured gathers its meaning from today's digitally mediated marketplace of ideas, forms and anxieties; only by doing so can it address today's man and woman, who stare at screens far more than they look through glass walls.

16 For just a small sample of studies into the value of white space on computer screens, see J. H. Huang and T.K. Yang, 'The Impacts of Homepage Screen Density on Website Evaluations: The Moderating Role of Personality Type', *Social Behavior and Personality*, vol. 39, no. 3, 2011, p. 381–390; D. Mortelmans, 'Visualizing Emptiness', *Visual Anthropology*, vol. 18, no. 1, 2005, p. 19–45; J.W. Pracejus, G.D. Olsen, and T.C. O'Guinn, 'How Nothing Became Something: White Space, Rhetoric, History, and Meaning', *Journal of Consumer Research*, vol. 33, no. 1, 2006, p. 82–90; and Y.D. Wang and H.H. Emurian, 'Trust in E-commerce: Consideration of Interface Design Factors', *Journal of Electronic Commerce in Organizations*, vol. 3, no. 4 (2005): 42–60.

17 Benjamin, 'Experience and Poverty', p. 733.

18 Cited in F. Bertoni, *Minimalist Architecture*, trans. Lucinda Byatt, Basel, Birkhäuser, 2002, p. 134.

19 Bertoni (p. 134) suggests Pawson's influences include Zen philosophy, an ascetic Calvinism, the reductive logic of Mies van der Rohe, "Shaker puritanism" and Wilhelm Worringer's comments on abstraction as a psychological oasis in a tumultuous modern world. Pawson himself refers back to the negative space evident in traditional Chinese scroll painting.

To be sure, this is no more than an image of trust and should not be confused with architectural austerity chic, the carefully constructed asceticism—"The glossy and overdesigned minimalism of Pawson", as Pier Vittorio Aureli quips—and studied humility that permeates the work of a number of practitioners today. In many such instances, the formal asceticism announces a rather elite subscription to purportedly egalitarian ideals.[20] Rather, the inevitability of exchange, the whole calculus of capitalist value, is built into the premise of these interiors. They are built to be owned, as well as lived in, just as a single creatively presented item surrounded by white space on your screen is as much about sales as a knock-off product in a dollar store. Nonetheless, such interiors speak a language of serenity and breathing room that is, at the very least, familiar and, amidst the din of the our own age, can even feel refreshing. Where modernist interiors once put forward a fresh standard to oppose a world awash in cheap goods, petrified design and social inequity, the minimalist modernism of today's interiors postulate that there is something underlying the shifting sands of the everyday, something one can trust: space itself. ■

20 P. V. Aureli, *Less is Enough. On Architecture and Asceticism,* Moscow, Strelka Press, 2013, location 340, (Kindle edition).

# Almost Nothing

Michael Hill

The unremarkable interiors of contemporary Swiss apartments are typified by a number. 240cm is the minimum floor-to-ceiling height according to building codes not only in Switzerland but much of the industrial world. This minimum is the intersection between human comfort and profit: any lower, and tall people would feel oppressed; any higher, and developers would cry poor. The number, in turn, governs internal scale, from the doorway to the kitchen bench. The curators imagine that the ignorable 240cm-high apartment can be made visible by treating it as if it were a sculptural space that shrinks or enlarges in relation to a person moving through it.

The authors refer to these interiors as "background architecture". The word "background" in this sense is normally associated with Muzak, the low-volume music company founded by George Owen Squier in 1922. Squier had invented multiplexing while working in the US Army Signal Corps; his understanding about how information travelled down the wire was behind the business model, originally called Wired Radio, that continuous music could be available to anyone with electricity. Wireless radio eventually cornered the market, but Muzak, as it was named in 1934, survived by repurposing itself as something other than entertainment. Its Stimulus Progression system of the 1940s consisted of sequences of instrumental arrangements that were meant to keep workers keen across the natural rhythm of the day. This may or may not have been effective, but it did create a good mood, and in the following decades Muzak was transformed into a general soundtrack for the bland affluence of post-war American life. It was heard everywhere, from shopping centres to waiting rooms, the audio equivalent of *horror vacui*: advertisements for Muzak in the 1960s claimed that "it filled the deadly silences", while shortly before it folded in 2009, a spokesperson acknowledged that "our biggest competitor is silence".[1] Yet it seemed to come from nowhere. Indeed, one Muzak nickname was "potted plant" music, as this was where speakers were often hidden. It was also a lullaby for waking sleep, with the mollification of fear never far away: the commonest nickname for Muzak derived from its presence in otherwise unnerving elevators.

Muzak was moderate in tempo, voiceless and familiar-sounding without being wholly unoriginal. But in the 1970s, a rival called Yesco began to offer background music made of popular "foreground songs": the environment of happiness became evermore dense. This is where Brian Eno enters the scene. Waiting in Cologne airport one day and irritated by the upbeat tunes playing through the speakers, Eno began to imagine the sound that might accompany air travel. He decided it should be "interruptible (because there will be announcements), it has to work ... at a different speed to speech patterns, so as not to confuse communication, and it has to accommodate all the noises that airports produce".[2] The resulting *Ambient 1: Music for Airports* (1978) went on and on like space, without centre and often seeming without end. Comprised of sequences played in loops, here was music that made itself. Eno called it "ambience". Unlike the aural paste of Muzak, silence was used effectively, with oftentimes immense distances between notes; and being empty of the plaintive emotions typical of pop, the mind was unharassed and free to wander. Compared to normal background music, ambience did not so much dull feeling as sensitise thought. It was an environment in which worry was trite; since the fear of flying was common then, it would be good for people in airports to realise it was no big deal if they should live or die. Yet when *Music for Airports* was played in airports, travellers famously complained that it made them uneasy; either Eno's otherworldliness sounded funereal, or nonchalance was as troubling as the prospect of being in the air.[3]

Not only background, but barely audible. Eno recalled that he was once stuck on the couch listening to eighteenth-century harp music with the volume so low he couldn't tell the difference between the music and the rain falling on the window. It seemed like music had dissolved into the space of its listening. Notes made by strings demanded no priority over other sounds, including those of his own body; music and life had intermingled and he could hear everything. Simone Weil thought of such attention as akin to a living prayer.[4] It can't last, and can be broken by a hiccup. This is the deeper sense of Eno's wish for ambience to be interruptible, beyond the practical need to accommodate messages; namely that the jolt back to the here and now might not be so violent if the reverie occurs in the present and takes the form of the commonplace. Returning to the Swiss apartment, it appears that the new generation of architects has rejected bespoke materials and privileged sightlines in favour of standardised elements experienced by a moving viewer. In so doing, the authors suggest, an interior domestic design has been created that, echoing Mies van der Rohe, is "almost nothing".

In line with this quiet approach is the flattening of components into the skin of the interior walls, which is part of a trend where switches, knobs, joins and gaps are eliminated to fashion a surface that seems to be all of a piece. This is an instance of the ancient yet recurrent ideal of the building so perfect that it appears to be made from a single stone. But different as well: *ex uno lapide* refers to the coherence of a body, whether building or poem, whose integration of parts ultimately speaks of its organic vitality. In the case of the apartments, however, the process of making interiors appear seamless has as much to do with suppressing tactility. Concealed also are the electronics of sensors and smart appliances. Gentle finger pressure and voice commands are all that will be needed to open cupboards and operate lighting systems. Instead of clumsy hands, the functions of the home may one day flow as if they were extensions of the mind.

→

1 D. Owens, 'The Soundtrack of Your Life: Muzak in the Realm of Retail Theatre', *The New Yorker*, 10 April 2006
2 P. Roquet, 'Ambient Landscapes from Brian Eno to Tetsu Inoue', *Journal of Popular Music Studies*, vol. 21, no. 4, 2009, p. 367.
3 V. Szabo, 'Unsettling Brian Eno's Music for Airports', *Twentieth Century Music*, vol. 14, no. 2, 2017, p. 311.
4 J. Delaruelle, 'Attention as Prayer: Simone Weil', *Literature and Aesthetics: Journal of the Sydney Society of Literature and Aesthetics*, vol. 13, no. 2, 2003, p. 19–27.

This sounds like a dream, particularly of the sort encountered, again, in the spaces of air travel. The apartments of the House Tour have white walls, cabinets, doors, tiles and ceilings. The only darker elements are timber floors and stone or melamine kitchen benches. In places with long winters, like Switzerland, there are good reasons for the preference for white. However, there is more to it than practicality. Modern architects love dressing buildings in white. Architects want to see the form, and white reveals the most in this respect. They apply this perspective to the past as well: the recent restoration of Borromini's masterpiece San Carlo alle Quattro Fontane included the removal of the nineteenth-century polychromy from the stucco walls; no longer coloured like other Baroque churches, San Carlo seemed to speak directly of its architectural condition to the modern practitioner. In this sense, white's significance is that it is a colourless, original state, implying the future. Precious few photographs of Swiss interiors show them with furniture and people. The apartments await the vitality—the colour—of life. At this register, one should not over-interpret whiteness, which might simply mean that the interiors are pristine. We don't read books by imagining what the page looked like before it was written on, and it is good to remember that these rooms will not stay unspoiled for long. They will be smudged by dirty children and left uncleaned by harried adults.

In addition to its lack of colour, white is also the expression of light; that is, the material embodiment of something out of this world.[5] The earliest temples of Mesopotamia were mud-brick brown, but when gleaming plaster was applied to one in Uruk in the fourth millennium BC, it seemed to lift from the earth. If white is regarded as pure, it's because of light. However, seeing is difficult in pure light; and vice versa, it is shade that makes something visible, defining an occupation of space and thereby suggesting weight. The purity of white, a resonance that is found in the deepest depths of religion and poetry, renders the whiteness of the Swiss apartments somewhat spectral. Suggesting more than the colourful future, white is the promise of a life free of encumbrance, one of movement that floats, of a reality that keeps getting better. Architecture is presented as an ideal, as if occupants will conform to its cues. They will be trim and content and organised according to an intelligent understanding of what is important. Although empty, the interiors offer a glimpse of people at their best.

Another effect of white is that of sameness. White 240cm spaces are, throughout the industrial world, pressed into existence by economics. The communication theorist Joshua Meyrowitz has written about how the process of an individual's self-definition within physical localities such as home and neighbourhood was redefined with the rise of global media, such that everyone "has images in their heads of other people [which] help to shape the imagined elsewhere from which each person's somewhere is conceived".[6] Meyrowitz describes the picturing of other ways of life as "a negative mirror" against which the self stands out. But if we were to live in spaces that look the same, the negative mirror for the self would be en route to being simply a mirror.

No matter where you are, white rooms tell you that it is the same as before. Sameness is not always comforting. The Danish artist Jesper Rasmussen digitally repaints his photographs of cities to remove people, who at any rate rarely feature in architectural photography, and the parts long understood to characterise the human quality of architecture, namely doors and windows. His distressing civic vision could be the future: human beings have been evicted from their home; they're not welcome anymore. Rasmussen avoids darkness, inspired by Stanley Kubrick's *The Shining*, in which terror occurs within brightly lit rooms.[7] The "aesthetic hygiene" that results from cleaning away traces of life in the city and its buildings means that everything is revealed. There are no secret rooms and no hiding places, like contemporary society, which, thanks to the media and electronic surveillance, makes everywhere and everyone accessible. Little is left that is unfamiliar and the dark realms

5 F. Barry, 'A Whiter Shade of Pale: Relative and Absolute Light in Roman Sculpture and Architecture', in S. Clerbois and M. Droth (eds.), *Revival and Invention: Sculpture through its Material Histories*, Oxford, Peter Lang 2011, p. 31–62.

6 J. Meyrowitz, 'The Rise of Glocality', in K. Nyiri ed., *A Sense of Place: The Global and the Local in Mobile Communication*, Vienna, Passagen Verlag, 2005, p. 22.

7 J. Rasmussen, *Another Sense of Place*, 2013, Copenhagen, p. 71.

of the sort that were once used to store our anxieties have been fully aired. And yet fears remain, lurking now in plain sight. For anyone still wary of Big Brother, the endless white interiors in the House Tour look creepy.

Instead of being threatened by the off-the-shelf componentry and the ubiquitous ceiling height, the interiors are imagined on an allegorical level. Undistracted by conventional appearance, the viewer is freed to enjoy surface, space and light. And rather than judging them by the standards of domestic design, forms can be apprehended as social representation. The painter Peter Halley engaged with modernist abstraction in this manner, not as refuge from society but as an analogue of it, thinking of the flow charts of managerial capitalism as if they were artful geometric compositions. Likewise, these interiors—in which options are regulated by codes, and surfaces determined by supply chains of existing fittings and materials—might be seen as akin to the procedural generation of game design, where spaces automatically open before the exploring player. Decision-making formulas do all the work and despite our stubborn manner of speaking that puts humans in command, it would appear that society is designing itself like a virtual world.

In the House Tour, architecture assumes the shape of sculpture witnessed from within, inverting minimalist sculptural theory that allowed the object to be viewed as a component of a situation. Donald Judd declared in 1965 that it was time to stop thinking of sculpture as material transformed into something pleasing. Instead, he implored, regard the medium. A plywood box can be just that. Soon after, Robert Morris insisted that the relevant issue was not what the thing is, but how it is seen, and in that sense it is critical whether the viewer is stationary or mobile, and if he or she is larger or smaller than the viewed object. Minimalism turned sculpture inside out. Minimalism was a part of a larger movement in art and criticism that bound the beholder to the beholden. What began with a simple premise that the site might be relevant to understanding an artwork—from testing possible viewing angles to accounting for the prestige of a museum—ended with the feeling that environment is all. Meanwhile, the distinction between looking and comprehending got thornier, such that it seemed there were as many lookers as meanings. The post-object sculptors that emerged in the following decades made the world their topic: work occurred on the floor rather than atop the plinth; it was scattered about rather than gathered together and lying down rather than standing up; it went disguised as civic furniture; it included the surrounding air. In short, sculpture dissolved into the space of its viewing, becoming, like ambient music, almost nothing. ■

# The Banality of 240cm

John Macarthur

It is not necessarily a bad thing that aspects of building culture are generic, but there is fine print in the contract we make in the standardisation of life. Considerable building and planning efficiency results from the near-universal agreement that 240cm should separate ceilings from floors in domestic space. Certainly, some scope for spatial design is lost in following this rule, but the problems of standardisation go beyond limits to creativity. *Svizzera 240: House Tour* reveals a broader issue, which is the degree to which we think empirical reality can be measured against the human body. The body might work as a metric of things, such as rocks and trees, but the world is equally constructed by the reification of rules and measures, ideas we have had. Our agreement to fit within the 240cm of contemporary living space is, to a degree, consoling, suggesting as it does that we live in a world that was intended for us. However, the anthropometrics of 240cm should not be taken to be an anthropomorphism; other standards could well accommodate the human body and its social normalisation. It is the ubiquity of 240cm, not its dimension, that makes it seem to be a natural likeness of us.[1] The existential issues of this flattening out of space, of scale and repetition, confront us all directly, but for architects there is the further reverberation of the relation of modernist architecture to the minimalist sculpture of the late twentieth century. This is both a precedent and a critical armoury for the architects of *Svizzera 240.*

Alessandro Bosshard, Li Tavor, Matthew van der Ploeg and Ani Vihervaara address in *Svizzera 240* the topic of housing, but not as it is usually presented; rather, they build segments of typical apartments inside the Swiss Pavilion, at a variety of scales. They write:

> Each individual room is scaled so that it deviates slightly from the 240 standard. These scalar operations result in interior models at scales of 2:1, 1,5:1, 1.3:1, 1.2:1, 1.1:1, 1:1, 1:1.1, 1:1.2 1:1.3 and 1:1.4. Only the front-entrance corridor is constructed at 1:1 with a true ceiling height of 240cm, thereby acting as a "control" or normative condition against which to compare the other under- or oversized spaces. In this way, the exhibition of *Svizzera 240* borrows a trick from the minimalist sculptors like Robert Morris and Tony Smith for whom "scale" was a form of content in and of itself.[2]

These changes of scale reveal not only the standardisation of the interior and its components, but also how close the blank or empty apartment is to minimalist sculpture, which too relied on scaling against the body to foreground the conditions of perception.

We might imagine 240cm ceilings to be an example of the natural standardisation of products which Le Corbusier called *objet-types,* but this is not the case. Corbusier proposed that, just as the briar pipe and Thonet bentwood chair were ubiquitous standardised forms of his time, the aggregate choices of architects and clients would settle on a happy norm, and domestic space would eventually achieve such a classic condition under modernism; one announced *avant la lettre* by his Pavillon de l'Esprit Nouveau. Whereas the Thonet is a popular choice among chair designs, the 240cm standard ceiling height of housing today is not so much a choice as a rule. The experiential discomfort of the scale shifts of *Svizzera 240* point to the tremendous social and economic unstitching that would be required to free the building section from this standardised height. To remove this one basic presupposition of multiple-dwelling construction would impact too dramatically on the economics of construction and city planning, let alone the sizing of furniture, fittings and electrical switches that *Svizzera 240* makes acutely visible. Efficiency in housing provision would be lost, but it is also the case that the mundane commonality of our existence would become apparent; the various appendages of domestic life would coalesce into a form that is other to us. 240cm is generic but it is not an *objet-type,* an empirically derived norm; it is a rule that we might better describe as *banal.*

Today we use the word "banal" for the mundane and trivial. The banality of everyday life is made up of those common and mostly unremarked-upon experiences that become visible when we name them as "banal" and make them a question of value and valuation. The pejorative aspect of naming someone's life, possessions and aspirations as banal lies in suggesting that such a person is bound to the mundane aspects of their existence. This signification lies in the etymology of the word. In Old French and mediaeval English, "the banal" refers to feudal agriculture, and particularly the seigneurial right of *banalité* which obliged peasants to grind their grain in mills controlled and taxed by the lord of the manor. Banal has the same root in the German and Old English, *bannan,* as the modern word 'ban' in the sense of an interdict or summons. To say, then, that the 240cm ceiling height of the modern apartment is banal is to say that it is commonplace, not through the fact of it being a frequent occurrence or popular choice, but as an obligation, and by edict. To design for the 240cm apartment is to tacitly accede to the authority of the construction industry to determine the metrological order of life.[3]

In France at the time of the Revolution, the politics of *banalité* were tied up in the adoption of the decimal metric system, because the power to oblige peasants to use the common mill extended to the choice of the units of grain measurement employed there. Increasing the size of the sacks in which grain was accepted at the mill increased the lord's rent, and the question of whether a bushel of grain in the sack was "heaped" or "struck" level was contentious for buyers and sellers alike.[4] Under the Ancien Régime, it is estimated that a quarter of a million different units of measurement were used. The successful imposition in 1795 of a national standard of measures—which became the →

1 I live in a house with 11'6" (350.5cm) ceilings. It was built at a time (1907) when ceilings of the timber villa houses of Brisbane in northern Australia were constructed at one of three heights, 10'6", 11'6", or 12'6", depending on social class and overall proportions. Mine is a middle-class house. More recently built houses in Queensland have 240cm ceilings, like apartments.

2 Author's correspondence, quote drawn from the competition brief

3 My interest in the etymology of the banal derives from reading Meaghan Morris's excellent essay, which treats the concept with regard to a quite different topic. Meaghan Morris, 'Banality in Cultural Studies', *Discourse,* vol. 10, no. 2, 1988, p. 3–29.

4 W. Kula, *Measures and Men,* Princeton New Jersey, Princeton University Press, 1986.

International System of Units—was and still is understood as a blow against feudalism and the injustices that could occur under opaque customary practices. Should we be grateful, then, that Swiss centimetres are the same as those in France, or India?

In sociology, there is a concept of "banal cosmopolitanism", which describes the experience of globalisation by members of metropolitan cultures when they listen to "world music" and expect to have a variety of cuisines available in their neighbourhoods.[5] 240 cm could be an aspect of this process; not the imagination of a cosmopolitan world presented in the ubiquitous choice between Italian and Indian restaurants, but rather a banal metropolitanism where, across the globe, bourgeois domestic life becomes more homogenised as cultural difference also becomes more managed and banal.

There has been a flattening out of housing that goes beyond the standardisation of the sectional dimension. The image economy in which housing is caught up also lends it some of the flatness of a picture. the *House Tour* archive shows photographs of empty, freshly finished apartments taken by their architects, and this documents a startling sameness. Apartments are consumer items, and one's choice of an address, price point and internal plan expresses class position and economic means. The staging of the apartment—its modern furniture and heirloom pieces, artworks, books and perhaps a piano (or valve amplifier for the smaller apartment)—provides buyers with the scope to become the inhabitants the apartment calls for. But in between the macroeconomics of apartment location and size, and the microeconomics of furnishing—with all the semantic potential that these offer—the apartments themselves are strangely the same. In the time of Facebook and Instagram, the homemaking work we must do to produce ourselves has changed; it is as if the apartment were an Internet platform, a blank screen, an empty account calling out for images and experiences to be shared. It is the place where, awake on a sleepless night, we will like our friends' witty Instagrams. A metropolitan banality is, of course, no longer part of the feudal mode of production, but we are still turning millstones. Under neoliberal capitalism our fealty is not to the local lord but to ourselves, or to our responsibility to fully exercise the freedoms that are allowed us. The flatness of housing lies not only in the limited range of spatial variation that 240cm imposes, but also in the image of housing. Less and less is one's home an expression of self: more and more, it is like other shareable, monetisable forms of cultural content production at which we must toil. What is revealed in our clothing, online lives and housing is not only us, but also how successful we have been as entrepreneurs of ourselves.

The facts of the banality of our existence, facts that we recognise when we use the term pejoratively, are also familiar at another level in critical art practice. The photographs of empty apartments exhibited in the *House Tour* archive also reveal a fascination with blankness, seriality and ambiguity of scale which reveals a common ground with aspects of art, from minimalist sculpture, to the matter-of-factness of photographers such as the "new topographers", Bernd and Hilla Becher and their contemporary followers.[6] Thus the seriality of the apartment form and its ambiguous scale when photographed empty has as much to do with the relationship of art and architecture as disciplines as it does with the subject of the contemporary interior. As Hal Foster puts it: "Not long ago, a near prerequisite for vanguard architecture was an engagement with theory; lately it has become an acquaintance with art."[7] This leads to the difficult question of whether the contemporary apartment is a cultural trickle-down of lessons learned in the Minimalism art movement last century, into the style that architects and popular interiors publications now call "minimalism". But the banality of this observation can also be hardened and sharpened by recalling the archaic meaning of banal; it is a confrontation of obligations and rights, of categories and practices, that is involved in these two minimalisms. In the architects' photographs, the issue of the constrained condition of building the domestic interior becomes an agonistic relation

5 U. Beck, 'Cosmopolitical Realism: On the Distinction between Cosmopolitanism in Philosophy and the Social Sciences', *Global Networks*, vol. 4, no. 2, 2004, p. 131–56.

6 E. Shinkle, 'Boredom, Repetition, Inertia: Contemporary Photography and the Aesthetics of the Banal', *Mosaic: An Interdisciplinary Critical Journal*, vol. 37, no. 4, 2004, p. 165–84.
R. Hawker, 'Repopulating the Street: Contemporary Photography and Urban Experience', *History of Photography*, vol. 37, no. 3, 2013, p. 341–52.

7 H. Foster, *The Art-Architecture Complex*, London, Verso, 2011, p. 2.

between architecture and visual art, and vice versa, debates about the differential specificity of art disciplines bears on how we live.

One of the various apologies for minimalism in architecture is, like that of the *objet-type*, that a process of abstraction and reduction can lead to classic forms that satisfyingly combine a high degree of formal closure with simplicity scaled to the body. *Svizzera 240* shows the limits of this idea through the bodily discomfort that the same arrangements can produce at different scales. The more sophisticated accounts of minimalist architecture suggest that blankness and apparent uneventfulness in building form can make an observer attend more closely to the structure and temporality of their own perception, but *Svizzera 240* shows that this, too, is a poor explanation of architecture. If the simplicity of the modern apartment were a finely calibrated phenomenology, then we would not be so struck by the sameness and reiteration of the interiors. If some true address to the perceiving body were possible, we would not be so struck by the self-consisting thingness that an apartment is, even when its scale is varied as by *Svizzera 240*. In this way, as Foster writes, *Svizzera 240* is "acquainted" with the plays on scale and objecthood that we know from the sculpture of Robert Morris and Tony Smith. But to use these strategies in architecture is not simple appropriation. While a critique of the singularity of the body clearly has a precedent in Minimalism, a new question about the relation of art and architecture and the empirical existence of art objects emerges: what is an art concept of seriality when exercised in the actual modularity of the built environment?

Michael Fried's criticism of Minimalism in its heyday has itself become a kind of theory of contemporary art practice and its limits.[8] It is worth remembering that he called the body of work he criticised "literalism", a term that brings it in closer parallel to our present concern. Fried thought that the nominalism by which mundane objects were said to be art was only part of the problem of literalism, which extended to the kind of subjectivity it constructed for the art viewer, one that was, as Fried writes, "vaguely monstrous".[9] This monstrosity lay in the hidden or latent anthropomorphism of literalist objects. The cubes, boxes and beams of Morris, Smith and Donald Judd seem to be generic, featureless, with no address to a viewer, and thus in the phenomenological theory of Minimalism, are objects that would throw a viewer back into an awareness of their apperception. Fried argued this was a kind of theatricality, a display of being affected, or being affectable, that he later connected to sentimental paintings of the eighteenth century and which is common today in the cultivation of online personas or the self-conscious staging of the apartment. In literalist sculpture, Fried argued that this theatre relied on a certain anthropomorphism. However unhuman in form and unadapted to use these objects were, they were hollow; they supposed a relation of figure and interior like that of the human body. The monstrosity lay in the objecthood of the artwork being both like and unlike the object of our bodies. The apartment is hollow, but in a different way.

The empty, just-finished apartment is a blank and hollow interior that we can fill with our lives. Certain dimensions make that possible: the height of benches, sills and door handles, and ceilings that can make domestic space seem as prosthetic as clothing. Unlike the covert anthropomorphism of minimalist objecthood, the apartment is explicit; what it hides are the abstract standards of a socioeconomic system to which we are bound. Of course, we see the door handle as a relation to a hand, and the ceiling as a roof over us, but they are also strange and monstrous objects, coded standards and the economy of supply chains that have become things. To understand the fit of the apartment to the body is to see housing completed in its relation with us. This is what the scale shifts of *Svizzera 240* disrupt, like an ill-fitting prosthesis. What we see, then, is the objecthood in which lies the image of domestic space that we cannot measure with our bodies. This banality of housing shows us something of the obligations under which we live, and which we might easily mistake as comfort. ■

8 M. Fried, 'Art and Objecthood', *Artforum,* vol. 5, no. 10, Summer 1967.
9 For a discussion of Fried's charge of the monstrosity of Minimalism see T. Ross, 'Art and Objecthood Three Decades On', *Australian and New Zealand Journal of Art,* vol. 1, no. 1, 2000, p. 149–61.

# Custom Vanity

Claire Lehmann

RN Richard Nixon
NK Nikita Khrushchev

RN I want to show you this kitchen. It is like those of our houses in California. *[Nixon points to dishwasher.]*

NK We have such things.

RN This is our newest model. This is the kind which is built in thousands of units for direct installations in the houses. In America, we like to make life easier for women ...

NK Your capitalistic attitude toward women does not occur under Communism.

RN I think that this attitude towards women is universal. What we want to do is make life more easy for our housewives ...

NK Your American houses are built to last only twenty years so builders could sell new houses at the end. We build firmly. We build for our children and grandchildren.

RN American houses last for more than twenty years, but, even so, after twenty years, many Americans want a new house or a new kitchen. Their kitchen is obsolete by that time ... The American system is designed to take advantage of new inventions and new techniques.

NK This theory does not hold water. Some things never get out of date—houses, for instance, and furniture, furnishings—perhaps—but not houses. I have read much about America and American houses, and I do not think that this exhibit and what you say is strictly accurate ...

RN This exhibit was not designed to astound but to interest. Diversity, the right to choose, the fact that we have a thousand builders building a thousand different houses is the most important thing. We don't have one decision made at the top by one government official. This is the difference.

—'Kitchen Debate', American National Exhibition at Sokolniki Park, Moscow, 24 July 1959

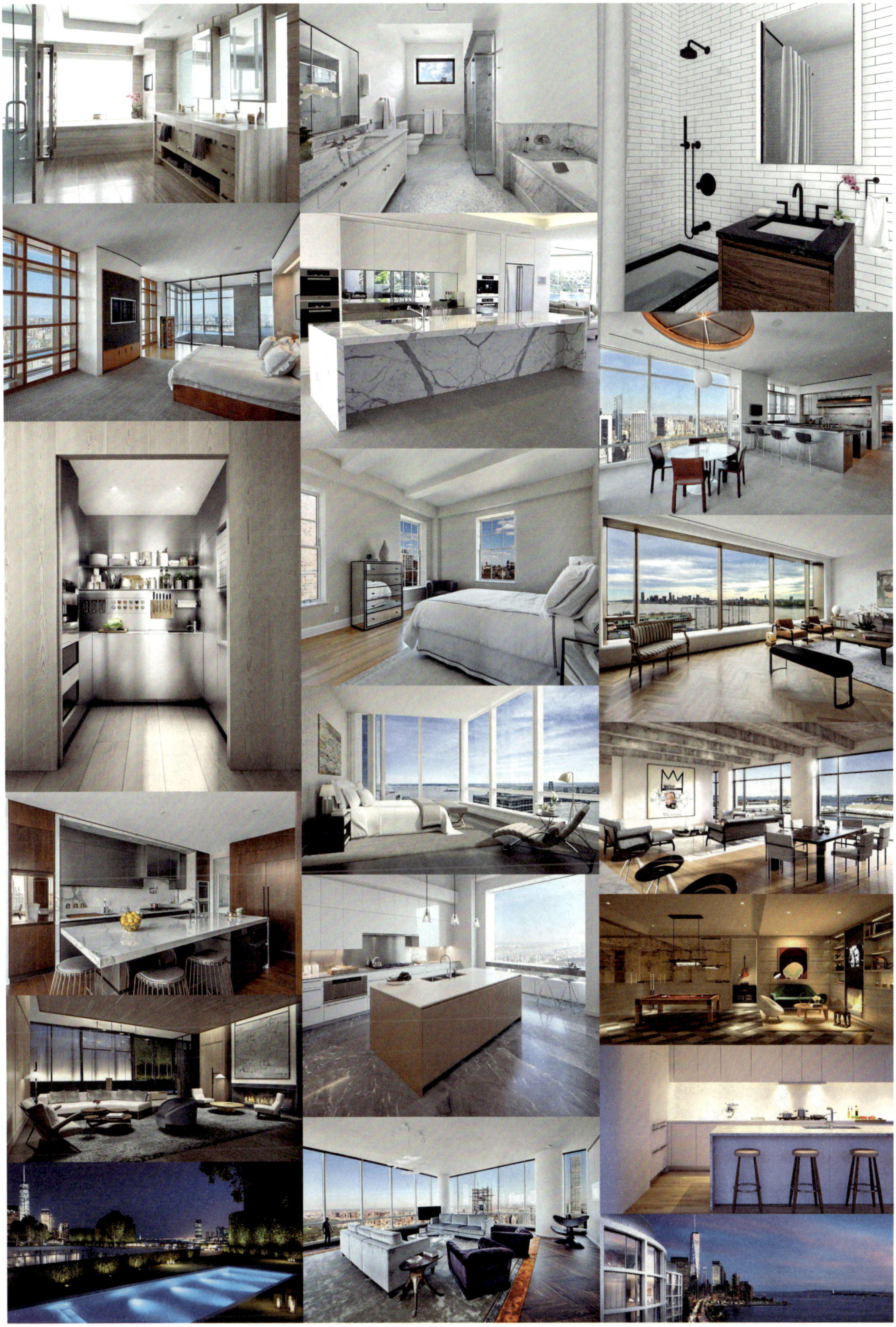

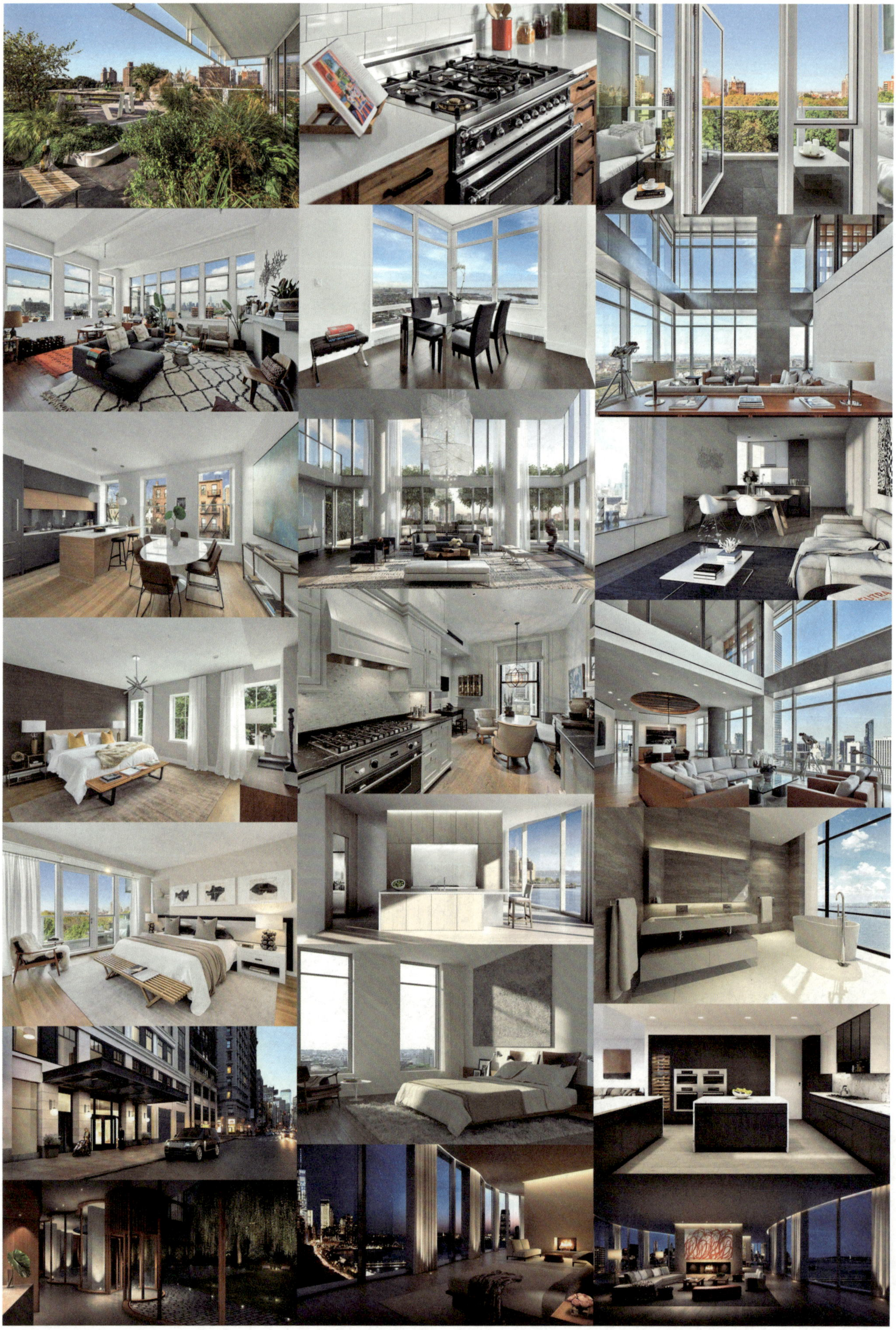

House Tour:
Views of the Unfurnished Apartment

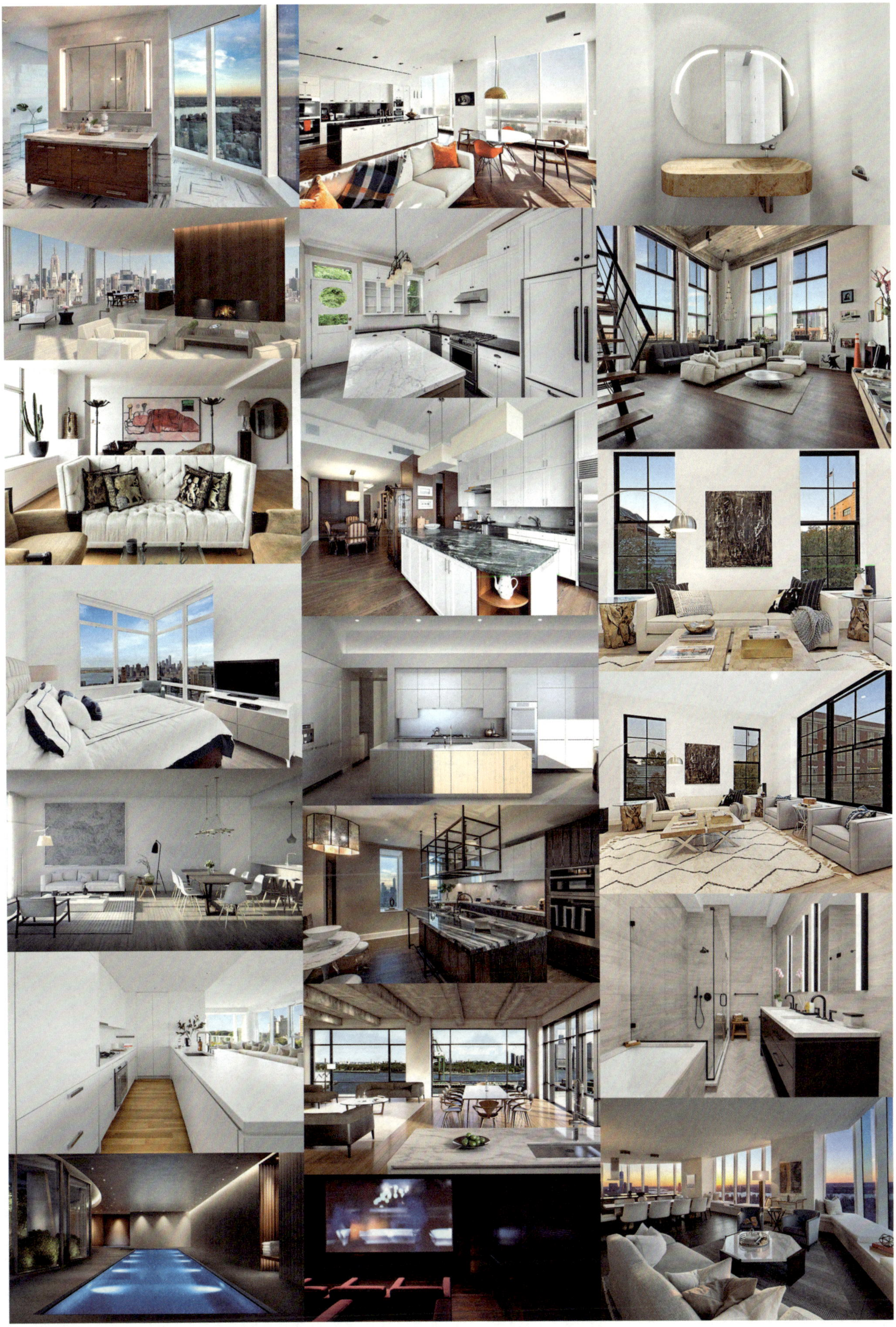

Reference images found by the author on various real-estate marketing websites.

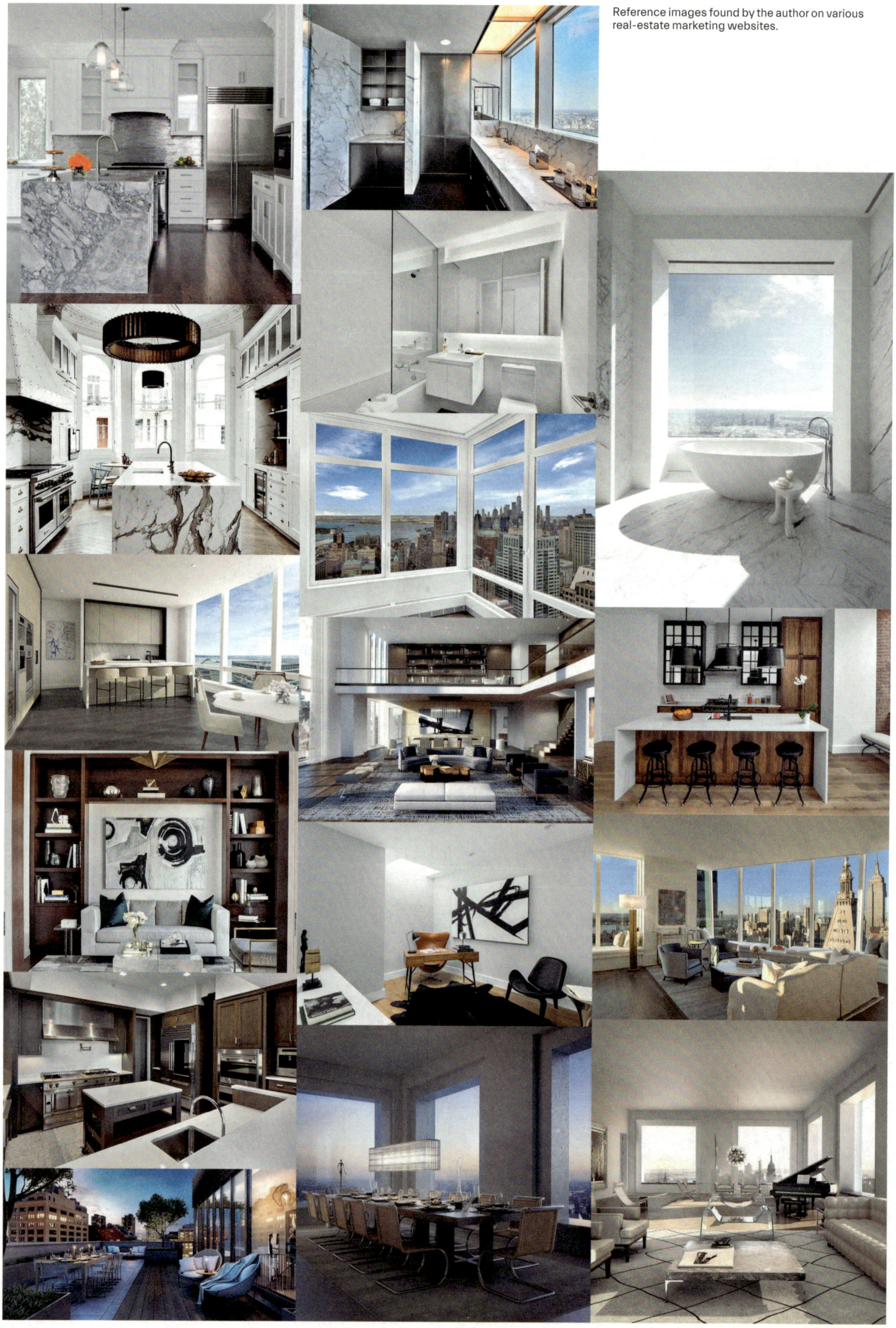

1.

In the real-estate listing photos, the kitchen will be faceted in richly veined stones of variegated colours. Through the windows, the cyan sky will have a typical average RGB screen value of 135–175–240. That blue will fade as it descends, via a gentle gradient, toward a distant stand of treetops. The trees, though far off, will be crystalline in focus and vivid in colour; simultaneously sharp is the well-lit interior, with its waterfall-style island, its blossoming countertop orchid, its row of Bertoia stools. The appliance suite will be Gaggenau, Liebherr, Miele, Bertazzoni or Bosch, depending on the price per square foot, the neighbourhood and the target demographic. The cabinets will be a classic lacquered white or gray, or, if the desired buyer is appropriately high-income, will be fronted with rift-sawn oak or walnut—the priciest cut due to the high wastage in milling a 45-degree linear grain pattern from lumber. If the stove is a Viking or a Wolf, the cabinet fronts are more likely to have wide chamfers and finish beading (rather than flat, minimalist planes), the drawer pulls likely to be “apothecary style”, and the ceiling more apt to feature crown molding, for such heroically sized cooking ranges tend to appeal to the buyer who prefers a rustic, arcadian feel to the kitchen.[1] There will be a modernist bowl of citrus fruits on the island, and perhaps a couplet of croissants and a French press on the rear counter. If we are viewing the kitchen at dusk, wine glasses and even a CGI cheese plate may appear. The apartment is new, or will be in the near future: it is unfinished at the moment, but the listing agent is currently accepting offers on the basis of slick photos and the building’s sole completed model unit. It is located in downtown or midtown Manhattan, or in the northwestern quadrant of Brooklyn; legally speaking, it is a condominium, not a cooperative building, meaning that there will be an absence of the irritating regulations and shareholder meetings endemic to the latter.

This apartment—the New York new-construction condo—is coveted and reviled in equal measure. Its desirability can be inferred by robust sales numbers and the sizable transfer-tax premium that buyers willingly pay for virgin occupancy; its vilification easily noted in essays and social-media chatter, in which it regularly appears as an easy metonym for vulgar taste and an insufficient appreciation of history. (The new-construction condo is the *ne plus ultra* symbol of the changing city, that once-feral creature undergoing a quite literal process of domestication.) The city’s modern residential construction boom began waxing in the 1980s, as the city came out of bankruptcy into the frenzy of Reagan-era money; in the current millennium, New York’s growth (and that of similar cities across the country) exploded, as people shunned the suburbs in favour of the cosmopolitan attributes that celebrity urbanists enumerated: walkability, diversity, density and, above all, proximity to culture, to perceived bohemianism, to all that posits itself in opposition to life in the suburbs—the very desires that led to intensifying gentrification, ballooning home prices and the inevitable eradication of the very diversity and heterogeneity that had been so alluring. As the United States’ most expensive housing market, New York’s high volume of new residential buildings and its constant sales froth arguably situate its real-estate scene as the most elaborate expression of the similar structures deployed in such markets across the globe: the design trends, financial calculations, marketing signifiers and imaging styles that together form the aesthetics of the contemporary interior.

A small coterie of institutional players brings such structures to life: sponsors, developers, consultants, stagers, photographers, retouchers. A building’s design specifics must be determined two to three years before it will come to market, and will depend primarily on the most significant considerations, i.e., the target neighbourhood, the desired demographics of the potential buyers, the range of bedrooms required by those buyers, the acceptable floor layouts and the combined package of building-wide amenities. Once the building has transitioned to the finish-work stage, at least one apartment will be fully completed ahead of the rest, so that it can be used as the model; the stager will then transform its bare cubic volumes into refined →

1 For helpful insight regarding developers’ habits, apartment-staging concerns and real-estate photography, I thank broker Deborah Rieders, stager Nicole Rueda-Watts and photographer Al Siedman. All quoted listing copy is sourced from the websites of the Corcoran Group or Douglas Elliman Real Estate, two leading New York City real-estate firms.

salons, filling them with strenuously neutral furnishings and careful accents of texture and colour that signal a bland but knowing elegance. This set of rooms will then be documented in bright daylight—and, occasionally, also at dusk—by a photographer using a lens with a focal length ranging on average from 17 to 24mm, who will shoot multiple exposures for compositing in postproduction, so that every element in the image—from the high-flying clouds in the windows to the polished wood floors just a few feet from the lens—will be evenly lit and perfectly in focus.

> [Our] proprietary Clearshot technology assures that all parts of the image, even what's seen through the windows, will be colorful and ultra-sharp, with multiple exposures skillfully combined to create one stunning, brilliant image.[2]

2.

A front entrance photograph of the building will feature a white-gloved doorman, a Range Rover parked at the curb, and an attractive blonde woman pushing a baby carriage while staring down at her cell phone. On closer inspection, the blonde is identifiable as Gisele Bündchen, the Brazilian supermodel, in an appropriated paparazzi shot from 2012 (from which the figure has been silhouetted, reduced in size, and digitally flipped). If the new building is a high-rise, there will also be several seconds of animation of the morning or late-afternoon sun falling gently on its exterior, and then dusk descending as the city glows with a million illuminated windows. At this magical hour, living room lamps in the interior shots will create pools of warm light around the sofas, which, as one real-estate industry website advised, will encourage the buyer to "think that could be an eternal sunset"—an endless quiescence that is, apparently, enviable.

This is how desire is conjured from a set of empty cubes. As one longtime real-estate photographer ruefully described it, New York's interiors are just "boxes stacked next to each other, side by side, or on top of each other". This is, of course, true of most residential architecture the world over: boxes that must be ordered, aligned and configured for living. But in a market as teeming with activity as New York City's, the challenge is one of differentiation. How to summon, from blocks rising out of a particular patch of ground—out of thin air, truly—a home that will distinguish itself from the others, that will cut through the froth?

The interior photographs have their own conventions; so too does the listing language. The marketing copy will be a thicket of signifiers, a canny bid to the particular market rung of the buyer. Exploring such texts over time will yield a sort of rough index, revealing which appliances correlate with which price brackets, which amenities will be included with what amount of total square footage.

> Surprisingly large open chef's kitchens feature European wood and lacquer cabinetry with fully paneled Bosch and Liebherr appliances and dramatic, honed Caesarstone countertops for both the work areas and breakfast bars.
>
> Representing the utmost in artisanal merit, experience a new level of culinary excellence in your handcrafted Brookman's kitchen from Smallbone of Devizes, a global purveyor of bespoke British craftsmanship.
>
> 1" thick Cristallo gold quartz countertops with "waterfall" feature and backsplash have been hand selected from Italy.
>
> The open kitchen boasts custom walnut cabinetry, Caesarstone countertops, a 5-burner Viking gas range, a SubZero refrigerator, a Bosch dishwasher, a SubZero wine cooler, and a vibrantly tiled backsplash.
>
> Chef's kitchens are outfitted with Miele appliance packages, custom light-gray cabinetry, walnut pulls, and Italian marble countertops.

2 Copy from VHT Studios, the US's number-one real-estate photography service.

The flurry of brand names, amenities and design features that so defines this era of new-construction interiors came into being not through the input of architects, but through the consistent need, on the part of developers and consultants, to boost the per-square-foot price. The apartment-hunter will come to understand a fuzzy yet not inaccurate taxonomy: that Gaggenau is strictly for one-per-centers; Miele for the moneyed, practical-minded buyer who disdains the flaunting of affluence—a genteel, trust-funded Yankee, say; Bertazzoni for the design-conscious hipster who enjoys the pedigree of Italian manufacture along with the frisson of the up-and-coming neighbourhood. Developers must choose these signifiers with care, however, and with no small feat of data interpolation: years in advance of the building's completion, they must determine how to distinguish their building through such choices, imbued with both real and symbolic value; they must design a building that will feel at once fresh yet timeless without knowing precisely where the market will be or what the tastes of that future date will dictate. Jumping on a widespread trend can have its own risks, for whenever a trend tips over into the realm of overexposure, it risks being duplicated at a much lower cost by the home-improvement giants (Home Depot, Lowes, Ikea) and becoming irreparably tainted. Such was the case with cherry-wood kitchen cabinets, a style all the rage fifteen years ago: noticing the widespread demand, Home Depot developed a cherry veneer set, flooding the lower tier of the market; the cherry cabinet thus became stylistically toxic, in unspeakably bad taste.

Thus, the perennial quandary for developers is this: for any given space, in any given neighbourhood, how to construct a building in which each square foot can justifiably command the highest rate the market will bear, while staying carefully ahead of the trend curve? How to eke a two-bedroom, two-bath floor plan out of a mere thousand square feet, or, conversely, how to fashion a four-bedroom, five-and-a-half-bath apartment out of six thousand square feet—and moreover, how to determine what brands of bathroom tile would appeal to these two vastly different buyers? For, as Fredrik Eklund, one of Manhattan's top real-estate brokers (over $5 billion in property sold to date), notes, "We not only sell property, we sell a lifestyle."

3.

Not all real-estate brokers write their own listing copy; this work can be outsourced to one of the many such online services. One business boasts a copywriting team that "will write copy unique to your property within just 24-hours *with no property inspection required*".[3] No property inspection is required not only because photos will be available for the writer's perusal, but also because the language is entirely standardised. The appropriate adjectives, or the knowledge of which brand names to emphasise and which to suppress, can be easily gleaned by the attentive reader after an hour or two on a listings website. Whoever composes successful copy knows that the best features must be "seen to be believed," that the views are "sweeping" and "magical," that the home is *both* "gracious and grand."

beautifully outfitted
generously proportioned
imported from France
hand-selected
stunning
rare
private
coveted
iconic
majestic
exceptional
sumptuous

All this would suggest, then, that the central irony in what the marketing language for the new-construction condo must do—i.e., differentiate—is a task based on the inherent uniformity of what buyers are looking for. Or, put another way, in order to differentiate, the marketing must indicate that the →

3 BoxBrownie, a market leader in real-estate photo editing. Emphasis mine.

new-construction condo has exactly the same things as all the other condos in its class have, but that these same things are better: copy must therefore be garnished with adjectives that indicate the qualities of refinement, abundance, elevation from the norm. The high-end, new-construction condo must *conform while exceeding* what is offered by other buildings—a condo development is just a series of "boxes stacked next to each other", sure, and equipped with the standards of its class, but *its* marble countertops are hand-selected; *its* mantels are imported from France; *its* views are majestic. Within the building itself, the residences could be easily analogised to a suburban prefab subdivision: a handful of floor plans are applied to a vast number of apartments, uniform along the same vertical axis. You live in an identical apartment to that of your upstairs or downstairs neighbour—those who live on the same "line" (2B, 3B, 4B). All of you share the same taste, a similar income bracket, and consistent aesthetic values. Your apartment may be *grand, coveted* and *rare*, but you are in fact living in an upright queue of selfsame "rarities" reaching skyward, as formulaic as the production-line homes on a suburban cul-de-sac—a new, elitist mass vernacular.

4.

> Spa bathrooms feature Waterworks fixtures, Ruscello Fosso Picollo marble floors, and walnut and brushed nickel vanities.
>
> Spa-like bathrooms offer clean lines and feature custom wood vanities topped with Caesarstone, glass-enclosed showers, and large-format floor-to-ceiling wall tile.
>
> The master bathroom features a steam shower, Waterworks fixtures and radiant heated, hand laid marble floors in Chevron pattern. The richly hued walnut vanity is topped with a continuous slab of Zeus black marble.
>
> The gracious Master Bedroom suite … [is] completed with a lavish spa master bath with a deep Kaldewei soaking tub, radiant heated floors, double Sivec marble vanity, large stall shower, and separate water closet, all clad in slabs of pure Sivec marble.

A lifestyle frequently depicted in listings is one in which everyday ablutions are conducted in a warm, steam-filled *spa*, a word seen constantly in the copy describing high-end bathrooms. The marketing photos will focus lovingly on the lavish master bath, which, like the kitchen, is a tour de force of marmoreal outlay, boasting vast planes of lineated stone. The custom vanity features stacks of plush towels spiraled into neat rolls, a row of bath products (Aesop), and a candle (Diptyque). There will be city views from the bathtub, and there will also be a single stalk of monstera in a cylindrical minimalist vase.

In the sleeping chamber to which this spa environment is adjoined, the furniture will be sparse but handsomely accoutred. On the bed, three layers of pillows in descending sizes will be stacked against the headboard, with the first or second row providing a bright accent hue against the radiantly white sheets. At the foot, overlaying the main coverlet, a folded blanket supplies a horizontal stripe of coordinated colour, breaking up the plane to give the mattress depth. A fiddle-leaf fig tree in the corner of the room will add a pop of green, and the bedside lamp will be an articulated industrial classic. An abstract painting above the phalanx of pillows will be a passable take on the work of Franz Kline.

This bedroom—the quantity of such bedrooms, more specifically—is a key aspect of the marketing of the new-construction condo. To make the proposed square-foot-price of a new building a successful proposition, the total price point for the bedroom *count* has to match the demographic of the buyer. (Who is that buyer, and how many offspring do they have; are they rich enough to afford a guest room?) Standard, overstandard and substandard bedroom sizes will be designed based on the neighbourhood and purchasing power of the targeted buyer. If the total square footage is too high for a given bedroom count, the overall price will exceed the buyer's capacity; if too many bedrooms have been carved from too small a footprint, the buyer will likewise be deterred.

Matching the price per square foot to the correct buying demographic is thus the art of the thriving development team. Some standard considerations apply across the board: good closet space is essential; it is important to lay out the living room to fit both a sofa and a dining table comfortably, and to consider where the TV might be placed in relation to the couch. Certain trend-proof truths about new buildings remain durable: in New York, the thirty-something first-time buyer is delighted by a garbage disposal, a new bathroom, a good shower head and a plethora of outlets. The DUMBO buyer wants a loft-like, open-plan kitchen for family-style entertaining. The Upper East Side buyer wants a closed kitchen, where their domestic staff will labour unseen.

5.

Step off your private elevator vestibule and embrace the impeccable Great Room with a fireplace and wetbar on the waterfront with idyllic sunrise and sunset views.

A private elevator landing invites you into an elegant entry gallery, beyond which awaits artfully-designed living space graced by solid oak flooring and massive 10'× 10' picture windows that bathe the ambience in natural light. The dramatic 29'× 29' corner living / dining room affords a glamorous setting for entertaining with a backdrop of stretching views.

Masterfully planned for the contemporary lifestyle, the residence's open floor plan accommodates gracious living and formal entertaining while maximizing light and offering an abundance of wall space for art.

In the living room, the coffee-table books contribute illustrated histories of *Vogue* or the fashions of Manolo Blahnik; an artful stack on the side table boasts spines with straightforward titles like ART or MODERN ART or PICASSO. An assemblage of pendant chandeliers lights the dining table; the chairs are mid-century. The throw pillows on the couch will be orderly, and ideally will not be so excessive in number that they extend too far forward on the seat cushion, for this would subtly alter the potential buyer's mental perception that they could sit down and feel at home here. All the views from the windows will feature abundant sky; the attentive photo retoucher will have ensured that the blue in the window, if reflected in other planes in the room—a highly polished coffee table, a decorative mirror, an ebonised finish on the floors—will be matched in chromatic intensity.

If the photographs of the apartment are virtually staged, the selection of art will rise to another stratosphere altogether. A recent perusal of high-end listings yielded the following parade of blue-chip hits: in one apartment ($82 million) living room sported Botticelli's *Primavera* and one of Brancusi's bronze *Birds in Space*. A Lower East Side condo ($23.5 million) had a virtual version version of Gerhard Richter's 1982 painting *Three Candles*, covering the wall at a size about ten times larger than the area of the actual painting. In a Brooklyn condo ($2.55 million), a Yayoi Kusama rests both above the dining table and the headboard in the master bed- →

room. In the waiting area of one particularly chic lobby, a Tom Ford book on the coffee table was paired with a Christopher Wool (unit cost: $18.9 million).

6.

The essential sameness of mass-construction American homes is one of the most long-running and potent symbols for late-capitalist conformity and its attendant anomie. Cultural scrutiny of the state of American real estate proliferated in the latter half of the twentieth century, in light of white flight and the hollowing out of the nation's cities in favour of the newly sprouting surrounding towns. Amid the proliferation of uniform towns rose a collective notice of the crushing squareness they engender: the neatly subdivided Levittowns, sprouting negligibly iterative model homes; the acerbic bedroom-community fiction of John Cheever, John Updike or Richard Yates, the former of whom delighted in detailing the habits of "stupid, depressed, and uncreative" suburbanites; the deadpan photography of Dan Graham's *Homes for America,* Lewis Baltz's *The Tract Houses* or Bill Owens's *Suburbia.* Post-war home ownership has been propped up by tax policy, morally deformed by racially restrictive covenants and pushed to the brink by the mid-aughts housing bubble, but it remains ever-durable as the symbol of the American Dream—and, by extension, American capitalism itself.

Khruschev and Nixon's impromptu 'Kitchen Debate', at the 1959 American Exhibition in Moscow, after all, began with Nixon directing Khruschev to inspect a brand-new dishwasher installed in the cutaway kitchen of a suburban model house, constructed on-site and billed as a home that "anyone" in the US could afford. Irritated by Nixon's insinuation that such things were not available under Communism, Khruschev accused the American construction industry of shoddy workmanship motivated by the profit imperative of planned obsolescence, while Nixon in turn lionised the American desire for innovation and variety, noting that in the US there are "a thousand builders building a thousand different houses ... We don't have one decision made at the top by one government official. This is the difference." This emphasis on variation and choice was by no means uncontroversial: just three years later, in 1962, Malvina Reynolds composed the song "Little Boxes," made famous by Pete Seeger:

> Little boxes on the hillside
> Little boxes made of ticky-tacky
> Little boxes on the hillside
> Little boxes all the same
> There's a pink one and a green one
> And a blue one and a yellow one
> And they're all made out of ticky-tacky
> And they all look just the same
> And the people in the houses
> All went to the university
> Where they were put in boxes
> And they came out all the same
> And there's doctors and lawyers
> And business executives
> And they're all made out of ticky-tacky
> And they all look just the same.

If there is difference in the mass vernacular of post-war American housing, Reynolds suggests, it is merely superficial ("a pink one and a green one"); the essential sameness at its core is reflected in the similitude of the citizens it produces. While the initial widespread move to the suburbs (by white Americans) was driven by the notion that such towns offered relief from the city's press of bodies, filth and noise, in reality (or as endless cultural commentary has posited) such towns offered an opportunity for its inhabitants' dreams to be supplanted—by keeping up with the Joneses, by the socially pacifying effects of the monthly mortgage. As the Marxist geographer David Harvey explains,

> The suburbanization of the United States was not merely a matter of new infrastructures ... It entailed a radical transformation in lifestyles and produced a whole new way of life in which new products from housing to refrigerators and air conditioners as well as two cars in the driveway and an enormous increase in the consumption of oil, all played their part ... It also altered the political landscape as subsidized homeownership for the middle classes changed the focus of community action towards the defense of property values and individualized identities (turning the suburban vote towards conservative republicanism). In any case, it was argued, debt-encumbered homeowners are less likely to go on strike.

After the initial post-war rush of suburbanisation, it was going *back* to the city that provided a suitable nod to liberation, at least in certain pop-cultural representations: by the late 1960s, *Mad Men*'s Don Draper leaves his wife and their shared home in Westchester County in order to begin life anew with Megan, wife number-two, in the city. There they live in a flawless mid-century high-rise on Park Avenue, with a balcony, sunken living room, teakwood built-ins and breakfast bar. The thrusting-off of convention demands—on a symbolic level—city living, even if the apartments there remain just as standardised.

The seasoned real-estate photographer tells of shooting images "of an L-shaped studio, going ten blocks away to shoot another apartment … and it's the same floor plan." It is inescapable. The developer interpolates the market's data points, but the sameness of what they produce is no deterrent: the buyer has already interpellated the prevailing values of the market. She will take the cookie-cutter L-shaped studio, but she knows her taste, and prefers the one ten blocks further uptown, the one with the Miele stove, not the Bertazzoni.

7.

What essential promise does any newly constructed home hold for its inhabitants, from the mid-century boxes of the suburban subdivision to the multimillion-dollar condo high above the city streets? If the standards of design and amenities for a new home shift constantly over the years, where does its enduring appeal lie? Who, moreover, is the notional resident of these newly constructed dwellings? At the frothiest, highest end of the market, I visualise the denizens of such apartments as characterised by the writer Lucinda Rosenfeld, in a novel whose narrator imagines moving in with a new beau, and how they'd soon be "lying around on the floor in their androgynous Calvin Klein underwear … snacking on seaweed while debating the relative merits of the latest Don DeLillo novel." (This vision can only be contrasted with a vision of the suburban Babbitts, who presumably spend their leisure time freshening up the white paint on their fence pickets before tucking into their Saturday-night baked potato and pot roast.) So much of the task of understanding the codes that govern American new construction lies in looking at images of unpopulated rooms—but what of those rooms when they are occupied, when the task of living there begins?

Initially, the aesthetic language of the listing photographs of such residences—the typicality of the floor plans, the benign, staged furnishings, the carefully stacked pillows—seem absurd: redolent of a chic but bland residential hotel, pleasing to anyone but no one in particular. And then, after looking at dozens or scores of such listings, the possible freedom that this newness affords, its infectious sense of potentiality, starts to creep into your bloodstream like a slow-moving contagion, quickening your heartbeat as you project yourself into the spa, the living room, the master bed. To say that such imagery provides a sense of pure possibility is commonplace, but it's actually impossible, or at least undesirable, to imagine *living* in a newly constructed home at all. Thinking of a future beyond the initial projection implies that the space would become … used. Real-estate images of a new home seem effective because of the easy projection they allow, but their true effectiveness lies in the fact that their perfection dispels all thoughts of quotidian existence thereafter, obviating the mortal need for seaweed snacks and pot roast alike. That is to say, they make it easy to imagine a lifestyle, but hard to imagine a life. This conundrum becomes clear upon encountering images of a previously occupied residence. In for-sale photographs of inhabited homes, the slightly out-of-date furnishings—specific to the tastes of an actual occupant—no matter how smartly edited or staged, seem to foretell that such an apartment may only be suitable for a slightly out-of-date person: superannuated, obsolescent.

In the newly constructed home, the paint is fresh, the floors are clean; not merely clean, but flawless, varnished just weeks ago. You can be certain that the interior doors will close with a satisfying click. No hinges will squeak or stick. If dust must fall upon the baseboards during your tenancy, the dust will be yours alone. But think not of dust: "This is our newest model", said Nixon. You will be free from such things, for you will exist surrounded by the newest-model spa shower, the newest-model dishwasher, the newest-model everything. Of course, to maintain this image, you couldn't possibly use any of it. You must stand perfectly still in the centre of the room that you had imagined yourself in, suspended in sharp focus, waiting for the eternal sunset to arrive. ▪

# Antagonistic Exchange

Charles Rice

It is a one-minute scene in episode eight of season three of the American sitcom *Curb Your Enthusiasm:* Larry David visits the house Susie and Jeff Greene have just moved into. On stepping into the entrance hall, Larry is politely effusive: "Look at this place—amazing." Susie then enters past the removalists' boxes and greets him with new homeowner's pride: "Hey Lar! Huh, is this something!" and then she offers him "the tour". Her use of the definite article is worth noting. It's not just *a* tour, it's *the* tour, the ritual all new homeowners impose on first-time visitors. Larry politely demurs, explaining that it's not necessary: "It's bedrooms, bathrooms ... I get it." Susie is aghast, and fires back a vehement riposte (Larry and Susie's ongoing antagonism is part of the comic setup): "Alright, get the fuck out of my house, OK, Larry, just get the fuck out. Right now." It's not that Larry has refused the tour, he's refused to engage with the desire that drives home ownership—the desire for personal identity and pride in achievement expressed spatially and materially. In refusing, Larry confirms that her house is like every other one up and down the street. He can see past the tchotchkes and decorations being unpacked from boxes, clearly the focus of Susie's libidinal investment, to what makes her new dwelling just another example of suburban housing. Susie is "turned off" at Larry's refusal, despite—or perhaps because of—his peacemaking entreaties. In Susie's terms, what "freak of fucking nature" wouldn't want the house tour, wouldn't want to understand the domestic as the natural habitat for the cultivation of personal identity, where everyone's difference is put on display?

I take house tours all the time, as I'm mildly addicted to a smartphone app called Domain. A genius amalgam of Tinder and Instagram, it matches you with a lifestyle. I check it about three or four times a day, which, it must be said, is not all that often in the context of smartphone apps. But when you consider that it's selling real estate, such frequency of checking is a little worrying. I'm not actually looking to buy an apartment—I already found my match on Domain—but I'm drawn back there all the time for updates on the way people present their places. The app's scrollable listings provide instant gratification. I can set preferences for postcode, dwelling type, price and number of bedrooms and bathrooms, and specify keywords such as "study" or "pool", or even "architect-designed". My personalised selections materialise as a constantly updated list, with each dwelling presented by a headline image underscored by its attributes: address, guide price, and icons for number of bedrooms, bathrooms and parking spaces. These are the parameters of real estate in Sydney.

Domain was spun out from the classified section of the *Sydney Morning Herald*, the daily newspaper of a city famously obsessed with real estate. Most domestic properties in Sydney are sold via public auction, and realtors are required to indicate a realistic guide price to anyone who inquires. Like an experienced investor, via Domain I can calibrate the guide price against the specific qualities of the apartment for sale, determining in a fraction of a second whether it's too high or low. It's often the latter—realtors want to drive interest towards their properties and show success to clients by exceeding expectations with the eventual sale price.

Listings typically have eight to ten photographs and a plan. All photography is professional, and most apartments have been styled specifically to be sold. Renting out tasteful modern furniture for this purpose is a lucrative business. But the photography goes further than just professional presentation. What is being posted for sale is not simply a piece of real estate; it is, as mentioned above, a lifestyle. While wide-angle shots are the norm, giving an expansive feeling to the smallest of spaces, and the obligatory hero shots of renovated kitchens and luxury bathrooms abound, particular kinds of detailed shots have become popular. These consist of vignettes such as: a close-up of a side table with a succulent delicately balanced on a stack of art and design books; framed prints leaned up against a wall in a nonchalant array; and a sunny corner where dappled light plays on oak floorboards. Posed models have also begun to appear: a hipster lounging on a couch balancing a laptop; a blurry figure disappearing up a staircase; a pair of high heels abandoned by a sofa; or a monsoon shower head gushing. Libidinally, we chase our proxies through these images, all the time fretting that the guide price really is too low, and that we don't stand a chance with this listing we're beginning to crave.

It's a dramatic switch to turn away from my smartphone, and Sydney's styled apartment obsession, to these contemporary images of unfurnished Swiss interiors. Most obviously, it's a switch from fullness to emptiness, from inhabitation to vacancy. It's also a move away from domesticity understood through the lens of the market, to one where "architecture" is clearly in the frame. After the constancy of checking indicators of value, the lack of these cues is refreshing. It's as if in banishing furniture, hipsters and the taint of the sale, I can now take in something more fundamental. I've moved away from libidinal investment to the clarity of spatial abstraction. But the sheer amount and repetition of these images is alarming. I start to scroll as quickly as I would on Domain, without reaching the end of the archive. And to my surprise, in this action, a code starts to emerge, and I begin to be able to calibrate very subtle markers of differentiation against a pattern that sets the context for a determination of value. To put this another way, these images clearly belong as a set that holds together because distinctions can be made between each image. I think I'm making progress in understanding them when Susie's admonishment rings in my ears: "freak of fucking nature" (→ p. 151). I feel it acutely. I'm wavering. I can't decide whose side I'm on, and it's not turning out to be very funny. Am I still interested in the house tour, in the display of identity this implies? If so, I should accept the *House Tour* images as potential sites of investment. In my imagination, I should start unpacking my things and moving in, accepting the fact that my search for "architect-designed" has come good. Or are the subtle differentiations I'm registering alerting me to a larger pattern emerging? Do I get it without needing to dwell for any length of time in any one situation? Do I even need to take the house tour? Whose side am I on? I can't sit back and laugh because Susie and Larry's antagonism is all too real for me. It encapsulates the academic discourse on domesticity in all its polarised glory.

Larry embodies those we might call the New Typologists: scholars who are interested in the problem of domesticity as the problem of housing. They aren't interested in anyone's house in particular, or what it means to live there. Rather, they see housing as a pattern. At →

a glance, they get what constitutes the larger configuration within any given instance. Rather than be detained by particularity, scholars of this ilk track the emergence and development of the domestic subject per se. They do this through understanding housing configurations that reveal both stability and change across time and location. Not an individual whose personal preferences or taste are of interest, this subject is a kind of resultant, formed despite their conscious choices within a larger mosaic of possibility and constraint, wherein questions of identity are framed in politico-historical terms.

Susie, in her appeal to the particular and the personal—in her appeal to Larry to invest in her investment—captures the interest of those we might call the Apologists of Identity: scholars who are interested in the way individual preference and desire is formed from and through the material culture of domesticity. Important here are practices and rituals, like the house tour, which underpin a personal account of "home", one which is nonetheless claimed as trans-historical and cross-cultural. The subject is the inhabitant, an individual who triumphs in negotiating his or her daily life, securing an identity amid things accreted on surfaces whose significance is at once personal and part of a universally understood condition. Architecture is relatively unimportant in this discourse, or sometimes the object of barely concealed antagonism. At times it is appreciated for the way it provides "affordances", a kind of self-effacing structuring of everyday life. And in its best manifestations, to the Apologists of Identity, domestic architecture is "poetic", not a machine for living, but an artisanally crafted mechanism in which to dwell.

Each pole of this discourse would have a standard approach to the images that begin this book. The Apologists would understand that these interiors are empty in a negative sense, only waiting for inhabitants to move in with their stuff, making these generic spaces their own. The Typologists would see that the archive reveals a pattern of consistency, telling us something more broadly about the architecture of Swiss domesticity. I waver between these poles because my sense is that neither provides a sufficient framing for what makes these images compelling. At a basic level, neither account can quite come to grips with who these images are for. The photographic composition of each is far too precise to appeal to would-be inhabitants, or to scholars interested in the everyday affordances of domestic architecture. Hardly any image actually shows the kinds of spatial contiguities necessary for a proper, invested, imaginary inhabitation. Though Domain images might be crowded out by good-taste furniture, it's possible to work between each image to build a synthetic understanding of the spaces of the dwelling on show. The problem is the same for the pattern-hunting Typologists. The pattern emerging from the *House Tour* archive has to do with incidental details rather than spatial consistencies: window frames, skirting boards, the positioning of light switches and power sockets, the placement of ovens and sinks, whether or not cupboard door pulls are recessed or stand proud (if you're wondering, it's clearly the former). The archive presents nothing other than a taxonomy of aspects of the dwelling which fall below conscious registration, and it's enough to infuriate both Apologists and Typologists. But it should present pure visual joy to those who can see, understand and compare these things: the architects who brought these apartments into being. It's for them that the archive exists.

Acknowledging architects as creators is tricky for both poles of scholarship on domesticity. Each tends to steer clear of questions of architectural intention, probably for good reason. Indeed, the Apologists have taken a deliberate stance in this respect, with the Typologists more concerned with global effect rather than individual intention. But it might be interesting to imagine a different comedic scene, a fictional dialogue between architects vis-à-vis what they see in this archive which, after all, is an archive of their own handiwork. First, they would agree on the house tour, being drawn to it for the same reason I'm drawn to Domain—by an interest in how difference is displayed within tightly framed consistency. So, for some parallel-reality sitcom, on a channel only architects would watch, I have imagined a series of short dialogues between pairs of architects, one noticing certain details, and the other attempting to explain them, as they scroll (stroll?) together through the archive. These would not be the principals of firms, but the project architects who are employed to solve the problems of the particular job and see it through. In this way, we are engaging with a domain of architectural production not normally accorded significance, trying to find in the obvious comedy of a specialist language some truthful account of the production of domestic architecture.

A1 Architect 1
A2 Architect 2

A1 Why do you think the kitchen counter extends along the wall in that fashion?

A2 It has to do with defining the counter as an object and not just a return, as it needs to face into the living room in a convincing way.

A1 An enfilade that ends in the bathroom!

A2 The subversion of a grand gesture, or just weird planning?

A1 The way those rooms read as boxes placed within a larger room is very subtle.

A2 It's the shadow gap, detailed so that the ceiling appears to extend, rather than the walls.

A1 I count four different flooring materials in that image.

A2 I think what you see as the fourth is just a trick of the light. At any rate, if you're going for variance, you may as well go for it.

A1 How odd, to see an eat-in kitchen.

A2 A return to the sanctity of rooms and their functions.

A1 What is inside and outside seems to oscillate due to the way the outdoor terrace space intrudes into the living space.

A2 It's because of the way the frames are detailed. The terrace is more inside than the living room which, in fact, seems to project outward via the corner window.

A1 That door appears to sit on the wall almost as an object.

A2 It's because the rest of the spatial transitions are managed via sliding doors concealed within the walls. It returns to the door its doorness.

A1 Concrete floor, timber ceiling. There's a curious inversion there.

A2 "Curious inversion"? Mistake in the specification, I'd say.

Perhaps I have unwittingly given voice to a secret society of project architects for whom the *House Tour* archive makes absolute sense, and finally gives them the chance to talk about what they really do all day. That's their identity on show! I can imagine our polarised scholars marshalling their arguments. On the one hand: "This is just obfuscatory formalism. What does it mean to the people who have to move into these blank white boxes?" Yet these architects have an investment on par with any libidinal attachment to a dwelling. Or on the other hand: "These minutiae reveal nothing of consequence for the question of housing." Yet this way of talking about decisions does say something about the constraints of the generic.

The images pulled together here, as well as those constantly updated on Domain and its ilk, force together the two poles of domestic discourse. Both sets of images promote a calibration or sensitivity to fluctuation or irreducible individuality, at the same time as an attention to what emerges as a pattern within constraint—whether that be the perverse constraint of market presentation and all it implies about how we "invest" in domesticity, or the constraint of the 2.4m ceiling height, and all that implies about the practical codes of domestic production. Whether it's easier to imagine living in a flat where furniture and belongings channel desire and identity, or in an empty shell where shadow gaps and threshold details set the mood, is a moot point; yet by conjuring up the figure of the project architect, whose Domain counterpart might be the real-estate stylist, I now see how I can enjoy both archives equally, as each gives full reign to a sophisticated image culture that has framed domesticity in modernity. And in this we must understand that there is no identity or typology to be found beyond this play of images, no real essence of domesticity dissimulated by real-estate images or revealed in dwelling patterns, or even honed through perfecting shadow gaps, flush cabinetry, or the perfectly thrown cushion. We have always been given images as they appear and reappear on new formats and in new collections. And we'll invest or coolly analyse as the mood takes us. ■

# Off White, Please

Hans-Christian Dany

There is more than one way to use a thing. Even so, many things present themselves as if there were only one proper way to handle them. Packaging, photographs and users manuals instruct us to use a thing in one way, and one way only. Things *could* be different. "Codetermination", a variant of adaptive re-use, was around long before digitalisation made everybody a *user*. You could always adapt a lighter as a bottle opener, instead of just using it to light up a cigarette. Analogue tools are often more stable when diverted from their planned purpose. They don't usually malfunction after being used contrary to plan, whereas computer programs often go on strike when the buttons are pressed in the wrong order.

In the everyday of capitalism, people are less likely to encounter the naked thing than its costumed appearance as a commodity. Karl Marx illustrated the point with a surreal revue starring a table. Once commodified, the table doesn't stay a tangible thing standing in the apartment:

> so soon as it steps forth as a commodity, it is changed into something transcendent. It not only stands with its feet on the ground, but, in relation to all other commodities, it stands on its head, and evolves out of its wooden brain grotesque ideas, far more wonderful than "table-turning" ever was.[1]

Marx's dancing table could be viewed as threatening, but it might also be taken as an opportunity. We, the audience, can sit back and observe, or we can participate in the table's metamorphosis. Half a century ago, the

Situationist International proposed taking an active role, and called it *détournement,* intentional misuse. Repurposing, a latent potential of any mutant commodity-thing, always served a clear goal in the SI model: for instance, a popular comic strip could be reused as a targeted political subversion by replacing the dialogue in the speech bubbles, or a job could be dissipated via aimless drifting. At home, your desires should get off the sofa and onto the street. Detournement opposed purpose-driven action and sought to supplant it with a purposeless game; the SI imagined this as an escape route into a freer life. "Functional means practical. The only thing that is really practical is the resolution of our fundamental problem: our self-realisation."[2] The defunctionalised table turns into a rocking-horse that you could ride into a more autonomous life.

For the SI, the home constitutes a central arena of conflict. Within the home, questions about who determines usage, and how self-determination could look in practice, become very pointed:

> We have invented the architecture and the urbanism that cannot be realised without the revolution of everyday life— without the appropriation of conditioning by everyone, its endless enrichment and fulfillment.[3]

The SI's playful detournements didn't just make them co-authors of the 1968 uprisings; they would also influence various experiments in how to live in the decade that followed.

The big game proposed by the SI persisted into the early 1980s: squatters across Europe configured models of autonomous living. Evil capitalism wasn't the sole enemy; people also objected to centralised planning, to being locked up in the standardised sleeping cells of social housing projects. Their dwellings were the managed heritage of the planning the Bauhaus believed would build workers a better life. In his 1981 essay *From Bauhaus to Our House,* Tom Wolfe made fun of planning ideas in which "workers should be spared high ceilings and wide hallways, too, along with all of the various outmoded objects and decorations. ... Seven-foot ceilings and thirty-six-inch-wide hallways were about right for ... recreating the world. *Starting from zero!"*[4] The Bauhaus architects weren't interested in input from the "culturally underdeveloped" (Gropius) residents for whom housing projects were designed, until the proletariat was "re-educated" (Corbusier). That re-education, which some called revolution, would never come to pass.

In the shadow of the creeping demise of the welfare state and the neoliberal reforms of the 1980s, the Situationist vocabulary broadened, as did ideas about consumer co-determination. During that time, the pioneers of capitalism—in St. Gallen, amongst other places—began to reading texts by the SI and cybernetic autonomists. Futurist Alvin Toffler introduced the term *prosumer* in his book *The Third Wave* (1980). Toffler envisioned consumers of the future no longer simply consuming things and environments, but participating in the production process as well; they would supply their own planning. His dream came true twenty years later in social network content coproduced by its consumers. More than anyone else, the future belongs to weak prosumers who pump information out to suppliers about how they live and what they might possibly want to suppliers via formalised feedback loops. All live together in a big consumption panopticon.[5]

In his book *L'Invention du Quotidien* (1980, translated as *The Practice of Everyday Life,* 1984) historian Michel de Certeau added a profusion of poetics, rhetoric, tricks, ruses and lists to the Situationist vocabulary. De Certeau conceived of putting alternate usages for things into practice as being a tactic of defiance: "Sly as a fox and twice as quick: there are countless ways of 'making do.'"[6] The conflict is between strategies that want to reduce spaces to one concept of use, versus forms of resistance that manipulate and repurpose the rules:

> Thus a North African living in Paris or Roubaix (France) insinuates into the system imposed on him by the construction of a low-income housing development or of the French language the ways of "dwelling" →

1 K. Marx, F. Engels (ed.), *Capital: A Critical Analysis of Capitalist Production,* trans. S. Moore and E. Aveling, London, Swan Sonnenschein, 1887.
2 A. Kotànyi and R. Vaneigem, 'Basic Program of the Bureau of Unitary Urbanism', trans. K. Knabb, Internationale Situationniste #6, August 1961, http://www.cddc.vt.edu/sionline/si/bureau.html (accessed 11 February 2018)
3 A. Kotànyi and R. Vaneigem
4 T. Wolfe, *From Bauhaus to Our House,* New York, Washington Square Press, 1986.
5 A. Toffler, *The Third Wave,* New York, William Morrow, 1980.
6 M. de Certeau, *The Practice of Everyday Life,* trans. S. F. Rendall, Berkley and Los Angeles, University of California Press, 1984, p. 29.

> (in a house or a language) peculiar to his native Kabylia. He superimposes them and, by that combination, creates for himself a space in which he can find ways of using the constraining order of the place or of the language.[7]

Planning faced resistance; planners were hopelessly out of touch with the people whose worlds they were supposed to plan. Misplanned populaces pushed for a say in shaping the worlds they inhabited, and their demand initially got picked up along two main lines. Firstly, the architecture of the self-satisfied liberal left channeled desires into participatory planning. Their round-table talks asking everybody what they wanted may have been temporarily interesting experiments, but ultimately were mired in bland compromises and tired rehashes, none of which held out any hope of adding to existing knowledge. Few still expect much of such organised participation. The other line was a triumph of the freedom-of-the-fittest narrative. Whoever put in enough effort, whoever was strong enough, could obtain the freedom to live as they wished. Economic success is the key to self-determination in life; that's relatively realistic inside the system we now inhabit. Self-determination has been reduced to a "lifestyle," or self-realisation through consuming better quality goods.

It is said that a picture says more than a thousand words. So instead of talking about what everybody really wants, people started taking pictures of it. Concurrently with all these theories of autonomy, codetermination, prosumerism, participation and the practice of everyday life, a photographic practice emerged that would radically alter what it was observing—and what it observed was fashion. I'm talking about street-style photography, another product of the 1980s; these pictures didn't show studio-lit models striking choreographed poses, but young people on city streets wearing what they wore, and acting in whatever way they thought was *cool*. A London magazine called *i-D* was an early disseminator of this fresh treatment of clothing. The outfits were a mix of flea market finds, industrially manufactured sportswear, ready-to-wear apparel and homemade accessories. Their "straight-up" shots claimed to document fashion as it really was, outfits of the wearer's own invention, and document desires that got out of apartments and onto the streets. The emergence of street style marked the creative appropriation of the language of fashion by those who were supposed only to parrot it. It was curiosity about the ways of the street that made the rise of streetwear possible in the first place. Photography was a crucial factor in this fundamental shift in what is called fashion; if producers previously dictated trends, they were now compelled to follow the consumers' lead, or rather, the consumer zeitgeist, the collective unconscious. In the place of the photographic gaze—that has meanwhile widened from street photography to the panoptic ocular machine Instagram—has stepped the digital analysis of patterns. The ramifications have been diverse, culminating in the textile industry scaling back a globalised structure too slow to keep up with fickle consumer behaviour. Fashion is no longer seasonal; now it updates itself continuously. Throughout all these gradual steps, something was transpiring that ultimately blossomed in the summer of 2017 as street style's triumph over prêt-à-porter.

This last phase has one star, although many had a hand in preparing the stage. He's called Virgil Abloh, and he runs a company with a brand by the name of Off White. Abloh also brings us back to the question of how to live (in the residential sense) because, as a consultant for IKEA, he also deals in speculations about how every new crop of young people will furnish their first apartments. That Abloh knows what young people will want this summer is beyond a shadow of a doubt; the clothing he designs is perfectly attuned to what's hanging in the air between twelve year olds. Basically, he decorates relatively standardised cuts—moderately modified street fashion basics—with an oversized logo. This logo isn't a set form, but variations on diagonal white stripes, like the ones used to indicate road hazards. The logo ornament is embellished with words and phrases typeset in Helvetica and enclosed in quotation marks. Helvetica is the ultimate postmodern font, and refers to the cultural era of the sec-

7 de Certeau, p. 30.

ond half of the twentieth century. The texts also quote verbatim art from that time—for example, that a bag is a sculpture, borrowed from the artist group Art & Language. Long before this, Marcel Duchamp illustrated for his imaginary attorney through the "readymade" why it's no longer a matter of inventing anything, but merely of fashioning just the right references.

Abloh's elevation of the typical to the status of high fashion constitutes a conscious vulgarisation—an indispensable move in eliminating fashion's hierarchies. The old order must be destroyed to make space for the new. De Certeau defines "cultural decline" as an exaggerated act of vengeance, and many among the older generation have called what is currently unfolding in fashion "cultural decline". Architecture has been through that at least once—it was called *Learning from Las Vegas*, although at the moment "austerity" is doing more damage. In the case of fashion, government spending can't play much of a role. Still, for some reason, the standard gear of an Off White hoodie or the uniforms by Vêtements look so much more attractive than the standard white, unfurnished apartment. It may be because courage comes a lot easier in the transient play of fashion—every style will always go right back out of style—whereas an apartment building will stand around for much longer.

Despite being an admirer of Swiss concrete construction—a wonderful act of vengeance against the innocuously cute architecture that preceded it—as well as generally believing myself able to spot a latent opportunity for freedom within the standard, I am not attracted to Switzerland's piles of light-drenched cells. The empty white residential cube may imply that, beyond just having a say, its future inhabitants will have their way. But this is baloney: the spaces may be empty, but we are not able to use them as we wish. What with the virginal non-colour and the nothing inside, the order of the place presents us with a clearly preconceived idea of life. Images of blank apartments and condos operate within larger contexts, wherein the promise of freedom comes paired with claims of a self-reliance that no longer seems honest. Late capitalism has induced a scepticism toward any promise of freedom laid on too thick. An empty apartment seems only to offer a limited opportunity for total self-determination within its confines. But it's simply an advertising ploy, and the game is given away by the floor plan, which sets out the real program of the space. The promise of a void that will never really be empty can't do it for people used to repelling a daily onslaught of deceptive images. Perhaps it would be more rewarding to conceive of apartments—the term itself is restrictive—as something more than just places to live a standardised life. Perhaps dwelling could also offer surreal possibilities. ■

# Real Estate Fiction

Marija Marić

About Reality

High resolution, straight lines, mostly white colour scheme. Standardised elements are rendered invisible, turning into geometry and abstraction. When singular, they do not say much. When together, they fit perfectly into the minimal layouts of the meticulously curated websites and Instagram timelines. What language do the silent images of the unfurnished apartment interiors speak? Could the logic of the distribution be the content of that being distributed?

Describing the visual world of low-resolution copies, thumbnails and previews that emerged with the proliferation of the Internet, artist and theorist Hito Steyerl introduced the concept of a "poor image". Compressed and pixelated free versions of the original, "poor images are poor because they are not assigned any value within the class society of images", she writes.[1] They tend towards abstraction, not only in terms of bad image quality, but also in terms of their ephemeral existence, anonymous production and fragmented distribution. Nevertheless, curated, edited and maintained by various online communities, these pieces of "digital folk art" are successfully destabilising traditional understandings of authorship, distribution and property. In this light, Steyerl calls for new ways of defining the value of an image; value that goes beyond resolutions and art markets, and is instead based on spread, speed and distribution capacity. "Poor image" reminds us that digital information is no longer about authenticity and originality; instead, "it is about its own real conditions of existence: about swarm circulation, digital dispersion, fractured and flexible temporalities ... In short: it is about reality."[2]

Starting from "white images", I turn towards "white texts" in an attempt to understand real-estate advertisements as forms of infrastructure that circulate architecture as information and value. Real-estate ads, perhaps more than any other writings on buildings and cities, are about their own conditions of existence—fast circulation, far-reaching dispersion and universal language. In short: about architectural reality.

## Fiction as Infrastructure

Real estate advertisements probably constitute the majority of the existing body of texts written on architecture and cities. Still, the ways in which real-estate agents and developers describe their products are often neglected by architects as trash talk or generic patter, and are therefore systematically excluded from architectural discussions.

In her book *Extrastatecraft*, architect and theorist Keller Easterling studies how repeatable "spatial formulas" constituting what she describes as the global "infrastructure space" play a role in shaping new forms of power and governance beyond the state. "More than grids of pipes and wires ... infrastructure is now the overt point of contact and access between us all—the rules governing the space of everyday life", she writes.[3] Within this broad definition of global infrastructure space, real-estate advertisements appear as a set of fluid multipliers able to productively employ seemingly disconnected scales and ideas. Merging progress with nostalgia, regional myths with smart-city parameters, English with non-English speaking localities, real-estate fictions zoom in and zoom out, scale up and scale down, efficiently engaging local fears with global dreams, and the other way around.

The language of real estate is, therefore, performative on multiple levels. Such language operates on a discursive technology, described by the anthropologist Anna Tsing as "the economy of appearances", referring to the "self-conscious making of a spectacle ... necessary for gathering investment funds."[4] Profit must be imagined before it is to be obtained. The same goes for property. And while architecture makes real estate real, real estate often makes architecture fictional, opening ways for an economically productive confusion between its reality and speculative potential.

Still, writes Easterling, "The things that make infrastructure space powerful—its multipliers, its irrational fictions, or its undeclared consequential activities—are perhaps the very things that make it immune to righteous declaration and prescription."[5] Infrastructure, therefore, is able to generate tools for both its own expansion and shrinkage. Only by "becoming its own medium—by becoming infrastructural",[6] architecture could escape the limitations of a singular, isolated intervention. This leads to the question: using only the very tools of real estate, could we learn to understand its mechanisms more productively? Can fiction itself be a means of accessing the fictional materialities of real estate? Could we, through the act of decontextualisation, achieve the opposite, namely contextualise real-estate fictions within architectural discussions?

## New Literary Genre[7]

Could texts on architecture and cities, written to sell, be considered a new and unexpected source of fiction and poetry? *Real Estate Fiction* is an outline for a new literary genre; one that is solely based on real-estate advertisements. Ads, seen as ephemeral texts soon to be obsolete after the product is sold, are collected and transcribed, displaced as readymades and eread as literary works of fiction.

Instead of writing; displacing texts. Instead of hiding, deleting and skipping; reframing, curating and publishing again. Managing the existing. Moving texts around. Unciting. Rewriting. Renaming. Transcribing. Appropriating by exhibiting. Reclaiming by reading.

The American poet Kenneth Goldsmith, whose work draws from the practices of plagiarism, copying and appropriation, argues that the distribution of information and →

1 H. Steyerl, 'In Defense of the Poor Image', *e-flux Journal*, no. 10, November 2009. http://www.e-flux.com/journal/10/61362/in-defense-of-the-poor-image/.
2 Steyerl, 'In Defense of the Poor Image'.
3 K. Easterling, *Extrastatecraft: The Power of Infrastructure Space*, London, Verso, 2014, p. 11.
4 A. T. Lowenhaupt, *Friction: An Ethnography of Global Connection*, Princeton, NJ, Princeton University Press, 2005, p. 57.
5 Easterling, *Extrastatecraft*, p. 22–23.
6 K. Easterling, *The Action Is the Form. Victor Hugo's TED Talk*, Moscow: Strelka Press, 2012.
7 Parts of this essay will be published in M. Marić, 'Real Estate Fiction: An Outline for a New Literary Genre', *Thresholds*, no. 46 (forthcoming in April 2018).

knowledge on the Web makes traditional understandings of authorship and originality outdated. "While the author won't die, we might begin to view authorship in a more conceptual way", he writes. "Perhaps the best authors of the future will be ones who can write the best programs with which to manipulate, parse and distribute language-based practices."[8] To appropriate texts is to recognise the vastness of the digital information and its free flows, as well as copying and pasting as basics of any digital reading or writing. To retype, however, is to appropriate in detail; not just to take over the text, but to take over every word of it. Retyping real-estate advertisements means writing them again, only this time as real-estate fictions.

Architecture moves around as real estate. Its modes of distribution, dispersion, travel and inhabitation constitute the invisible "other" of architecture as a profession. And while the reality of buildings, after the design work is done, is mostly shaped by developers and agents as well as by the institutions of property, profit and speculation, the question remains open: what role do these "other stories" play in the histories of architecture? What are the histories of global infrastructure space? How about those histories of anonymous production and speculative distribution that are at the very base of not only professional reality, but also everyday life?

*Real Estate Fiction* is a proposal for a new literary genre. This, obviously, is a paradoxical task. It revolves around the question: could we talk about architecture, drawing from its disciplinary trash bins? Where does displaced knowledge, such as *Real Estate Fiction(s)*, belong? What would its archive look like? And finally, who would claim to be its authority—real-estate agents or real-estate poets?

8 K. Goldsmith, *Uncreative Writing: Managing Language in the Digital Age*, New York, Columbia University Press, 2011, p. 11.

## Seven Real Estate Fictions[9]

Zurich works here, Zurich lives here, and Zurich goes out here. The bright and modern two-and-a-half-room apartment with excellent transport connections is located in the heart of the popular, trendy district of Kreis Five.[10]

9 *Seven Real Estate Fictions* is a text installation in seven parts. Each piece of fiction is a transcribed real estate advertisement for an existing unfurnished apartment in Switzerland. Advertisements were subsequently translated from German to English by Erik Smith.

10 Urban Living im Kreis 5 on neubauprojekte.ch. (accessed 18 February 2018)

True living is possible here. There are many reasons to choose Zug as your home—whether it's the charming old town, the modern city center, the low tax rates or its centralized location within Switzerland. The most important of these reasons are easy to see from Bernoldweg: the fantastic view of Lake Zug and the world-famous Zug sunsets, adding to your enjoyment here. Located on a hillside just outside the city center, the beautiful residential district of Liebfrauenhof Guggital is easily accessible with private and public transportation. Your new home. The architectural design reflects current tastes, even though the elegant houses are already eleven years old. High-quality materials like dark-slate facades reinforce first impressions. Shifting sunlight constantly alters the views. Large, floor-to-ceiling windows allow sunlight into all rooms. And they provide incredible vistas. The five, four-unit buildings each feature an elevator and direct access to the underground car park. Let yourself be inspired by the quality of life in this well-kept, intimate, multifamily residence in a quiet location.[11]

11 Schöner Wohnen on newhome.ch. (accessed 18 February 2018)

We are renting this fabulous, three-room attic apartment by appointment only. You can't miss the merits of this building—it is difficult to put into words. Our virtual tour can give you a first impression; for example, the twenty-seven-square-metre bedroom with a dressing room, or the spacious, forty-one-square-metre living area with approx. five-metre ceiling heights. Or the two bathrooms, each with a stacked washer and dryer, an elevator with apartment access and the amazing views from the terrace. The surrounding neighbourhood of this outstanding property also speaks for itself: the subway station is only five minutes away. From there with the S-nine, it takes eleven minutes to reach Zurich main station or eighteen minutes to reach Winterthur. Shops are also within walking distance. Do you want to go for a swim after work? No problem, the Freibad Oberdorf pool is just around the corner. Or perhaps a romantic stroll along the Glatt? You're only five minutes away.[12]

12 Top of Dübendorf—Ihr neues Zuhause on neubauprojekte.ch. (accessed 18 February 2018)

The location. With its international aura, the idyllic location on Lake Zug, and the surrounding central Swiss Alps, the city of Zug is a preferred place of residence offering a high quality of life. Live here in an appealing, easy-access setting with unique lake views in a quiet residential district. This is what's most important. The two-and-a-half-room apartment is located on an attractive hillside, in a natural-stone-facade building constructed in two thousand and thirteen. The approx. one-hundred-and-five-square-metre apartment features a top-quality and stylish interior. The partially glazed outdoor terrace invites you to linger and unwind. The financial matters. We are happy to personally discuss the financial terms with prospective buyers. What's special: enjoy exclusive ambience in a prime location in the city of Zug with unique lake views and a spacious garden area with plenty of privacy.[13]

13 2.5-Zimmerwohnung an schönster Lage on newhome.ch. (accessed 18 February 2018)

Located in a quiet residential area, this newly constructed residential gem easily impresses with its top-quality construction standards that satisfy even the most stringent demands. This gem begins with the bright foyer, which also features a wet room with a rain shower and toilet. Then you'll enter an open-plan living, dining and kitchen area, where you'll immediately notice a perfectly equipped kitchen that leaves nothing to be desired. The cozy loggia provides another highlight in this area, inviting you linger and unwind. The spacious master bedroom ensures a restful night sleep, and scores extra points with a private bathroom featuring a bath, a shower and a toilet. Two additional rooms for personal use and an amply sized storage space are also present. If this is not enough, two basement storage compartments for non-everyday things are also a must.[14]

14 Wohnung zu Mieten in Reinach (BL) on homegate.ch. (accessed 18 February 2018)

Located in the heart of Zurich West, the Zolly offers perfect access to the public transport network—the kind you've come to expect from the most dynamic district in the city. The interior design is tailor-made for well-connected urban dwellers who value communication and appreciate modern architecture's distinctive features. Large-scale tile flooring and reduced, clear forms generate an airy, understated atmosphere, leaving creative room for the occupant's individual lifestyle. Located on the eleventh floor, the one-hundred-and-twenty-square-metre, light-flooded, four-and-a-half-room apartment is generously proportioned. Ceiling heights are two metres sixty centimetres. Offering spectacular views to the south and west, the living area exudes peace and tranquility from sunrise to late at night. High above the hustle and bustle of everyday life, there's no one here to block your sunlight or disturb your privacy. Controlled ventilation provides refreshing air in the middle of the city around the clock. In summer, the apartment can also be cooled via environmentally friendly means. All living areas and rooms are equipped with electric blinds. The bedrooms feature oiled parquet flooring. High-quality Italian porcelain stoneware tiling is installed in the living area, bathrooms, and kitchen. The open-plan, modern Warendorf kitchen features a natural-stone work top and all the creature comforts. The rooms are heated and cooled individually with adjustable floor heating. Temperature, ventilation, lighting, slat blinds and main entry access are easily controlled via the state-of-the-art Smarthome touch panel. An additional storage room in the basement supplements the ample space allowance. An underground parking and/or motorcycle parking space can be rented along with the apartment. Electricity connection available on request. Come and see this apartment for yourself to envision your future prospects.[15]

15 4.5-Zimmerwohnung mit Split-Level und überhohem Raum im Zoelly Hochhaus on neubauprojekte.ch. (accessed 18 February 2018)

With one hundred and fifty-five residential units, the Westlink Tower is your modern home. Perfect workmanship down to the last detail, high-quality building materials, state-of-the-art technology, and full-height windows make the one-and-a-half to four-and-a-half-room apartments, spread over twenty-three floors, the ideal retreat for city dwellers, families, singles and couples. Its proximity to Altstetten station, allowing unparalleled connection to public transport, and extensive shopping and recreational offerings, makes this a highly exclusive location. Available in three different models—"fresh", "smart" and "extra"—the residential units represent a new kind of living experience in Zurich West: urbanity paired with a sense of security.[16] ■

16 Westlink Tower: Die neue Skyline Altstettens on neubauprojekte.ch. (accessed 18 February 2018)

# Modern Gers

Ariell Ahearn
Stephen Lezak

From the outside, every ger in Mongolia looks more or less the same: squat, round tents, with vertical walls and conical roofs. They are reminiscent of circus pavilions, only smaller, and with stovepipes protruding from the top. And they are all white.

Gers, or yurts, are ubiquitous in the Mongolian countryside; any other type of residence is rare and usually a bold and unwelcome statement of wealth. Their design evolved as a seasonal structure for nomadic herders, sturdy enough to withstand the Mongolian winter but easily taken down, moved, and rebuilt in a day. Even in contemporary Mongolia, they remain the dwelling of choice for at least half the country's residents.

Remarkably, the ger has retained its functionality as a temporary structure that is easy to disassemble and transport, despite an increasing number of Mongolians choosing to leave nomadism behind.[1] Modern gers, even those that have not moved in many years, are still effectively tents, providing only modest, yet efficient, shelter from the elements. The ability to quickly relocate at a moment's notice is retained by an extraordinary share of Mongolian families. The ger offers assurance that no matter what the future brings, there will always be a link with the past. Mobility is a response to environmental variation and social flux and a symbol of belonging for a proud national community.

We live in England, where the long rows of two-story brick homes only offer a partial parallel. In cities across the country, many roads look largely identical with this archetypal housing, but walking through the neighbourhoods after sunset, one notices that the anonymous red facades barely conceal the diversity of life behind the windows. Paintings, pianos, bookshelves and assorted kitsch make each flat a raucously individual, curated reflection of its inhabitants.

By contrast, the insides of gers barely reflect their owners. Instead, there are a number of strict rules governing how the physical orientation of the ger relates to the outside environment and the physical orientation of people and things inside the ger itself. It is a general cultural rule that households build their ger with the door facing south-southeast. Marco Polo identified this practice in the thirteenth century: "Whenever they erect these huts the door is always to the south."[2] In rural Mongolia, both people and objects have "socially-designated places" determined by seniority, status and gender.[3]

Enter any ger and to your left you'll find a washbasin. Look clockwise from there and you will see a compact wooden bed, then an altar, perhaps a television or a bureau, then another bed, a small kitchen with a gas burner, a cabinet, and a sink, which is just to your right. The small iron stove sits in the centre; next to it is a store of fuel-wood or dried dung. A chimney will always protrude from the ceiling, surrounded by 108 orange and blue spokes; an umbilical connection to the sky through which fortune and balance flow. Lashed to the wooden spokes of the vaulted ceiling is a blue silk scarf, a two-string horsehead fiddle and perhaps an old Soviet rifle if you're out in the countryside. The decorations on the walls will show images of horses, Genghis Khan and fields of tall grass. The altar will have family photos, medals dating back generations and perhaps pictures of Buddhist gods or religious mandalas with an offering of fresh dairy products or milk tea presented next to them.

The western side of the circular interior is designated as the "male" space, reserved for guests, the head of household, and tools associated with men's work tasks. The opening of the stove faces the women's side of the ger, the eastern side; this is also the space for children, the elderly, and for dairy products and kitchen supplies to rest.

The ger is additionally divided into vertical upper and lower sections; this provides the architecture for maintaining and attracting household spiritual well-being and prosperity. Bumochir describes the items hung from the roof-ring, which is considered to be the most spiritually significant piece of the ger:

> As I noticed in the Deed Mongol [from Upper Mongolia] gers, only two things are hung from the "crown", with the exception of the wool rope *chagtaga.* One is the ceremonial silk scarf *hadag,* which is considered the "highest thing among the goods" *(ediin deed hadag)* and the other is the *malyn im.* These are pieces of the ears of one-year-old sheep and goats that are left over when marking ownership by cutting the animals' ears. All the small pieces of ear have to be treated with great respect, in order not to lose the *malyn zaya buyan,* good fortune in animal husbandry. Similarly, in some parts of Mongolia the *chagtaga* is also festooned with tufts of hair or wool. Whenever a Mongol sells one of his animals, he takes a tuft from it, wipes it on the animal's nose, and fastens it to the rope so as to preserve the vitality of his herds. Another sign of the respect in which this space is held is the fact that the crown, the roof-ring, is made of suhai (tamarisk), the most respected tree, used as a sacred offering to deities.[4]

By arranging axes of cardinal direction, verticality and gender orientations, the ger participates in the material and spiritual livelihoods of its residents, structuring physical and social dynamics according to archetypes cemented in honoured traditions.

The relatively spartan nature of gers is not accidental. Rural Mongolians accumulate wealth by buying more animals, adding to their herd. It is a functional provision of material security. This is critically important in a nation where currency and banks are historically unreliable; the best way to preserve wealth in this environment is to convert it into an object with durable value, sheltered from political and economic disturbances.[5] What's more, the uniformity of ger sizes and the →

1 O. Myadar, 'Imaginary Nomads: Deconstructing the Representation of Mongolia as a Land of Nomads', *Inner Asia,* vol. 13, no. 2, 2011, p. 335–62.
2 W. B. Dinsmoor, 'Mongol Housing: with an Emphasis on Architectural Forms of the "Ger"', PhD diss., Indiana University, Department of Uralic and Altaic Studies, 1985.
3 C. Humphrey, 'Inside a Mongolian Tent', *New Society,* 31, 1974.
4 D. Bumochir, *Power of Respect: Political Lives of Mongols in the Qinghai Tibetan Plateau,* forthcoming, p. 103.
5 R. Empson, *Harnessing Fortune,* Oxford, Oxford University Press, 2011.

strict conventions that govern their interior arrangements actively discourage material accumulation. There is room for a fridge and a television, but not much else beyond the traditional arrangements. Indoor plumbing is unheard of.

The accumulation of wealth in the West is less concerned with the creation of durable objects than with the making of personal identity. Clothes, furniture and wall art constitute a vocabulary of self-creation in a world where individuality is valued more than communitarianism. The white wall of a newly built apartment offers itself up to the Western consumer as a vehicle for individual expression. In its virgin state it says nothing, but rather awaits the touch of its inhabitant to transform it into something that communicates her unimpeachable individuality. The wall (perhaps no longer white), adorned with photographs, sconces or cabinetry, is now an allegory for its owner; but in its model-unit state it is nothing more than the spectre of what it might become. It is a blank canvas, a blanketing of fresh snow, an undisturbed potentiality for material self-expression. In this way, it is optimistic; it suggests a future of abundance. It is unobtrusive and versatile, looking ahead to a life where each day is different, and better than its predecessor, as movie posters are replaced in adulthood by paintings.

But while the white wall looks ahead to the future, the white ger signifies a temporality grounded in the past. Mongolian society has a deeply embedded wariness of what's to come that the ger-space reassures. The ger is a container for relations and memories layered over time.[6] If the white wall signals potentiality, then the ger offers stability, a link to the past that steadies an uncertain present. The ger is surrounded by ritual and tradition; rituals for securing future fortune and prosperity for the family unit are directed in and through the physical space of the ger. Humphrey writes: "Time here is ideologically constructed in invariant repetition. Each category of person occupies a certain social space, which is conceived as unambiguous and invariant, repeated at each stopping place, in a trajectory through time."[7] This repetition serves to blend cycles of production and reproduction, mirroring beliefs in reincarnation where old folds into new. The individuals and interactions become abstracted to enable the stabilisation of rituals and social form.

Empty white rooms are scrubbed of memories and relations. They situate nature as something to be gazed at though the security of a neutral space. Rather than a permeable vessel which spirits might enter the home through the rooftop from the surrounding landscape, the modernist apartment space incorporates the natural world as an arena of potential leisure and increasing property value—these are places with "views". In stark contrast to this neutrality, the Mongolian ger has a specific temporality associated with its movement in response to seasonal work and migrations. The home-space, in this sense, is not a fixed point. Humphrey writes, "'The centre' is established anew when people make a halt.It is, in other words, not a place but an action."[8]

Even in the unregulated sprawl of neighbourhoods surrounding Ulaanbaatar, gers still rely on barely transformed raw materials like felt and wood, providing physical and temporal links beyond the capital city. Each piece of the dwelling is made largely of materials native to the steppe landscape: wood (willow and larch), camel and horse hair, and felt. Layers of the soft thick material, made from Mongolian livestock wool, envelope the lattice-wall framework. This lightweight, flexible and warm insulating felt encapsulates the home and provides protection from high winds and temperatures that dip below 30°C. The natural fibre is aesthetically, materially and physically connected to the livestock outside the door. The sweet smells of dairy products and dried-dung fire from a central hearth soak into the walls.

In Mongolia, the desert is always outside. It is not dead in the way Westerners might imagine, but neither is it welcoming. Its vastness provides for livelihoods but equally threatens them with drought, dust and the vicious winter storms called *zud*. The ger functions as a vessel—containing ritual, tradition and fortune—that might otherwise spill out. Permeable felt walls allow the exchange of sounds and sensations between the inter-

6 R. Empson, 'Movement and Stasis: Shifting Subjectivities on the Mongolian Border', in P. Rawes (ed.), *Relational Architectural Ecologies: Architecture, Nature and Subjectivity*, London, Routledge, 2013.

7 C. Humphrey, 'Chiefly and Shamanist Landscapes in Mongolia', in E. Hirsch and M. O'Hanlon (eds.) *The Anthropology of Landscape: Perspectives on Place and Space*, Oxford, Clarendon Press, 2003, p. 143.

8 Humphrey, 'Chiefly and Shamanist Landscapes in Mongolia', p. 142.

nal space and external environment. Laying down on the ger bed in the dark, one can sometimes feel the bodies of sheep and goats pressing against the outside walls, sleeping or scratching their heads against the canvas. When it rains, goats will huddle against the front door and knock with their horns and tough hooves to be let inside. On stormy nights, the wind will rush past the round walls, whistling and causing the roof flap to tap against the canvas. This rhythm of homemaking reflects something about Mongolian concepts of *baigal* (nature), which is related to the verb "to be".

In some respects, the ger could hardly be more different from the new-built apartment. With the absence of anything immediately identifiable as earthly, the apartment curates an ethereality that seems to divorce object from substance. It is as if its chief aspiration is to create space that can be filled and fulfilled, while rejecting its own materiality or temporality. If the ger is a mountain cairn, then perhaps the modern urban home is a passing cloud. And if the ger has come to reflect the realities of its environment, might it reveal how the modern home has done the same?

The two openings in the Mongolian ger—the roof skylight *toono* and the door—provide a means to look out, to watch the changes in the sky or the movement of herds and people, but also for the outside world to look in. If deserted, the ger will become the roost of steppe pigeons flying through the open roof. Dairy products left to dry on the beds become covered in guano and dust, blown in through the cracks under the wall-lattice, layering the patterned linoleum ground cover. One must occupy the ger and perform daily maintenance for it to reflect human habitation. The divides between present and future, human and nature, physical and spiritual, are themselves flexible, precarious and easily rearranged at a moment's notice.

The white-walled apartment is poised in expectation, in anticipation of the future; it too generates an urban material culture where the contents may be seen as merely place markers for social forms. It too is perhaps a vessel to temporarily protect against precarious jobs and the uncertainty of modern relationships—gigs, furniture, intimate partners and fashion seem to change with the season. The mobility of goods and information makes this shelter and its contents easily disposable and replicated. At the same time, the modern urban home exists within a vastly different ecology. Shop windows and billboards announce a post-industrial cornucopia, where a relatively small share of a person's income is spent on food, housing and goods. Productive hours are primarily in service of status, recreation or travel. This cycle of consumption rituals become an abstract blur where shelter is no longer a way to mediate the relationship between human and nature, but to provide a tribute to individual tastes and an anchor point in in the spectacle of postmodernity. The empty home is designed with minimalist aesthetics which hint at transience, but this is a matter of style, and it is in a lonely orbit around the temples of mass consumption. Nature abhors a vacuum, and the impulse to accumulate can be felt pressing inwards on the empty white walls in the same way that the cold winter air lashes at a ger's canvas. If the ger is meant to hold something in, then perhaps the modern home is meant to keep things out—but only for the time being. ■

# Svizzera 240: House Tour

Matthew van der Ploeg
Ani Vihervaara
Li Tavor
Alessandro Bosshard

Successful Architecture

The most widespread achievements of the constructed world are not to be found in books celebrating architectural history—the success of these architectures may even depend on the extent to which they are *overlooked.*

For the 2018 Biennale Architettura, the Swiss Pavilion draws attention to an architecture that is hidden-in-plain-sight—the interior of contemporary housing. The apartment's interior enclosure is one of modernity's most successful exports. With only slight variations due to culture or climate, a new flat is very flat indeed—it routinely consists of a volume 240cm in height, dressed with white walls, parquet or tile flooring, and off-the-shelf fittings.

This envelope is one of the most stable and consistent *appearances* in architecture. Over the past century, housing's interior surface has not only survived fluctuations in architectural styles, but it has also been promoted in the name of sharply contrasting ideologies. This interior has been austere or luxurious, Marxist or fascist, artistic or clinical, fulfilling the wishes of every client with the same answer. Like all great architectures, it does not seem to change. It sells itself as timeless and inevitable. Its appearance has only become more uniform and seamless over time as domestic elements—radiators, appliances, wardrobes, cornices and curtain rods—have become background by disappearing into the architectural surface. In pursuit of integration and consistency, it is an appearance that *appears* less and less.

## The House Tour
### *Looking at Empty Apartments*

S Susie
L Larry

S I'll give you the tour.
L No, that's OK. I get it.
S What do you mean?
L You know, it's bedrooms, bathrooms ... I get it.
S You don't want a tour?
L You don't need to walk me around ...
S Get the ... out of my house. Get the ... out right now!
L All right, fine, I'll take the house tour
S I'm done. I'm over it. I'm turned off. Leave! Freak of ... nature, doesn't want a house tour ...

—HBO's *Curb Your Enthusiasm,* Season Three, Episode Eight

An unexpected opponent threatens the anonymity of the interior. It is called *the house tour.* The house tour offers a meandering, eye-level view of the apartment interior, placing its inconspicuous interior shell under direct scrutiny.

For some, the house tour is merely a social formality. For others, it is a cherished ritual. For Swiss architects, the house tour has become an integral aspect of architectural production and dissemination.

A house tour can be experienced in person or simulated through film or virtual reality, but the format gaining the most traction in Swiss architectural discourse is the photography of unfurnished apartments. These images of empty apartments not only feature on the websites of architectural offices, but they have also recently begun to appear in publications on housing architecture. Such publications were once limited to floor plans and technical drawings. The occasional photograph captured the facade or, if lucky, the stairwell. Now, interior views celebrate the extruded reality of the floor plan.

## The Inscrutable Interior
### *An Architectural Rorschach Test*

As architectural documents, unfurnished apartment photographs are somewhat odd. It is surprising how something so obvious, presented in such a straightforward manner, could trigger so many *other* thoughts.

Images in architecture are typically cherished for their memorability; these photos reveal an architecture that we have collectively decided to forget. Like the whitewashed walls of art galleries and Protestant churches, the walls of a flat were never meant to be *looked at.* Perhaps this is why images of an empty apartment are a genre more common to real estate rather than architecture. And yet, with only bare walls, doors, windows and floors, few images could be more *architectural.* The photos offer a matter-of-fact portrayal of architecture itself, but what actually *matters* here? Such images cannot speak of *organisation, use* or *efficiency.* The reliable crutches we typically use when discussing housing come up short.

Do the images depict *space*? Perhaps, but it is difficult to see beyond the surface. The photos propose an architecture designed for as-yet-unknown occupants, who possess unknown objects and live unknown lives. This assertion of uncertainty liberates the shell from its purpose, granting it a level of autonomy. Increasingly free of facts, the enclosure becomes the main protagonist in these images. The interior shell not only looks back at you, but starts to ask questions.

Adjectives applied to such an interior—"standardised", "neutral", "background"—only succeed at first glance. As in a Rorschach test, the background continually threatens to flip into foreground. Emptiness suddenly becomes very full. Images of the pure and empty bring forth questions about its opposite: Yves Klein's *Le Vide* was immediately followed by Arman's *Le Plein.* Leonardo da Vinci advised painters to seek inspiration in irregular blotches on a wall. Le Corbusier's *Law of Ripolin* ordered us to cover them up. It takes more than a coat of whitewash for us to stop hallucinating.

Taking a photograph of almost nothing creates an image of something, of pure potentiality. *Svizzera 240* embraces the unfurnished interior photograph as a plastic representational medium that encourages reflection on a supposedly settled topic. →

### Built Representation

*Constructing a Foreign Territory*

What has been built in the Swiss Pavilion is not a "house" but a *house tour*. What is offered for your pleasure is latent in the strange potentiality of the images themselves. Instead of *representing building*, we *build representation*.

You enter an impossible dwelling—the construction of the installation is determined by *images* of apartments, not by real homes. The photograph's inability to convey scale, dimension, depth or spatial adjacency is presented in built form, creating a labyrinth of interior perspectives. The interior of housing is reimagined, not as an array of private volumes, but as a single, topological surface.

The credibility promised by the 1:1 model is discarded in favour of an entirely futile set of scales. Rooms oscillate between 1:5, 1:2, 1:1.6, 1:1.3, 1:1.2, 1:1, 1.1:1, 1.3:1, 1.5:1 and 2:1. The elements of the continuous space are banal, but they refuse to become familiar. This is called "defamiliarisation", "estrangement" or sometimes, "alienation". Welcome to your new home. Let us show you around.

### Becoming a House Tourist

*Drawing the Wrong Conclusion*

On this tour, there is little to do but *look* at an architecture that has never been known for its looks. A cast of supporting characters have been dragged into the spotlight: door handles, skirting boards, window frames, power outlets, light switches, countertops and cupboard doors.

This is not a question of architectural criticism but of architectural discovery. A tour through this alien landscape loosens the grip of your judgments. You are no longer an apartment dweller, builder or buyer—you are not an academic or even an architect—you become a new subject, a *House Tourist*.

You gaze at what you already know, but now the magic stupidity of the tourist opens the door to erroneous interpretations. Subjectivity enters the scene, paving the way for alternate readings. What's public? Anything private? Where's the facade? You're looking at it. And who lives here? We all do. ■

About the Curators:
The architects Alessandro Bosshard (MSc, ETH Arch.), Li Tavor (MSc, ETH Arch.), Matthew van der Ploeg (M.Arch, UIC) and Ani Vihervaara (M.Arch, BAS) live and work in Zurich. They have been working together since 2015 as assistant lecturers and researchers at the Swiss Federal Institute of Technology Zurich, ETH. Alessandro, Li and Matthew currently work with Prof. Dr. Alex Lehnerer in the chair of Architecture and Urban Design.

# Epilogue

Marianne Burki
Head of Visual Arts,
Pro Helvetia

With their *Svizzera 240: House Tour,* Alessandro Bosshard, Li Tavor, Matthew van der Ploeg and Ani Vihervaara extend an invitation to visitors of the Biennale in Venice to take a house tour. Even more precisely: the project is an invitation to indulge in a photographic gaze upon a flat. While visiting the apartment built within the Pavilion, guests experience the camera's view at the same time. As crazy as this might sound on paper, the refined and playful approach taken by the team of young architects plays on perspective and represents the starting point of their project.

In our time of the Internet, photographic views of living spaces are normally found at the beginning of any search for a new apartment or house. Naturally we get to see far more images of flats than actual apartments. What sort of norms, of preconceived ideas and feelings, to do with interiors are such images intended to convey? What efforts go into their fabrication? What architectural and/or professional documentation standards do they need to meet? Photographs also help architects to convey and document their performance. In "House Tour", visitors are invited to follow the architecture "backwards": from the image back to the model. "House Tour" further confronts us with aesthetic as much as societal questions, addressing both outside and inside perception as a way of affording a momentary grasp of the ever-fluctuating frontier between private and public realms.

Numerous authors found inspiration in the project's development process, motivating them to join the discourse by contributing texts of their own. The resulting publication features their approach to a site set up by society for individuals above and beyond public space. Further still, this publication is something of a cultural history of the inside of our living quarters: our living needs, our living dreams and our living spaces ... plus those of today's architects.

The 2018 Swiss Pavilion and this publication are at once the starting point for that critical discourse and the initial "product". This is the first year that the Swiss Arts Council Pro Helvetia has established the project for the Swiss Pavilion via a competition open to the public. With this, Pro Helvetia has included an element which is part of all architectural practice. Generally, architectural competitions don't only take place in order to establish a winning project, but also offer an understanding of the current architectural discourse by enabling the public a deeper insight into the jury's criteria and scores. By representing this process, the Swiss Arts Council also provides insight into the work of their Architecture Biennial Jury. The project also went on a "roadshow" prior to its opening. This was set up jointly with the SIA (Swiss Society of Engineers and Architects) with the aim of encouraging a discussion and reflection and further developing the project. It took place at the Swiss Architecture Museum in Basel, the F'ar (forum d'architectures Lausanne) and the Accademia di architettura Mendrisio.

In addition, all the applications are published on the www.biennials.ch website, making them available for public discussion.

My heartfelt thanks go first and foremost to the team responsible for this year's contribution, to Alessandro Bosshard, Li Tavor, Matthew van der Ploeg and Ani Vihervaara. I am also most grateful to all the authors who have contributed to the experimental dimension of this publication.

I would further like to thank the Pro Helvetia Visual Arts Biennial Team—namely, Sandi Paucic and Rachele Giudici.

# Index to the House Tour

p. 1–48

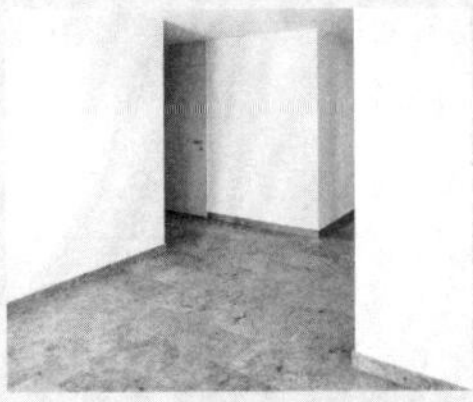

1 Planergemeinschaft Meier Hug mit Semadeni Architekten
Alterswohnungen GAIWO
Year: 2014 / Height: 246 cm
Photo: Roman Keller, Zürich
© Meier Hug

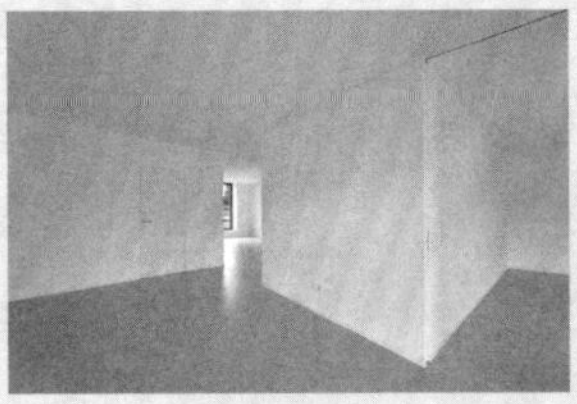

2 L3P Architekten AG
Mehrfamilienhaus Glättlistrasse
Year: 2011 / Height: 250 cm
Photo: Sabrina Scheja, Rebstein
© L3P Architekten AG

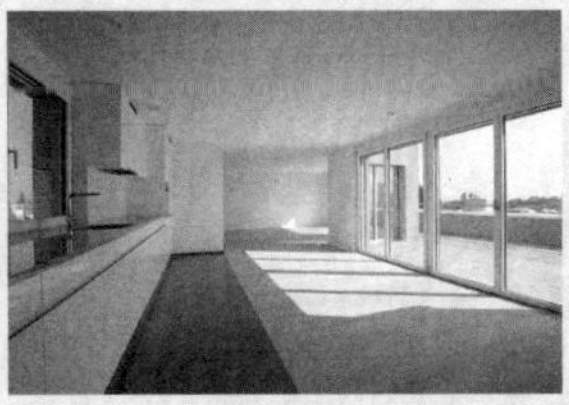

3 Felix Partner Architektur AG
Wohn-Gewerbeüberbauung Witenzelg
Year: 2017 / Height: 240 cm
Photo: Fotohalle, Heinz Unger
© Heinz Unger

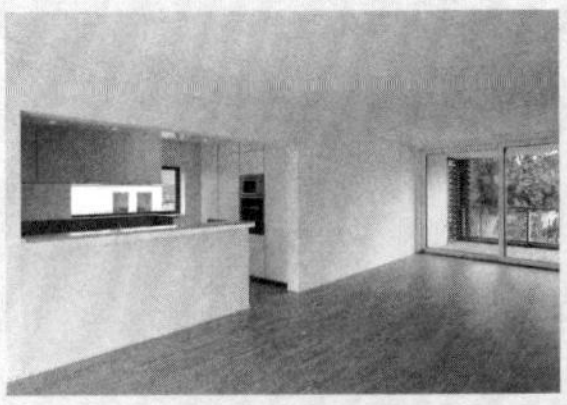

4 ADP Architekten
Wohn- und Geschäftshaus Feldeggstrasse
Year: 2012 / Height: 255 cm
Photo: Daniel Sutter, Zürich
© Daniel Sutter

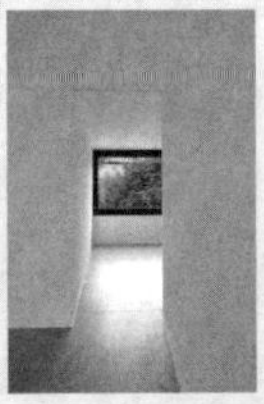

5 L3P Architekten AG
Mehrfamilienhaus Glättlistrasse
Year: 2011 / Height: 250 cm
Photo: Sabrina Scheja, Rebstein
© L3P Architekten AG

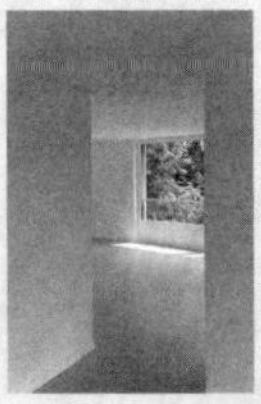

6 Igual & Guggenheim Architekten
Wohnhäuser Am Ättenberg
Year: 2014 / Height: 240 cm
Photo: Sancho Igual
© Igual & Guggenheim Architekten

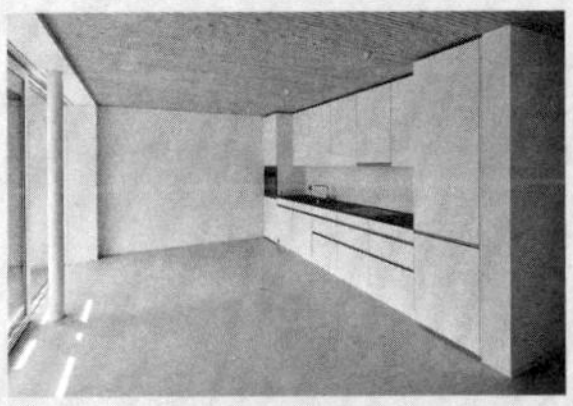

7 Carlos Martinez Architekten
Haus Albin Pedrotti
Year: 2017 / Height: 250 cm
Photo: Hannes Thalmann, St. Gallen
© Hannes Thalmann

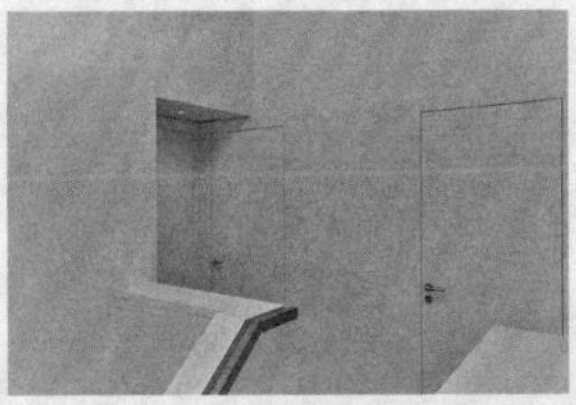

8 Forster & Uhl Architekten GmbH
Aufstockung / Ersatzbau Wohnhaus Buckstrasse
Year: 2017 / Height: 240 cm
Photo: Forster & Uhl Architekten GmbH
© Forster & Uhl Architekten GmbH

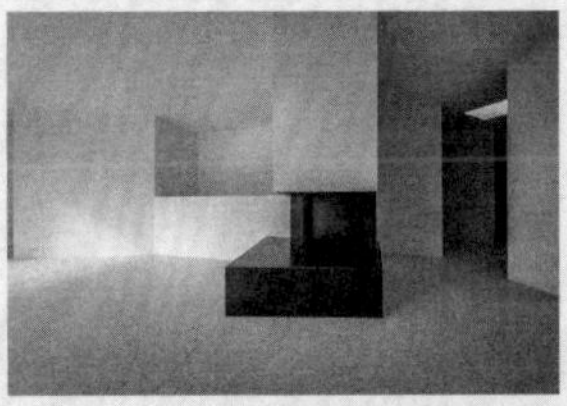

9 Think Architecture
Haus für drei Familien
Year: 2015 / Height: 250 cm
Photo: Think Architecture
© Think Architecture

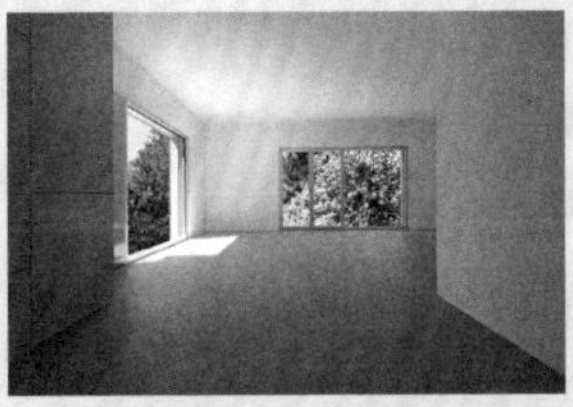

10 Lukas Meyer e Ira Piattini Architetti
Quartiere abitativo Ronchetto
Year: 2004 / Height: 250 cm
Photo: Enrico Cano, Lugano
© Enrico Cano

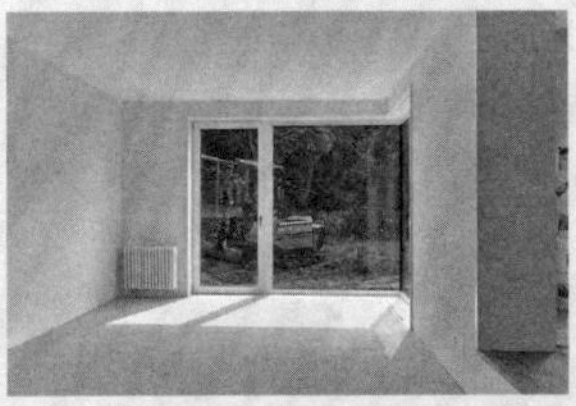

11 Forster & Uhl Architekten GmbH
Erweiterung Wohnhaus Enge
Year: 2017 / Height: 235 cm
Photo: Forster & Uhl Architekten GmbH
© Forster & Uhl Architekten GmbH

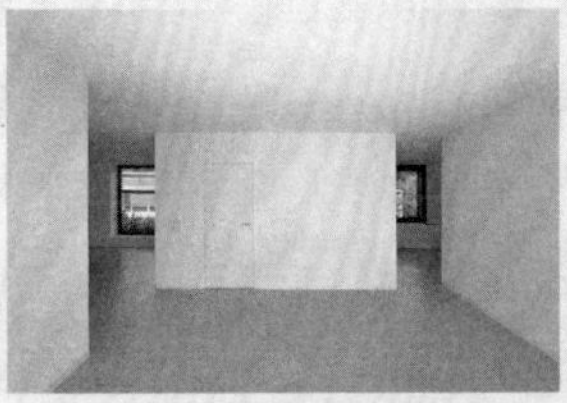

12 L3P Architekten AG
Mehrfamilienhaus Glättlistrasse
Year: 2011 / Height: 250 cm
Photo: Sabrina Scheja, Rebstein
© L3P Architekten AG

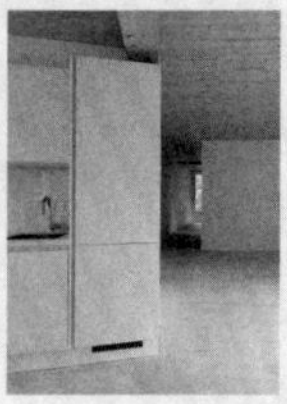

13 Slik Architekten
Konkordiastrasse
Year: 2017 / Height: 248 cm
Photo: Daniel Erne, Horgen
© Daniel Erne

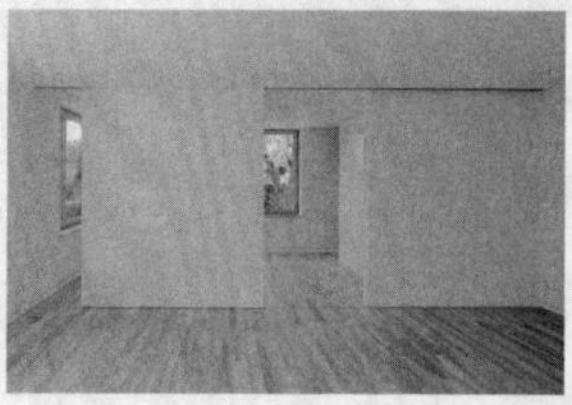

14 Schneider Gmür Architekten
Harmonika
Year: 2015 / Height: 246 cm
Photo: Pit Brunner, Winterthur
© Pit Brunner

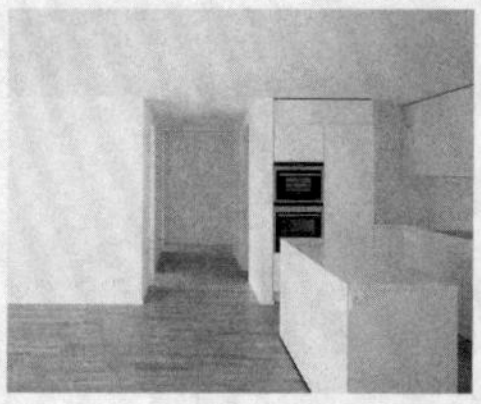

15 Phalt Architekten AG
Mehrfamilienhaus
Lohn-Ammannsegg
Year: 2011 / Height: 241 cm
Photo: Joël Tettamanti, Lausanne
© Joël Tettamanti

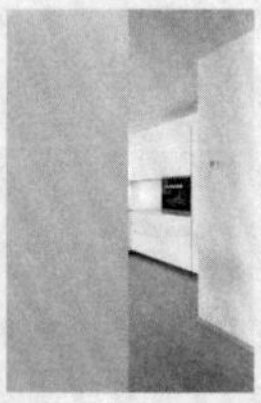

16 Enrico Sassi
Appartamento sul Lago di Lugano
Year: 2016 / Height: 252 cm
Photo: Alberto Canepa, Mendrisio
© Alberto Canepa

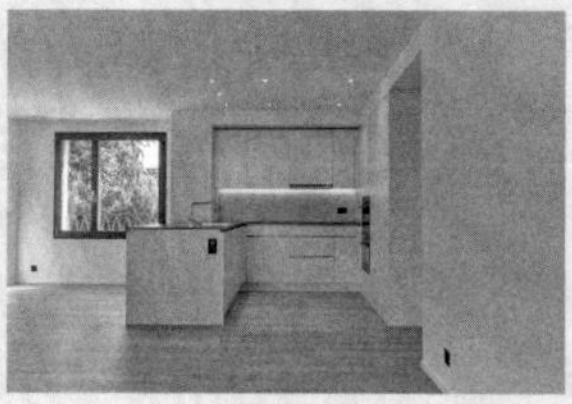

17 Forster & Uhl Architekten GmbH
Aufstockung/Ersatzbau
Wohnhaus Buckstrasse
Year: 2017 / Height: 235 cm
Photo: Forster & Uhl Architekten GmbH
© Forster & Uhl Architekten GmbH

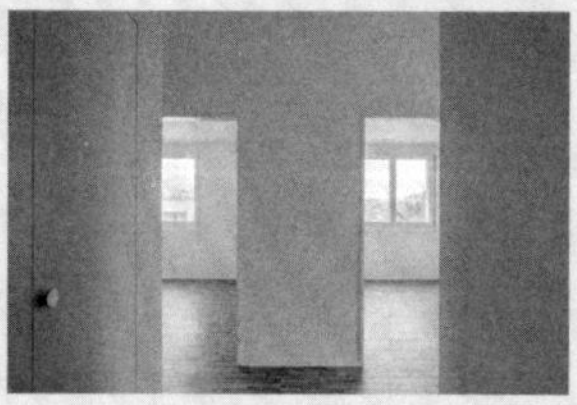

18 Husistein & Partner AG
Wohnüberbauung Oberdorf
Year: 2017 / Height: 242 cm
Photo: Goran Potkonjak, Uster
© Husistein & Partner AG

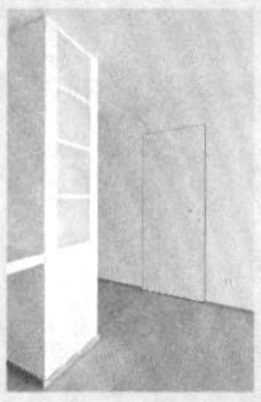

19 Enrico Sassi
Appartamento sul Lago di Lugano
Year: 2016 / Height: 252 cm
Photo: Alberto Canepa, Mendrisio
© Alberto Canepa

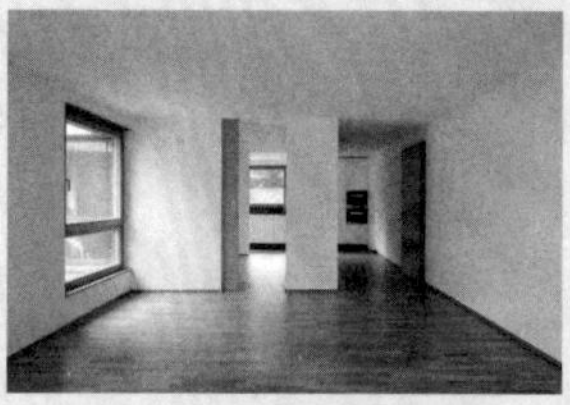

20 ADP Architekten
Mehrfamilienhaus
Breitensteinstrasse
Year: 2016 / Height: 242 cm
Photo: Daniel Sutter, Zürich
© Daniel Sutter

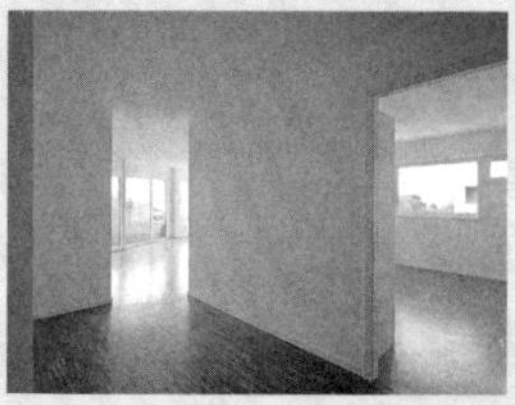

21 Bonhôte Zapata
La Chapelle, Chemin de Compostelle
Year: 2014 / Height: 250 cm
Photo: Johannes Marburg, Genève
© Johannes Marburg

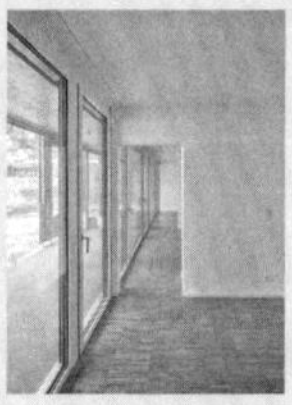

22 Bonhôte Zapata
Rigaud
Year: 2017 / Height: 250 cm
Photo: Johannes Marburg, Genève
© Johannes Marburg

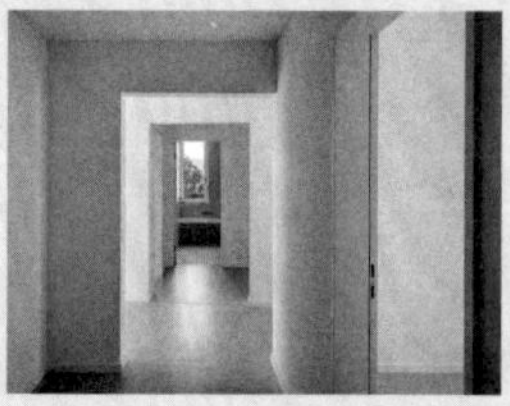

23 Phalt Architekten AG
Wohnsiedlung Sandfelsen Erlenbach
Year: 2014 / Height: 243 cm
Photo: Roger Frei, Zürich
© Roger Frei

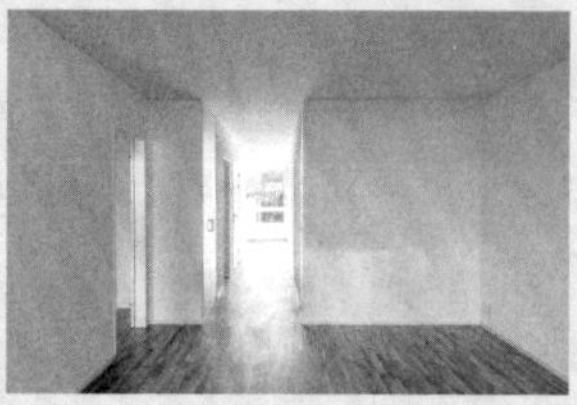

24 Luca Selva Architekten
Wohnübebauung Widmi 2
Year: 2016 / Height: 255 cm
Photo: Adriano Biondo, Basel
© Adriano Biondo

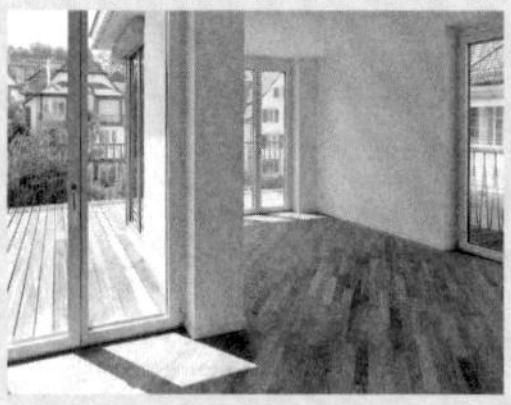

25 Guignard & Saner Architekten AG
Wohnheim Humanitas
Year: 2013 / Height: 240 cm
Photo: Roland Bernath, Zürich
© Roland Bernath

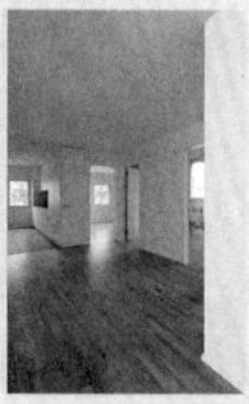

26 Coon Architekten GmbH
Mehrfamilienhaus Wiesenstrasse
Year: 2013 / Height: 242 cm
Photo: Christian Schwager, Winterthur
© Christian Schwager

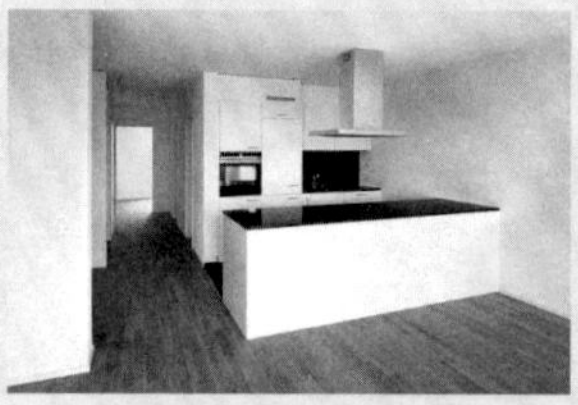

27 Carlos Martinez Architekten
Abitar
Year: 2017 / Height: 248 cm
Photo: Hannes Thalmann, St. Gallen
© Carlos Martinez Architekten

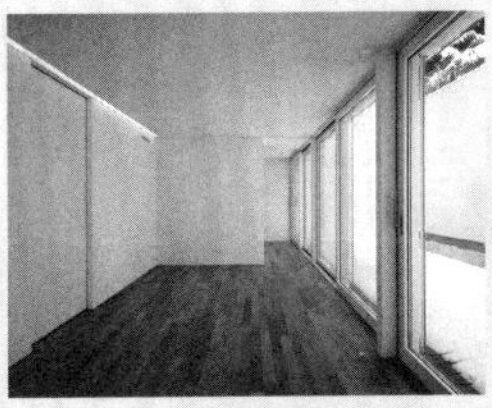

28 Think Architecture
Haus S Erlenbach
Year: 2008 / Height: 240 cm
Photo: Roger Frei, Zürich


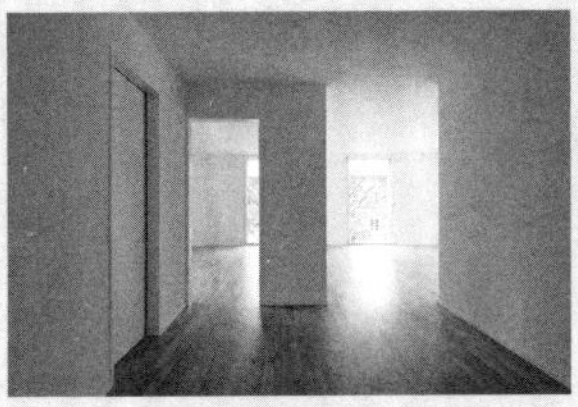

29 Coon Architekten GmbH
Mehrfamilienhaus Wiesenstrasse
Year: 2013 / Height: 242 cm
Photo: Christian Schwager, Winterthur


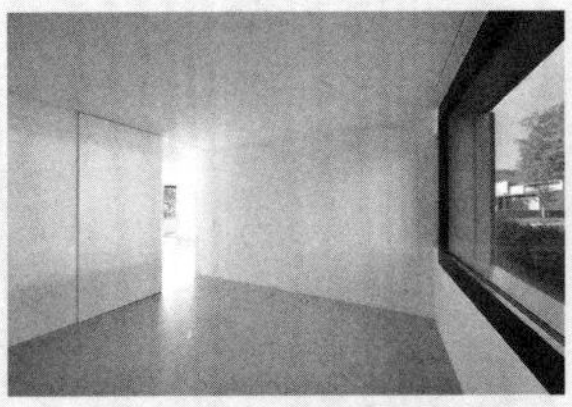

30 L3P Architekten AG
Mehrfamilienhaus Glättlistrasse
Year: 2011 / Height: 250 cm
Photo: Sabrina Scheja, Rebstein


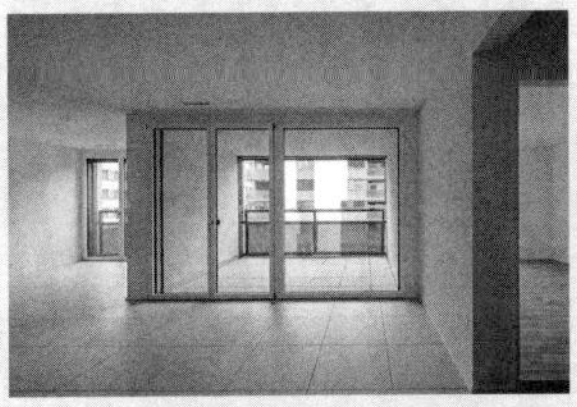

31 Think Architecture
Wohn und Gewerbehaus
Glattpark Mitte
Year: 2015 / Height: 245 cm
Photo: Radek Brunecky, Zürich


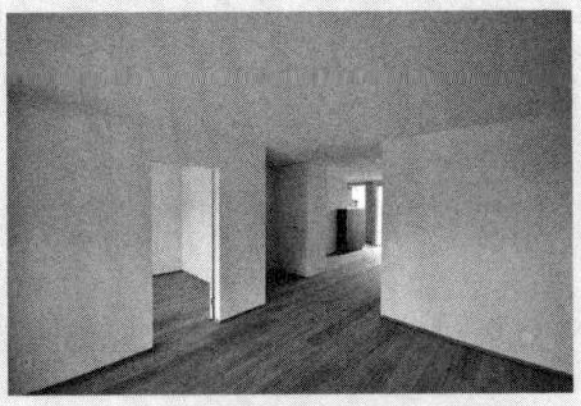

32 Meyer Architecture
Immeuble Dixence
Year: 2017 / Height: 250 cm
Photo: Meyer Architecture


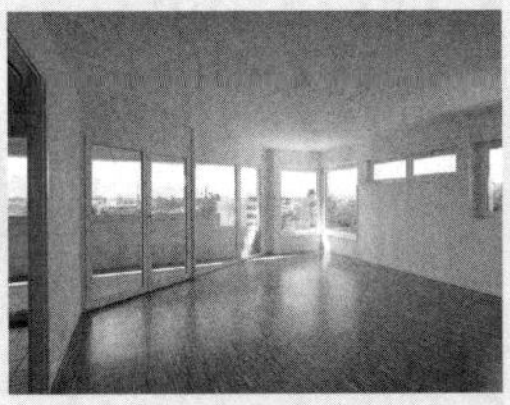

33 Bonhôte Zapata
La Chapelle, Chemin de Compostelle
Year: 2014 / Height: 250 cm
Photo: Johannes Marburg, Genève


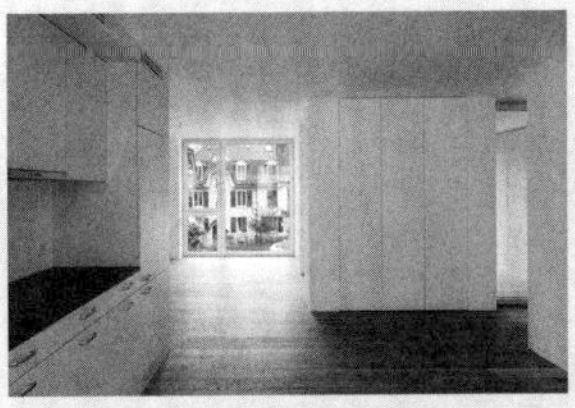

34 Bart & Buchhofer Architekten AG
Freiburgstrasse
Year: 2016 / Height: 250 cm
Photo: Markus Frietsch, Zürich


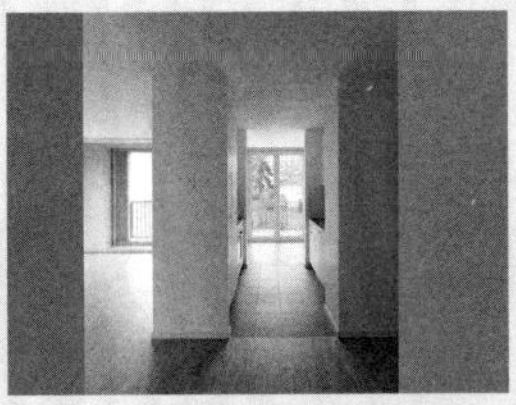

35 Burckhardt+Partner AG
Wohnüberbauung Sous-Bois
Year: 2015 / Height: 256 cm
Photo: Thomas Jantscher, Neuchâtel


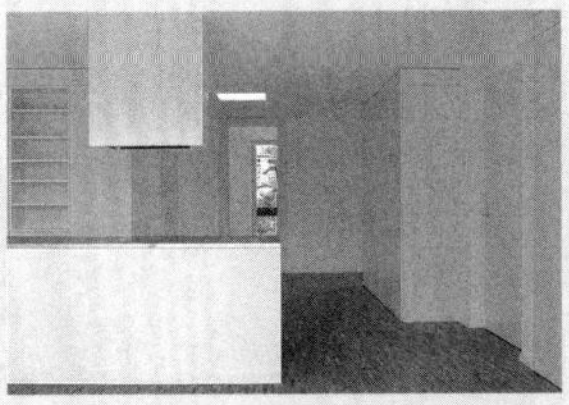

36 Bart & Buchhofer Architekten AG
Büttenbergstrasse
Year: 2009 / Height: 247 cm
Photo: Nadja Frey, Bern


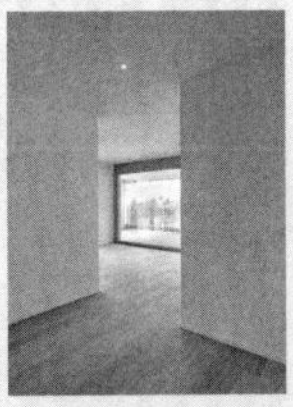

37 Husistein & Partner AG
Wohnüberbauung am Lindenweg
Year: 2017 / Height: 242 cm
Photo: Goran Potkonjak, Uster


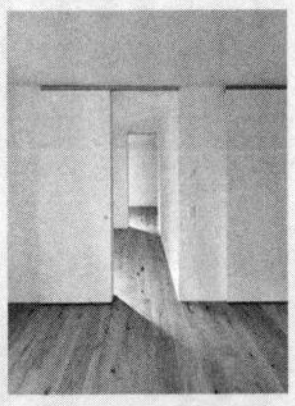

38 Sven Stucki Architekten AG
Neubau MFH Schönberg Ost
Year: 2016 / Height: 247 cm
Photo: Manuel Stettler, Bern


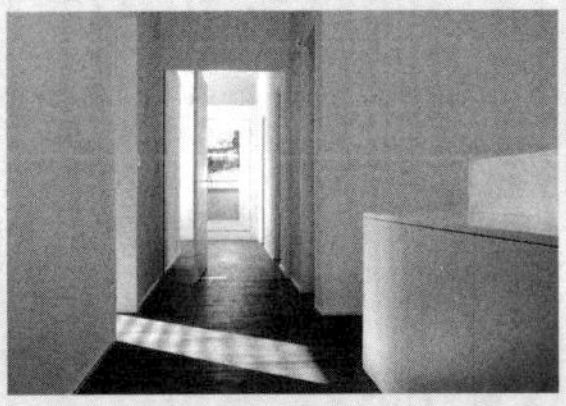

39 W2H Architekten
Neubau Wohnhaus Riggisberg
Year: 2007 / Height: 242 cm
Photo: Marco Frauchiger, Bern


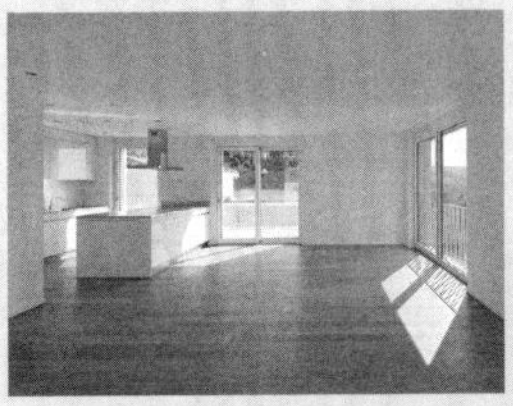

40 Felix Partner Architektur AG
Überbauung Drusberg
Year: 2016 / Height: 240 cm
Photo: Thomas Aus der Au, Winterthur


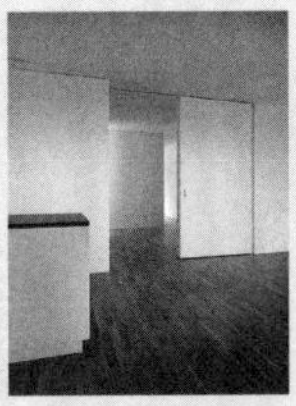

41 Frundgallina Architectes
Réalisation de 20 Logements
Year: 2009 / Height: 250 cm
Photo: Milo Keller, Fribourg


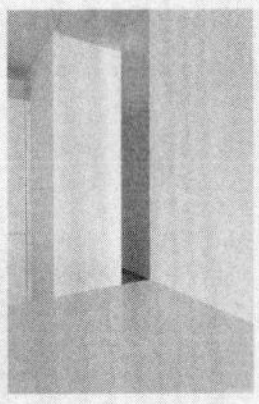

42 Enrico Sassi
Appartamento sul Lago di Lugano
Year: 2016 / Height: 252 cm
Photo: Alberto Canepa, Mendrisio

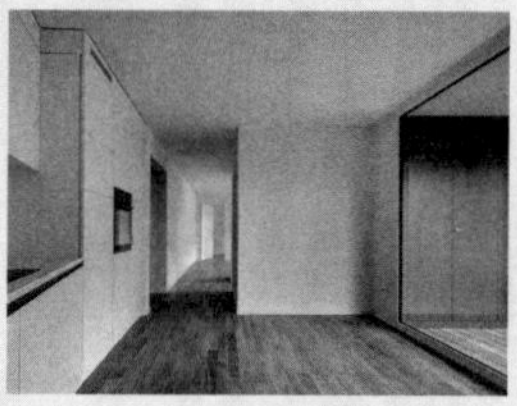

43 Phalt Architekten AG
Wohnüberbauung Hofstatt Zuchwil
Year: 2014 / Height: 245 cm
Photo: Roger Frei, Zürich
© Roger Frei

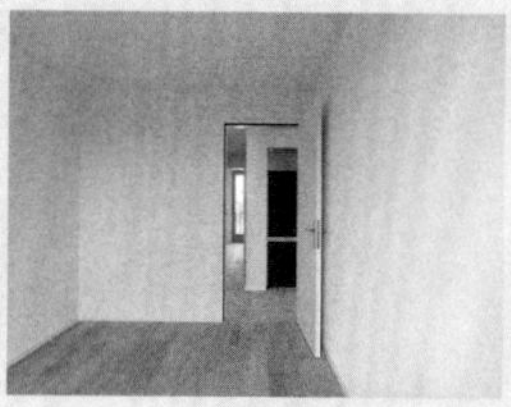

44 Husistein & Partner AG
Wohnüberbauung am Lindenweg
Year: 2017 / Height: 242 cm
Photo: Goran Potkonjak, Uster
© Husistein & Partner AG

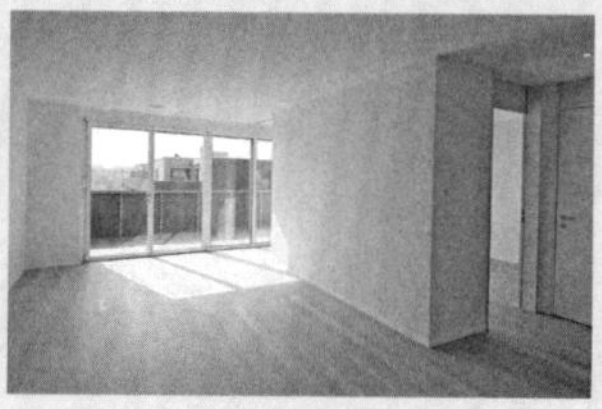

45 Felix Partner Architektur AG
Wohn- und Gewerbeüberbauung
Witenzelg
Year: 2017 / Height: 240 cm
Photo: Fotohalle, Heinz Unger
© Heinz Unger

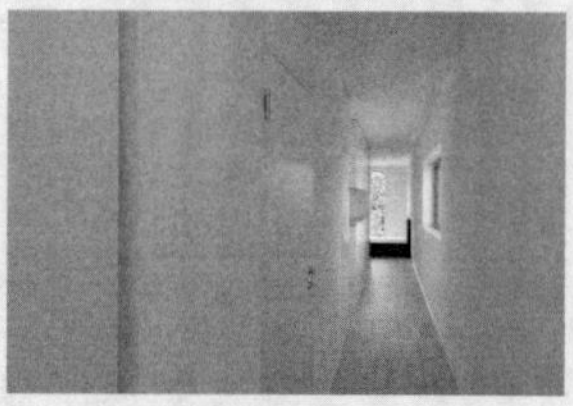

46 ADP Architekten
Wohn- und Geschäftshaus
Feldeggstrasse
Year: 2012 / Height: 255 cm
Photo: Daniel Sutter, Zürich
© Daniel Sutter

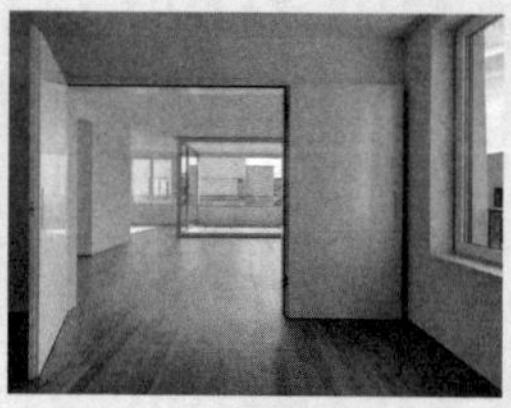

47 Schneider & Schneider
Wohnhäuser Rössligut
Year: 2012 / Height: 250 cm
Photo: Roger Frei, Zürich
© Schneider & Schneider

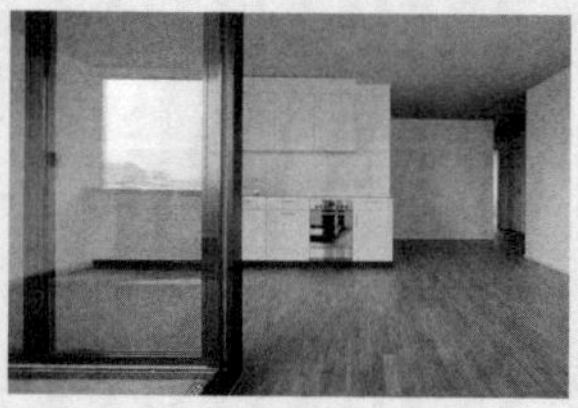

48 Galli Rudolf
Haus A3 am Rietpark
Year: 2011 / Height: 247 cm
Photo: Dominique Marc Wehrli, Winterthur
© Dominique Marc Wehrli

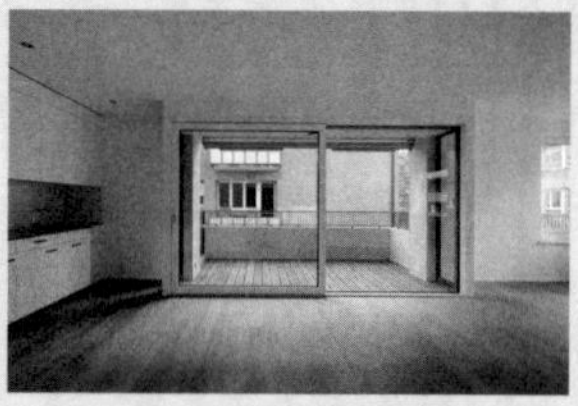

49 Forster & Uhl Architekten GmbH
Neubau Wohnhaus Delphinstrasse
Year: 2017 / Height: 240 cm
Photo: Beat Bühler, Zürich
© Forster & Uhl Architekten GmbH

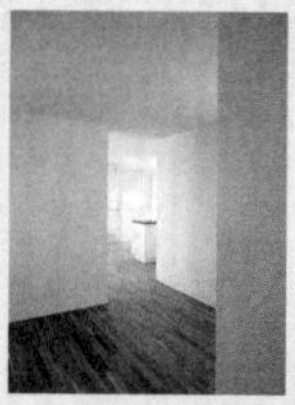

50 Frundgallina Architectes
Réalisation de 20 Logements
Year: 2009 / Height: 250 cm
Photo: Milo Keller, Fribourg
© Milo Keller

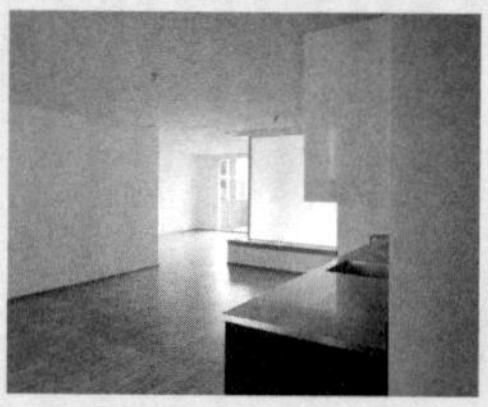

51 Kaschka Knapkiewicz + Axel Fickert AG
Wohnüberbauung Klee
Year: 2011 / Height: 244 cm
Photo: Ruedi Walti, Basel
© Ruedi Walti

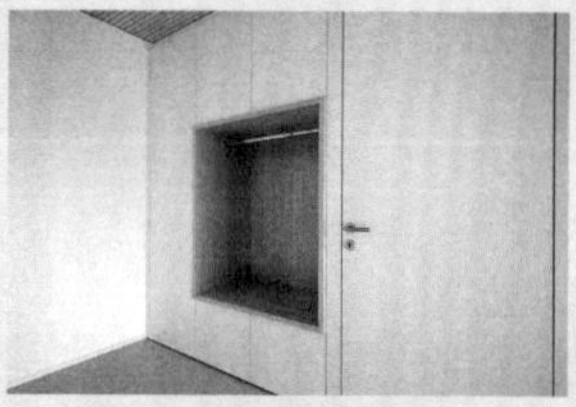

52 Carlos Martinez Architekten
Haus Albin Pedrotti
Year: 2017 / Height: 250 cm
Photo: Hannes Thalmann, St. Gallen
© Hannes Thalmann

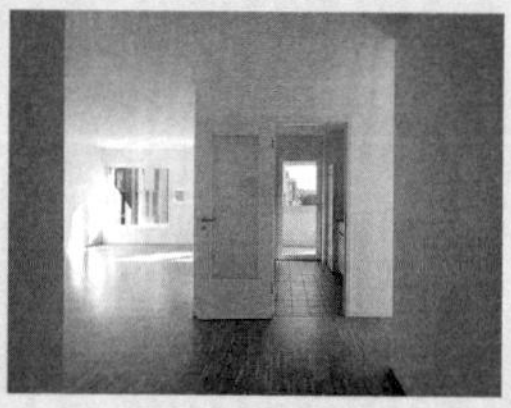

53 Bonhôte Zapata
La Chapelle, Chemin de Compostelle
Year: 2014 / Height: 250 cm
Photo: Johannes Marburg, Genève
© Johannes Marburg

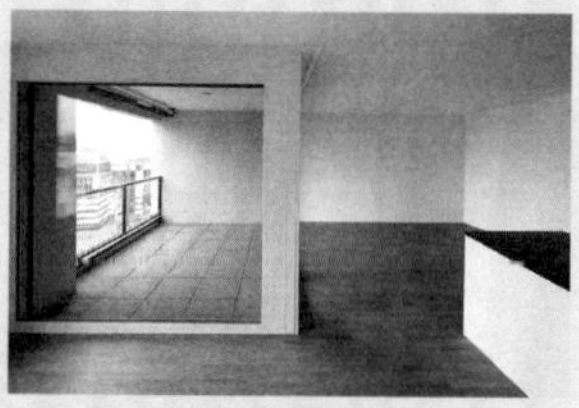

54 Carlos Martinez Architekten
Abitar
Year: 2017 / Height: 248 cm
Photo: Hannes Thalmann, St. Gallen
© Hannes Thalmann

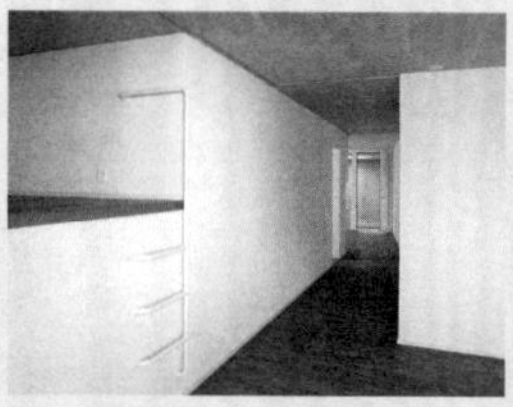

55 JOM architekten
Neubau Mehrgenerationenhaus
Im Morgen
Year: 2015 / Height: 106–248 cm
Photo: Thomas Stöckli, Zürich
© Thomas Stöckli

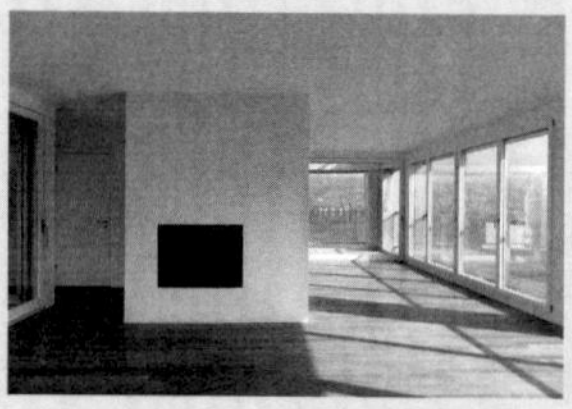

56 Gigon Guyer
Wohn- und Bürogebäude
Färberei-Areal, Haus 1
Year: 2008 / Height: 260 cm
Photo: Lucas Peters, Zürich
© Lucas Peters

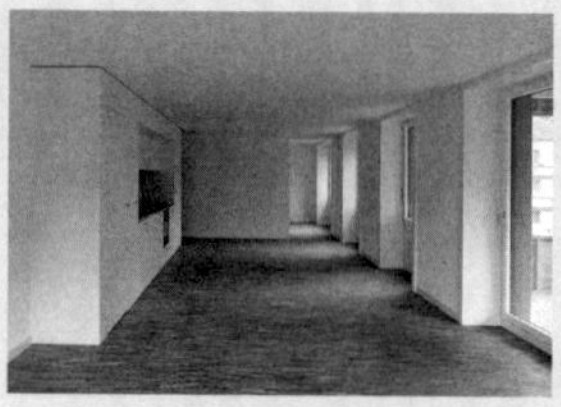

57 Bart & Buchhofer Architekten AG
Ankerweg
Year: 2012 / Height: 238 cm
Photo: Thomas Jantscher, Neuchâtel
© Bart & Buchhofer Architekten AG

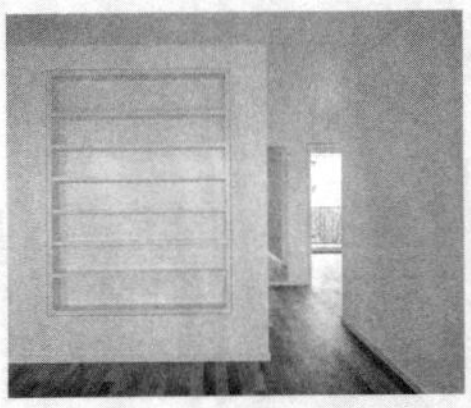

58 GFA Gruppe für Architektur GmbH
Umbau Wohnung Baker Cowling
Year: 2009 / Height: 248 cm
Photo: Roger Frei, Zürich
© Roger Frei

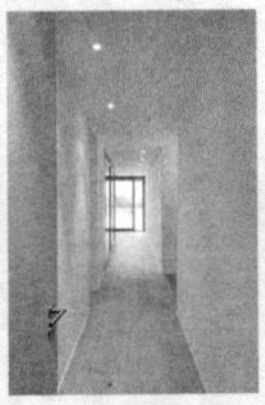

59 Burckhardt+Partner AG
Wohnüberbauung Elco Park
Year: 2012 / Height: 251 cm
Photo: Beat Ernst, Basel
© Beat Ernst

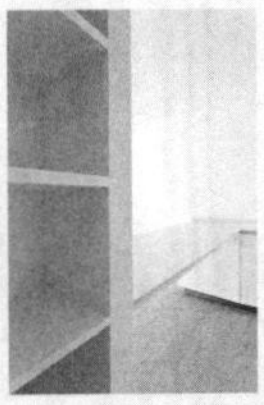

60 Enrico Sassi
Appartamento sul Lago di Lugano
Year: 2016 / Height: 252 cm
Photo: Alberto Canepa, Mendrisio
© Alberto Canepa

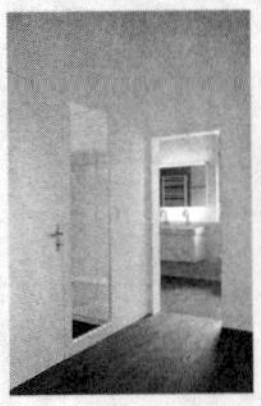

61 3B Architekten AG
Aebnitweg
Year: 2015 / Height: 242 cm
Photo: 3B Architekten AG
© 3B Architekten AG

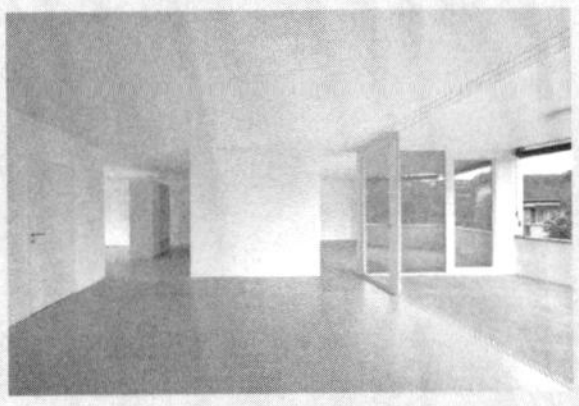

62 L3P Architekten AG
Mehrfamilienhaus Glättlistrasse
Year: 2011 / Height: 250 cm
Photo: Sabrina Scheja, Rebstein
© L3P Architekten AG

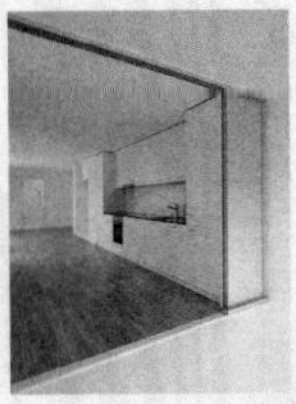

63 Tribu Architecture
Boissonnet
Year: 2013 / Height: 240 cm
Photo: Michel Bonvin, Lausanne
© Michel Bonvin

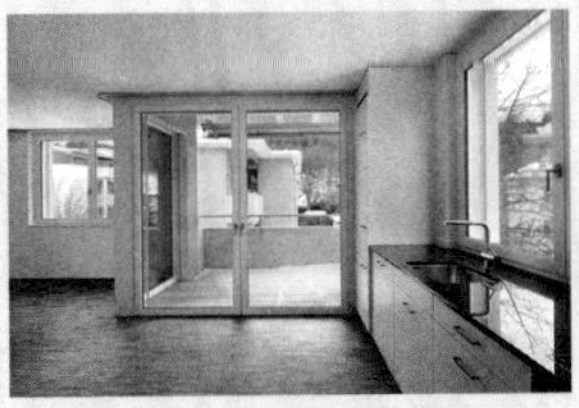

64 Slik Architekten
Wohnhäuser Frohburgstrasse
Year: 2017 / Height: 250 cm
Photo: Daniel Erne, Horgen
© Daniel Erne

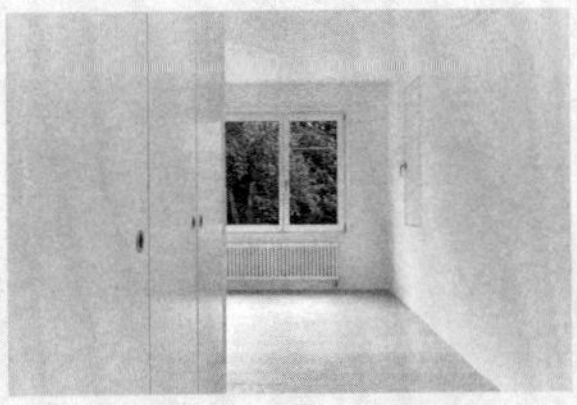

65 Forster & Uhl Architekten GmbH
Erweiterung Wohnhaus Enge
Year: 2017 / Height: 225 cm
Photo: Forster & Uhl Architekten GmbH
© Forster & Uhl Architekten GmbH

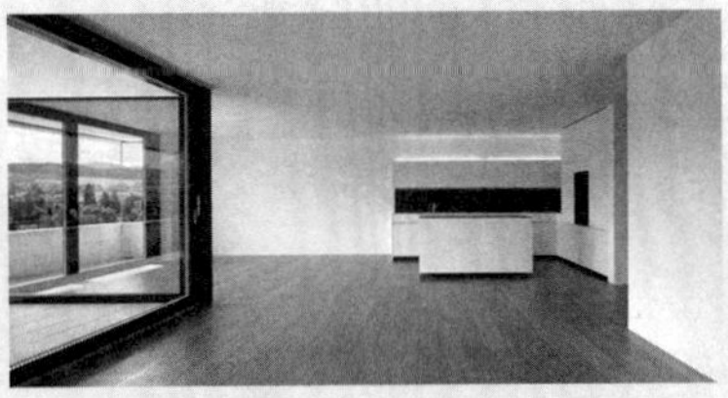

66 Rosenmund + Rieder Architekten
Wohnen am alten Rebberg
Year: 2014 / Height: 255 cm
Photo: Tom Bisig, Basel
© Tom Bisig, Basel

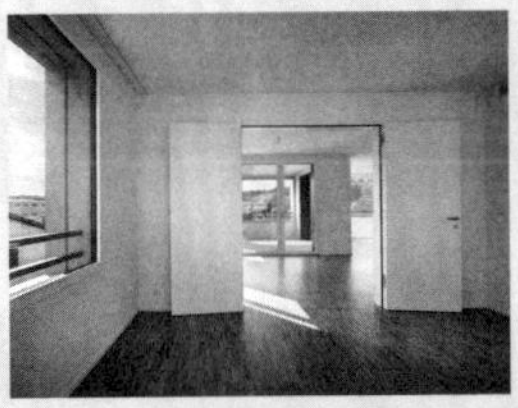

67 Bauart Architekten und Planer AG
Swisswoodhouse Nebikon
Year: 2014 / Height: 250 cm
Photo: Ruedi Walti, Basel
© Bauart Architekten und Planer AG

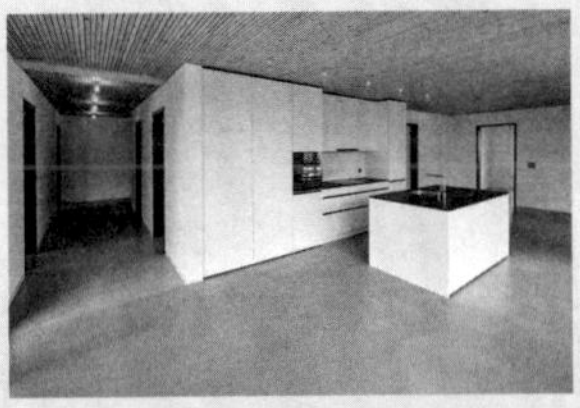

68 Carlos Martinez Architekten
Haus Albin Pedrotti
Year: 2017 / Height: 250 cm
Photo: Hannes Thalmann, St. Gallen
© Hannes Thalmann

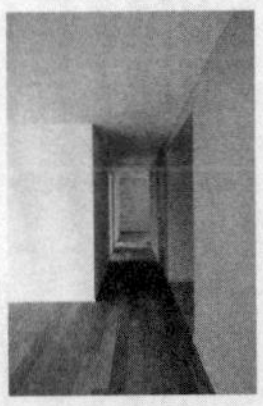

69 Philipp Wieting Werknetz
Grossmatt 4
Year: 2016 / Height: 251 cm
Photo: Philipp Wieting
© Philipp Wieting

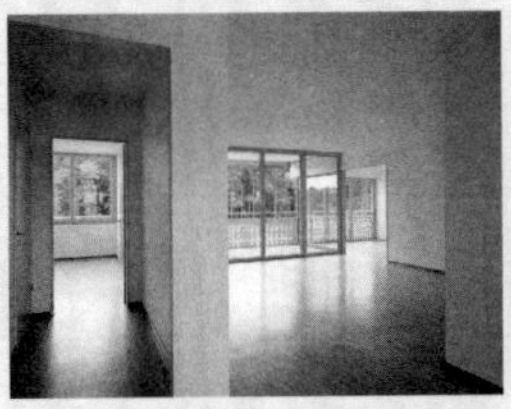

70 Esch Sintzel Architekten
Wohnüberbauung Stähelimatt
Year: 2007 / Height: 255 cm
Photo: Walter Mair, Basel
© Walter Mair

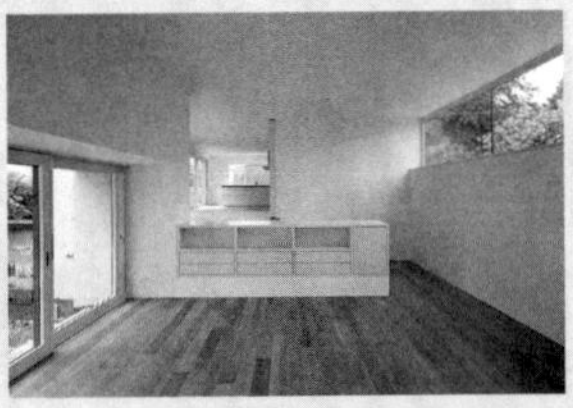

71 Baumann Roserens Architekten
Haus Weinberg
Year: 2004 / Height: 360 cm
Photo: Jürg Zimmermann, Zürich
© Jürg Zimmermann

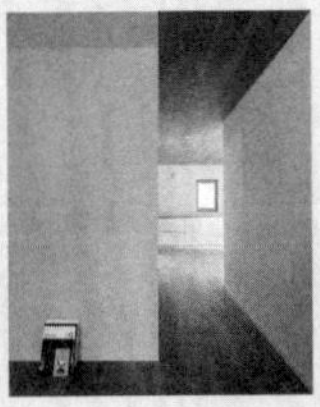

72 Inches Geleta Architetti Sagl
Casa Desgraz
Year: 2015 / Height: 240 cm
Photo: Simone Bossi, Milano
© Simone Bossi

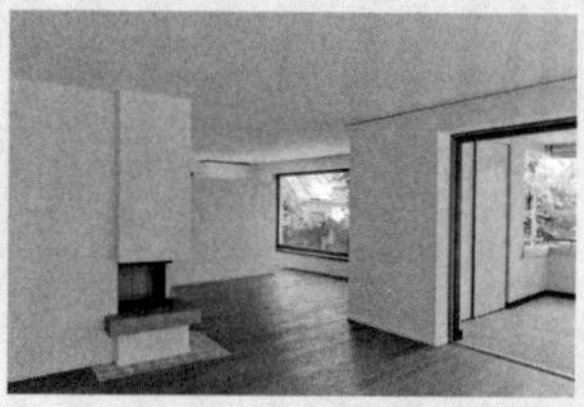

73 Bollhalder Eberle Architektur
Wohnhäuser Goethestrasse
Year: 2014 / Height: 255 cm
Photo: Marco Kistler, Zürich
© Bollhalder Eberle Architektur

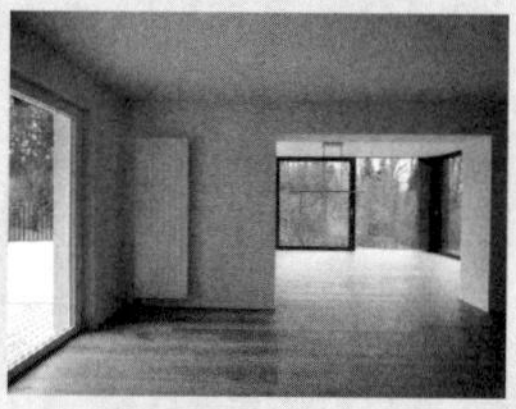

74 Schoch Tavli Architekten
Wohnhaus Frauenfeld
Year: 2016 / Height: 242 cm
Photo: Schoch Tavli Architekten
© Schoch Tavli Architekten

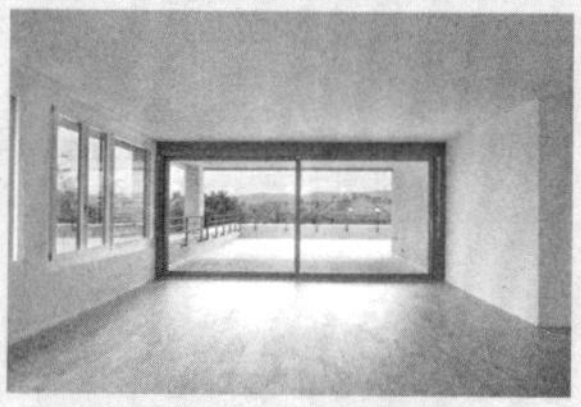

75 Burckhardt+Partner AG
Wohnüberbauung Elco Park
Year: 2012 / Height: 251 cm
Photo: Beat Ernst, Basel
© Beat Ernst

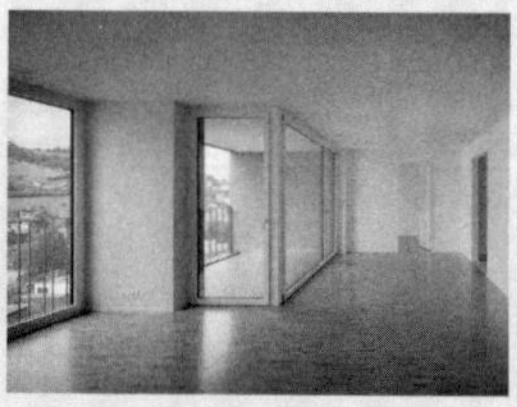

76 ARGE Ciriacidis Architekten GmbH, Forster & Uhl Architekten GmbH
Erweiterung Sunnehof
Year: 2015 / Height: 240 cm
Photo: Karin Gauch, Fabien Schwartz, Zug
© Forster & Uhl Architekten GmbH

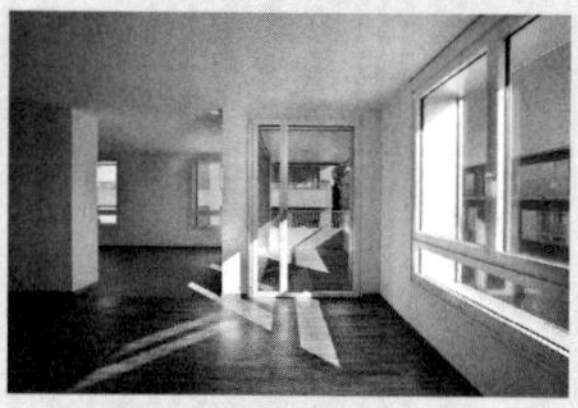

77 Bonhôte Zapata
Victor Ruffy
Year: 2010 / Height: 248 cm
Photo: Lignum
© Lignum

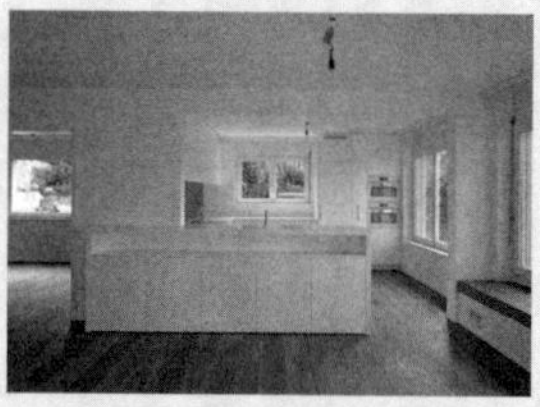

78 3B Architekten AG
Aebnitweg
Year: 2015 / Height: 242 cm
Photo: 3B Architekten AG
© 3B Architekten AG

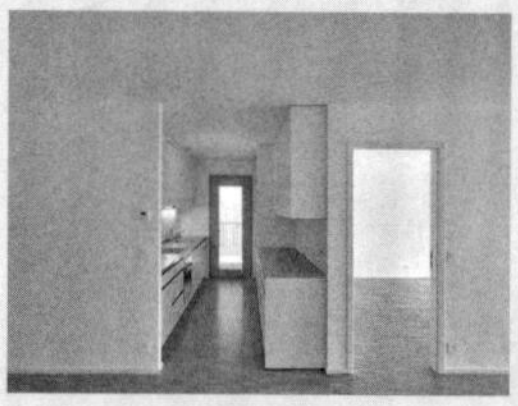

79 Bonhôte Zapata
Rigaud
Year: 2017 / Height: 250 cm
Photo: Johannes Marburg, Genève
© Johannes Marburg

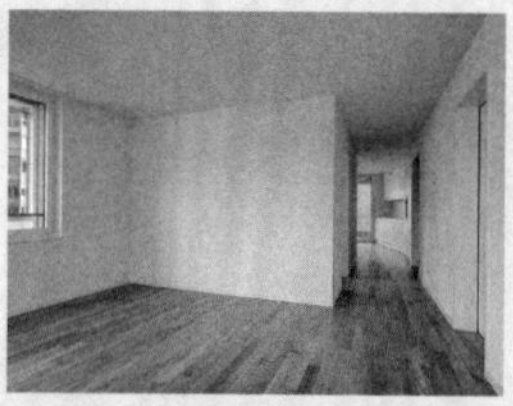

80 Phalt Architekten AG
Wohnüberbauung Hofstatt Zuchwil
Year: 2014 / Height: 245 cm
Photo: Roger Frei, Zürich
© Roger Frei

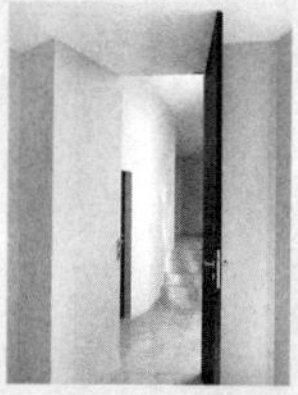

81 Edelaar Mosayebi Inderbitzin Architekten
Wohnhaus Steinwies- / Irisstrasse
Year: 2015 / Height: 274 cm
Photo: Roland Bernath, Zürich
© Roland Bernath

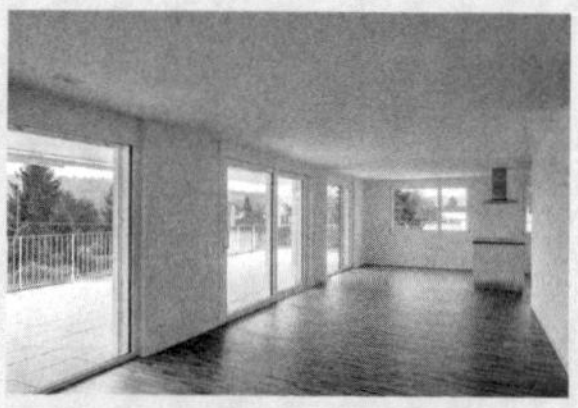

82 Husistein & Partner AG
Wohnüberbauung Oberdorf
Year: 2016 / Height: 244 cm
Photo: Radek Brunecky, Zürich
© Husistein & Partner AG

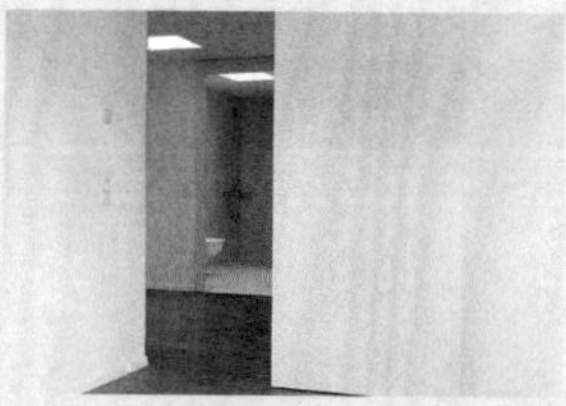

83 Bart & Buchhofer Architekten AG
Büttenbergstrasse
Year: 2009 / Height: 244 cm
Photo: Nadja Frey, Bern
© Bart & Buchhofer Architekten AG

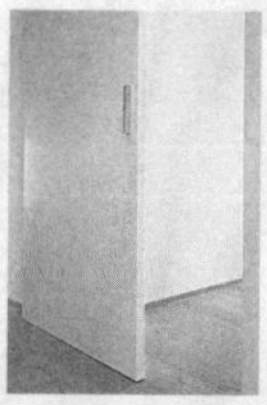

84 Enrico Sassi
Appartamento sul Lago di Lugano
Year: 2016 / Height: 252 cm
Photo: Alberto Canepa, Mendrisio
© Alberto Canepa

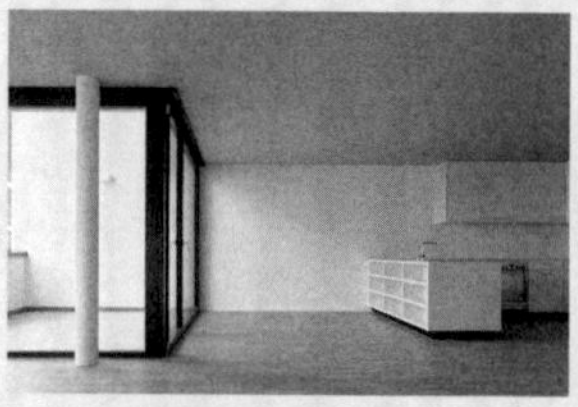

85 Galli Rudolf
Haus A3 am Rietpark
Year: 2011 / Height: 247 cm
Photo: Dominique M. Wehrli, Zürich
© Dominique M. Wehrli

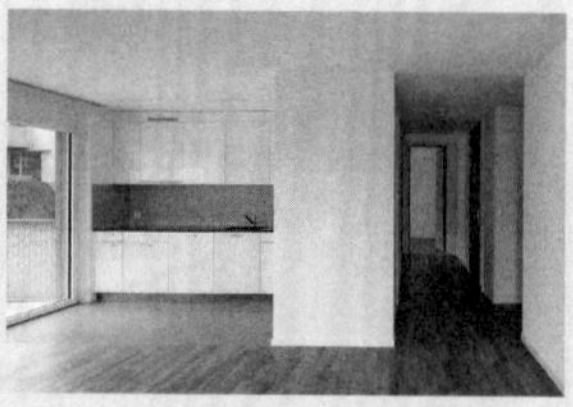

86 Beat Rothen Architektur
Hohfurristrasse / Eichenweg, Winterthur
Year: 2014 / Height: 250 cm
Photo: Claudia Luperto, Winterthur
© Claudia Luperto

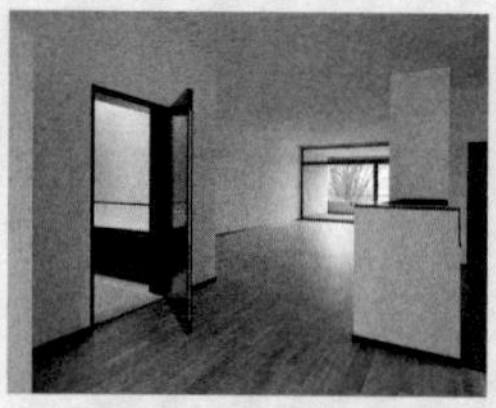

87 Gmür & Steib Architekten AG
Mehrfamilienhaus Imbisbühlstrasse
Year: 2008 / Height: 302 cm
Photo: Roger Frei, Zürich
© Roger Frei

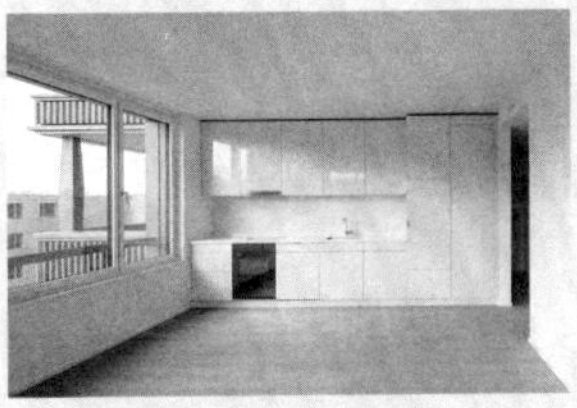

88 Müller Sigrist Architekten
Suurstoffi, Risch-Rotkreuz
Year: 2015 / Height: 260 cm
Photo: Claudia Luperto, Winterthur
© Müller Sigrist Architekten

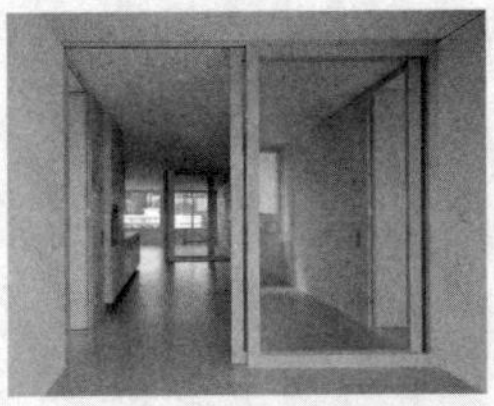

89 Adrian Streich Architekten AG
Wohnhaus Diener-Areal
Year: 2009 / Height: 270 cm
Photo: Roger Frei, Zürich
© Roger Frei

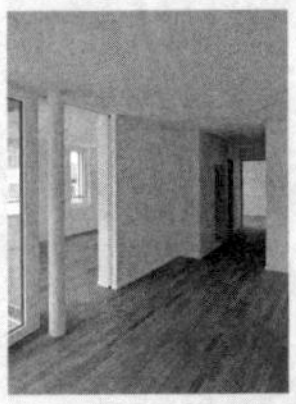

90 ERP Architekten
Mehrfamilienhaus Spirgartenstrasse
Year: 2014 / Height: 240 cm
Photo: Ariel Huber, Lausanne
© Ariel Huber

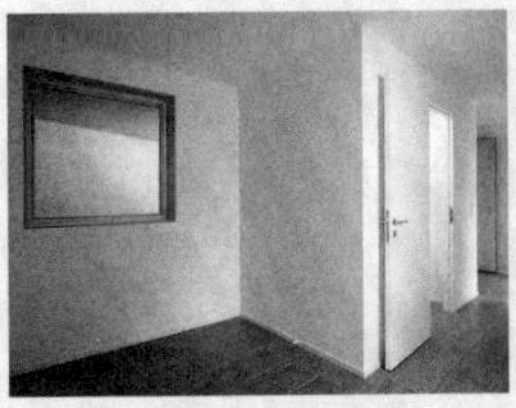

91 Tribu Architecture
Bonne-Espèrance
Year: 2013 / Height: 241 cm
Photo: Michel Bonvin, Lausanne
© Michel Bonvin

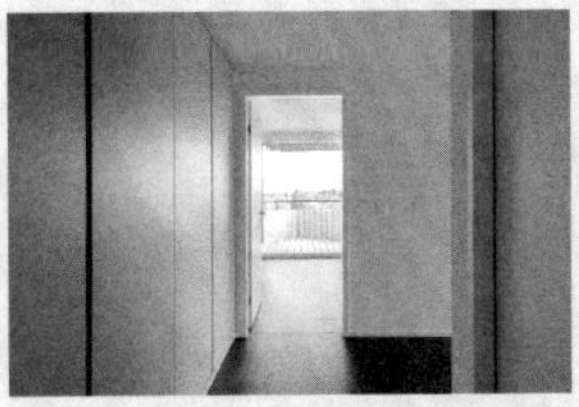

92 Huggenbergerfries Architekten AG
Umbau Wohnhochhaus Bachstrasse
Year: 2013 / Height: 232 cm
Photo: Beat Bühler, Zürich
© Huggenbergerfries Architekten AG

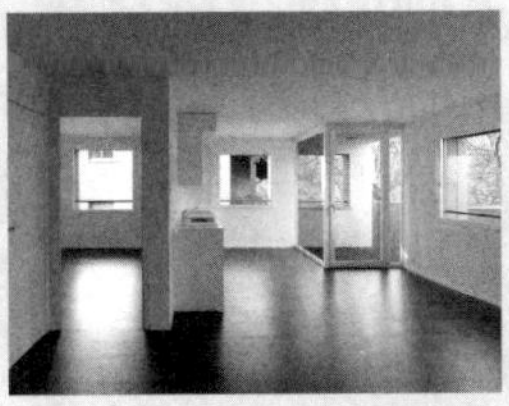

93 Meyer Architecture
Immeuble Habitation
Year: 2013 / Height: 240 cm
Photo: Thomas Jantscher, Neuchâtel
© Thomas Jantscher

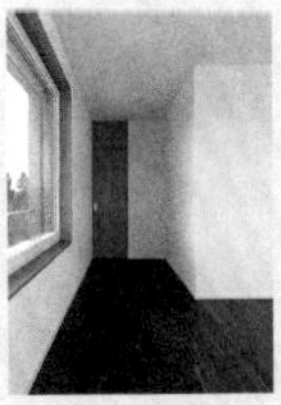

94 Furrer Jud Architekten
Ersatzneubau Mühle Freudenau
Year: 2014 / Hight: 268 cm
Photo: Benedikt Redmann, Zürich
© Furrer Jud Architekten

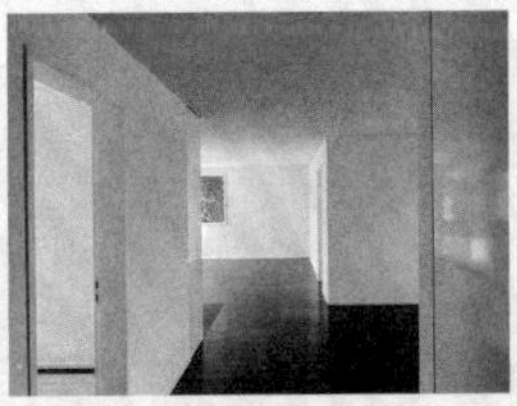

95 pool
Kosakenweg
Year: 2014 / Height: 240 cm
Photo: Georg Aerni, Zürich
© Georg Aerni

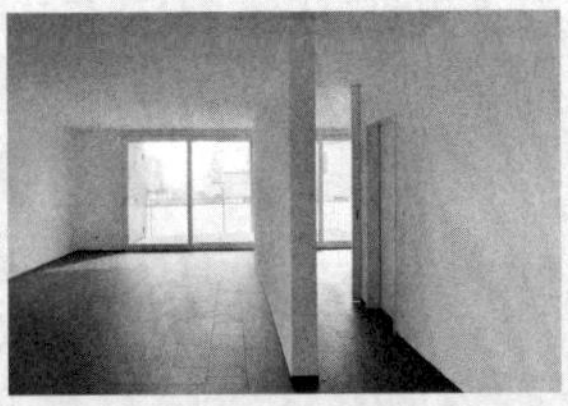

96 Schoop de Santis Architekten
Wohn- und Geschäftshaus Wohlen
Year: 2009 / Height: 240 cm
Photo: René Rötheli, Baden
© René Rötheli

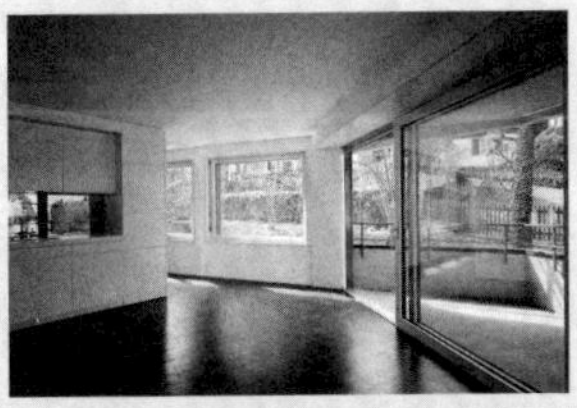

97 Guagliardi Ruoss
Wohnsiedlung Papillon
Year: 2010 / Height: 241 cm
Photo: Andrea Helbling, Zürich
© Andrea Helbling

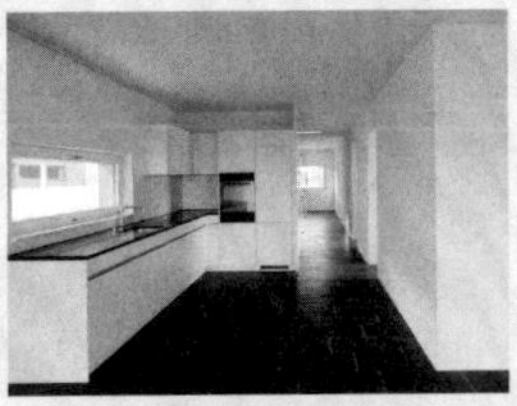

98 ERP Architekten
Wohnüberbauung Zelgweg
Year: 2012 / Height: 240 cm
Photo: Ariel Huber, Lausanne
© Ariel Huber

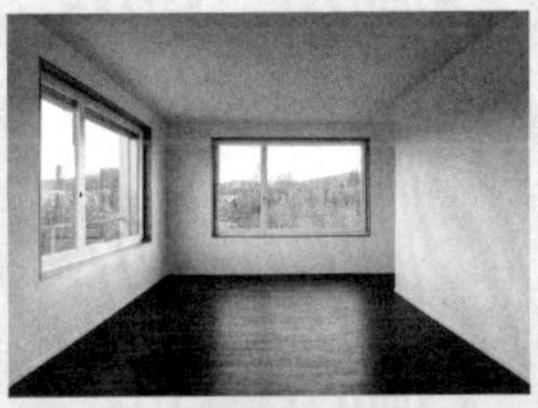

99 Furrer Jud Architekten
Ersatzneubau Mühle Freudenau
Year: 2014 / Height: 268 cm
Photo: Benedikt Redmann, Zürich
© Furrer Jud Architekten

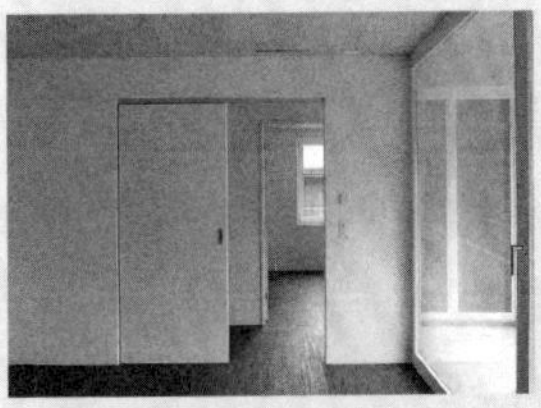

100 Schneider Gmür Architekten
Mehrfamilienhaus Stettbachstrasse
Year: 2008 / Height: 245 cm
Photo: Andre Schneider, Winterthur
© Andre Schneider

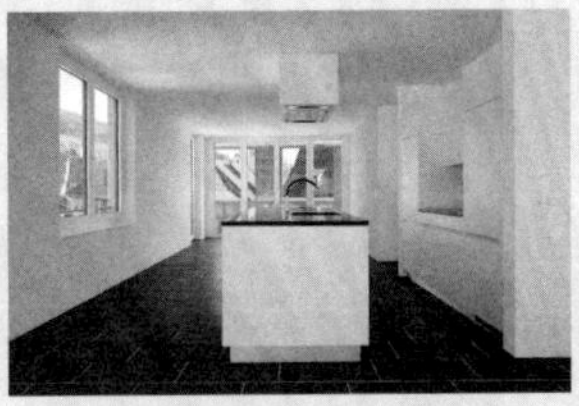

101 Rosenmund + Rieder Architekten
Wohnen am Diegterbach
Year: 2013 / Height: 245 cm
Photo: Tom Bisig, Basel
© Tom Bisig, Basel

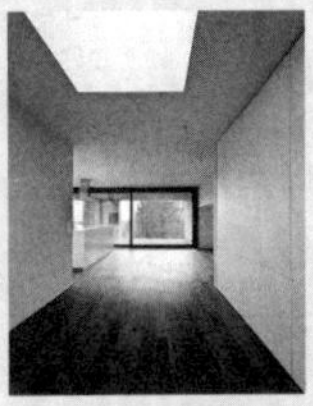

102 Think Architecture
Monolith
Year: 2013 / Height: 245 cm
Photo: Think Architecture
© Think Architecture

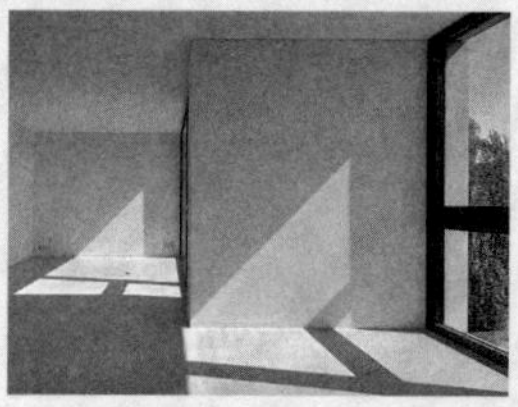

103 Spillmann Echsle Architekten
Aufstockung Rauti Huus
Year: 2014 / Height: 260 cm
Photo: Roger Frei, Zürich
© Roger Frei

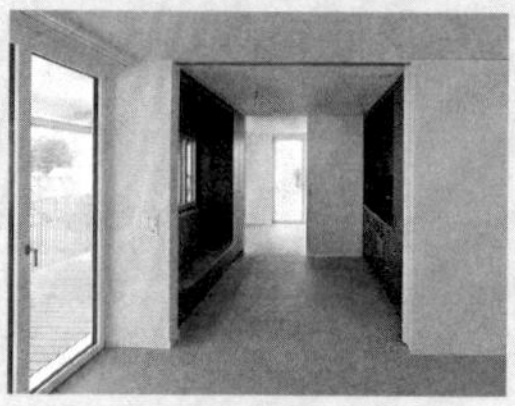

104 Haerle Hubacher
Hofächer Dietikon
Year: 2015 / Height: 252 cm
Photo: Theodor Stalder, Zürich
© Theodor Stalder

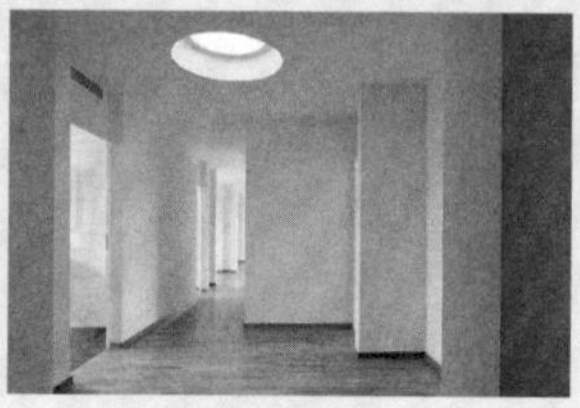

105 Galli Rudolf
Wohnsiedlung Paradies
Year: 2017 / Height: 248 cm
Photo: Ralph Feiner, Malans
© Ralph Feiner

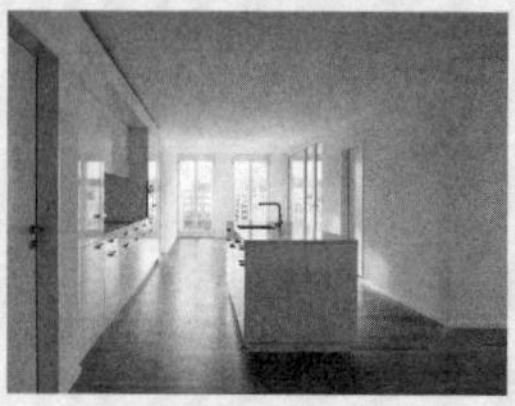

106 Giuliani Hönger
Wohn- und Gewerbehaus Weidenhof
Year: 2015 / Height: 250 cm
Photo: David Willen, Zürich
© David Willen

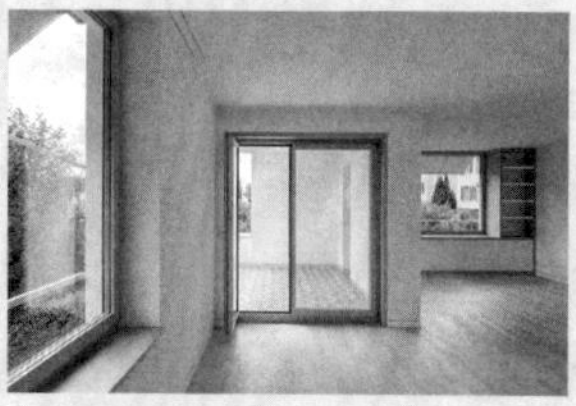

107 Schneider Gmür Architekten
Harmonika
Year: 2015 / Height: 246 cm
Photo: Pit Brunner, Winterthur
© Pit Brunner

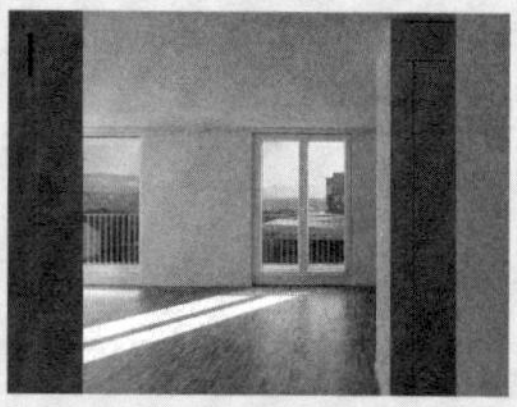

108 Burckhardt+Partner AG
Wohnüberbauung Sous-Bois
Year: 2015 / Height: 256 cm
Photo: Thomas Jantscher, Neuchâtel
© Thomas Jantscher

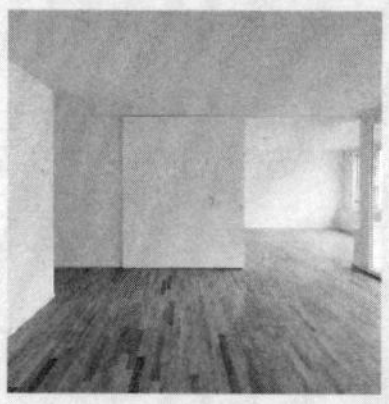

109 Guignard & Saner Architekten AG
Überbauung Station Illnau
Year: 2010 / Height: 250 cm
Photo: Roman Keller, Zürich
© Roman Keller

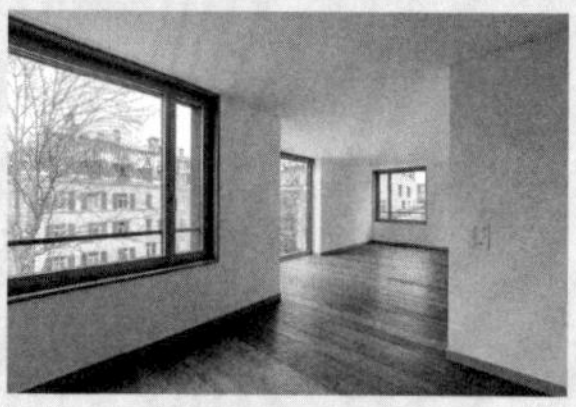

110 Igual & Guggenheim Architekten
Stadtvilla Am Rossberg
Year: 2017 / Height: 240 cm
Photo: Beat Bühler, Zürich
© Beat Bühler

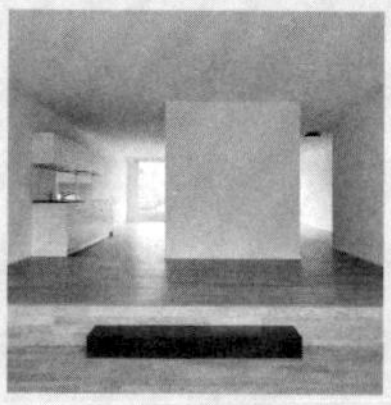

111 Guignard & Saner Architekten AG
Überbauung Station Illnau
Year: 2010 / Height: 250 cm
Photo: Roman Keller, Zürich
© Roman Keller

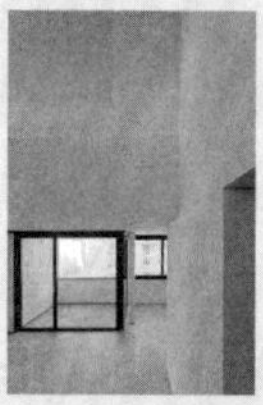

112 Galli Rudolf
Haus A3 am Rietpark
Year: 2012 / Height: 544 cm
Photo: Dominique Marc Wehrli, Winterthur
© Dominique Marc Wehrli

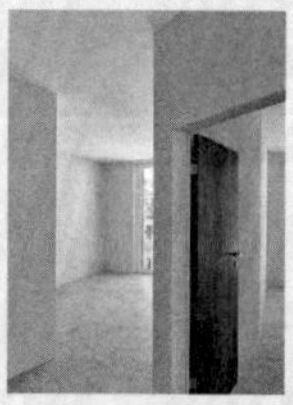

113 Edelaar Mosayebi Inderbitzin Architekten
Wohnhaus Steinwies- / Irisstrasse
Year: 2015 / Height: 274 cm
Photo: Roland Bernath, Zürich
© Roland Bernath

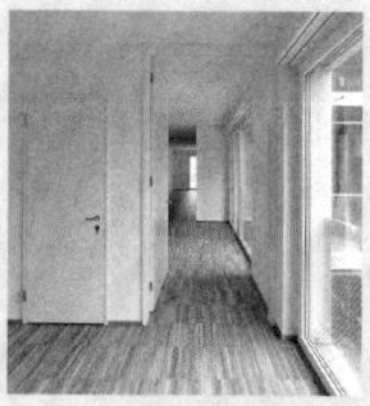

114 BS+EMI Architektenpartner
Wohnsiedlung Brüggliäcker
Year: 2014 / Height: 277 cm
Photo: Roland Bernath, Zürich
© Roland Bernath

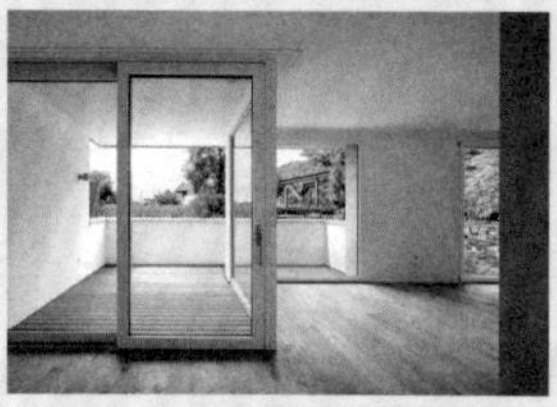

115 Burckhardt+Partner AG
Wohnüberbauung Schorenstadt
Year: 2015 / Height: 260–314 cm
Photo: Tom Bisig, Basel
© Tom Bisig

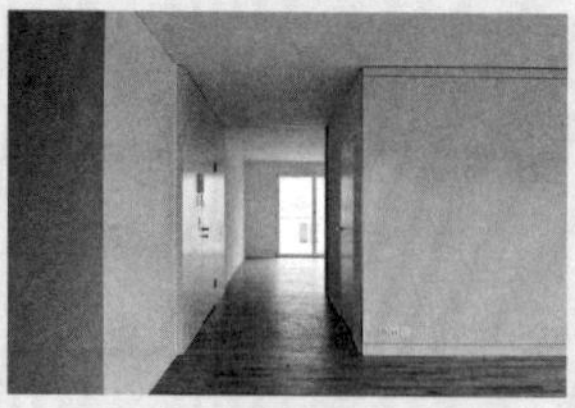

116 pool
Siedlung Frieden
Year: 2013 / Height: 246 cm
Photo: Andrea Helbling, Zürich
© Andrea Helbling

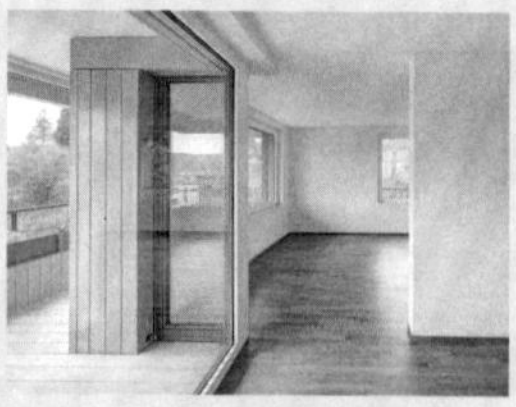

117 Arge ERP Architekten AG /
stehrenberger architektur gmbh
Wohnsiedlung Frankental
Year: 2015 / Height: 240 cm
Photo: Jürg Zimmermann, Zürich
© Jürg Zimmermann

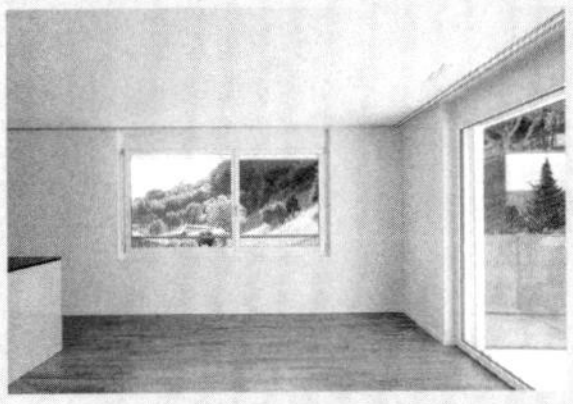

118 Beat Rothen Architektur
Hohfurristrasse / Eichenweg, Winterthur
Year: 2014 / Height: 250 cm
Photo: Claudia Luperto, Winterthur
© Claudia Luperto

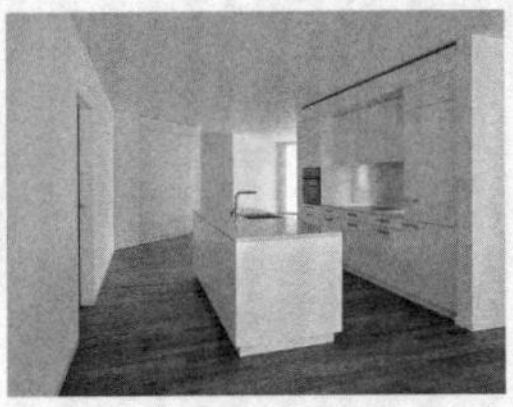

119 Giuliani Hönger
Wohn- und Gewerbehaus Weidenhof
Year: 2015 / Height: 250 cm
Photo: David Willen, Zürich
© David Willen

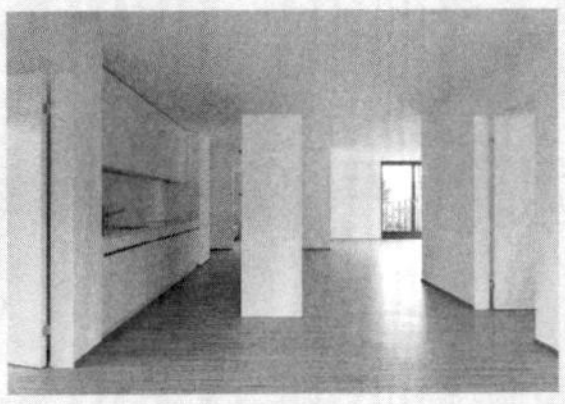

120 pool
Wohnhaus Limmattalstrasse
Year: 2013 / Height: 243 cm
Photo: Martin Stollenwerk, Zürich
© Martin Stollenwerk

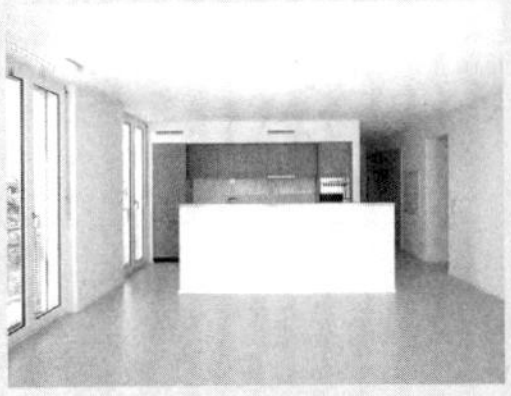

121 ADP Architekten
Wohnsiedlung Bramen Etappe B
Year: 2011 / Height: 250 cm
Photo: Hannes Henz, Zürich
© Hannes Henz

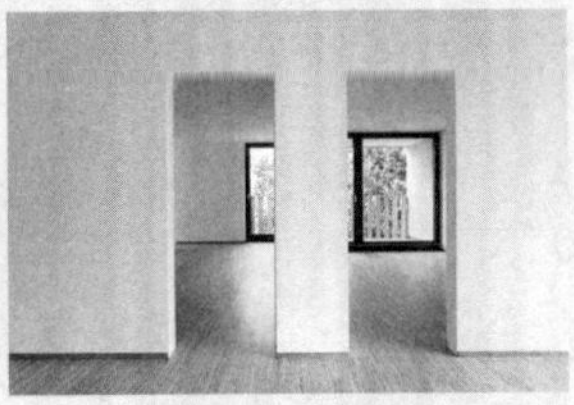

122 pool
Wohnhaus Limmattalstrasse
Year: 2013 / Height: 243 cm
Photo: Martin Stollenwerk, Zürich
© Martin Stollenwerk

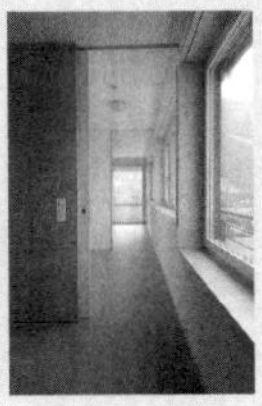

123 BUR Architekten AG
Alterswohnungen Kantengut
Year: 2009 / Height: 253 cm
Photo: Menga von Sprecher, Maienfeld
© Menga von Sprecher

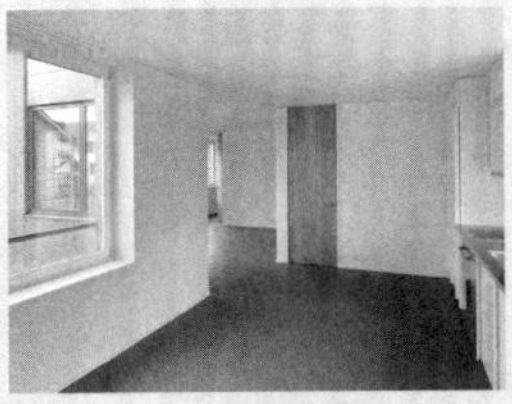

124 Edelaar Mosayebi Inderbitzin Architekten
Wohnsiedlung Avellana
Year: 2012 / Height: 245 cm
Photo: Roland Bernath, Zürich
© Roland Bernath

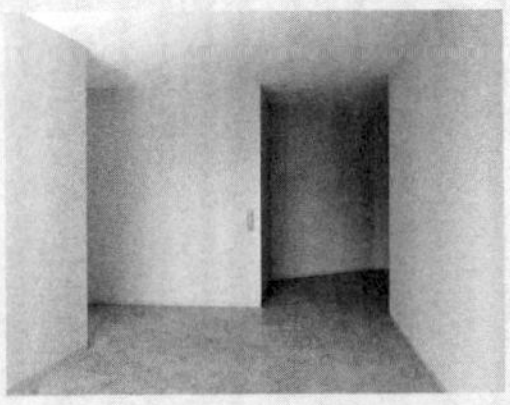

125 Edelaar Mosayebi Inderbitzin Architekten
Wohnhaus Steinwies- / Irisstrasse
Year: 2015 / Height: 274 cm
Photo: Roland Bernath, Zürich
© Roland Bernath

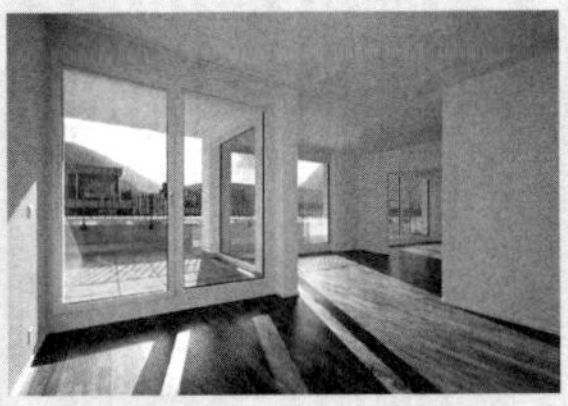

126 Ritter Schumacher AG
Segantini Haus F
Year: 2009 / Height: 254 cm
Photo: Ralph Feiner, Malans
© Ralph Feiner

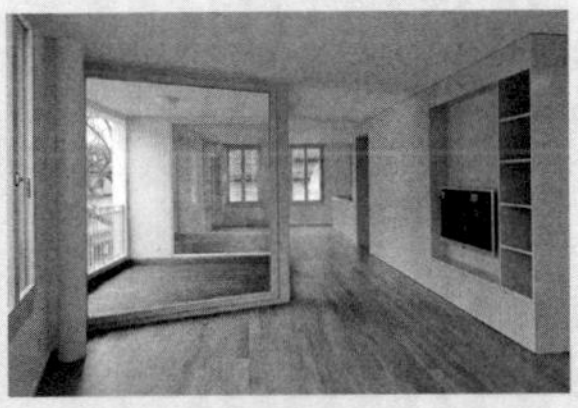

127 Seiler Linhart Architekten
Wohn- und Geschäftshaus Tschanz
Year: 2011 / Height: 250 cm
Photo: Jean-Pierre Grüter, Luzern
© Seiler Linhart Architekten

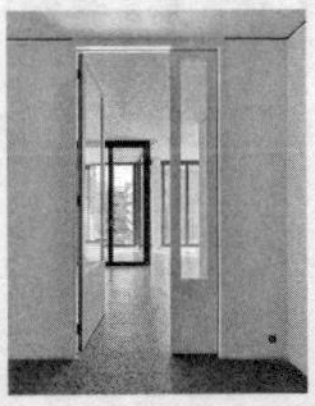

128 Edelaar Mosayebi Inderbitzin Architekten
Wohn- und Geschäftshaus Min Max
Year: 2016 / Height: 295 cm
Photo: Roland Bernath, Zürich
© Roland Bernath

# House Tour: Views of the Unfurnished Interior

# Catalogue

This publication is produced to accompany the 2018 exhibition titled *Svizzera 240: House Tour,* which takes place from May 26 to November 24, 2018 at the 16th International Architecture Exhibition — La Biennale di Venezia. It is commissoned by the Swiss Arts Council Pro Helvetia.

Editorial Director:
Adam Jasper

Co-Editors:
Ani Vihervaara, Matthew van der Ploeg, Li Tavor, Alessandro Bosshard

Copy-Editing:
Guy Weress

Translations:
Carrie Roseland, Yves Alexandre Jaquier, Erik Smith, Margie Mounier

Proofreading:
Christen Jamar

Image Research:
Milena Buchwalder

Visual Concept and Graphic Design:
Studio Martin Stoecklin, Zurich with Adrian Schnegg

Typeface:
Everett, Nolan Paparelli

Lithography, Printing and Binding:
Musumeci S.p.A., Quart (Aosta)

Paper:
Magno Gloss 100g/m²
Munken Polar Rough 100g/m²
Constellation Snow E/11 Lime 280g/m²



Park Books
Niederdorfstrasse 54
8001 Zürich
Switzerland
www.park-books.com

Park Books is being supported by the Federal Office of Culture with a general subsidy for the years 2016–2020.



ISBN 978-3-03860-114-2

Authors:
Ariell Ahearn, Marianne Burki, Hans-Christian Dany, Michael Hill, Francesca Hughes, Sandy Isenstadt, Emma Jones, Christophe Joud and Lorraine Beaudoin, Claire Lehmann, John Macarthur, Marija Marić, Nicholas de Monchaux, Charles Rice, Martin Steinmann, Georges Teyssot

## Svizzera 240: House Tour

swiss arts council
prohelvetia

The Swiss Arts Council Pro Helvetia is mandated by the Swiss Confederation to promote artistic creation in Switzerland, contribute to cultural exchange at home, promote the dissemination of Swiss culture abroad and foster cultural outreach. It is responsible for Swiss contributions to the several editions of art and architecture biennials in Venice. Switzerland has taken part in the Biennale Arte since 1920 and in the Biennale Architettura since 1991.

Commissioners,
Swiss Arts Council Pro Helvetia:
Marianne Burki, Head of Visual Arts,
Sandi Paucic, Project Leader,
Rachele Giudici, Project Coordinator

Biennials Jury Architecture,
Swiss Arts Council Pro Helvetia:
Marco Bakker, Architect at Bakker & Blanc architectes, Lausanne and Zurich, and Prof. EPFL ENAC,
Francesco Buzzi, Architectural Director at Buzzi studio d'architettura, Locarno and President of the FAS Ticino,
Irina Davidovici, Architect and Academic Researcher, ETH Zurich,
Céline Guibat, Architect sia, mijong architecture design, Sion and Zurich,
Isa Stürm, Architect at Isa Stürm Urs Wolf SA, Zurich

Project Collaboration,
Swiss Arts Council Pro Helvetia:
Cleoriana Benacloche, Martina Lughi,
Jacqueline Wolf

Press Office Switzerland,
Swiss Arts Council Pro Helvetia:
Marlène Mauris, Lisa Stadler

Press Office International:
Pickles PR, Caroline Widmer,
Camille Regli

## Installation

la Biennale di Venezia
16. Mostra Internazionale di Architettura
Partecipazioni Nazionali

16th International Architecture Exhibition — La Biennale di Venezia

Curators and Exhibitors:
Alessandro Bosshard, Li Tavor,
Matthew van der Ploeg, Ani Vihervaara

Project Architect:
Milena Buchwalder

Sound Installation:
Nicolas Buzzi, Li Tavor

Artwork:
Shirana Shahbazi

Photo Laboratory:
Tricolor Bildproduktion

Graphic Design Exhibition:
Studio Martin Stoecklin, Zurich
with Adrian Schnegg

Pavilion Photography:
Tobias Wootton

Architectural Consultant, Pavilion:
Alvise Draghi

Exhibition Contractor:
Adunic, Sandro Usznula

Construction Manager:
Adunic, Billy Beck

Fittings and Components:
Kunstgiesserei St. Gallen, Noel Hochuli
Glutz AG, Renato Caccivio

Lighting:
Neuco, Thomas Lack

Fundraising:
Manuela Schlumpf, Aline Feichtinger

www.svizzera240.ch
www.prohelvetia.ch
www.biennials.ch

# Sponsors and Support

## Main Sponsors

ETH zürich

Implenia

## Sponsors

Glutz since 1863

RENGGLI SMART BUILDING

Feller by Schneider Electric

neuco

FOTOBODEN™

ADUNIC

Basler & Hofmann

REInvest Capital

## With the Support of

ERNST GÖHNER STIFTUNG

Ikea Stiftung Schweiz
Fondation Ikea Suisse
Ikea Foundation Switzerland

vitra.

BSA FAS Bund Schweizer Architekten
Fédération des Architectes Suisses
Federazione Architetti Svizzeri

# Thanks!

Alex Lehnerer
Savvas Ciriacidis
Philip Ursprung
Adam Jasper
Shirana Shahbazi
Sascha Roesler
Billy Beck
Sandro Usznula
Philipp Brühwiler
Martin Joos
Dominik Courtin
Marco Leuenberger
Patrik Koller
Noel Hochuli
Katalin Deér
Felix Lehner
Jens Vollmar
Luzi Gruber
Martin Bosshard
Manuela Schlumpf
Seraina Winzeler
Martin Steinmann
Hans-Christian Dany
Marija Marić
Christophe Joud
Lorraine Beaudoin
Dubravka Sekulić
Valérie Knoll
Aline Feichtinger
Sandra Oehy
Sira Löpfe
Samia Henni
Nina Zschocke
Benjamin Dillenburger
Uta Hassler
Elisabetta Giordano
Brigitte Beck
Jared Macken
Klara Bindl
Katharina Ehrenklau
Lorenzo Steiger
Tibor Bielicky
Paul Preissner
Beat von Allmen
Corinne Gerber
Renato Caccivio
Stefan Auer
Jakob Felix
Thomas Lemp
Cello Duff
Denise Erni
Giovanna Bellini
Thomas Lack
Helena Roivainen

Architects:

3B Architekten AG
Adrian Streich Architekten AG
ADP Architekten
ARGE Ciriacidis Architekten GmbH Forster & Uhl Architekten GmbH
Arge ERP Architekten AG /stehrenberger architektur gmbh
Bart & Buchhofer Architekten AG
Bauart Architekten und Planer AG
Baumann Roserens Architekten
Beat Rothen Architektur
Bollhalder Eberle Architektur
Bonhôte Zapata BS+ EMI Architekten-partner
Burckhardt+Partner AG
Carlos Martinez Architekten
Coon Architekten GmbH
Edelaar Mosayebi Inderbitzin Architekten
Enrico Sassi
ERP Architekten
Esch Sintzel Architekten
Felix Partner Architektur AG
Forster & Uhl Architekten GmbH
Frundgallina Architectes
Furrer Jud Architekten
Galli Rudolf
GFA Gruppe für Architektur GmbH
Gigon Guyer
Giuliani Hönger
Gmür & Steib Architekten AG
Guagliardi Ruoss
Guignard & Saner Architekten AG
Haerle Hubacher
Huggenbergerfries Architekten AG
Husistein & Partner AG
Inches Geleta Architetti Sagl
Igual & Guggenheim Architekten
JOM architekten
Kaschka Knapkiewicz + Axel Fickert AG
L3P Architekten AG Luca Selva Architekten
Lukas Meyer e Ira Piattini Architetti
Meyer Architecture
Müller Sigrist Architekten
Phalt Architekten AG
Philipp Wieting Werknetz
Planergemeinschaft Meier Hug mit Semadeni Architekten pool
Rosenmund + Rieder Architekten
Ritter Schumacher AG
Schneider & Schneider
Schneider Gmür Architekten
Schoch Tavli Architekten
Schoop de Santis Architekten
Seiler Linhart Architekten
Slik Architekten
Spillmann Echsle Architekten
Sven Stucki Architekten AG
Think Architecture
Tribu Architecture
W2H Architekten

Photographers:

Georg Aerni
Thomas Aus der Au
Roland Bernath
Adriano Biondo
Tom Bisig
Michel Bonvin
Simone Bossi
Radek Brunecky
Pit Brunner
Beat Bühler
Alberto Canepa
Enrico Cano
Daniel Erne
Beat Ernst
Ralph Feiner
Marco Frauchiger
Roger Frei
Nadja Frey
Markus Frietsch
Jean-Pierre Grüter
Andrea Helbling
Hannes Henz
Ariel Huber
Thomas Jantscher
Milo Keller
Roman Keller
Marco Kistler
Lignum
Claudia Luperto
Walter Mair
Johannes Marburg
Lucas Peters
Goran Potkonjak
Benedikt Redmann
René Rötheli
Sabrina Scheja
Andre Schneider
Theodor Stalder
Christian Schwager
Fabien Schwartz
Manuel Stettler
Thomas Stöckli
Martin Stollenwerk
Daniel Sutter
Joël Tettamanti
Hannes Thalmann
Heinz Unger
Menga von Sprecher
Ruedi Walti
Dominique
Marc Wehrli
David Willen
Jürg Zimmermann